THE
OFFICIAL
ACT
MATHEMATICS GUIDE

THE
OFFICIAL
ACT

MATHEMATICS GUIDE

ACT

WILEY

Contents

Introduction

So you want to do well on the ACT mathematics test. That's a good goal to have! Whether you've already taken the test once or are planning to do so in the near or even distant future, this book will help you achieve your goal. There are three major factors that will determine how well you do on the ACT math test:

- Focus
- Effort
- Guidance

You need to be focused and diligent in your studies and preparation for the ACT mathematics test. There is no getting around that. You need to put the time and effort into fully practicing the skills the test will be looking for. If you are reading this book, it can be assumed that you are focused on achieving your goal of success and that you are willing to put the necessary time and effort into making it happen.

The third factor, guidance, is where this book comes into play. Guidance is difficult to supply to yourself. This book covers just about every math topic that you're likely to see on the ACT mathemtics test, so by going through this book, you'll know what to expect on test day.

The ACT math test can be daunting because of the sheer number of math topics. Fortunately, the test is based on topics covered in high school, so nothing here is new. Even in high school math, the ACT mathematics test only asks questions about certain topics, and only these topics are in this book. There are topics that you may see on the test, such as exponents, and topics that you won't see, such as Venn diagrams. If you see an unfamiliar topic in this book, you'll probably see that topic again, in class, before the year is over.

The plan is simple. Start with chapter 1 and become familiar with the reporting categories on the test, which are the foundation for your math score. Continue with chapters 2 through 6 and refresh your math progressively while working the practice ACT questions that accompany most topics. Be sure to note anything you struggle with to review later. Finally, work through chapter 7, which includes the practice ACT questions from the text along with additional questions directly from the ACT. Review chapter 8 for a detailed and thorough breakdown of the solution to each question.

If you struggle with certain math topics, you're not alone, but now you have an edge: you know the scope of the ACT math test and which topics you need to review. Most students who score well on the ACT had to practice first, and this is something that you can do. Almost no one gets a perfect score, but with the guidance in this book, you can score well enough to be a competitive applicant to a good university.

You definitely want to pick up the other ACT subject guides, and you'll eventually want to take at least one full-length practice exam from *The Official ACT Prep Guide*, but this is a good start for the math. You can and will succeed with your goal of doing well on the ACT math test. You provide the focus and the effort, and this book will provide the guidance. So read on, and let's get started.

Chapter 1:
The ACT
Math Test

The ACT mathematics test is a 60-question, 60-minute test designed to assess the mathematical reasoning skills that you've acquired in courses taken up to the beginning of grade 12. Most questions are self-contained, but some may belong to a set of several questions (e.g., about the same graph or chart).

The questions cover a wide variety of concepts, techniques, and procedures that emphasize the major content areas requisite to successful performance in entry-level courses in college mathematics. Some questions require computation, but the questions are designed to emphasize your ability to reason mathematically, not your ability to compute numbers or recall complex formulas.

You may use a calculator. See www.act.org/calculator-policy.html for details about models and features that are permitted or prohibited.

Reporting Categories: Score Reporting

Nine scores are reported for the mathematics test: a total test score based on all 60 questions and eight reporting category scores based on specific mathematical knowledge and skills. The approximate number of questions and percentage of the test devoted to each reporting category is shown in Table 1.1.

Table 1.1: Number of Questions per Reporting Category

Reporting Category/Reported Score	Number of Questions	Percentage of Test
Integrating Essential Skills	24–26	40–43
Preparing for Higher Mathematics	34–36	57–60
Number and Quantity	4–6	7–10
Algebra	7–9	12–15
Functions	7–9	12–15
Geometry	7–9	12–15
Statistics and Probability	5–7	8–12
Modeling	≥ 16	≥ 27
Total Math Test Score	**60**	**100**

Reporting Categories: Topic Overview

Integrating Essential Skills measures how well you can synthesize and apply your understanding and skills from previously learned concepts to solve more complex problems. These questions ask you to address topics such as rates and percentages; proportional relationships; area, surface area, and volume; average and median; and the expression of numbers in different ways. You will be asked to solve nonroutine problems that involve combining skills in longer chains of steps in more varied contexts, while understanding conceptual connections and demonstrating fluency of skills.

Preparing for Higher Mathematics covers mathematics that you recently learned, starting with the use of algebra as a general way of expressing and solving equations. This category has its own reported score and is divided into five discrete categories, each with its own reported score:

- **Number and Quantity** asks about real and complex number systems. You will be asked to apply your understanding and fluency with rational numbers and the four basic operations (addition, subtraction, multiplication, and division) to irrational numbers by manipulating rational numbers and delving deeper into properties of the real number system. You will be asked to apply your knowledge of integer exponents to rational exponents. Questions also involve vectors and matrices, which can be treated as number systems with properties, operations, and applications.

- **Algebra** asks you to solve, graph, and model different types of expressions. You will be asked to interpret and use various equations based on linear, polynomial, radical, and exponential relationships in the context of equations and inequalities. Questions will ask you to apply your understanding of expressions to strategically solve problems, and you will be asked to apply polynomial relationships in applications to create expressions, equations, and inequalities that represent problems and constraints in real-world contexts.

- **Functions** questions are based on the definition, notation, representation, and application of functions in linear, radical, piecewise, polynomial, and logarithmic forms. These questions provide a framework for modeling real-world phenomena, and you will be asked to interpret the characteristics of a function in the context of a problem while recognizing the difference between a model and reality. You will also be asked to manipulate and translate functions as well as interpret and use key features of graphs.

- **Geometry** asks you to apply your knowledge of shapes and solids to spatial concepts that include congruence and similarity relationships and surface area and volume measurements. You will be asked to apply your understanding of geometric objects to model and solve problems as well as find missing values in triangles, circles, and other figures. You will also be asked to apply trigonometric ratios as functions of right triangles and apply these concepts to the coordinate plane. Questions may also ask about trigonometric concepts of non-right triangles based on the law of sines and the law of cosines.

- **Statistics and Probability** is based on the distribution of data. You will be asked about data collection methods and relationship models in bivariate data. You will also be asked to calculate probabilities by recognizing the related sample spaces.

Modeling represents all questions that involve producing, interpreting, understanding, evaluating, and improving models, which are representations of complex mathematical concepts. This category is an overall measure of how well you use modeling skills across mathematical topics. Each Modeling question is also counted in other appropriate reporting categories; thus, the Modeling category is an overall measure of how well you use modeling skills across mathematical topics.

Tips for Taking the Mathematics Test

If you use a calculator, use it wisely.
All of the mathematics problems can be solved without a calculator. Many of the problems are best done without a calculator. Use good judgment in deciding when, and when not, to use a calculator. For example, for some problems you may wish to do scratch work to clarify your thoughts on the question before you begin using a calculator to do computations.

Solve the problem.
To work out solutions to the problems, you will usually do scratch work in the space provided. You may wish to glance over the answer choices after reading the questions. However, working backwards from all five answer choices can take a lot of time and may not be effective.

Find your solution among the answer choices.
Once you have solved the problem, look for your answer among the choices. If your answer is not included among the choices, carefully reread the problem to see whether you missed important information. Pay careful attention to the question being asked. If an equation is to be selected, check to see whether the equation you think is best can be transformed into one of the answer choices provided.

Make sure you answer the question.
The solutions to many questions on the test will involve several steps. Make sure your answer accounts for all the necessary steps. Frequently, an answer choice is an intermediate result, not the final answer.

Make sure your answer is reasonable.
Sometimes an error in computation will result in an answer that is not practically possible for the situation described. Always think about your answer to determine whether it is reasonable.

Check your answer.
You may arrive at an incorrect solution by making common errors in the problem-solving process. If there is time remaining before the end of the mathematics test, it is important that you reread the questions and check your answers to make sure they are correct.

Chapter 2: Number and Quantity

Number and Quantity tests your ability to apply real and complex number systems in various forms, including integer and rational exponents, vectors, and matrices.

Real and Complex Number Systems

A **real number** is any number that appears on the number line, whether positive or negative. This includes every fraction, decimal, whole number, and zero.

A **non-real number** is a number that can't exist in real math and therefore isn't on the number line. Two types of non-real number may appear on the ACT mathematic test: any number divided by zero and the square root of a negative number, also known as an *imaginary number* or *i*, covered later in this chapter.

A **rational number** is any number or fraction that can be expressed as a terminating or repeating decimal. For example, the fraction $\frac{1}{4}$ can be expressed as the decimal 0.25, which both terminates and expresses the true value of the decimal. The fraction $\frac{1}{3}$ can be expressed as the decimal $0.\overline{33}$, which doesn't terminate but is considered rational because it repeats. The fraction $\frac{7}{22}$, equivalent to $0.3\overline{18}$, is also considered rational because the 18 in the decimal repeats.

A **non-rational** or **irrational number** is a real number that cannot be written as a fraction or a terminating or repeating decimal. Examples of non-rational numbers are $\sqrt{2}$ and π.

Number Line and Absolute Value

The **number line** represents the spectrum of all real numbers and symbolically extends infinitely in both directions.

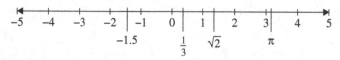

Absolute value represents an expression's distance from 0 on the number line. Absolute value is always positive, because a distance is always positive. Because −5 is 5 units from 0, the absolute value of −5, written as $|-5|$, is 5.

You can take the negative of an absolute value, but the absolute value itself is always positive. For example, $-|-7|$ is the same thing as $-(+7)$, which equals −7. The trick is to take the calculations step by step: $|-7| = 7$, and the negative of that is −7.

Reporting Category Quiz: Preparing for Higher Mathematics | Number and Quantity

DO YOUR FIGURING HERE.

1. On the real number line, what is the midpoint of −5 and 17?

   A. −11

   B. 6

   C. 11

   D. 12

   E. 22

2. On the real number line below, with coordinates as labeled, an object moves according to the following set of instructions: from point P the object moves right to Q, then left to R, then right to S, and finally left until it returns to its original position at P. What is the closest estimate of the total length, in coordinate units, of the movements this object makes?

   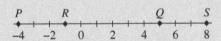

   A. 0

   B. 4

   C. 12

   D. 22

   E. 36

3. If the inequality $|a| > |b|$ is true, then which of the following must be true?

   A. $a = b$

   B. $a \neq b$

   C. $a < b$

   D. $a > b$

   E. $a > 0$

Whole Numbers

An **integer** is any number, positive, negative, or zero, that can be written without a fractional or decimal component. A **whole number** is any positive integer and doesn't include zero.

Multiples, Factors, and Prime Numbers

A **multiple** is a whole number that results from the product of two other whole numbers. For example, to find multiples of 7, multiply 7 by 1, 2, 3, and so on, resulting in 7, 14, 21, and so on. Note that every whole number is a multiple of itself: 23 is a multiple of 23.

A **factor** is a whole number that results from dividing two other whole numbers. For example, to find the factors of 30, find the pairs of numbers that multiply to 30: 5 and 6, 3 and 10, 2 and 15, and 1 and 30. Note that 1 is a factor of every whole number, and every whole number is a factor of itself. For example, factors of 52 include 1 and 52.

A **prime number** is a whole number that has exactly two factors: 1 and itself. For example, 13 is a prime number, because its only factors are 1 and 13. Note that 2 is the only even prime number, and 1 and 0 are not considered prime.

A **composite number** is a whole number that isn't prime; that is, it has more than two factors. For example, 12 is a composite number, because its factors are 1, 2, 3, 4, 6, and 12.

Prime factorization is the factoring of a composite number to its primes, including duplicates. For example, the prime factorization of 30 is $2 \times 3 \times 5$. Note that prime factorization doesn't include 1 as a factor.

These composite numbers can be prime factored:

1.   20

2.   36

3.   48

Results:

1. $20 = 2 \times 2 \times 5$

2. $36 = 2 \times 2 \times 3 \times 3$

3. $48 = 2 \times 2 \times 2 \times 2 \times 3$

Reporting Category Quiz: Integrating Essential Skills

4. Mr. Dietz is a teacher whose salary is $22,570 for this school year, which has 185 days. In Mr. Dietz's school district, substitute teachers are paid $80 per day. If Mr. Dietz takes a day off without pay and a substitute teacher is paid to teach Mr. Dietz's classes, how much less does the school district pay in salary by paying a substitute teacher instead of paying Mr. Dietz for that day?

   A. $42

   B. $80

   C. $97

   D. $105

   E. $122

5. The following chart shows the current enrollment in all the mathematics classes offered by Eastside High School.

Course title	Section	Period	Enrollment
Pre-Algebra	A	3	23
Algebra I	A	2	24
	B	3	25
	C	4	29
Geometry	A	1	21
	B	2	22
Algebra II	A	4	28
Pre-Calculus	A	6	19

The school owns 2 classroom sets of 30 calculators each, which students are required to have during their mathematics class. There are 2 calculators from one set and 6 calculators from the other set that are not available for use by the students because these calculators are being repaired.

(continued)

(*continued*)

For which of the following class periods, if any, are there NOT enough calculators available for each student to use a school-owned calculator without having to share?

　A. Period 2 only

　B. Period 3 only

　C. Period 4 only

　D. Periods 3 and 4 only

　E. There are enough calculators for each class period.

6. Nick needs to order 500 pens from his supplier. The catalog shows that these pens come in cases of 24 boxes with 10 pens in each box. Nick knows that he may NOT order partial cases. What is the fewest number of cases he should order?

　A. 2

　B. 3

　C. 18

　D. 21

　E. 50

DO YOUR FIGURING HERE.

Reporting Category Quiz: Preparing for Higher Mathematics | Number and Quantity

7. Kareem has 4 sweaters, 6 shirts, and 3 pairs of slacks. How many distinct outfits, each consisting of a sweater, a shirt, and a pair of slacks, can Kareem select?

　A. 13

　B. 36

　C. 42

　D. 72

　E. 216

DO YOUR FIGURING HERE.

8. How many prime numbers are there between 30 and 50?

   A. 4

   B. 5

   C. 6

   D. 7

   E. 8

DO YOUR FIGURING HERE.

Decimals and Percents

A **decimal** represents a fraction where the denominator is a multiple of 10. For example, 0.3 is equivalent to $\frac{3}{10}$, and 2.19 is equivalent to $2\frac{19}{100}$ or $\frac{219}{100}$.

A **percent** represents the first two decimal places of a decimal, or a fraction over 100. For example, 21% is equivalent to 0.21 or $\frac{21}{100}$. To convert a decimal amount to a percent, multiply the decimal amount by 100. For example, $0.35 \times 100 = 35\%$. To convert a fraction to a percent, convert the fraction so that it has a denominator of 100, and use the numerator. For example, $\frac{3}{20} = \frac{15}{100} = 15\%$.

Percent of Change

To find the **percent of change**, place the quantity of change over the starting quantity, and convert this to a fraction with a denominator of 100.

For example, to find the percent of change of the price of a calculator that increased from $20 to $25, place the quantity of change, 5, over the starting quantity for $\frac{5}{20}$, and convert this to a fraction with a denominator of 100: $\frac{25}{100}$, for 25%.

If that calculator goes on sale from $25 to $20, find the new percent of change: place the quantity of change, 5, over the starting quantity for $\frac{5}{25}$, and convert this to a fraction with a denominator of 100: $\frac{20}{100}$, for 20%.

Note that the same $5 price change yields a different percent of change when starting from different amounts. Also, a percent of change is always positive: the price didn't change negative 20%; it went down (positive) 20%.

These are examples of numbers with percents of change:

   1.   From 5 to 3

   2.   From 50 to 66

   3.   From 20 to 70

Results:

1.   40%.
The quantity of change is 2 and the starting quantity is 5: $\frac{2}{5} = \frac{40}{100}$.

2.   32%.
The quantity of change is 16 and the starting quantity is 50: $\frac{16}{50} = \frac{32}{100}$.

3.   250%.
The quantity of change is 50 and the starting quantity is 20: $\frac{50}{20} = \frac{250}{100}$.

Percent of a Group

To find the **percent of a group,** place the number of the subgroup over the entire group and convert the fraction. For example, if 7 of the 20 job applicants have college degrees, find the percent who have college degrees:

1.   The number of the subgroup: 7

2.   Over the entire group: $\frac{7}{20}$

3.   Converted fraction: $\frac{35}{100}$

7 out of 20 is 35%.

These are examples of percents of groups:

1.   6 out of 25 dogs are Labs.

2.   170 out of 200 flights are on time.

3.   28 out of 40 cars are electric.

Results:

1.   24%.
The number of the subgroup is 6 and the entire group is 25: $\frac{6}{25} = \frac{24}{100}$.

2.   85%.
The number of the subgroup is 170 and the entire group is 200: $\frac{170}{200} = \frac{85}{100}$.

3.   70%.
The number of the subgroup is 28 and the entire group is 40: $\frac{28}{40} = \frac{70}{100}$.

Reporting Category Quiz: Integrating Essential Skills

DO YOUR FIGURING HERE.

9. The oxygen saturation level of a river is found by dividing the amount of dissolved oxygen the river water currently has per liter by the dissolved oxygen capacity per liter of the water and then converting to a percent. If the river currently has 7.3 milligrams of dissolved oxygen per liter of water and the dissolved oxygen capacity is 9.8 milligrams per liter, what is the oxygen saturation level, to the nearest percent?

A. 34%

B. 70%

C. 73%

D. 74%

E. 98%

Fractions and Ratios

A **fraction** is a numerical quantity that is not a whole number, such as $\frac{5}{8}$. The **reciprocal** of a fraction is the switching of its numerator and denominator. For example, the reciprocal of $\frac{2}{5}$ is $\frac{5}{2}$. Placing a 1 on top of a fraction yields its reciprocal. For example, $\frac{1}{\frac{5}{7}} = \frac{7}{5}$.

- Add and subtract fractions by giving them common denominators: $\frac{5}{8} + \frac{3}{4} \rightarrow \frac{5}{8} + \frac{3(2)}{4(2)} \rightarrow \frac{5}{8} + \frac{6}{8} = \frac{11}{8}$.

- Multiply fractions by multiplying the numerators then the denominators: $\frac{2}{3} \times \frac{5}{7} \rightarrow \frac{2 \times 5}{3 \times 7} = \frac{10}{21}$.

- Divide fractions by multiplying the first fraction by the reciprocal of the second fraction: $\frac{4}{5} \div \frac{1}{2} \rightarrow \frac{4}{5} \times \frac{2}{1} = \frac{8}{5}$.

If an ACT mathematics test question involves multiplying fractions that have large numerators or denominators, you can often simplify the math work by reducing and cancelling the numbers before multiplying. In this example, the numerator 500 is a multiple of the denominator 250, so reducing these numbers saves math work: $\frac{500}{5} \times \frac{3}{250} \rightarrow \frac{2}{5} \times \frac{3}{1} = \frac{6}{5}$.

A **ratio** compares the quantities of two groups as a reduced fraction. For example, if the sports center has 24 baseballs and 16 footballs, then the fraction of quantities $\frac{24}{16}$ is reduced to a ratio of $\frac{3}{2}$.

Find the actual quantities from the ratio by multiplying each ratio number by x, adding them together, and setting them equal to the total. For example, if the ratio of gloves to bats is 2:3 and there are 30 goods total, find the number of each good:

$$2x + 3x = 30$$
$$5x = 30$$
$$x = 6$$

Now substitute 6 for x in the original equation:

$$2(6) + 3(6) = 12 + 18$$

And there are 12 gloves and 18 bats.

These are examples of ratios from quantities:

1.   The ratio of classical to electric guitars is 3:4, and there are 35 guitars total. The ratio and quantity can be used to determine the numbers of classical and electric guitars.

2.   The ratio of mountain bikes to road bikes is 5:3, and there are 20 mountain bikes. The ratio and number of mountain bikes can be used to determine the number of road bikes.

3.   There are 15 cars and 35 trucks. The quantities of cars and trucks can be used to determine the ratio.

Results:

1.   15 and 20.

   Multiply 3 and 4 each by x, add them together, and set that equal to the total. After finding that $x = 5$ multiply that by 3 and 4 from the ratio to determine that there are 15 classical and 20 electric guitars:

$$3x + 4x = 35$$
$$7x = 35$$
$$x = 5$$
$$3(5) + 4(5) = 35$$
$$15 + 20 = 35$$

2.   12.

Multiply 5 and 3 each by x, add them together, and set that equal to the total. After finding that $x = 4$, multiply that by 3 to determine that there are 12 road bikes:

$$5x + 3x = 20 + 3x$$
$$5x = 20$$
$$x = 4$$
$$3(4) = 12$$

3.   3:7.

Set the proportion up as a fraction and reduce it to find the ratio: $\frac{15}{35} = \frac{3}{7}$

Reporting Category Quiz: Integrating Essential Skills

DO YOUR FIGURING HERE.

10.   If 12 vases cost $18.00, what is the cost of 1 vase?

   F. $0.67

   G. $1.05

   H. $1.33

   J. $1.50

   K. $1.60

11.   Company A sells 60 pens for $15.00. Company B sells the same type of pens in packs of 40 for $8.00. Which company's price per pen is cheaper, and what is that price?

   A. Company A, at $0.20

   B. Company A, at $0.23

   C. Company A, at $0.25

   D. Company B, at $0.20

   E. Company B, at $0.25

(*continued*)

(*continued*)

12. At a refinery, 100,000 tons of sand are required to produce each 60,000 barrels of a tarry material. How many tons of sand are required to produce 3,000 barrels of this tarry material?

 A. 5,000

 B. 18,000

 C. 20,000

 D. 40,000

 E. 50,000

DO YOUR FIGURING HERE.

Reporting Category Quiz: Integrating Essential Skills | Modeling

13. Of the 804 graduating seniors in a certain high school, approximately $\frac{2}{5}$ are going to college and approximately $\frac{1}{4}$ of those going to college are going to a state university. Which of the following is the closest estimate for how many of the graduating seniors are going to a state university?

 F. 80

 G. 90

 H. 160

 J. 200

 K. 320

DO YOUR FIGURING HERE.

DO YOUR FIGURING HERE.

14. What is the least common denominator
    when adding the fractions $\frac{a}{2}, \frac{b}{3}, \frac{c}{9}$,
    and $\frac{d}{15}$?

    A. 45

    B. 90

    C. 135

    D. 270

    E. 810

15. A ramp for wheelchair access to the gym
    has a slope of 5% (that is, the ramp rises
    5 feet vertically for every 100 feet of
    horizontal distance). The entire ramp is
    built on level ground, and the entrance
    to the gym is 2 feet above the ground.
    What is the *horizontal* distance, in feet,
    between the ends of the ramp?

    A. 4

    B. 10

    C. 40

    D. 100

    E. 400

Exponents

An **exponent** refers to a base number multiplied by itself a certain number of times. For example, 5^3 refers to the base number 5 multiplied by itself 3 times: $5^3 = 5 \times 5 \times 5 = 125$. A *negative exponent*, such as 5^{-3}, is the reciprocal of a positive exponent: $5^{-3} = \frac{1}{5^3}$.

Multiplication and Division

Exponential expressions that have the same base number can be multiplied and divided.

To multiply, add the exponents: $(x^2)(x^3) = x^{2+3} = x^5$. To divide, subtract the exponents: $\frac{x^7}{x^4} = x^{7-4} = x^3$.

These are examples of expressions that can be simplified:

1. $(x^5)(x^4)$

2. $(x^2)(x^{-5})$

3. $\dfrac{x^8}{x^2}$

Results:

1. x^9.

    When multiplying like terms, add the exponents: $(x^5)(x^4) = x^{5+4} = x^9$.

2. x^{-3} or $\dfrac{1}{x^3}$.

    Add the exponents: $(x^2)(x^{-5}) = x^{2-5} = x^{-3}$ or $\dfrac{1}{x^3}$.

3. x^6.

    When dividing like terms, subtract the exponents: $\dfrac{x^8}{x^2} = x^{8-2} = x^6$.

Exponents of Exponents

Simplify an exponent of an exponent by multiplying the exponents: $(x^3)^4 = x^{3\times4} = x^{12}$.

These are examples of expressions that can be simplified:

1. $(x^2)^5$

2. $(y^4)^{-3}$

3. $\left(z^{\frac{1}{2}}\right)^{\frac{3}{5}}$

Results:

1. x^{10}.

    When taking the exponent of an exponent, multiply the exponents: $(x^2)^5 = x^{2\times5} = x^{10}$.

2. y^{-12} or $\dfrac{1}{y^{12}}$.

    Multiply the exponents, even when negative: $(y^4)^{-3} = y^{(4)(-3)} = y^{-12}$ or $\dfrac{1}{y^{12}}$.

3. $z^{\frac{3}{10}}$.

    Multiply the exponents, even as fractions: $\left(z^{\frac{1}{2}}\right)^{\frac{3}{5}} = z^{\frac{1}{2}\times\frac{3}{5}} = z^{\frac{3}{10}}$.

Variations on Exponents

These are variations of exponents that can be simplified:

1. $(-4)^2$

2. -5^2

3. 3^{-2}

4. $\left(\frac{2}{5}\right)^2$

5. $(0.4)^2$

6. $(x+2)^2$

7. 6^0

8. $(x^3)(x^{-3})$

Results:

1. 16.

    The exponent multiplies the entire expression containing the -4:
    $(-4)^2 = (-4)(-4) = 16$.

2. -25.

    The exponent multiplies only the 5; the negative is outside this: $-5^2 = -(5\times5) = -25$.

3. $\frac{1}{9}$.

    The negative exponent yields the reciprocal of the positive exponent: $3^{-2} = \frac{1}{3^2} = \frac{1}{9}$.

4. $\frac{4}{25}$.

    An exponent of a fraction multiplies the entire fraction: $\left(\frac{2}{5}\right)^2 = \frac{2}{5}\times\frac{2}{5} = \frac{4}{25}$.

5. 0.16.

    This is 0.4 multiplied by itself. Note that $\frac{2}{5}$ is equivalent to 0.4 and $\frac{4}{25}$ is equivalent to 0.16: $(0.4)^2 = 0.4\times0.4 = 0.16$.

6. $x^2 + 4x + 4$.

    Don't just distribute the exponent for $x^2 + 4$, which is a common mistake. Instead, multiply the expressions using the FOIL method, which is covered further in chapter 3, "Algebra": $(x+2)^2 = (x+2)(x+2) = x^2 + 4x + 4$.

7. 1.

    Any quantity raised to the 0 power equals 1: $6^0 = 1$.

8. 1.

    $$(x^3)(x^{-3}) = x^{3-3} = x^0 = 1.$$

These are additional variations that can be simplified:

1. $(-7)^2$

2. -8^2

3. 9^{-2}

4. $\left(\frac{3}{10}\right)^2$

5. $(0.3)^2$

6. $(x-3)^2$

7. 7.3^0

8. $(y^2)(y^3)(y^{-5})$

Results:

1. 49.

   The exponent multiplies the entire expression containing the –7:
   $(-7)^2 = (-7)(-7) = 49$.

2. –64.

   The exponent multiplies only the 8; the negative is outside this: $-8^2 = -(8 \times 8) = -64$.

3. $\frac{1}{81}$.

   The negative exponent yields the reciprocal of the positive exponent: $9^{-2} = \frac{1}{9^2} = \frac{1}{81}$.

4. $\frac{9}{100}$.

   An exponent of a fraction multiplies the entire fraction: $\left(\frac{3}{10}\right)^2 = \frac{3}{10} \times \frac{3}{10} = \frac{9}{100}$.

5. 0.09.

   This is 0.3 multiplied by itself: $(0.3)^2 = 0.3 \times 0.3 = 0.09$.

6. $x^2 - 6x + 9$.

   Multiply the expressions using the FOIL method:
   $(x-3)^2 = (x-3)(x-3) = x^2 - 6x + 9$.

7. 1.

   Any quantity raised to the 0 power equals 1: $7.3^0 = 1$.

8. 1.

   $(y^2)(y^3)(y^{-5}) = y^{2+3-5} = y^0 = 1$.

Reporting Category Quiz: Preparing for Higher Mathematics | Number and Quantity

DO YOUR FIGURING HERE.

16. $3x^3 \cdot 2x^2y \cdot 4x^2y$ is equivalent to:

F. $9x^7y^2$

G. $9x^{12}y^2$

H. $24x^7y^2$

J. $24x^{12}y$

K. $24x^{12}y^2$

17. Which of the following expressions is equivalent to $(-2x^5y^2)^4$?

A. $-16x^{20}y^8$

B. $-8x^{20}y^8$

C. $-8x^9y^6$

D. $16x^9y^6$

E. $16x^{20}y^8$

18. Which real number satisfies $(2^x)(4) = 8^3$?

F. 2

G. 3

H. 4

J. 4.5

K. 7

Imaginary and Complex Numbers

An **imaginary number** is represented by i, where $i = \sqrt{-1}$ or $i^2 = -1$. Because a square root can only be of a positive number, the square root of a negative number isn't possible and is therefore an imaginary number. For example, $\sqrt{-25}$ is an imaginary number, but it can be simplified:

$$\sqrt{-25}$$
$$\sqrt{25} \times \sqrt{-1}$$
$$5 \times i$$
$$5i$$

These are examples of imaginary numbers that can be written in terms of i:

1. $\sqrt{-9}$

2. $\sqrt{-36}$

3. $\sqrt{-5}$

Results:

1. $\sqrt{-9} = \sqrt{9} \times \sqrt{-1} = 3i$

2. $\sqrt{-36} = \sqrt{36} \times \sqrt{-1} = 6i$

3. $\sqrt{-5} = \sqrt{5} \times \sqrt{-1} = \sqrt{5}i$

To find the value of an imaginary number, use $i^2 = -1$. To find the value of $(3i)^2$, use $(3i)(3i)$, and multiply the 3s separately from the is: $(3 \times 3)(i \times i) = (9)(-1) = -9$.

These are imaginary numbers that can be simplified:

1. $(5i)^2$

2. $(2i)^4$

3. $(2i)^3$

4. $3i \times 5i$

5. $(2i)(-3i)$

Results:

1. -25.

   Multiply the numbers and the is separately: $(5 \times 5)(i \times i) = (25)(-1) = -25$.

2.   16.

   Multiply the numbers and the is separately. The 4 is multiplied together become positive 1: $(2 \times 2 \times 2 \times 2)(i \times i \times i \times i) = (4)(4)(-1)(-1) = (16)(1) = 16$.

3. $-8i$.

   Multiply them separately: $(2 \times 2 \times 2)(i \times i \times i) = (8)(-1)(i) = -8i$.

4. -15.

   $3 \times 5 \times i \times i = 15 \times (-1) = -15$

5.   6.

   $(2)(-3)(i)(i) = (-6)(-1) = 6$

A **complex number** includes the imaginary number i in the form $a + bi$, such as $3 + 2i$. You can represent the complex number as a graph on the number plane, where the horizontal axis, labeled r, represents the real component and the vertical axis, labeled i, represents the imaginary component. For example, to represent the complex number $3+2i$, plot the point 3 spaces right and 2 spaces up for the coordinates $(3,2)$:

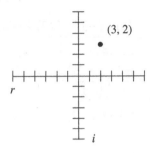

Distance and Midpoint

Find the **distance**, also called the **modulus**, between two graphed complex numbers with the *distance formula*, where a and b are the coordinates of one point and s and t are the coordinates of the other:

$$d = \sqrt{(s-a)^2 + (t-b)^2}$$

To find the distance between $3+2i$ and $-5-4i$, place 3 and 2 for a and b, respectively, and -5 and -4, as s and t, respectively, into the formula:

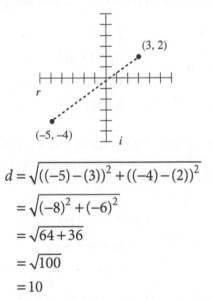

$$d = \sqrt{((-5)-(3))^2 + ((-4)-(2))^2}$$
$$= \sqrt{(-8)^2 + (-6)^2}$$
$$= \sqrt{64+36}$$
$$= \sqrt{100}$$
$$= 10$$

Find the **average** or **midpoint** in the complex plane between two graphed complex numbers with the *midpoint formula*:

$$mid = \frac{a+s}{2} + \left(\frac{b+t}{2}\right)i$$

To find the distance between $3+2i$ and $-5-4i$, place 3 and 2 for a and b, respectively, and -5 and -4, as s and t, respectively, into the formula:

$$mid = \frac{(3)+(-5)}{2} + \left(\frac{(2)+(-4)}{2} \right)i$$

$$= \frac{-2}{2} + \left(\frac{-2}{2} \right)i$$

$$= -1 - i$$

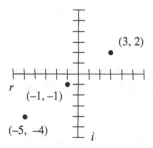

Multiplication

Multiply or square complex numbers with the FOIL method as you would a quadratic expression:

$$(3+2i)^2$$
$$(3+2i)(3+2i)$$
$$9+6i+6i-4$$
$$5+12i$$

Find the **conjugate** of a complex number by reversing the sign of the imaginary component. For example, the conjugate of $3+2i$ is $3-2i$. When a complex number is multiplied by its conjugate, the imaginary component cancels and the real component remains. For example, multiply $3+2i$ by its conjugate $3-2i$:

$$(3+2i)(3-2i)$$
$$9-6i+6i+4$$
$$13$$

These are examples of complex numbers that can be simplified:

1. $(5+4i)^2$

2. $(2+3i)(4-5i)$

3. $(3+4i)(3-4i)$

Results:

1. $9 + 40i.$

   FOIL the expression and combine like terms:

   $$(5 + 4i)^2$$
   $$(5 + 4i)(5 + 4i)$$
   $$25 + 20i + 20i - 16$$
   $$9 + 40i$$

2. $23 + 2i.$

   $$(2 + 3i)(4 - 5i)$$
   $$8 - 10i + 12i + 15$$
   $$23 + 2i$$

3. 25.

   $$(3 + 4i)(3 - 4i)$$
   $$9 - 12i + 12i + 16$$
   $$25$$

Vectors

A **vector** is an object, represented by an arrow, that has both magnitude and direction. It's written in the *component form* as $\langle a,b \rangle$, where, from any starting point, a represents the number of units that it moves right and b represents the number of units that it moves up. In this way, the component form represents changes in its x- and y-values. For example, the vector $\langle 4,3 \rangle$ moves 4 units right and 3 units up:

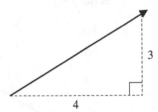

The distance between the starting point and ending point is the *magnitude*, which can be found using the Pythagorean theorem of its component form. Place the component numbers in the theorem as a and b, with c as the magnitude:

$$c^2 = a^2 + b^2$$
$$c^2 = (4)^2 + (3)^2$$
$$c^2 = 16 + 9$$
$$c^2 = 25$$
$$c = 5$$

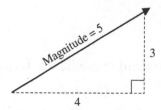

Think of the vector as a right triangle, with its component form as the sides and its magnitude as the hypotenuse. The component form can have negative values, meaning the vector moves left and/or down. However, the magnitude is always positive:

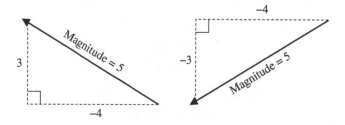

Multiplication

The vector can be multiplied by a number, known as a *scalar*. For example, to multiply the previous vector by a scalar of 2, write it as $2\langle 4,3 \rangle = \langle 8,6 \rangle$, in which case the vector moves 8 units right and 6 units up. Find the magnitude by placing these component numbers into the Pythagorean theorem:

$$c^2 = a^2 + b^2$$
$$c^2 = (8)^2 + (6)^2$$
$$c^2 = 64 + 36$$
$$c^2 = 100$$
$$c = 10$$

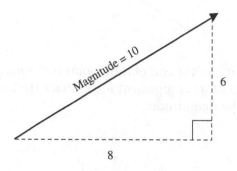

These vectors can be multiplied:

1.   Find 2**a** where vector $a = \langle 2,5 \rangle$.

2.   Find -3**b** where vector $b = \langle 3,-6 \rangle$.

Results:

1.　　$\langle 4,10 \rangle$.

　　　　Multiply $\langle 2,5 \rangle$ by 2: $2\langle 2,5 \rangle = \langle 4,10 \rangle$.

2.　　$\langle -9,18 \rangle$.

　　　　Multiply $\langle 3,-6 \rangle$ by -3: $-3\langle 3,-6 \rangle = \langle -9,18 \rangle$.

Addition and Subtraction

To add or subtract vectors, use their component forms to separately add or subtract the x-values and y-values. For example, to add the vectors $\langle 2,3 \rangle$ and $\langle 5,1 \rangle$, add the 2 and the 5 for the shift in x-value and the 3 and the 1 for the shift in y-value, like this: $\langle 2,3 \rangle + \langle 5,1 \rangle = \langle 7,4 \rangle$.

In other words, if vector **a** moves right 2 and up 3, and vector **b** moves right 5 and up 1, and $a + b = c$, then vector **c** moves right $2 + 5 = 7$ and up $3 + 1 = 4$:

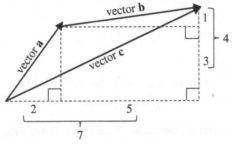

Note that the second vector begins where the first one ends.

These are examples of vectors that can be multiplied and added:

1.　　Find vector **c** where vectors a $= \langle 3,7 \rangle$, b $= \langle -4,5 \rangle$, and c $= a + b$.

2.　　Find vector **c** where vectors a $= \langle 2,1 \rangle$, b $= \langle -5,3 \rangle$, and c $= 2a + 3b$.

Results:

1.　　$\langle -1,12 \rangle$.

　　　　$\langle 3,7 \rangle + \langle -4,5 \rangle = \langle -1,12 \rangle$

2.　　$\langle -11,11 \rangle$.

　　　　$2\langle 2,1 \rangle = \langle 4,2 \rangle$

　　　　$3\langle -5,3 \rangle = \langle -15,9 \rangle$

　　　　$\langle 4,2 \rangle + \langle -15,9 \rangle = \langle -11,11 \rangle$

Note that the resulting magnitude isn't the sum of the two starting magnitudes. It's calculated from the component form of the new vector with the Pythagorean theorem.

Reporting Category Quiz: Preparing for Higher Mathematics | Number and Quantity

DO YOUR FIGURING HERE.

19. The component forms of vectors **u** and **v** are given by u = $\langle 5,3 \rangle$ and v = $\langle 2,-7 \rangle$. Given that $2u + (-3v) + w = 0$, what is the component form of **w**?

F. $\langle -16,15 \rangle$

G. $\langle -4,-27 \rangle$

H. $\langle 3,10 \rangle$

J. $\langle 4,27 \rangle$

K. $\langle 16,-15 \rangle$

Matrices

A **matrix** is a rectangular array of letters or numbers that represents data. The matrix facilitates data manipulation, making it ideal for use in complex applications such as statistics or computer operations.

For example, $\begin{bmatrix} 2 & 3 & 4 \\ 1 & 2 & x \end{bmatrix}$ is a 2×3 matrix, because it has two rows and three columns.

Addition and Subtraction

Matrices can only be added or subtracted when they have the same dimensions. For example, a 3×2 matrix can only be added or subtracted to another 3×2 matrix. To do this, add (or subtract) the quantities in each corresponding position. For example, to add $\begin{bmatrix} 2 & 3 \\ 4 & 5 \\ 6 & x \end{bmatrix}$ and $\begin{bmatrix} 0.1 & 0.2 \\ 0.3 & 0.4 \\ 0.5 & x \end{bmatrix}$, add the

values in each position (top left, top right, etc.) for the result of $\begin{bmatrix} 2.1 & 3.2 \\ 4.3 & 5.4 \\ 6.5 & 2x \end{bmatrix}$.

Questions: Add or subtract these matrices:

1. $\begin{bmatrix} 3 & 6 & x \\ 5 & 8 & y \end{bmatrix} + \begin{bmatrix} 4 & 3 & x \\ 3 & 2 & y \end{bmatrix}$

2. $\begin{bmatrix} 4 & 6 & 2 \\ 3 & 5 & 1 \end{bmatrix} - \begin{bmatrix} 3 & 4 & 5 \\ 0 & 1 & 6 \end{bmatrix}$

Answers:

1. $\begin{bmatrix} 7 & 9 & 2x \\ 8 & 10 & 2y \end{bmatrix}$

2. $\begin{bmatrix} 1 & 2 & -3 \\ 3 & 4 & -5 \end{bmatrix}$

Multiplication

A matrix can be multiplied by a single quantity, also known as a *scalar*. To do this, distribute the scalar among the values in the matrix, and the result is a *scalar multiple*. For example, to multiply the matrix $\begin{bmatrix} 3 & 4 & 5 \\ 2 & x & y \end{bmatrix}$ by the scalar 3, written as $3\begin{bmatrix} 3 & 4 & 5 \\ 2 & x & y \end{bmatrix}$, multiply each value in the matrix by 3 for the scalar multiple: $\begin{bmatrix} 9 & 12 & 15 \\ 6 & 3x & 3y \end{bmatrix}$.

A matrix can be multiplied by another matrix when the number of columns in the first matrix matches the number of rows in the second matrix. For example, $\begin{bmatrix} 1 & 2 \\ 3 & 4 \\ 5 & 6 \end{bmatrix}$ has two columns and $\begin{bmatrix} x & y & z \\ 2x & 2y & 2z \end{bmatrix}$ has two rows, so these can be multiplied.

The resulting matrix has the number of rows from the first matrix and the number of columns from the second, so the order matters when multiplying matrices: $\begin{bmatrix} 1 & 2 \\ 3 & 4 \\ 5 & 6 \end{bmatrix} \times \begin{bmatrix} x & y & z \\ 2x & 2y & 2z \end{bmatrix}$, with 3 rows in the first matrix and 3 columns in the second, produces a 3×3 answer. Now switch the order: $\begin{bmatrix} x & y & z \\ 2x & 2y & 2z \end{bmatrix} \times \begin{bmatrix} 1 & 2 \\ 3 & 4 \\ 5 & 6 \end{bmatrix}$, having 2 rows in the first matrix and 2 columns in the second, produces a 2×2 answer.

To multiply $\begin{bmatrix} 1 & 2 \\ 3 & 4 \\ 5 & 6 \end{bmatrix} \times \begin{bmatrix} x & y & z \\ 2x & 2y & 2z \end{bmatrix}$, draw a blank 3×3 matrix:

. Start with the first row of the answer: Multiply 1 from the first matrix by x from the second matrix, and add this to the product of 2 from the first matrix and $2x$ from the second matrix. Place the resulting $5x$ in the top left position:

$5x$		

. Multiply 1 from the first matrix by y in the second matrix, and add this to the product of 2 from the first matrix and $2y$ in the second matrix. Place the resulting $5y$ in the top middle position:

$5x$	$5y$	

. The 1 and 2 from the first matrix are similarly

multiplied by z and $2z$ from the second matrix, and that sum is placed in the top right position:

$5x$	$5y$	$5z$

Now for the second row of the answer: add $(3 \cdot x)$ to $(4 \cdot 2x)$ for $11x$, $(3 \cdot y) + (4 \cdot 2y) = 11y$ and

$(3 \cdot z) + (4 \cdot 2z) = 11z$:

$5x$	$5y$	$5z$
$11x$	$11y$	$11z$

. The third row is similar: add $(5 \cdot x)$ to $(6 \cdot 2x)$ for $17x$,

$(5 \cdot y) + (6 \cdot 2y) = 17y$ and $(5 \cdot z) + (6 \cdot 2z) = 17z$:

$5x$	$5y$	$5z$
$11x$	$11y$	$11z$
$17x$	$17y$	$17z$

.

These are examples of matrices that can be multiplied:

1. $2 \begin{bmatrix} 5 & 3 & x \\ 4 & 2 & y \end{bmatrix}$

2. $\begin{bmatrix} 1 & 2 \\ 3 & 4 \\ 5 & 7 \end{bmatrix} \begin{bmatrix} 3 & 5 & x \\ 2 & 4 & x \end{bmatrix}$

3. $\begin{bmatrix} 5 & 4 & 3 \\ 2 & 1 & 7 \end{bmatrix} \begin{bmatrix} 4 & y \\ 3 & y \\ 2 & y \end{bmatrix}$

Results:

1. $\begin{bmatrix} 10 & 6 & 2x \\ 8 & 4 & 2y \end{bmatrix}$.

    Distribute the 2 by each quantity in the matrix.

2. $\begin{bmatrix} 7 & 13 & 3x \\ 17 & 31 & 7x \\ 29 & 53 & 12x \end{bmatrix}$.

    Three rows in the first matrix by three columns in the second produce a 3×3

    answer: $\begin{bmatrix} (1 \cdot 3) + (2 \cdot 2) & (1 \cdot 5) + (2 \cdot 4) & (1 \cdot x) + (2 \cdot x) \\ (3 \cdot 3) + (4 \cdot 2) & (3 \cdot 5) + (4 \cdot 4) & (3 \cdot x) + (4 \cdot x) \\ (5 \cdot 3) + (7 \cdot 2) & (5 \cdot 5) + (7 \cdot 4) & (5 \cdot x) + (7 \cdot x) \end{bmatrix}$.

3. $\begin{bmatrix} 38 & 12y \\ 25 & 10y \end{bmatrix}.$

Two rows in the first matrix by two columns in the second produce a 2×2 answer:

$$\begin{bmatrix} (5\cdot4)+(4\cdot3)+(3\cdot2) & (5\cdot y)+(4\cdot y)+(3\cdot y) \\ (2\cdot4)+(1\cdot3)+(7\cdot2) & (2\cdot y)+(1\cdot y)+(7\cdot y) \end{bmatrix}.$$

Reporting Category Quiz: Preparing for Higher Mathematics | Number and Quantity

DO YOUR FIGURING HERE.

20. The number of students participating in fall sports at a certain high school is shown by the following matrix.

Tennis   Soccer   Cross-Country   Football
[40   60   80   80]

The athletic director estimates the ratio of the number of sports awards that will be earned to the number of students participating with the following matrix.

$$\begin{matrix} \text{Tennis} \\ \text{Soccer} \\ \text{Cross-Country} \\ \text{Football} \end{matrix}\begin{bmatrix} 0.3 \\ 0.4 \\ 0.2 \\ 0.5 \end{bmatrix}$$

Given these matrices, what is the athletic director's estimate for the number of sports awards that will be earned for these fall sports?

   A. 80

   B. 88

   C. 91

   D. 92

   E. 99

Determinant

The **determinant** that appears in the ACT mathematics test is based on a 2×2 matrix, where the determinant of $\begin{bmatrix} a & b \\ c & d \end{bmatrix}$ is $ad - bc$. If the matrix has numbers, find the determinant by placing the numbers into the equation. For example, the determinant of $\begin{bmatrix} 2 & 3 \\ 4 & 5 \end{bmatrix}$ is $(2 \cdot 5) - (3 \cdot 4) = -2$.

Here are examples:

1. The determinant of $\begin{bmatrix} 5 & 4 \\ 6 & 3 \end{bmatrix}$ can be found.

2. The value of k can be found if the determinant of $\begin{bmatrix} 8 & 5 \\ 3 & k \end{bmatrix}$ is 1.

Answers:

1. -5.

    To find the determinant of $\begin{bmatrix} 5 & 4 \\ 6 & 3 \end{bmatrix}$, use $(5 \cdot 3) - (4 \cdot 6) = -5$.

2. 2.

    If the determinant of $\begin{bmatrix} 8 & 5 \\ 3 & k \end{bmatrix}$ is 1, then $(8 \cdot k) - (5 \cdot 3) = 1$. Solve for k:

    $$(8 \cdot k) - (5 \cdot 3) = 1$$
    $$8k - 15 = 1$$
    $$8k = 16$$
    $$k = 2$$

Reporting Category Quiz: Preparing for Higher Mathematics | Number and Quantity

DO YOUR FIGURING HERE.

21. By definition, the determinant $\begin{bmatrix} a & b \\ c & d \end{bmatrix} = ad - bc$. What is the value of $\begin{bmatrix} 2x & 3y \\ 5x & 4y \end{bmatrix}$ when $x = -3$ and $y = 2$?

    F. -138

    G. -42

    H. 12

    J. 42

    K. 138

Chapter 2: Quiz Answers

1. The correct answer is B. Draw a picture:

On the number line, −5 and 17 are 22 units apart. Half this distance is 11, so either go right 11 units from −5 or left 11 units from 17 to land at 6.

2. The correct answer is E. Just count the spaces. From P to Q is 9, Q to R is 6, R to S is 9, and S back to P is 12. The total is $9+6+9+12=36$.

3. The correct answer is B. Pick a number for a and b, such as 3. If $a=3$ and $b=3$, then $|a|=|b|$. Pick any number at all for a and b, and you'll see this is always true. As long as $|a|$ doesn't equal $|b|$, then a can't equal b.

4. The correct answer is A. Find Mr. Dietz's daily pay by dividing his salary by the number of school days: $22,570 \div 185 = \$122$. If for one day, the school district pays the substitute teacher $80 instead of Mr. Dietz's regular $122, then the school district saves the difference in these amounts: $122 − \$80 = \$42$.

5. The correct answer is C. The school owns 30×2 calculators, of which 8 are being repaired, leaving 52 available. Add up the calculators needed for each period:

Period	1	2	3	4	6
Calculators Needed	21	46	48	57	19

The 52 available calculators will suffice for each period except for Period 4.

6. The correct answer is B. Each case has $24 \times 10 = 240$ pens. An order of 2 cases would have 480 pens, which isn't enough: Nick needs to order 3 cases to get 300 pens.

7. The correct answer is D. Multiply the numbers of the 3 different clothing pieces for $4 \times 6 \times 3 = 72$ distinct outfits. For each sweater, there are 6 shirts, and for each shirt, there are 3 pairs of slacks.

8. The correct answer is G. This one is solved by elimination. Any even number greater than 2 isn't prime, so write out the remaining odd numbers: 31, 33, 35, 37, 39, 41, 43, 45, 47, and 49. Divide these by 3, 5, and 7 and cross off anything that divides evenly. You don't have to try dividing them by anything greater than 7, because 7 times anything greater than 7 is greater than 49 and not in this list. The remaining numbers are prime: 31, 37, 41, 43, and 47, for a count of 5.

9. The correct answer is D. To find the oxygen saturation loss, divide the current number of milligrams of dissolved oxygen per liter of water by the dissolved oxygen capacity in milligrams per liter of water: $\frac{7.3}{9.8} = .07449 \approx 74\%$. Note the key words *nearest percent*. True, this could be close to 75%, but that's not an answer choice, and it wouldn't be 73%.

10. **The correct answer is J.** To find the cost of 1 vase, divide the cost of $18 by the 12 vases: $\frac{\$18.00}{12} = \$1.50$.

11. **The correct answer is D.** Find the price per pen for each company. For Company A, divide the pack cost of $15 by the 60 pens: $\frac{\$15.00}{60} = \$0.25$. For Company B, divide the pack cost of $8 by the 40 pens: $\frac{\$8.00}{40} = \$0.20$.

12. **The correct answer is A.** Set this one up as a ratio: 100,000 tons of sand per 60,000 barrels is the same as x tons of sand per 3,000 barrels. Reduce the fractions and cross multiply:

$$\frac{100,000}{60,000} = \frac{x}{3,000}$$
$$\frac{5}{3} = \frac{x}{3,000}$$
$$3x = 15,000$$
$$x = 5,000$$

13. **The correct answer is F.** Multiply the number of seniors graduating by the fraction going to college: $804 \times \frac{2}{5} = 321.6$. Next, multiply that number by the fraction going to a state university: $321.6 \times \frac{1}{4} = 80.4 \approx 80$. Note the key words in this question, *closest estimate*.

14. **The correct answer is B.** The least common denominator is the smallest common multiple of 2, 3, 9, and 15. Don't worry about the 3, because any number that's a multiple of 9 is also a multiple of 3.

    Factor the 2, 9, and 15 to their primes: 2, 3×3, and 3×5. Next, write down the fewest primes needed to multiply out any of these. 2×3×3×5 has the primes to multiply out any one of 2, 9, and 15. Multiply these together for the lowest common multiple: 2×3×3×5 = 90.

15. **The correct answer is C.** Set this one up as a ratio: 100 feet of distance per 5 feet of rise is the same as x feet of distance per 2 feet of rise. Reduce the fractions and cross multiply:

$$\frac{100}{5} = \frac{x}{2}$$
$$\frac{20}{1} = \frac{x}{2}$$
$$x = 40$$

16. **The correct answer is H.** To find an equivalent expression, multiply the constants $(3 \cdot 2 \cdot 4)$ and combine the x terms $(x^3 x^2 x^2 = x^{3+2+2} = x^7$ and y terms $(y \cdot y = y^2)$.

17. The correct answer is E. Each value inside the parentheses is to the 4th power:

$$(-2x^5y^2)^4 = (-2)^4(x^5)^4(y^2)^4 = 16x^{20}y^8.$$

18. The correct answer is K. Each base (2, 4, and 8) is a power of 2, so rewrite the equation with the 4 as 2^2 and the 8 as 2^3, and solve for x:

$$(2^x)(2^2) = (2^3)^3$$
$$(2^{x+2}) = (2^9)$$
$$x + 2 = 9$$
$$x = 7$$

You could also solve this one by working the straight math:

$$(2^x)(4) = 8^3$$
$$(2^x)(4) = 512$$
$$2^x = 128$$
$$2^7 = 128$$

19. The correct answer is G. Start with 2**u** and –3**v**: $2\langle 5,3 \rangle = \langle 10,6 \rangle$ and $-3\langle 2,-7 \rangle = \langle -6,21 \rangle$, respectively. Thus $2u + (-3v) = \langle 10,6 \rangle + \langle -6,21 \rangle = \langle 4,27 \rangle$. Place this in the equation and solve for **w**:

$$2u + (-3v) + w = 0$$
$$\langle 4,27 \rangle + w = 0$$
$$\langle 4,27 \rangle = -w$$
$$w = \langle -4,-27 \rangle$$

20. The correct answer is D. To find the number of sports awards earned, multiply the number of participants in each sport by the ratio for that sport and add the 4 products. This is a matrix multiplication:

$$\begin{bmatrix} 40\ 60\ 80\ 80 \end{bmatrix} \begin{bmatrix} 0.3 \\ 0.4 \\ 0.2 \\ 0.5 \end{bmatrix} = 40(0.3) + 60(0.4) + 80(0.2) + 80(0.5)$$
$$= 12 + 24 + 16 + 40$$
$$= 92$$

21. The correct answer is J. Place −3 and 2 for x and y, respectively, and solve with the arrangement $\begin{bmatrix} a & b \\ c & d \end{bmatrix} = ad - bc$:

$$\begin{bmatrix} 2(-3)3(2) \\ 5(-3)4(2) \end{bmatrix} =$$

$$\begin{bmatrix} -66 \\ -158 \end{bmatrix} = (-6)(8) - (6)(-15)$$

$$= -48 - (-90)$$

$$= 42$$

3 Chapter 3: Algebra

Algebra expands on Number and Quantity by asking you to solve, graph, and model expressions with equations that reflect linear, polynomial, radical, and exponential relationships. It also asks you to find solutions to systems of equations.

Scientific Notation

Scientific notation is used for very small decimals or very large numbers. It's a number, usually between 1 and 10, with a single decimal place, multiplied by a power of 10.

For example, the sun is approximately 93,000,000 miles from the earth. In scientific notation, this is 9.3×10^7 which is equivalent to $9.3 \times 10,000,000$.

The width of a carbon fiber strand is approximately 0.0003 inches, which in scientific notation is 3.0×10^{-4}. This is equivalent to 3.0×0.0001.

A shortcut method for converting scientific notation to standard notation is to move the number's decimal point by the power of the 10. In the sun example, where the distance is 9.3×10^7, move the 9.3 decimal point to the right 7 spaces for the numeric value of 93,000,000. In the carbon fiber example, where the width is 3.0×10^{-4}, move the 3.0 decimal point to the left 4 spaces for the numeric value of 0.0003.

These are examples of numbers that can be converted from scientific notation to standard notation:

1. 2.3×10^4

2. 4.4×10^5

3. 3.2×10^{-3}

Results:

1.   23,000.

   $2.3 \times 10^4 = 2.3 \times 10,000 = 23,000$. Multiplying 2.3 by 10,000 is the equivalent of moving the decimal 4 spaces to the right.

2.   440,000.

   $4.4 \times 10^5 = 4.4 \times 100,000 = 440,000$. Multiplying 4.4 by 100,000 is the equivalent of moving the decimal 5 spaces to the right.

3.   0.0032.

   $3.2 \times 10^{-3} = 3.2 \times 0.001 = 0.0032$. Multiplying 3.2 by 0.001 is the equivalent of moving the decimal 3 spaces to the left.

These are examples of numbers that can be converted from standard notation to scientific notation:

1.   160,000

2.   5,400,000

3.   0.00087

Results:

1. 1.6×10^5.

   $160,000 = 1.6 \times 100,000 = 1.6 \times 10^5$. Multiplying 1.6 by 100,000 is the equivalent of moving the decimal 5 spaces to the right.

2. 5.4×10^6.

   $5,400,000 = 5.4 \times 1,000,000 = 5.4 \times 10^6$. Multiplying 5.4 by 1,000,000 is the equivalent of moving the decimal 6 spaces to the right.

3. 8.7×10^{-4}.

   $0.00087 = 8.7 \times 0.0001 = 8.7 \times 10^{-4}$. Multiplying 8.7 by 0.0001 is the equivalent of moving the decimal 4 spaces to the left.

Reporting Category Quiz: Preparing for Higher Mathematics | Algebra

DO YOUR FIGURING HERE.

1. The normal amount of lead in a certain water supply is 1.5×10^{-5} milligrams per liter. Today, when the water was tested, the lead level found was exactly 100 times as great as the normal level, still well below the Environmental Protection Agency's action level. What concentration of lead, in milligrams per liter, was in the water tested today?

   A. 1.5×10^{-105}

   B. 1.5×10^{-10}

   C. 1.5×10^{-7}

   D. 1.5×10^{-3}

   E. $1.5 \times 10^{-\frac{5}{2}}$

Equations

An **equation,** such as $x = 2$, is a pair of expressions that are equal in size, meaning one side equals the other side. A **system of equations** is two or more equations in a single instance. Note that an **inequality,** such as $x < 5$, isn't considered an equation.

An **unknown** or **variable** is a number that might not be known and is typically represented by a letter, usually x. The letter could represent a fixed value, where only one value solves the equation, or it could represent a changing value, where two or more values solve the equation. For example, where $x = 2$, only one value for x solves the equation, but where $y^2 = 9$, two values for y solve it: 3 and –3.

A **coefficient** is the quantity of like unknowns. For example, with $3x$, the coefficient 3 tells you that there are three xs.

Some letters have standard meanings. For example:

- x and y typically represent the coordinates of a point on the rectangular coordinate system, covered further in this chapter.

- m and b typically represent the slope and y-intercept, respectively, of a linear equation, also covered further in this chapter.

- h and k typically represent the x- and y-positions, respectively, of the center of a circle or the vertex of a parabola. These are covered further in this chapter and in chapter 5, "Geometry."

- k could also represent a **constant,** which is a number that doesn't change.

- i typically represents the **imaginary number** $\sqrt{-1}$, which is a number that cannot exist in real math and is covered further in chapter 2, "Number and Quantity."

- a, b, and c typically represent the coefficients of a quadratic equation, covered further in this chapter, or the sides of a triangle, covered further in chapter 5.

- π, pronounced *pi*, represents the ratio of a circle's circumference to its diameter, roughly 3.14 or $\frac{22}{7}$, covered further in chapter 5.

- θ, pronounced *theta*, represents the degree measure of an angle, often within a unit circle, also covered further in chapter 5.

Solution

To solve an equation, move the unknown to one side of the equation, and divide both sides of the equation by the coefficient. For example, where $3x = x + 6$, subtract x from both sides of the equation for $2x = 6$. Divide both sides by the coefficient 2, for $x = 3$, and the solution is 3.

Reporting Category Quiz: Preparing for Higher Mathematics | Algebra

DO YOUR FIGURING HERE.

2. If $4x + 3 = 9x - 4$, then $x = ?$

F. $\dfrac{7}{5}$

G. $\dfrac{5}{7}$

H. $\dfrac{7}{13}$

J. $\dfrac{1}{5}$

K. $-\dfrac{7}{5}$

3. What is the value of x that satisfies the equation $2(x+4)=5x-7$?

   A. -1

   B. $\dfrac{1}{3}$

   C. $\dfrac{11}{3}$

   D. 5

   E. $\dfrac{45}{3}$

4. If $3\dfrac{3}{5}=x+2\dfrac{2}{3}$, then $x=?$

   F. $\dfrac{4}{5}$

   G. $\dfrac{14}{15}$

   H. $1\dfrac{1}{2}$

   I. $1\dfrac{6}{15}$

   J. $6\dfrac{4}{15}$

DO YOUR FIGURING HERE.

Substitution

Substitution refers to placing the given value of a letter into the equation. Substitute the numeric value for the letter or letters and simplify the equation. For example, if $y=2x^2+3x+5$ and $x=3$, you can find the value of y by substituting 3 for x:

$$y=2x^2+3x+5$$
$$=2(3)^2+3(3)+5$$
$$=18+9+5$$
$$=32$$

Reporting Category Quiz: Preparing for Higher Mathematics | Algebra

DO YOUR FIGURING HERE.

5. What is the value of the expression $g \cdot (g+1)^2$ for $g = 2$?

F. 10

G. 12

H. 18

J. 20

K. 36

6. When $a + b = 6$, what is the value of

$2(a+b) + \frac{a+b}{6} + (a+b)^2 - 2$?

F. 23

G. 37

H. 38

J. 43

K. 47

7. If $a = b + 2$, then $(b-a)^4 = ?$

F. −16

G. −8

H. 1

J. 8

K. 16

Multiplication

A letter or variable can be multiplied like a number. For example, if $x = 5$, then $2x = 10$, because $2 \times 5 = 10$. Note that when $y^2 = 16$, y could equal either 4 or −4, because both $4^2 = 16$ and $(-4)^2 = 16$.

Reporting Category Quiz: Preparing for Higher Mathematics | Algebra

DO YOUR FIGURING HERE.

8. If $a^2 = 49$ and $b^2 = 64$, which of the following CANNOT be a value of $a + b$?

F. -15

G. -1

H. 1

J. 15

K. 113

9. If x is a real number such that $x^3 = 64$, then $x^2 + \sqrt{x} = ?$

F. 4

G. 10

H. 18

J. 20

K. 47

10. The expression $a[b + (c - d)]$ is equivalent to:

A. $ab + ac - ad$

B. $ab + ac + ad$

C. $ab + ac - d$

D. $ab + c + d$

E. $ab + c - d$

Answers with Unknowns

The answer could include an unknown. For example, if a box holds x pieces, then 3 boxes hold $3x$ pieces, and the actual number of pieces isn't known or solved.

Reporting Category Quiz: Preparing for Higher Mathematics | Algebra

11. For all pairs of real numbers M and V where $M = 3V + 6$, $V = ?$

    F. $\dfrac{M}{3} - 6$

    G. $\dfrac{M}{3} + 6$

    H. $3M - 6$

    J. $\dfrac{M - 6}{3}$

    K. $\dfrac{M + 6}{3}$

12. For all positive integers x, y, and z, which of the following expressions is equivalent to $\dfrac{x}{y}$?

    A. $\dfrac{x \cdot z}{y \cdot z}$

    B. $\dfrac{x \cdot x}{y \cdot y}$

    C. $\dfrac{y \cdot x}{x \cdot y}$

    D. $\dfrac{x - z}{y - z}$

    E. $\dfrac{x + z}{y + z}$

Construction of Equations

A word problem could require you to construct an equation using a letter as the number you're looking for. For example, if Betty has 5 more dollars than Andy, and Andy has $15, how much does Betty have? Set this up with b as the amount that Betty has:

$$b = 5 + 15$$

$$b = 20$$

When constructing an equation, treat the word *is* or any variation of it as an equal sign. For example, if Joey is 2 years older than Billy, set up the equation as $j = 2 + b$.

Reporting Category Quiz: Preparing for Higher Mathematics | Algebra

DO YOUR FIGURING HERE.

13. So far, a student has earned the following scores on four 100-point tests this grading period: 65, 73, 81, and 82. What score must the student earn on the fifth and last 100-point test of the grading period to earn an average test grade of 80 for the 5 tests?

    F. 75

    G. 76

    H. 78

    J. 99

    K. The student cannot earn an average of 80.

14. What expression must the center cell of the table below contain so that the sums of each row, each column, and each diagonal are equivalent?

x	$8x$	$-3x$
$-2x$	?	$6x$
$7x$	$-4x$	$3x$

    F. $6x$

    G. $4x$

    H. $2x$

    J. $-2x$

    K. $-4x$

Linear Equations

A **linear equation** is any equation with one or more unknowns, usually x and y, and no exponents, such as $y = 2x + 3$. The equation has infinite solutions, because for any given value of x, there's a corresponding value of y. For example, with $y = 2x + 3$, when $x = 0$, $y = 3$; when $x = 1$, $y = 5$; and so on. These x- and y-values form a line, and each x-value and corresponding y-value falls on the line:

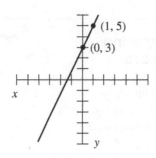

This equation can model a simple real-life scenario. For example, if a 3-foot-tall tree is planted and grows 2 feet each year, the height of the tree can be expressed as $h = 2t + 3$, where h is the tree's height and t is the number of years. When the tree is planted, no time has passed, so $t = 0$, and the corresponding $h = 3$. Note that a linear equation model question may not necessarily be within the Modeling reporting category.

Reporting Category Quiz: Integrating Essential Skills

DO YOUR FIGURING HERE.

15. A city utility department charges residential customers $2.50 per 1,000 gallons of water and $16.00 per month for trash pickup. Which of the following expressions gives a residential customer's total monthly charges, in dollars, for use of g thousand gallons of water and trash pickup?

   F. $2.50g + 16.00$

   G. $2.50g + 1,016.00$

   H. $16.00g + 2.50$

   J. $18.50g$

   K. $2,500.00g + 16.00$

Reporting Category Quiz: Preparing for Higher Mathematics | Algebra

16. A company rents moving vans for a rental fee of $25.00 per day with an additional charge of $0.30 per mile that the van is driven. Which of the following expressions represents the cost, in dollars, of renting a van for 1 day and driving it m miles?

    A. $0.30m + 25$
    B. $25m + 30$
    C. $30m + 25$
    D. $25.30m$
    E. $55m$

17. The relationship between temperature in degrees Fahrenheit, F, and temperature in degrees Celsius, C, is expressed by

    the formula $F = \frac{9}{5}C + 32$. Calvin reads

    a temperature of 38° on a Celsius thermometer. To the nearest degree, what is the equivalent temperature on a Fahrenheit thermometer?

    F. 36°
    G. 53°
    H. 68°
    J. 70°
    K. 100°

18. The length L, in meters, of a spring is

    given by the equation $L = \frac{2}{3}F + 0.03$,

    where F is the applied force in newtons. What force, in newtons, must be applied for the spring's length to be 0.18 meters?

    F. 0.13
    G. 0.15
    H. 0.225
    J. 0.255
    K. 0.27

System of Equations

A **system of equations** is two or more equations in a single instance. A system of equations can have zero, one, or more than one solution.

Linear Systems

The instance can have two linear equations, and the question can ask for the solution to these equations. For example, $y = 2x + 3$ and $y = x + 2$ each has infinite solutions, but together they have one solution for x and y, because there is only one x and corresponding y value that satisfies both equations.

The simplest way to find the solution is to subtract one equation from the other:

$$y = 2x + 3$$
$$\underline{-(y = x + 2)}$$
$$0 = x + 1$$
$$x = -1$$

Now that you know $x = -1$, place -1 for x in one of the equations and find the value of y. You should get the same result from either equation: both $y = 2(-1) + 3$ and $y = (-1) + 2$ result in $y = 1$. The solution to these equations is thus $(-1, 1)$, because those are the only x and y values that satisfy both equations. If you graph the equations, those are the coordinates where the lines intersect.

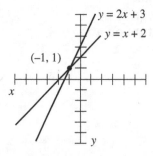

Note that when subtracting the equations, you could have to first multiply one of the equations by a coefficient or a negative. The purpose is to eliminate one unknown so that you can solve for the other one. For example, subtracting $y = 2x + 1$ and $3y = -4x + 8$ won't eliminate an unknown, so start by multiplying the first equation by 3:

$$3(y = 2x + 1)$$
$$3y = 6x + 3$$

Now subtract them to eliminate the y:

$$3y = -4x + 8$$
$$-(3y = 6x + 3)$$
$$\overline{0 = -10x + 5}$$
$$x = \frac{1}{2}$$

These are examples of systems of linear equations that each has a single solution:

1. $y = x + 2$ and $y = -2x + 5$

2. $3y = 5x + 7$ and $2y = 3x + 5$

Results:

1. $(1, 3)$.

First subtract the first equation from the second equation:

$$y = -2x + 5$$
$$-(y = x + 2)$$
$$\overline{0 = -3x + 3}$$
$$x = 1$$

Then substitute the value of x into one of the equations:

$$y = (1) + 2$$
$$y = 3$$

2. $(1, 4)$.

First multiply the first equation by 2 and the second one by 3, then subtract them:

$$2(3y = 5x + 7) \rightarrow 6y = 10x + 14$$
$$3(2y = 3x + 5) \rightarrow 6y = 9x + 15$$

Next, subtract the second result from the first one:

$$6y = 10x + 14$$
$$-(6y = 9x + 15)$$
$$\overline{0 = x - 1}$$
$$x = 1$$

Finally, substitute the value of x into one of the equations:

$$2y = 3(1) + 5$$
$$y = 4$$

Reporting Category Quiz: Preparing for Higher Mathematics | Algebra

19. What is the x-coordinate of the point in the standard (x, y) coordinate plane at which the 2 lines $y = 2x + 6$ and $y = 3x + 4$ intersect?

    A. 1

    B. 2

    C. 4

    D. 6

    E. 10

20. The cost of a hamburger and a soft drink together is $2.10. The cost of 2 hamburgers and a soft drink together is $3.50. What is the cost of a soft drink?

    A. $0.50

    B. $0.55

    C. $0.70

    D. $1.05

    E. $1.40

Another way to find the solution to two equations is to substitute the value of one of the unknowns for that unknown in the other equation. For example, to find the solution to $y = 3x - 4$ and $y = 2x + 1$, y equals both $(3x - 4)$ and $(2x + 1)$, so the two expressions equal each other. Set them up and solve for x:

$$(3x - 4) = (2x + 1)$$
$$x = 5$$

Then place the value of x in one of the equations and solve for y:

$$y = 3(5) - 4$$
$$y = 11$$

The coordinates $(x, y) = (5, 11)$.

Reporting Category Quiz: Preparing for Higher Mathematics | Algebra

DO YOUR FIGURING HERE.

21. If $x = 2t - 9$ and $y = 5 - t$, which of the following expresses y in terms of x?

A. $y = \dfrac{1-x}{2}$

B. $y = \dfrac{19-x}{2}$

C. $y = 14 - 2x$

D. $y = 5 - x$

E. $y = 1 - x$

22. The larger of two numbers exceeds twice the smaller number by 8. The sum of twice the larger and 3 times the smaller number is 65. If x is the smaller number, which equation below determines the correct value of x?

F. $3(2x+8) + 2x = 65$

G. $3(2x-8) + 2x = 65$

H. $(4x+8) + 3x = 65$

J. $2(2x+8) + 3x = 65$

K. $2(2x-8) + 3x = 65$

Numbers of Solutions

Note that the two equations might not have a single solution.

- If the equations represent parallel lines, then the lines don't intersect and there is no solution, because there are no corresponding values for x and y that satisfy both equations. For example, $y = x + 3$ and $y = x + 5$ represent parallel lines. If you were to subtract these, the result would be $0 = 2$. Because $0 = 2$ is impossible, the system of parallel lines doesn't have a solution.

- If the equations represent the same line, then there are infinite solutions, because any corresponding value for x and y would satisfy both equations. For example, $y = x + 3$ and $2y = 2x + 6$ represent the same line. If you were to subtract these, the result would be $0 = 0$. Because the two equations represent one line, there are infinite solutions.

Look at the slopes of the lines. If the slopes are different, the lines intersect, and there is a single solution for the system of equations. If the slopes are the same, the lines are either parallel or identical, and there is either no solution or infinite solutions.

Reporting Category Quiz: Preparing for Higher Mathematics | Algebra

DO YOUR FIGURING HERE.

23. A system of linear equations is shown below.

$$3y = -2x + 8$$
$$3y = 2x + 8$$

Which of the following describes the graph of this system of linear equations in the standard (x, y) coordinate plane?

A. Two distinct intersecting lines

B. Two parallel lines with positive slope

C. Two parallel lines with negative slope

D. A single line with positive slope

E. A single line with negative slope

Variations on Linear Equations

Linear equations can have certain variations.

- A y value without an x value represents a horizontal line. For example, $y = 3$ is a horizontal line that crosses the y axis at 3. This line has a slope of 0.

- An x value without a y value represents a vertical line. For example, $x = 5$ is a vertical line that crosses the x axis at 5. This line has an undefined slope.

- An expression, whether linear or non-linear, can be an inequality. For example, $y < x + 5$ and $y \leq x + 3$ represent the area beneath the line, while $y > x + 5$ and $y \geq x + 3$ represent the area above the line. An expression of "less than" or "greater than," < or >, respectively, is graphed with a dashed line, while an expression of "or equal to," $\leq$ or $\geq$, is graphed with a solid line.

Reporting Category Quiz: Preparing for Higher Mathematics | Algebra

24. Which of the following systems of inequalities is represented by the shaded region of the graph below?

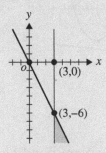

A. $y \leq -2x$ and $x \geq 3$

B. $y \leq -2x$ or $x \geq 3$

C. $y \geq -2x$ and $x \geq 3$

D. $y \geq -2x$ or $x \geq 3$

E. $y \geq -2x$ and $x \leq 3$

Non-Linear Systems

A system of equations can feature non-linear equations, in which case the system can have more than one solution. For example, the line and parabola cross twice, giving the system of equations two solutions.

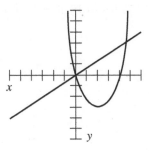

A line and parabola may cross once, as shown in the drawing on the left, giving the system of equations one solution; or they may not cross at all, as shown in the drawing on the right, in which case the system has no solution.

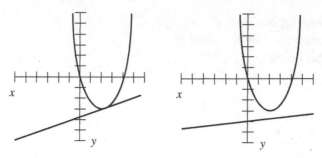

Quadratic Equations and Parabolas

A linear equation, such as $y = 2x + 3$, has no exponents and single corresponding values of x and y, but a **quadratic equation** has x^2, giving each value of y either zero, one, or two possible values of x. For example, with the quadratic equation $y = x^2$, when $y = 9$, x has two possible values, 3 or -3; when $y = 0$, x has one possible value, 0; and when $y = -4$, x has zero possible values. A quadratic equation graphs into a **parabola:**

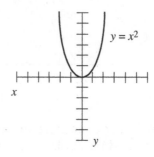

Note that $f(x)$ can be used in place of y, making $y = x^2$ the same as $f(x) = x^2$; this is covered further in chapter 4, "Functions."

Reporting Category Quiz: Preparing for Higher Mathematics | Algebra

25. Which of the following is the graph, in the standard (x, y) coordinate plane, of

$$y = \frac{2x^2 + x}{x}?$$

A.

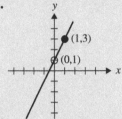

B.

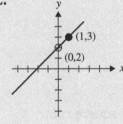

C.

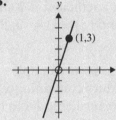

D.

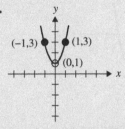

E.

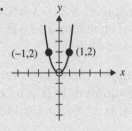

Quadratic Factors

A quadratic equation having a leading coefficient of 1, meaning it begins with x^2, not $2x^2$ or $3x^2$, can be factored simply. For example, $y = x^2 + 2x - 3$ factors into $y = (x+3)(x-1)$. To find the possible values of x, set y equal to 0, and $0 = x^2 + 2x - 3$ factors into $0 = (x+3)(x-1)$, meaning x could equal –3 or 1. If you graph the equation $y = x^2 + 2x - 3$, the parabola crosses the x-axis (where $y = 0$) at –3 and 1.

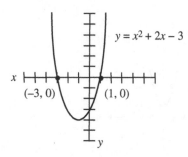

One simple method to factor a quadratic with a leading coefficient of 1 is to find two values whose sum is the x coefficient and product is the constant term. (The *constant term* is the number on the end that doesn't have an x.) With the example $x^2 + 2x - 3 = 0$, the x coefficient is 2 and the constant term is –3, so the two values are 3 and –1, because $3 + (-1) = 2$ and $(3)(-1) = -3$. Place these values into the factored expressions: $(x+3)$ and $(x-1)$.

Another method to factor the quadratic is to *complete the square*. With the same example $x^2 + 2x - 3 = 0$, look for an expression that, when squared, FOILs to a product containing $x^2 + 2x$: in this case, $(x+1)^2$. However, the FOIL of $(x+1)^2$ is $x^2 + 2x + 1$, so for this result, add 4 to both sides:

$$x^2 + 2x - 3 = 0$$
$$+4 \quad +4$$
$$x^2 + 2x + 1 = 4$$

Because $x^2 + 2x + 1 = (x+1)^2$, change the left side to $(x+1)^2$ and take the square root:

$$(x+1)^2 = 4$$
$$\sqrt{(x+1)^2} = \sqrt{4}$$
$$x + 1 = 2, -2$$
$$x = 1, -3$$

To check whether the equation was factored correctly, multiply the factors and see whether the product matches the original equation. Use the FOIL (**f**irst, **o**uter, **i**nner, **l**ast) method to multiply $(x+3)(x-1)$ back to x^2+2x-3:

$$(x+3)(x-1)$$
$$x^2-x+3x-3$$
$$x^2+2x-3$$

These are examples of quadratic equations that each has one or two possible solutions for x:

1. $x^2+3x-10=0$

2. $x^2-x-12=0$

3. $x^2+6x+9=0$

Results:

1. $x=-2,5$.

    The two values that add to 3 and multiply to –10 are 2 and –5; place these into the factored expressions:

    $$x^2+3x-10=0$$
    $$(x+2)(x-5)=0$$

2. $x=-3,4$.

    The two values that add to –1 and multiply to –12 are 3 and –4; place these into the factored expressions:

    $$x^2-x-12=0$$
    $$(x+3)(x-4)=0$$

3. $x=-3$.

    This is an example where the quadratic has a single value of x. $3+3=6$ and $3\times3=9$, so each number is 3: place 3s into the factored expression, and combine them into a single squared value:

    $$x^2+6x+9=0$$
    $$(x+3)(x+3)=0$$
    $$(x+3)^2=0$$

Reporting Category Quiz: Preparing for Higher Mathematics | Algebra

DO YOUR FIGURING HERE.

26. Which of the following quadratic equations has solutions $x = 6a$ and $x = -3b$?

F. $x^2 - 18ab = 0$

G. $x^2 - x(3b - 6a) - 18ab = 0$

H. $x^2 - x(3b + 6a) + 18ab = 0$

J. $x^2 + x(3b - 6a) - 18ab = 0$

K. $x^2 + x(3b + 6a) + 18ab = 0$

The x^2 in the quadratic $x^2 + 2x - 3 = 0$ is known as the *quadratic term*, and the $2x$ is known as the *linear term*. If the quadratic doesn't have a linear term, such as $x^2 - 25 = 0$, it can be solved by taking the square root. Isolate the quadratic term and take the square root of both sides:

$$x^2 - 25 = 0$$

$$x^2 = 25$$

$$x = 5, -5$$

If the quadratic equation cannot be factored simply, for example, if the leading coefficient is greater than 1, the **quadratic formula** is another option:

$$x = \frac{-b \pm \sqrt{b^2 - 4ac}}{2a}$$

The coefficients and numeric value from the quadratic equation are a, b, and c in the equation. For example, the equation $0 = x^2 + 2x - 3$ with coefficients showing is $0 = (1)x^2 + (2)x - 3$, so the values of a, b, and c are 1, 2, and –3, respectively. Place these into the quadratic formula and simplify:

$$x = \frac{-(2) \pm \sqrt{(2)^2 - 4(1)(-3)}}{2(1)}$$

$$= \frac{-2 \pm \sqrt{16}}{2}$$

$$= \frac{-2 \pm 4}{2}$$

$$= \frac{-2 - 4}{2}, \frac{-2 + 4}{2}$$

$$= -3, 1$$

You get the same solutions for x whether you factor the equation or solve it with the quadratic formula.

Note the expression $\pm\sqrt{b^2-4ac}$ within the quadratic equation: if b^2-4ac equals 0, x has one solution, and if b^2-4ac is negative, the equation cannot be solved or factored.

Multiplication

To multiply a quadratic by a coefficient, distribute the coefficient among the terms. For example, to multiply 3 by x^2+3x+2, written as $3(x^2+3x+2)$, distribute the 3 among the terms for $3x^2+9x+6$.

To multiply two expressions into a quadratic, use the FOIL method. For example, to multiply $(x-2)$ by $(x-3)$, multiply the first terms (each x), the inner terms (the –2 and x), the outer terms (the x and –3), and the last terms (the –2 and –3). Add the results for the answer:

$$(x-2)(x-3)$$

$$x^2-3x-2x+6$$

$$x^2-5x+6$$

To square an expression, write it out as two separate expressions for multiplying. For example, to simplify $(x+3)^2$, write it out as $(x+3)(x+3)$ and multiply using the FOIL method:

$$(x+3)^2$$

$$(x+3)(x+3)$$

$$x^2+3x+3x+9$$

$$x^2+6x+9$$

Note that when multiplying expressions that are identical except for the signs between the terms, the middle terms cancel out. For example, $(x+5)$ and $(x-5)$ are identical except that one has +5 and the other –5. When these are multiplied, the $5x$ and $-5x$ cancel, and the resulting quadratic has no middle term:

$$(x+5)(x-5)$$

$$x^2-5x+5x-25$$

$$x^2-25$$

This is called a **math conjugate** and also applies to factoring: the factors of a perfect square minus a perfect square are identical expressions of square roots but with differing signs. Common forms of this include x^2-9, which factors to $(x+3)(x-3)$, y^2-5, which factors to $\left(y+\sqrt{5}\right)\left(y-\sqrt{5}\right)$, and a^2-b^2, which factors to $(a+b)(a-b)$.

Reporting Category Quiz: Preparing for Higher Mathematics | Algebra

27. $(x^2 - 4x + 3) - (3x^2 - 4x - 3)$ is equivalent to:

   F. $2x^2 - 6$

   G. $2x^2 - 8x$

   H. $2x^2 - 8x - 6$

   J. $-2x^2 + 6$

   K. $-2x^2 - 8x$

28. Which of the following expressions is equivalent to $3x(x^2y + 2xy^2)$?

   F. $3x^2y + 6xy^2$

   G. $3x^3y + 2xy^2$

   H. $3x^3y + 6x^2y^2$

   J. $5x^4y^3$

   K. $9x^4y^3$

29. For all x, $(3x + 1)^2 = ?$

   F. $6x + 2$

   G. $6x^2 + 2$

   H. $9x^2 + 1$

   J. $9x^2 + 3x + 1$

   K. $9x^2 + 6x + 1$

30. $\left(\frac{1}{2}x - y\right)^2 = ?$

   A. $\frac{1}{4}x^2 + y^2$

   B. $\frac{1}{4}x^2 - xy + y^2$

   C. $\frac{1}{2}x^2 - xy + y^2$

   D. $x^2 + y^2$

   E. $x^2 - xy + y^2$

There are three common quadratic forms. The first is the *standard form*, which is the now-familiar $y = ax^2 + bx + c$, or $y = x^2 + 2x - 3$. The second is the *vertex form*, which is $y = a(x-h)^2 + k$, or with this example, $y = (x+1)^2 - 4$. Note that $a = 1$ in almost every ACT mathematics test parabola, so you can treat these as $y = x^2 + bx + c$ and $y = (x-h)^2 + k$. The advantage of the vertex form is that it gives you the parabola's vertex as h and k. If you FOIL the squared expression in the vertex form, it matches the standard form.

$$y = (x+1)^2 - 4$$
$$y = (x+1)(x+1) - 4$$
$$y = (x^2 + 2x + 1) - 4$$
$$y = x^2 + 2x - 3$$

The resulting graph of $y = (x+1)^2 - 4$ matches the graph of $y = x^2 + 2x - 3$.

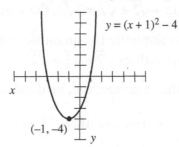

The third common quadratic form is the *factored form*, which is $y = (x-a)(x-b)$. For example, the factored form of $y = x^2 + 2x - 3$ is $y = (x-1)(x+3)$. The advantage of the factored form is that it tells you the x-intercepts as a and b.

Roots

A **square root** refers to a quantity that, when squared, yields the starting quantity. For example, $\sqrt{25} = 5$, because $5^2 = 25$. A **cube root** is similar, except the quantity is cubed to yield the starting quantity. For example, $\sqrt[3]{8} = 2$, because $2^3 = 8$.

A fractional exponent yields a root. For example, $3^{\frac{1}{2}} = \sqrt{3}$ and $5^{\frac{1}{3}} = \sqrt[3]{5}$. The denominator of the fraction becomes the *index number* (the small number outside the radical), and the numerator of the fraction stays as the exponent. For example, $7^{\frac{3}{5}} = \sqrt[5]{7^3}$.

Square Roots

A square root always yields a positive number, because a quantity times itself is never negative. The square root of any negative number is therefore not a real number and is referred to as i for *imaginary*. Where $\sqrt{36} = 6$ represents a real number, $\sqrt{-25} = \sqrt{25} \times \sqrt{-1} = 5i$ and is imaginary. Remember that $i = \sqrt{-1}$ and $i^2 = -1$.

Note that when $x^2 = 9$, x can equal either 3 or –3, because you're not taking the square root of x^2 or 9: you're finding values of x that satisfy the equation. However, $\sqrt{9}$ can only be 3, and not –3, because a square root can only be of a positive number.

To take the square root of a fraction, take the square roots of the numerator and denominator as separate numbers. For example, to take the square root of $\sqrt{\frac{4}{25}}$, take the square roots of 4 and 25 separately: $\frac{\sqrt{4}}{\sqrt{25}} = \frac{2}{5}$.

Multiplication and Division

You can multiply and divide square root quantities, but you cannot add or subtract them. For example, $\sqrt{3} \times \sqrt{5} = \sqrt{15}$, but $\sqrt{2} + \sqrt{3}$ cannot be simplified. However, if the square root quantities are the same, they can be counted: $\sqrt{2} + \sqrt{2} + \sqrt{2} = 3\sqrt{2}$, the same way that $x + x + x = 3x$.

Multiply square root quantities by multiplying the quantities within. In the same way that $7 \times 3 = 21$, multiply the square root quantities $\sqrt{7} \times \sqrt{3} = \sqrt{21}$.

Divide square root quantities with the same method, by dividing the quantities within. In the same way that $\frac{10}{2} = 5$, divide the square root quantities $\frac{\sqrt{10}}{\sqrt{2}} = \sqrt{5}$.

These are examples of roots that can be simplified:

1. $\sqrt{7} \times \sqrt{5}$
2. $\sqrt{10} + \sqrt{10}$
3. $\frac{\sqrt{21}}{\sqrt{7}}$

Results:

1. $\sqrt{35}$.

   Multiply the numbers under the radical: $\sqrt{7} \times \sqrt{5} = \sqrt{35}$.

2. $2\sqrt{10}$.

   Count the like radicals: $\sqrt{10} + \sqrt{10} = 2\sqrt{10}$.

3. $\sqrt{3}$.

   Divide the numbers under the radical: $\frac{\sqrt{21}}{\sqrt{7}} = \sqrt{3}$.

   If the roots have coefficients, multiply or divide the coefficients separately from the roots: $2\sqrt{3} \times 4\sqrt{5} \rightarrow (2 \times 4)(\sqrt{3} \times \sqrt{5}) = 8 \times \sqrt{15} = 8\sqrt{15}$.

Simplification

To simplify a square root, factor the quantity and simplify the perfect squares. For example, to simplify $\sqrt{18}$, factor it and simplify:

$$\sqrt{18}$$
$$\sqrt{9}\times\sqrt{2}$$
$$3\times\sqrt{2}$$
$$3\sqrt{2}$$

These are examples of roots that can be simplified:

1. $\sqrt{75}$
2. $\sqrt{32}$
3. $\sqrt{20}$

Results:

1. $5\sqrt{3}$.

   Factor out the perfect square, which is 25: $\sqrt{75}=\sqrt{25}\times\sqrt{3}=5\sqrt{3}$.
2. $4\sqrt{2}$.

   Factor out the perfect square, which is 16: $\sqrt{32}=\sqrt{16}\times\sqrt{2}=4\sqrt{2}$.
3. $2\sqrt{5}$.

   Factor out the perfect square, which is 4: $\sqrt{20}=\sqrt{4}\times\sqrt{5}=2\sqrt{5}$.

Cube Roots

A cube root can yield a positive or negative number, because a quantity times itself three times stays positive or negative. For example, $\sqrt[3]{27}=3$ and $\sqrt[3]{-64}=-4$, because $(-4)(-4)(-4)=-64$.

Multiplication and Division

Similar to square root quantities, cube root quantities can be multiplied, divided, and counted, but not added or subtracted.

These are examples of roots that can be simplified:

1. $\sqrt[3]{6}\times\sqrt[3]{3}$
2. $\sqrt[3]{8}+\sqrt[3]{8}$
3. $\dfrac{\sqrt[3]{35}}{\sqrt[3]{7}}$

Results:

1. $\sqrt[3]{18}$.

   Multiply the numbers under the radicals: $\sqrt[3]{6} \times \sqrt[3]{3} = \sqrt[3]{18}$.

2. $2\sqrt[3]{8}$.

   Add the like radicals: $\sqrt[3]{8} + \sqrt[3]{8} = 2\sqrt[3]{8}$.

3. $\sqrt[3]{5}$.

   Divide the numbers under the radicals: $\dfrac{\sqrt[3]{35}}{\sqrt[3]{7}} = \sqrt[3]{5}$.

Simplification

To simplify a cube root, factor the quantity and simplify the perfect cubes. For example, to simplify $\sqrt[3]{54}$, factor it out and simplify:

$$\sqrt[3]{54}$$

$$\sqrt[3]{27} \times \sqrt[3]{2}$$

$$3 \times \sqrt[3]{2}$$

$$3\sqrt[3]{2}$$

These are examples of roots that can be simplified:

1. $\sqrt[3]{16}$

2. $\sqrt[3]{24}$

3. $\sqrt[3]{81}$

Results:

1. $2\sqrt[3]{2}$.

   Factor out the perfect cube, which is 8: $\sqrt[3]{16} = \sqrt[3]{8} \times \sqrt[3]{2} = 2\sqrt[3]{2}$.

2. $2\sqrt[3]{3}$.

   Factor out the perfect cube, which again is 8: $\sqrt[3]{24} = \sqrt[3]{8} \times \sqrt[3]{3} = 2\sqrt[3]{3}$.

3. $3\sqrt[3]{3}$.

   Factor out the perfect cube, which is 27: $\sqrt[3]{81} = \sqrt[3]{27} \times \sqrt[3]{3} = 3\sqrt[3]{3}$.

Higher Roots

No index number indicates a square root and a 3 indicates a cube root, as in $\sqrt{9}$ and $\sqrt[3]{27}$. However, the index number can be any number, such as 4 or 5. It refers to the number of times the result is multiplied by itself to get the starting number. For example, $\sqrt[5]{32} = 2$, because $2^5 = 32$.

Logarithmic Equations

A **logarithmic equation** is the inverse function of an exponential equation. This means that the logarithm of a number is the exponent needed to produce that number from the base. For example, the logarithm of 16 from a base of 2 is 4, because the number 2 needs an exponent 4 to produce 16. This is written as $\log_2 16 = 4$, which is the same as $2^4 = 16$.

To solve for an unknown in a logarithmic equation, rewrite the equation in its exponential form. For example, rewrite $\log_3 9 = 2$ as $3^2 = 9$.

These are examples of logarithmic equations where the unknowns can be solved by rewriting the equations in their exponential forms:

1. $\log_3 81 = x$

2. $\log_2 x = 5$

3. $\log_x 25 = 2$

Results:

1. 4.

   Rewrite the equation in its exponential form:

   $$\log_3 81 = x$$
   $$3^x = 81$$
   $$x = 4$$

2. 32.

   Rewrite the equation in its exponential form:

   $$\log_2 x = 5$$
   $$2^5 = x$$
   $$x = 32$$

3. 5.

   Rewrite the equation in its exponential form:

   $$\log_x 25 = 2$$
   $$x^2 = 25$$
   $$x = 5$$

DO YOUR FIGURING HERE.

31. The value of $\log_5\left(5^{\frac{13}{2}}\right)$ is between which of the following pairs of consecutive integers?

A. 0 and 1

B. 4 and 5

C. 5 and 6

D. 6 and 7

E. 9 and 10

Chapter 3: Quiz Answers

1. The correct answer is D. Multiply 1.5×10^{-5} by 100, which is equivalent to 10^2:
$1.5\times10^{-5}\times10^2 = 1.5\times10^{(-5+2)} = 1.5\times10^{-3}$.

2. The correct answer is F. Move the xs to the left and the numbers to the right, then divide both sides by the x coefficient.

$$4x+3=9x-4$$
$$-5x=-7$$
$$x=\frac{7}{5}$$

3. The correct answer is D. First distribute the coefficient among the values in the expression, then move the xs to the left and the numbers to the right. Finally, divide both sides by the x coefficient.

$$2(x+4)=5x-7$$
$$2x+8=5x-7$$
$$-3x=-15$$
$$x=5$$

4. The correct answer is G. The x can stay on the right: subtract $2\frac{2}{3}$ from both sides.

$$3\frac{3}{5}-2\frac{2}{3}=x$$
$$3\frac{9}{15}-2\frac{10}{15}=x$$
$$\frac{14}{15}=x$$

5. The correct answer is H. Substitute 2 for g in the equation:

$$g \cdot (g+1)^2$$
$$(2) \cdot ((2)+1)^2$$
$$(2) \cdot (3)^2$$
$$(2) \cdot (9)$$
$$18$$

6. The correct answer is K. Substitute 6 for $a+b$ in the equation:

$$2(a+b)+\frac{a+b}{6}+(a+b)^2-2$$
$$2(6)+\frac{6}{6}+(6)^2-2$$
$$12+1+36-2$$
$$47$$

7. The correct answer is K. First find the value of $b-a$. Subtract b and multiply by -1:

$$a=b+2$$
$$a-b=2$$
$$b-a=-2$$

Then, substitute -2 for $b-a$ in the second expression:

$$(b-a)^4$$
$$(-2)^4$$
$$16$$

8. The correct answer is K. If $a^2=49$ and $b^2=64$, $a=7$ or -7, and $b=8$ or -8, giving $a+b$ four possibilities:

$$8+7=15$$
$$8-7=1$$
$$-8+7=-1$$
$$-8+-7=-15$$

The only one that's not a correct answer is 113.

9. The correct answer is H. If $x^3=64$, then $x=4$. Substitute 4 in the equation:

$$x^2+\sqrt{x}=$$
$$(4)^2+\sqrt{(4)}=$$
$$16+2=18$$

10. **The correct answer is A.** Distribute the a among the expression: $a\left[b+(c-d)\right]=ab+ac-ad$.

11. **The correct answer is J.** Set up the equation and solve for V:

$$M = 3V + 6$$
$$M - 6 = 3V$$
$$\frac{M-6}{3} = V$$

12. **The correct answer is A.** With the fraction $\frac{x\cdot z}{y\cdot z}$, the zs cancel, leaving $\frac{x}{y}$. Another way to work this question is to substitute numbers for the letters, such as $x=2$, $y=3$, and $z=5$. Then look for the answer choice equivalent to $\frac{2}{3}$.

13. **The correct answer is J.** For an average of 80 on 5 tests, the student needs $5 \times 80 = 400$ points. Set up the equation with x as the fifth test:

$$65+73+81+82+x = 400$$
$$301+x = 400$$
$$x = 99$$

14. **The correct answer is H.** You don't need to check each row, column, and diagonal: just set one complete row equal to the one with the missing value. Using the first row:

$$x+8x-3x = -2x+?+6x$$
$$6x = 4x+?$$
$$2x = ?$$

You could eliminate the xs and work with the coefficients:
$$1+8-3 = -2+?+6$$
$$6 = 4+?$$
$$2 = ?$$

15. **The correct answer is F.** This is a standard linear equation with g as the x and the value of the entire equation as the y. Set it up as $y = mx + b$ and add the numbers from the question. The customer pays a flat $16.00 regardless of the water used, so use $16.00 for b. The customer pays $2.50 per 1,000 gallons of water, and g represents 1,000 gallons, so use $2.50 for m. Last, place g for x, and the equation looks like this: $y = 2.50g + 16.00$. Eliminate the y for the answer.

16. **The correct answer is A.** This is a standard linear equation with m as the x and the value of the entire equation as the y. Because m is usually the slope of the equation, for this

explanation the slope will be *e*. Set up the equation as $y = ex + b$ and add the numbers from the question. The customer pays a flat $25.00 regardless of the miles driven, so use $25.00 for *b*. The customer pays $0.30 per mile, so use $0.30 for *e*. Last, place *m* for *x*, and the equation looks like this: $y = 0.30m + 25.00$. Eliminate the *y* for the answer.

17. **The correct answer is K.** Place 38 for *C* in the equation and solve for *F*:

$$F = \frac{9}{5}C + 32$$

$$= \frac{9}{5}(38) + 32$$

$$= 68.4 + 32$$

$$= 100.4$$

Note that the question reads, to the *nearest* degree.

18. **The correct answer is H.** Place 0.18 for *L* in the equation and solve for *F*:

$$L = \frac{2}{3}F + 0.03$$

$$(0.18) = \frac{2}{3}F + 0.03$$

$$0.15 = \frac{2}{3}F$$

$$0.225 = F$$

19. **The correct answer is B.** Subtract the first equation from the second one and solve for *x*:

$$y = 3x + 4$$

$$\underline{-(y = 2x + 6)}$$

$$0 = x - 2$$

$$2 = x$$

20. **The correct answer is C.** First, set up the two equations with *h* as the cost of a hamburger and *d* as the cost of a soft drink:

$$h + d = 2.10$$

$$2h + d = 3.50$$

Next, subtract the first equation from the second one:

$$2h + d = 3.50$$

$$\underline{-(h + d = 2.10)}$$

$$h = 1.40$$

Finally, place the value of h into the simpler equation:

$$h + d = 2.10$$
$$(1.40) + d = 2.10$$
$$d = 0.70$$

21. **The correct answer is A.** Substitute to eliminate the t. First, isolate the t in one equation:

$$y = 5 - t$$
$$t + y = 5$$
$$t = 5 - y$$

Next, substitute t with $5-y$ in the other equation:

$$x = 2t - 9$$
$$x = 2(5 - y) - 9$$
$$x = 10 - 2y - 9$$
$$x = 1 - 2y$$

Finally, isolate the y:

$$x = 1 - 2y$$
$$x + 2y = 1$$
$$2y = 1 - x$$
$$y = \frac{1 - x}{2}$$

22. **The correct answer is J.** First, set up two equations with b as the larger number and x as the smaller number. Use the words *exceeds* and *is* as the equal signs:

$$b = 2x + 8$$
$$2b + 3x = 65$$

Next, place the value of b from the first equation into the b in the second equation, so that the b is eliminated, and the result should match an answer choice:

$$2(2x + 8) + 3x = 65$$

23. **The correct answer is A.** The slopes of the lines are the x coefficients when y equals the equation. Because the slopes are different, the lines intersect.

24. **The correct answer is A.** Narrow down the answer. The shaded region represents constraints from line 1 *and* line 2, which narrows the answer down to choices **A, C,** and **E.** The shaded region is *below* the diagonal line, so the answer contains $y \le -2x$ and has to be choice **A.** Just to be sure, the shaded region is to the right of the vertical line, so the answer also contains $x \ge 3$, also in choice **A.**

25. The correct answer is A. Factor out the x to reduce the fraction:

$$y = \frac{2x^2 + x}{x}$$

$$= \frac{x(2x+1)}{x}$$

$$= 2x + 1$$

With no exponent, the graph is a line, which narrows the answer down to choices **A, B,** and **C.** The slope is 2 and y-intercept is 1, so the answer is **A.**

26. The correct answer is J. If the solutions to the equation are $x = 6a$ and $x = -3b$, then the factors of the equation are $(x - 6a)(x + 3b) = 0$. Multiply these using the FOIL method for the answer:

$$(x - 6a)(x + 3b) = 0$$

$$x^2 + 3bx - 6ax - 18ab = 0$$

$$x^2 + x(3b - 6a) - 18ab = 0$$

The two middle terms contain x, so this is factored out within the equation.

27. The correct answer is J. Distribute the negative among the second expression, and combine like terms:

$$\left(x^2 - 4x + 3\right) - \left(3x^2 - 4x - 3\right)$$

$$\left(x^2 - 4x + 3\right) - 3x^2 + 4x + 3$$

$$-2x^2 + 6$$

28. The correct answer is H. Distribute the $3x$ among the expression:

$$3x\left(x^2 y + 2xy^2\right)$$

$$\left(x^2 y \cdot 3x + 2xy^2 \cdot 3x\right)$$

$$3x^3 y + 6x^2 y^2$$

29. The correct answer is K. Set the expression times itself and multiply using the FOIL method:

$$(3x + 1)^2$$

$$(3x + 1)(3x + 1)$$

$$9x^2 + 3x + 3x + 1$$

$$9x^2 + 6x + 1$$

30. The correct answer is B. Set the expression times itself and multiply using the FOIL method:

$$\left(\frac{1}{2}x - y\right)^2$$

$$\left(\frac{1}{2}x - y\right)\left(\frac{1}{2}x - y\right)$$

$$\frac{1}{4}x^2 - \frac{1}{2}xy - \frac{1}{2}xy + y^2$$

$$\frac{1}{4}x^2 - xy + y^2$$

31. The correct answer is D. Set the equation equal to x and rewrite it in its exponential form:

$$\log_5\left(5^{\frac{13}{2}}\right) = x$$

$$5^x = 5^{\frac{13}{2}}$$

$$x = \frac{13}{2}$$

$$= 6\frac{1}{2}$$

Chapter 4:
Functions

The questions in this category test your ability to work with **functions**. Questions can ask you to manipulate and translate linear, radical, piecewise, polynomial, and logarithmic functions. They can also ask you to find and apply features of graphs.

Series, Sequences, and Consecutive Numbers

A **series** or **sequence** is the adding of many quantities, one after the other, to a given quantity, possibly in a repeating pattern. To discern a series or a sequence, look for the pattern or difference between each of the numbers. For example, to find the next number in series $\{1, 4, 7, 10, ...\}$, the common difference is 3, so you know that the next number after 10 is 13.

These are examples of series and sequences that can be completed:

1. $\{2, 7, 12, \_\_, 22, ...\}$

2. $\{3, 7, 15, 31, \_\_, ...\}$

3. $\{2, 5, 8, 5, 10, 2, 5, 8, \_\_, 10, ...\}$

Results:

1. 17.

    The common difference between each number is 5. Start with 2, and repeatedly add 5.

2. 63.

    The common difference between each number doubles: 4, 8, and 16. From this, you can discern that the next difference is 32:

$$3 + 4 = 7$$
$$7 + 8 = 15$$
$$15 + 16 = 31$$
$$31 + 32 = 63$$

3. 5.

    This sequence is the repetition of the numbers 2, 5, 8, 5, and 10.

Consecutive numbers are of a specific series where numbers follow each other in order, typically with a common difference of 1 between each number: $\{5, 6, 7, 8, 9, ...\}$. Consecutive numbers specified as *even* or *odd* have a common difference of 2 between each number: $\{2, 4, 6, 8, 10, ...\}$ or $\{1, 3, 5, 7, 9, ...\}$. Consecutive numbers can also be negative: $\{-3, -2, -1, 0, 1, 2, 3, ...\}$.

Reporting Category Quiz: Preparing for Higher Mathematics | Functions

1. What 2 numbers should be placed in the blanks below so that the difference between consecutive numbers is the same?

   17,____,____, 41

   A. 23, 29

   B. 24, 34

   C. 25, 33

   D. 26, 35

   E. 27, 31

2. Which of the following statements describes the total number of dots in the first n rows of the triangular arrangement illustrated below?

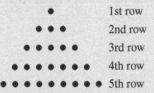

            ●   1st row
         ● ● ●   2nd row
       ● ● ● ● ●   3rd row
     ● ● ● ● ● ● ●   4th row
   ● ● ● ● ● ● ● ● ● 5th row

   A. This total number is always equal to 25 regardless of the number of rows.

   B. This total is equal to twice the number of rows.

   C. This total is equal to 5 times the number of rows.

   D. This total is equal to the square of the number of rows.

   E. There is no consistent relationship between this total and the number of rows.

(continued)

(continued)

3. Which of the following statements is NOT true about the arithmetic sequence $17, 12, 7, 2, ...$?

   A. The fifth term is -3.

   B. The sum of the first 5 terms is 35.

   C. The eighth term is -18.

   D. The common difference of consecutive terms is -5.

   E. The common ratio of consecutive terms is -5.

DO YOUR FIGURING HERE.

Slope-Intercept Form of a Linear Equation

The **slope-intercept form** of a linear equation is the form $y = mx + b$, where m is the slope and b is the y-intercept. With the line $y = 3x + 5$, the slope is 3 and the y-intercept is 5.

A linear equation can appear in a different form, such as $6x + 3y = 9$. To find the slope and y-intercept, convert it to the slope-intercept form by setting the equation equal to y:

$$6x + 3y = 9$$
$$3y = -6x + 9$$
$$y = -2x + 3$$

With this line, the slope is -2 and the y-intercept is 3.

Note that parallel lines have identical slopes, and perpendicular lines have negative reciprocal slopes. For example, $y = \frac{2}{3}x + 4$ is parallel to $y = \frac{2}{3}x + 2$ but perpendicular to $y = -\frac{3}{2}x + 4$.

Reporting Category Quiz: Preparing for Higher Mathematics | Functions

DO YOUR FIGURING HERE.

4. What is the slope-intercept form of $8x - y - 6 = 0$?

   F. $y = -8x - 6$
   G. $y = -8x + 6$
   H. $y = 8x - 6$
   J. $y = 8x + 6$
   K. $y = 6x - 8$

5. What is the slope of any line parallel to the
   line $7x + 9y = 6$?

DO YOUR FIGURING HERE.

   A. -7

   B. $-\dfrac{7}{9}$

   C. $\dfrac{7}{6}$

   D. 6

   E. 7

Slope and Intercept from a Line in the Coordinate Plane

Find the slope and y-intercept from the drawing to re-create the equation. Place the slope and y-intercept as the m and b, respectively, into the slope-intercept equation $y = mx + b$.

The y-intercept is the point where the line crosses the y-axis. In this example, the line crosses the y-axis at 3, so $b = 3$. The slope can be found using either *rise over run* or the *slope formula* $m = \frac{y_2 - y_1}{x_2 - x_1}$. Using rise over run, the line rises 3 and runs 2. Because the line goes down, the slope is negative, so $m = -\frac{3}{2}$.

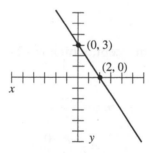

The slope formula captures the rise over run from any two points on the line. $y_2 - y_1$ refers to one y-coordinate minus the other, and $x_2 - x_1$ refers to one x-coordinate minus the other. In the following drawing, coordinate 2 is $(2,0)$ and coordinate 1 is $(0,3)$, so $y_2 - y_1$ is $0 - 3$ and $x_2 - x_1$ is $2 - 0$. It doesn't matter which point is coordinate 2 or 1, as long as the xs and ys are consistent.

Place these x- and y-values into the formula:

$$m = \frac{y_2 - y_1}{x_2 - x_1}$$

$$= \frac{0 - 3}{2 - 0}$$

$$= -\frac{3}{2}$$

The equation for this line is thus $y = -\frac{3}{2}x + 3$.

These are examples of lines from which the equations can be found:

1.

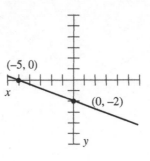

2.

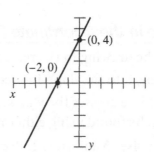

Results:

1. $y = -\frac{2}{5}x - 2$.

Find b from the y-intercept, which is –2, so $b = -2$. Find the slope from the slope formula:

$$m = \frac{y_2 - y_1}{x_2 - x_1}$$
$$= \frac{-2 - 0}{0 - (-5)}$$
$$= -\frac{2}{5}$$

2. $y = 2x + 4$.

Find b from the y-intercept, which is 4, so $b = 4$. Find the slope from the slope formula:

$$m = \frac{y_2 - y_1}{x_2 - x_1}$$
$$= \frac{4 - 0}{0 - (-2)}$$
$$= 2$$

Reporting Category Quiz: Preparing for Higher Mathematics | Functions

6. What is the slope of the line given by the equation $14x - 11y + 16 = 0$?

A. -11

B. $-\frac{14}{11}$

C. $-\frac{11}{14}$

D. $\frac{14}{11}$

E. 14

Patterns

A linear equation can model a real-life scenario. For example, sound travels at the constant speed of 1,125 feet per second, so to calculate the distance in feet, d, that a sound travels over a certain number of time in seconds, t, use the equation $d = 1,125t$. This is equivalent to a linear equation with a slope of 1,125 and an intercept of 0.

Reporting Category Quiz: Preparing for Higher Mathematics | Functions

7. When Jeff starts a math assignment, he spends 5 minutes getting out his book and a sheet of paper, sharpening his pencil, looking up the assignment in his assignment notebook, and turning to the correct page in his book. The equation $t = 10p + 5$ models the time, t minutes, Jeff budgets for a math assignment with p problems. Which of the following statements is necessarily true according to Jeff's model?

F. He budgets 15 minutes per problem.
G. He budgets 10 minutes per problem.
H. He budgets 5 minutes per problem.
J. He budgets 10 minutes per problem for the hard problems and 5 minutes per problem for the easy problems.
K. He budgets a 5-minute break after each problem.

If the pattern is complicated, simply place the input or inputs into the equation. For example, to use the speed of sound equation $d = 1,125t$ to find the distance that a sound travels in 200 seconds, place 200 for t: $d = 1,125(200) = 225,000$ feet.

Reporting Category Quiz: Preparing for Higher Mathematics | Functions

DO YOUR FIGURING HERE.

8. What is $\sin \frac{\pi}{12}$ given that $\frac{\pi}{12} = \frac{\pi}{3} - \frac{\pi}{4}$ and that
    $(\sin \alpha - \beta) = (\sin \alpha)(\cos \beta) - (\cos \alpha)(\sin \beta)$?

    (Note: You may use the following table of values.)

θ	$\sin \theta$	$\cos \theta$
$\frac{\pi}{6}$	$\frac{1}{2}$	$\frac{\sqrt{3}}{2}$
$\frac{\pi}{4}$	$\frac{\sqrt{2}}{2}$	$\frac{\sqrt{2}}{2}$
$\frac{\pi}{3}$	$\frac{\sqrt{3}}{2}$	$\frac{1}{2}$

F. $\dfrac{1}{4}$

G. $\dfrac{1}{2}$

H. $\dfrac{\sqrt{3}-2}{4}$

J. $\dfrac{\sqrt{3}-\sqrt{2}}{2}$

K. $\dfrac{\sqrt{6}-\sqrt{2}}{4}$

Graphed Equations in the *f(x)* Form

A function can be a graphed equation where *f(x)* takes the place of *y*. For example, the functions $y = 2x^2 + 1$ and $f(x) = 2x^2 + 1$ are the same. On the coordinate system, *x* is the lateral coordinate and *f(x)*, like *y*, is the vertical coordinate. The value of *x* is placed into the *f(x)*. For example, if $x = 3$, the function would appear as $f(3) = 2x^2 + 1$ or $f(3) = 2(3)^2 + 1$, so in this case $f(3) = 19$.

These are variations of functions that can be simplified where $f(x) = 2x + 1$.

1. $f(3)$

2. $\dfrac{1}{f(4)}$

3. $2f(5)$

4. $f(t)$

Results:

1. 7.

   Place the 3 for *x* in the function: $f(3) = 2(3) + 1 = 7$.

2. $\dfrac{1}{9}$.

   Solve for $f(4) = 2(4) + 1 = 9$ and place this under the 1.

3. 22.

   Solve for $f(5) = 2(5) + 1 = 11$ and multiply this by 2.

4. $f(t) = 2t + 1$.

   Place the *t* for *x* in the function.

Reporting Category Quiz: Preparing for Higher Mathematics | Functions

DO YOUR FIGURING HERE.

9. If $f(x) = x^2 - 2$, then $f(x + h) = ?$

F. $x^2 + h^2$

G. $x^2 - 2 + h$

H. $x^2 + h^2 - 2$

J. $x^2 + 2xh + h^2$

K. $x^2 + 2xh + h^2 - 2$

A function can use letters other than f and x, such as $g(h)$. Also, a function can be nested within another function. For example, if $f(x) = x^2 - 3$ and $g(h) = 2h - 1$, the question can ask the value of the nested functions $f(g(h))$ when $h = 5$. To solve this:

1. Find $g(h)$ by placing 5 for h: $g(5) = 2(5) - 1 = 9$.

2. Because $g(5) = 9$, place 9 for $g(5)$: $f(g(5)) = f(9)$.

3. Solve the final equation by placing 9 for x: $f(9) = (9)^2 - 3 = 78$.

System of Functions

A **system of functions** refers to two or more functions in a single instance. The number of solutions refers to the number of points where the functions cross. For example, this drawing of a system of functions shows two functions with two solutions, or two points where $f(x) = g(x)$.

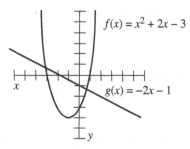

$$f(x) = x^2 + 2x - 3$$
$$g(x) = -2x - 1$$

Finding the coordinates of the solutions is covered further in chapter 3, "Algebra."

Trigonometric Functions

A **trigonometric function** is the graph of a continuous, smooth periodic oscillation. The simplest form is $y = \sin x$ or $f(x) = \sin x$, also known as a **sine wave**, shown in the following:

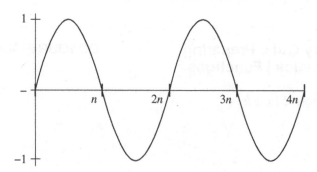

The terms describing a sine wave are *period*, *amplitude*, and *frequency*:

- **Period**, also known as **phase**, is the distance along the x-axis for the function to complete one full cycle. The function in the drawing of $y = \sin x$ has a period of 2π.

An x-coefficient reduces the period: for example, the graph of $y = \sin(2x)$ has a period of π.

- **Frequency** is the number of cycles, or periods, in a given interval. The interval shown of 4π has a frequency of 2. An x-coefficient increases the frequency. For example, the graph of $y = \sin(2x)$ in the same interval of 4π has a frequency of 4.

- **Amplitude** is the distance from the mean, in this case, the x-axis, to the maximum. The function in the drawing of $y = \sin x$ has an amplitude of 1. A coefficient on the $\sin x$ increases the amplitude. For example, the graph of $y = 2\sin x$ has an amplitude of 2.

Note that the graph of $y = \cos x$ produces a similar trigonometric function known as a **cosine wave**.

Reporting Category Quiz: Preparing for Higher Mathematics | Functions; Modeling

DO YOUR FIGURING HERE.

10. A trigonometric function with equation $y = a\sin(bx + c)$, where a, b, and c are real numbers, is graphed in the standard (x, y) coordinate plane below. The *period* of this function $f(x)$ is the smallest positive number p such that $f(x + p) = f(x)$ for every real number x. One of the following is the period of this function. Which one is it?

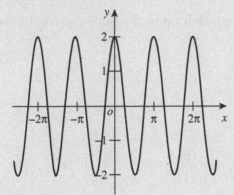

A. $\dfrac{\pi}{2}$

B. π

C. 2π

D. 4π

E. 2

Chapter 4: Quiz Answers

1. **The correct answer is C.** The difference between 17 and 41 is 24. That these are *consecutive numbers* indicates a common difference, so the space of 24 means that the common difference is 8: the missing numbers are 25 and 33.

2. **The correct answer is D.** The total of 25 dots is the square of the number of rows of 5, and without the last row, the revised total of 16 dots is the square of the new number of rows of 4.

3. **The correct answer is E.** The common difference between each number is –5, making each statement true except for the last one: The common ratio of the numbers 17, 12, 7, and 2 is not –5.

4. **The correct answer is H.** To find the slope-intercept form, set the equation equal to y:

$$8x - y - 6 = 0$$
$$8x - 6 = y$$
$$y = 8x - 6$$

5. **The correct answer is B.** To find the slope of any parallel line, start by setting the equation equal to y:

$$7x + 9y = 6$$
$$9y = -7x + 6$$
$$y = -\frac{7}{9}x + \frac{2}{3}$$

Any line with a slope of $-\frac{7}{9}$ is parallel to this line.

6. **The correct answer is J.** To find the slope, set the equation up in the *slope-intercept form*, which isolates the y. The slope is the x-coefficient.

$$14x - 11y + 16 = 0$$
$$14x - 16 = 11y$$
$$\frac{14}{11}x - \frac{16}{11} = y$$
$$y = \frac{14}{11}x - \frac{16}{11}$$

7. **The correct answer is G.** The equation $t = 10p + 5$ indicates that for each increment of p, the value of t increases by 10.

8. **The correct answer is K.** Don't worry about understanding the function. Place the values from the table into the equation and simplify. If $\frac{\pi}{12} = \frac{\pi}{3} - \frac{\pi}{4}$, then $\sin\left(\frac{\pi}{12}\right) = \sin\left(\frac{\pi}{3} - \frac{\pi}{4}\right)$. Consider

$\sin\left(\frac{\pi}{3}-\frac{\pi}{4}\right)$ as equivalent to $\sin(\alpha-\beta)$, so place the values of $\frac{\pi}{3}$ and $\frac{\pi}{4}$ from the table for α and β, respectively, in the equation:

$$\sin(\alpha-\beta)=(\sin\alpha)(\cos\beta)-(\cos\alpha)(\sin\beta)$$

$$=\left(\frac{\sqrt{3}}{2}\right)\left(\frac{\sqrt{2}}{2}\right)-\left(\frac{1}{2}\right)\left(\frac{\sqrt{2}}{2}\right)$$

$$=\left(\frac{\sqrt{6}}{4}\right)-\left(\frac{\sqrt{2}}{4}\right)$$

$$=\frac{\sqrt{6}-\sqrt{2}}{4}$$

9. The correct answer is K. Place the $x+h$ for x in the function:

$$f(x+h)=(x+h)^2-2$$
$$=(x+h)(x+h)-2$$
$$=x^2+2xh+h^2-2$$

10. The correct answer is B. The distance along the x-axis for this function to complete one full cycle is π.

5

Chapter 5: Geometry

Geometry questions are based on two-dimensional and three-dimensional shapes. They ask about the composition of objects and ask you to find the missing values in triangles, circles, and other figures. These questions also include trigonometric ratios.

Coordinate Geometry

Coordinate Geometry is a method of using algebraic equations to describe points, lines, and shapes on a (x, y) *coordinate plane*, also known as the *x-y rectangular grid*. This is a two-dimensional area defined by a horizontal x-axis and a vertical y-axis that intersect at the **origin**, which has coordinates $(0, 0)$, and forms **Quadrants I, II, III,** and **IV.**

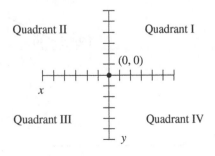

Each point on the grid is labeled using an ordered pair (x, y), with the x-value indicating the lateral position and the y-value indicating the vertical position. For example, this point has an x-value of 3 and a y-value of 2, for the coordinates $(3, 2)$:

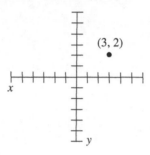

Lines and Angles

Lines and angles comprise most basic shapes.

A **line** is straight and continuous.

A **segment** is part of a line and can be indicated by its endpoints. This segment, with endpoints A and B, is indicated as $\overline{AB}$.

An **angle** is formed by the intersection of two lines or segments and can also be indicated by its endpoints. This angle, with endpoints C, D, and E, is indicated as $\angle CDE$.

Complementary angles total 90°.

Supplementary angles total 180°.

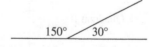

A **triangle** has angles totaling 180° and can be indicated by its endpoints. This triangle, with endpoints *F*, *G*, and *H*, is indicated as Δ*FGH*.

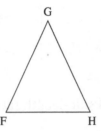

A **bisector** is a segment that *bisects*, or divides, an angle or another segment into two equal parts.

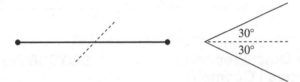

A **perpendicular bisector** is a segment that bisects another segment at 90°.

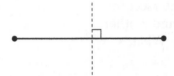

Any two lines or segments that cross create four angles. The opposite angles, also known as **vertical angles**, are equal, and all four angles total 360°.

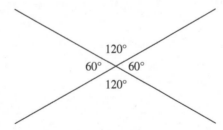

A **transversal** is a line that crosses two or more lines. If the two crossed lines are parallel, the transversal creates two identical sets of four angles.

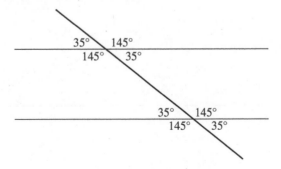

Congruent shapes are identical, though one shape can be rotated.

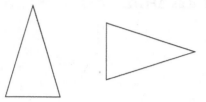

Similar shapes have the same angles and side-length ratios but have different sizes.

Reporting Category Quiz: Preparing for Higher Mathematics | Geometry

DO YOUR FIGURING HERE.

1. In the figure below, lines m and n are parallel, transversals r and s intersect to form an angle of measure $x°$, and 2 other angle measures are as marked. What is the value of x?

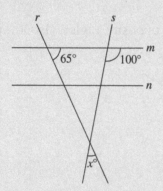

A. 15

B. 25

C. 35

D. 65

E. 80

2. In the figure below, *ABCD* is a trapezoid, *E* lies on $\overline{AD}$, and angle measures are as marked. What is the measure of ∠*BDC*?

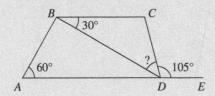

DO YOUR FIGURING HERE.

F. 15°

G. 25°

H. 30°

J. 35°

K. 45°

Two-Dimensional Shapes

Two-dimensional shapes are the foundation of all geometry and the basis of many questions in the Geometry reporting category.

A **polygon** is any complete shape having more than two sides and only straight sides.

The **angle total** is the sum of the angles of a polygon. The angle total can be found with the equation $a = (n-2)180°$, where *n* is the number of sides. For example, to find the angle total of this hexagon, use 6 for *n* in the equation:

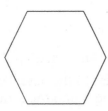

$$a = (n-2)180°$$
$$= ((6)-2)180°$$
$$= (4)180°$$
$$= 720°$$

The **perimeter** is the length of the outline of a shape. Find the perimeter by taking the sum of the side lengths.

Triangles

A **triangle** is a three-sided shape, and its angles always total 180°. With any triangle, the sum of any two side lengths is greater than the third side length.

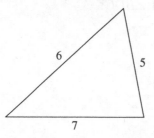

Reporting Category Quiz: Integrating Essential Skills

DO YOUR FIGURING HERE.

3. A triangle with a perimeter of 66 inches has one side that is 16 inches long. The lengths of the other two sides have a ratio of 2:3. What is the length, in inches, of the *longest* side of the triangle?

   A. 16
   B. 20
   C. 30
   D. 40
   E. 50

Area

The area of any triangle can be found with the equation $A = \frac{bh}{2}$, where b is the base and h is the height, represented by a line perpendicular to the base. For example, to find the area of this triangle, place the base and height of 5 and 4 into the b and h of the equation:

$$A = \frac{bh}{2}$$
$$= \frac{(5)(4)}{2}$$
$$= 10$$

Standard Forms

There are certain standard forms of triangles.

An **isosceles triangle** is a triangle that has two identical sides and angles. If two sides are identical, two angles will also be identical.

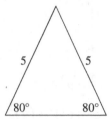

An **equilateral** triangle is a type of isosceles triangle where each side is identical and each angle is 60°.

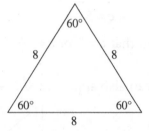

The area of an equilateral triangle can be found with the equation $A = \frac{s^2\sqrt{3}}{4}$, where s is a side length. For example, to find the area of this triangle, place the side length of 8 into the s of the equation:

$$A = \frac{s^2\sqrt{3}}{4}$$
$$= \frac{(8)^2\sqrt{3}}{4}$$
$$= \frac{64\sqrt{3}}{4}$$
$$= 16\sqrt{3}$$

A **right triangle** is a triangle where one angle is 90°, usually indicated by the right-angle symbol.

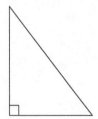

The side opposite the right angle is the longest side of the triangle and called the *hypotenuse*. Use the Pythagorean theorem to find the third side length from the two other side lengths, where c indicates the hypotenuse: $c^2 = a^2 + b^2$. With this right triangle, place the side lengths 3 and 4 as the a and b in the Pythagorean theorem:

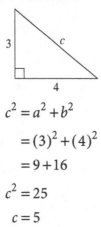

$$c^2 = a^2 + b^2$$
$$= (3)^2 + (4)^2$$
$$= 9 + 16$$
$$c^2 = 25$$
$$c = 5$$

Note that although $c^2 = 25$ could mean that $c = 5$ or $c = -5$, a distance or length is always positive, so use only the positive answer.

The hypotenuse of the right triangle can also appear as $\sqrt{a^2 + b^2}$, where $c = \sqrt{a^2 + b^2}$.

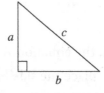   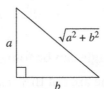

Reporting Category Quiz: Preparing for Higher Mathematics | Geometry

DO YOUR FIGURING HERE.

4. In the figure below, B is on $\overline{AC}$, E is on $\overline{DF}$, $\overline{AC}$ is parallel to $\overline{DF}$, and $\overline{BE}$ is congruent to $\overline{BF}$. What is the measure of $\angle DEB$?

   F. 35°

   G. 135°

   H. 145°

   J. 155°

   K. 215°

5. In $\triangle ABC$ below, D, E, and F are points on $\overline{AB}$, $\overline{BC}$, and $\overline{AC}$, respectively, and $\overline{DF}$ is congruent to $\overline{EF}$. What is the *sum* of the measures of the angles marked x and y?

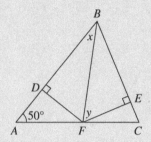

F. 40°

G. 80°

H. 90°

J. 100°

K. 130°

6. Which of the following lists gives 2 of the 3 interior angle measurements of a triangle for which the third angle measurement would be equal to 1 of the 2 given measurements?

F. 20°, 40°

G. 30°, 60°

H. 40°, 100°

J. 45°, 120°

K. 50°, 60°

Right Triangle Ratios

Some right triangles have common ratios:

- The **3:4:5** triangle has a side-length ratio of 3:4:5 as in the previous example. As a ratio, the side lengths of the triangle could also be 6:8:10 or 9:12:15. These numbers work in the Pythagorean theorem, but they're easier to calculate as a ratio: $3(3:4:5) = 9:12:15$.

- The **5:12:13** triangle has a side-length ratio of 5:12:13. As a ratio, the side lengths could also be $2(5:12:13) = 10:24:26$.

- The 30°-60°-90° triangle has angles measuring 30°, 60°, and 90° and a side-length ratio of $1 : 2 : \sqrt{3}$, where the hypotenuse ratio factor is 2. Note that the side lengths can appear as $\frac{1}{2} : 1 : \frac{\sqrt{3}}{2}$, which is consistent with the ratio.

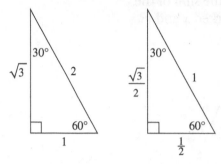

- The 45°-45°-90° triangle has angles measuring 45°, 45°, and 90° and a side-length ratio of $1 : 1 : \sqrt{2}$, where the hypotenuse ratio factor is $\sqrt{2}$.

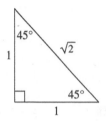

Reporting Category Quiz: Integrating Essential Skills

DO YOUR FIGURING HERE.

7. A ladder is 10 ft long and reaches 8 ft up a wall, as shown below. How many feet is the bottom of the ladder from the base of the wall?

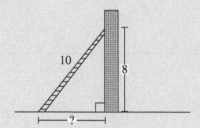

F. 2

G. 3

H. 6

J. $\sqrt{2}$

K. $\sqrt{164}$

8. The ratio of the side lengths for a triangle is exactly 12:14:15. In a second triangle similar to the first, the shortest side is 8 inches long. To the nearest tenth of an inch, what is the length of the longest side of the second triangle?

   A. 11.0

   B. 10.0

   C. 9.3

   D. 6.4

   E. Cannot be determined from the given information.

DO YOUR FIGURING HERE.

Reporting Category Quiz: Preparing for Higher Mathematics | Geometry

9. Members of the fire department lean a 30-foot ladder against a building. The side of the building is perpendicular to the level ground so that the base of the ladder is 10 feet away from the base of the building. To the nearest foot, how far up the building does the ladder reach?

   A. 10

   B. 20

   C. 28

   D. 31

   E. 40

DO YOUR FIGURING HERE.

(continued)

(continued)

10. Which of the following sets of 3 numbers could be the side lengths, in meters, of a 30°-60°-90° triangle?

    DO YOUR FIGURING HERE.

    A. 1, 1, 1
    B. 1, 1, $\sqrt{2}$
    C. 1, $\sqrt{2}$, $\sqrt{2}$
    D. 1, $\sqrt{2}$, $\sqrt{3}$
    E. 1, $\sqrt{3}$, 2

11. In the figure below, *ABCD* is a square and *E, F, G,* and *H* are the midpoints of its sides. If $\overline{AB}$ = 12 inches, what is the perimeter of *EFGH*, in inches?

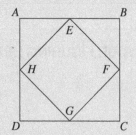

    F. 24
    G. $24\sqrt{2}$
    H. $36\sqrt{2}$
    J. $48\sqrt{2}$
    K. 72

On the Coordinate Plane

A right-triangle question can ask the distance or midpoint between two points on the coordinate plane. The points on the grid form a right triangle, and the side lengths can be determined by the (x, y) coordinates.

With any two points on the coordinate plane, you can find the distance and the midpoint.

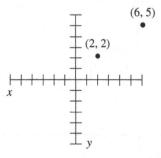

Distance

Draw right triangle connecting the points and use the Pythagorean theorem to calculate the distance. For example, to find the distance between these two points, draw a right triangle:

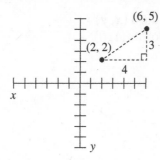

Now use the lengths of the two shorter sides and the Pythagorean theorem to find the third side, which is the hypotenuse:

$$c^2 = a^2 + b^2$$
$$= 3^2 + 4^2$$
$$= 9 + 16$$
$$c^2 = 25$$
$$c = 5$$

The *distance formula* automatically measures the right triangle and places the side lengths into the Pythagorean theorem. The distance formula is $d = \sqrt{(x_2 - x_1)^2 + (y_2 - y_1)^2}$, where one point is represented by (x_1, y_1) and the other by (x_2, y_2).

To use the distance formula to find the distance between these points, place the point coordinates into the formula:

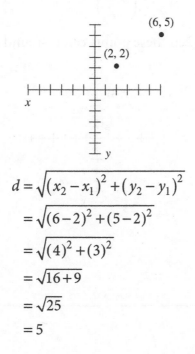

$$d = \sqrt{(x_2 - x_1)^2 + (y_2 - y_1)^2}$$
$$= \sqrt{(6-2)^2 + (5-2)^2}$$
$$= \sqrt{(4)^2 + (3)^2}$$
$$= \sqrt{16 + 9}$$
$$= \sqrt{25}$$
$$= 5$$

Reporting Category Quiz: Preparing for Higher Mathematics | Geometry

DO YOUR FIGURING HERE.

12. What is the distance in the standard (x, y) coordinate plane between the points $(1, 0)$ and $(0, 5)$?

A. 4

B. 6

C. 16

D. 36

E. $\sqrt{26}$

Midpoint

To find the midpoint between two points, use the *midpoint formula*, which separately measures the distances between the x- and y-coordinates. The midpoint formula is $mid = \left(\frac{x_1+x_2}{2}, \frac{y_1+y_2}{2}\right)$.

To find the midpoint between these two points, place the point coordinates into the formula:

$$
\begin{aligned}
mid &= \left(\frac{x_1+x_2}{2}, \frac{y_1+y_2}{2}\right) \\
&= \left(\frac{2+6}{2}, \frac{2+5}{2}\right) \\
&= \left(4, \frac{7}{2}\right)
\end{aligned}
$$

The distances and midpoints between these points can be found using the respective formulas:

1.

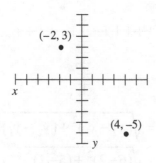

2.

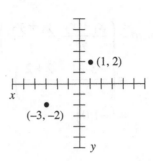

Results:

1.   Distance is 10 and midpoint is (1, –1).

$$d = \sqrt{(x_2 - x_1)^2 + (y_2 - y_1)^2}$$
$$= \sqrt{(4 - (-2))^2 + ((-5) - 3)^2}$$
$$= \sqrt{(6)^2 + (-8)^2}$$
$$= \sqrt{36 + 64}$$
$$= \sqrt{100}$$
$$= 10$$

$$mid = \left(\frac{x_1 + x_2}{2}, \frac{y_1 + y_2}{2} \right)$$
$$= \left(\frac{-2 + 4}{2}, \frac{3 - 5}{2} \right)$$
$$= (1, -1)$$

2.   Distance is $4\sqrt{2}$ and midpoint is (–1, 0).

$$d = \sqrt{(x_2 - x_1)^2 + (y_2 - y_1)^2}$$
$$= \sqrt{(1 - (-3))^2 + (2 - (-2))^2}$$
$$= \sqrt{(4)^2 + (4)^2}$$
$$= \sqrt{16 + 16}$$
$$= \sqrt{32}$$
$$= 4\sqrt{2}$$

$$mid = \left(\frac{x_1 + x_2}{2}, \frac{y_1 + y_2}{2} \right)$$
$$= \left(\frac{-3+1}{2}, \frac{-2+2}{2} \right)$$
$$= (-1, 0)$$

Quadrilaterals

A **quadrilateral** is any four-sided shape. Its angles always total 360°.

Perimeter

Find the perimeter by adding the side lengths. Certain quadrilaterals, including the square and rectangle, have opposite sides that are the same length.

Reporting Category Quiz: Integrating Essential Skills

DO YOUR FIGURING HERE.

13. Your friend shows you a scale drawing of her apartment. The drawing of the apartment is a rectangle 4 inches by 6 inches. Your friend wants to know the length of the shorter side of the apartment. If she knows that the length of the longer side of the apartment is 30 feet, how many feet long is the shorter side of her apartment?

A. 9

B. 20

C. 24

D. 30

E. 45

Reporting Category Quiz: Preparing for Higher Mathematics | Geometry

14. A rectangular lot that measures 150 ft by 200 ft is completely fenced. What is the approximate length, in feet, of the fence?

F. 300

G. 350

H. 400

J. 700

K. 1,400

15. In the figure shown below, each pair of intersecting line segments meets at a right angle, and all the lengths given are in inches. What is the perimeter, in inches, of the figure?

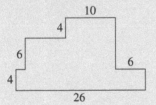

A. 40

B. 52

C. 56

D. 66

E. 80

Area

Certain quadrilaterals have different equations to find the areas. Common quadrilaterals and equations include the following:

- A **square**, where each angle is 90° and each side is the same length. Note that the drawing usually doesn't show a right-angle box in each corner: if three angles are right angles, the fourth must also be. The side length is referred to as *s*, and you can find the area by squaring the side length:

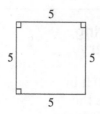

$$A = s^2$$
$$= (5)^2$$
$$= 25$$

- A **rectangle,** where each angle is 90° but only the opposite sides are the same length. The longer side is the length of the rectangle, or *l*, and the shorter side is the width, or *w*. Find the area by multiplying *l* by *w*:

$$A = lw$$
$$= (8)(5)$$
$$= 40$$

- A **parallelogram,** where opposite angles are the same measure and opposite sides are parallel and the same length. One of the side lengths is the *base*, or *b*, and its distance from its opposite side length is the *height*, or *h*, usually represented by a dashed line with a right-angle box. Find the area by multiplying the base by the height:

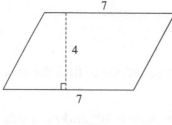

$$A = bh$$
$$= (7)(4)$$
$$= 28$$

- A **trapezoid,** where only two sides are parallel, and the sides might not have the same length and the opposite angles might not be the same. The parallel sides are called *bases*, or b_1 and b_2, and the distance between them is the *height*, or h. If a side is perpendicular to the bases, then its length is the height; otherwise, the height can be represented by a dashed line with a right-angle box. Find the area by multiplying the average of the two bases by the height:

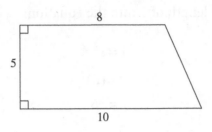

$$A = \left(\frac{b_1 + b_2}{2} \right) h$$
$$= \left(\frac{(8) + (10)}{2} \right)(5)$$
$$= 45$$

- A **rhombus** is a type of parallelogram where each side has the same length and opposite angles are equal. Find the area by multiplying the lengths of the *diagonals*, or d_1 and d_2, and dividing by 2:

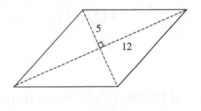

$$A = \frac{(d_1)(d_2)}{2}$$
$$= \frac{(5)(12)}{2}$$
$$= 30$$

These are examples of quadrilaterals where the areas can be found:

1. A square with a side length of 6

2. A rectangle with a length of 5 and a width of 3

3. A parallelogram with a base of 5 and a height of 4

4.   A trapezoid with bases of 3 and 7 and a height of 6

5.   A rhombus with diagonals of 6 and 8

Results:

1.   36.

Place the side length of 5 into the equation:

$$A = s^2$$
$$= (6)^2$$
$$= 36$$

2.   15.

Place the length and width of 5 and 3 into the equation:

$$A = lw$$
$$= (5)(3)$$
$$= 15$$

3.   20.

Place the base and height of 5 and 4 into the equation:

$$A = bh$$
$$= (5)(4)$$
$$= 20$$

4.   30.

Place the bases and height of 3, 7, and 6, respectively, into the equation:

$$A = \left(\frac{b_1 + b_2}{2}\right)h$$
$$= \left(\frac{(3) + (7)}{2}\right)(6)$$
$$= 30$$

5.   24.

Place the diagonals of 6 and 8 into the equation:

$$A = \frac{(d_1)(d_2)}{2}$$
$$= \frac{(6)(8)}{2}$$
$$= 24$$

Reporting Category Quiz: Preparing for Higher Mathematics | Geometry

DO YOUR FIGURING HERE.

16. Parallelogram *ABCD*, with dimensions in inches, is shown in the diagram below. What is the area of the parallelogram, in square inches?

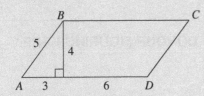

A. 18

B. 36

C. 39

D. 45

E. 72

17. If a rectangle measures 54 meters by 72 meters, what is the length, in meters, of the diagonal of the rectangle?

F. 48

G. 53

H. 90

J. 126

K. 252

(continued)

(continued)

18. Shannon is planning to tile a rectangular kitchen countertop that is 24 inches wide and 64 inches long. She determined that 1 tile will be needed for each 4-inch-by-4-inch region. What is the minimum number of tiles that will be needed to completely cover the countertop to its edges?

A. 44

B. 88

C. 96

D. 176

E. 384

DO YOUR FIGURING HERE.

Reporting Category Quiz: Preparing for Higher Mathematics | Geometry; Modeling

19. The trapezoid below is divided into 2 triangles and 1 rectangle. Lengths are given in inches. What is the combined area, in square inches, of the 2 shaded triangles?

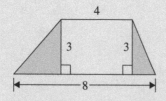

A. 4

B. 6

C. 9

D. 12

E. 18

DO YOUR FIGURING HERE.

Circles

A **circle** is a shape where each point on the shape is the same distance from the center. This distance is called the **radius**. A **chord** is a line or segment that cuts across the circle. The **diameter** is a chord that cuts across the center and is the width of the circle. The **circumference** is the distance around the circle, and a **tangent** is a line or segment that touches the circle at exactly one point.

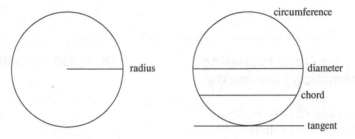

Circumference and Area

The ratio of the circumference to the diameter is approximately 3.14, also known as *pi* or π. To get the circumference from the diameter, multiply the diameter by π. For example, this circle has a diameter of 10:

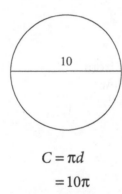

$$C = \pi d$$
$$= 10\pi$$

The radius is half the diameter, so to get the circumference from the radius, multiply the radius and π by 2:

$$C = 2\pi r$$
$$= 2\pi(5)$$
$$= 10\pi$$

Because $\pi \approx 3.14$, the circumference is actually closer to 31.4, but answers to ACT mathematics test questions are typically in terms of π.

To get the area of the circle, multiply π by the square of the radius:

$$A = \pi r^2$$
$$= \pi(5)^2$$
$$= 25\pi$$

Reporting Category Quiz: Preparing for Higher Mathematics | Geometry

DO YOUR FIGURING HERE.

20. The ratio of the radii of two circles is 4:9. What is the ratio of their circumferences?

   F. 2:3

   G. 4:9

   H. 16:81

   J. 4:8π

   K. 9:18π

21. A chord 24 inches long is 5 inches from the center of a circle, as shown below. What is the radius of the circle, to the nearest tenth of an inch?

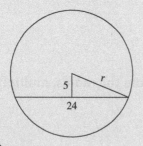

   A. 29.0

   B. 24.5

   C. 16.9

   D. 13.0

   E. 10.9

Circles on the Coordinate Plane

Circles also appear on the (x, y) coordinate plane. The equation for a circle is $(x-h)^2 + (y-k)^2 = r^2$, where h and k are the x- and y-coordinates, respectively, of the center and r is the radius. For example, the equation for this circle with a center of $(-1, 2)$ and radius 4 is $(x+1)^2 + (y-2)^2 = 16$.

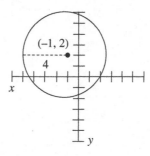

Reporting Category Quiz: Preparing for Higher Mathematics | Geometry

DO YOUR FIGURING HERE.

22. A circle in the standard (x, y) coordinate plane is tangent to the x-axis at 5 and tangent to the y-axis at 5. Which of the following is an equation to the circle?

   A. $x^2 + y = 5$

   B. $x^2 + y = 25$

   C. $(x-5)^2 + (y-5)^2 = 5$

   D. $(x-5)^2 + (y-5)^2 = 25$

   E. $(x+5)^2 + (y+5)^2 = 25$

(continued)

(continued)

23. In the standard (x, y) coordinate plane below, the vertices of the square have coordinates $(0, 0)$, $(6, 0)$, $(6, 6)$, and $(0, 6)$. Which of the following is an equation of the circle that is inscribed in the square?

DO YOUR FIGURING HERE.

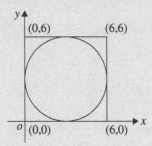

A. $(x-3)^2 + (y-3)^2 = 9$

B. $(x-3)^2 + (y-3)^2 = 3$

C. $(x+3)^2 + (y+3)^2 = 9$

D. $(x+3)^2 + (y+3)^2 = 6$

E. $(x+3)^2 + (y+3)^2 = 3$

Geospatial Elements in the Coordinate Grid

Coordinate grid questions in the Algebra reporting category ask about the result of an equation, but in the Geometry reporting category they ask about the placement and movement of points, lines, or shapes. Answer these questions by adjusting the x- or y-coordinates according to these concepts:

- **Reflection** across an axis: A point, line, or shape reflected across an axis appears as if the axis is a mirror with the reflection on the opposite side.

  ○ A reflection across the x-axis has the same x-coordinates but negative y-coordinates. For example, a point with coordinates $(2, 3)$ reflected across the x-axis has the coordinates $(2, -3)$.

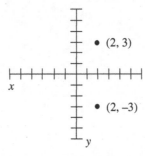

○ A reflection across the *y*-axis has negative *x*-coordinates but the same *y*-coordinates. For example, a point with coordinates (4, 5) reflected across the *y*-axis has the coordinates (−4, 5).

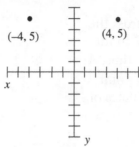

In this example, the trapezoid is reflected across the *y*-axis. Note that the *y*-coordinates are the same but the *x*-coordinates are negative.

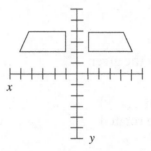

• **Rotation** about the origin: A point, line, or shape rotated about the origin of the graph appears as if the origin is an anchor and the items rotate about it, like the hands of a clock, only the items rotate counterclockwise. An item that rotates 180° results in negative *x*- and *y*-coordinates. For example, a point with coordinates (4, 3) rotates 180° to coordinates (−4, −3).

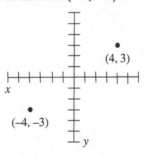

In this example, the trapezoid is rotated 180°. Note that the resulting shape is upside-down but otherwise unchanged and not flipped.

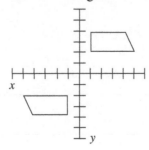

Reporting Category Quiz: Preparing for Higher Mathematics | Geometry

24. A triangle, $\triangle ABC$, is reflected across the x-axis to have the image $\triangle A'B'C'$ in the standard (x, y) coordinate plane; thus, A reflects to A'. The coordinates of point A are (c, d). What are the coordinates of point A'?

    F. $(c, -d)$

    G. $(-c, d)$

    H. $(-c, -d)$

    J. (d, c)

    K. Cannot be determined from the given information

25. The graph shown in the standard (x, y) coordinate plane below is to be rotated 180° about the origin.

    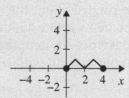

    One of the following graphs is the result of this rotation. Which one is it?

    A.

    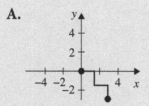

    B.

    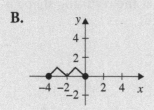

DO YOUR FIGURING HERE.

C.

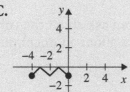

D.

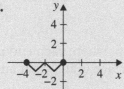

E.

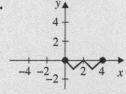

26 Point A is to be graphed in a quadrant, not on an axis, of the standard (x, y) coordinate plane below.

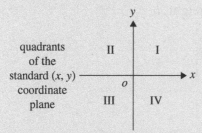

If the x-coordinate and the y-coordinate of point A are to have opposite signs, then point A *must* be located in:

A. Quadrant II only.

B. Quadrant IV only.

C. Quadrant I or III only.

D. Quadrant I or IV only.

E. Quadrant II or IV only.

Three-Dimensional Shapes

The ACT mathematics test questions on three-dimensional shapes often ask about the volume. Following are some common shapes and formulas. If the question asks about an uncommon shape, it provides the formula that you need to solve it.

Volume

Common shapes and volume equations include the following:

- A **cylinder** or *right-circular cylinder* is like a can of soup, where each end is a circle, the circular sides are parallel, and the curved surface is at a right angle to the circular sides.

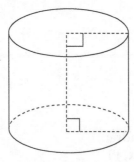

This cylinder has a radius of 3 and a height of 5. Find the volume by multiplying the area of a circular side, πr^2, by the height, h:

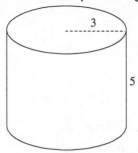

$$V = \pi r^2 h$$
$$= \pi (3)^2 (5)$$
$$= 45\pi$$

- A **rectangular solid** or *rectangular prism* is like a shoebox, where each side is a rectangle and opposite sides are parallel.

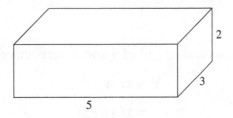

This rectangular solid has a length of 5, a width of 3, and a height of 2. Find the volume by multiplying these together as *l*, *w*, and *h*:

$$V = lwh$$
$$= (2)(3)(5)$$
$$= 30$$

- A **cube** is a type of rectangular solid where each side is a square. Because the length, width, and height are equal, each is called an *edge*. A six-sided die is an example of a cube.

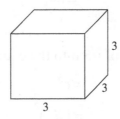

This cube has an edge length, or *e*, of 3. Find the volume by cubing the edge length:

$$V = e^3$$
$$= (3)^3$$
$$= 27$$

The following are examples of three-dimensional shapes for which the volumes can be found:

1. A right-circular cylinder with a radius of 4 and a height of 5

2. A rectangular solid with a length, width, and height of 3, 4, and 5, respectively

3. A cube with an edge length of 4

4. A cube with an edge length of $\sqrt[3]{5}$

Results:

1. 80π.

   Place the radius and height of 4 and 5, respectively, into the equation:

   $$V = \pi r^2 h$$
   $$= \pi (4)^2 (5)$$
   $$= 80\pi$$

2. 60.

   Place the length, width, and height of 3, 4, and 5 into the equation:

   $$V = lwh$$
   $$= (3)(4)(5)$$
   $$= 60$$

3. 64.

   Place the edge length of 4 into the equation:

   $$V = e^3$$
   $$= (4)^3$$
   $$= 64$$

4. 5.

   Place the edge length of $\sqrt[3]{5}$ into the equation:

   $$V = e^3$$
   $$= \left(\sqrt[3]{5}\right)^3$$
   $$= 5$$

Surface Area

An ACT mathematics test question can also ask for the surface area of a cube. Find this by squaring the edge and multiplying by 6:

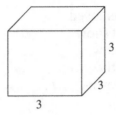

$$SA = 6e^2$$
$$= 6(3)^2$$
$$= 54$$

The following are examples of cubes for which the surface areas can be found:

1.   A cube with an edge length of 2

2.   A cube with an edge length of $\sqrt{7}$

Results:

1.   24.

Place the edge length of 2 into the equation:

$$SA = 6e^2$$
$$= 6(2)^2$$
$$= 24$$

2.   42.

Place the edge length of $\sqrt{7}$ into the equation:

$$SA = 6e^2$$
$$= 6\left(\sqrt{7}\right)^2$$
$$= 6(7)$$
$$= 42$$

Reporting Category Quiz: Preparing for Higher Mathematics | Geometry

27. After a snowstorm, city workers removed an estimated 10,000 cubic yards of snow from the downtown area. If this snow were spread in an even layer over the entire rectangular football field shown below, about how many yards deep would the layer of snow be?

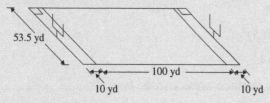

53.5 yd

100 yd

10 yd   10 yd

A. Less than 1

B. Between 1 and 2

C. Between 2 and 3

D. Between 3 and 4

E. More than 4

28. A formula for the volume V of a sphere is $V = \frac{4}{3}\pi r^3$. If the radius of a spherical rubber ball is $1\frac{1}{4}$ inches, what is its volume to the nearest cubic inch?

A. 5

B. 7

C. 8

D. 16

E. 65

29. When Angela was cleaning her refrigerator, she found 2 bottles of catsup. Looking at the labels, she noticed that the capacity of the larger bottle was twice the capacity of the smaller bottle. She estimated that the smaller bottle was about $\frac{1}{3}$ full of catsup and the larger bottle was about $\frac{2}{3}$ full of catsup. She poured all the catsup from the smaller bottle into the larger bottle. Then, about how full was the larger bottle?

A. $\frac{2}{9}$ full

B. $\frac{1}{2}$ full

C. $\frac{5}{6}$ full

D. Completely full

E. Overflowing

DO YOUR FIGURING HERE.

Trigonometry

Trigonometry is the study of the relationship between the side lengths and the angles of triangles. Most trigonometry questions in the ACT mathematics test are based on right triangles.

Right Triangles

A right triangle is any triangle where one angle measure is 90°. The side across from the 90° angle is the *hypotenuse*, and the other two sides are the *opposite* and *adjacent*. *Opposite* refers to *across from* and *adjacent* refers to *next to*, so the sides that are opposite or adjacent depend on the angle in question. In this triangle, for angle A, side $\overline{BC}$ is opposite and side $\overline{AC}$ is adjacent; but these switch for angle B, where side $\overline{AC}$ is opposite and side $\overline{BC}$ is adjacent.

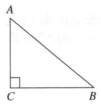

Sine, Cosine, and Tangent

Many trigonometry questions on the ACT mathematics test ask about the **sine**, **cosine**, and **tangent** functions of angles of a right triangle. The easiest way to remember the trigonometric relationships is with the acronym *SOH CAH TOA*, where O, A, and H refer to the side lengths of the *opposite*, *adjacent*, and *hypotenuse*:

- *SOH* refers to $\text{sine} = \dfrac{\text{opposite}}{\text{hypotenuse}}$, or $\sin = \dfrac{o}{h}$

- *CAH* refers to $\text{cosine} = \dfrac{\text{adjacent}}{\text{hypotenuse}}$, or $\cos = \dfrac{a}{h}$

- *TOA* refers to $\text{tangent} = \dfrac{\text{opposite}}{\text{adjacent}}$, or $\tan = \dfrac{o}{a}$

In this right triangle, the sine of angle A is $\frac{4}{5}$, because the side length opposite angle A is 4 and the hypotenuse is 5. The cosine of angle A is $\frac{3}{5}$, because the side length adjacent to angle A is 3, and the tangent of angle A is $\frac{4}{3}$.

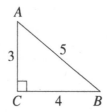

However, for angle B, the opposite and adjacent sides switch, so the respective sine, cosine, and tangent of angle B are different:

- $\sin B = \dfrac{o}{h} = \dfrac{3}{5}$

- $\cos B = \dfrac{a}{h} = \dfrac{4}{5}$

- $\tan B = \dfrac{o}{a} = \dfrac{3}{4}$

There are two trigonometric identities relevant to this concept:

- The sine of a non-right angle equals the cosine of the other non-right angle; in this case, the sine of A equals the cosine of B:

$$\sin A = \frac{o}{h} = \frac{4}{5}$$

$$\cos B = \frac{a}{h} = \frac{4}{5}$$

- For any angle in a right triangle, the square of the sine plus the square of the cosine equals 1:

$$\sin^2 B + \cos^2 B = 1$$

$$\left(\frac{3}{5}\right)^2 + \left(\frac{4}{5}\right)^2 = 1$$

$$\frac{9}{25} + \frac{16}{25} = 1$$

It is important to note that *SOH CAH TOA* and these two identities only apply to a right triangle.

Reporting Category Quiz: Preparing for Higher Mathematics | Geometry

DO YOUR FIGURING HERE.

30. For right triangle $\triangle RST$ shown below, what is tan R?

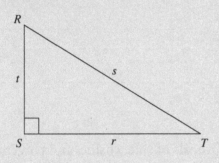

F. $\dfrac{r}{s}$

G. $\dfrac{r}{t}$

H. $\dfrac{t}{r}$

J. $\dfrac{t}{s}$

K. $\dfrac{s}{t}$

(continued)

(continued)

31. The hypotenuse of the right triangle △*PQR* shown below is 16 feet long. The sine of ∠*P* is $\frac{3}{5}$. About how many feet long is $\overline{QR}$?

DO YOUR FIGURING HERE.

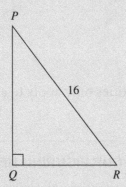

F. 8.0

G. 9.6

H. 12.4

J. 14.3

K. 15.4

Cosecant, Secant, and Cotangent

Cosecant, **secant**, and **cotangent** are the respective reciprocals of sine, cosine, and tangent. When an ACT mathematics test question involves one of these reciprocal functions, it's usually easier to convert the function back to its original form. These are the functions and their reciprocals:

- Cosecant: $\cos = \frac{1}{\sin}$

- Secant: $\sec = \frac{1}{\cos}$

- Cotangent: $\tan = \frac{1}{\cot}$

The easiest way to remember that *cosecant* is the reciprocal of *sine* and *secant* is the reciprocal of *cosine* is that the *c* is the reciprocal of the *s*, and vice versa: $\cos = \frac{1}{\sin}$ and $\sec = \frac{1}{\cos}$.

Reporting Category Quiz: Preparing for Higher Mathematics | Geometry

DO YOUR FIGURING HERE.

32. The lengths, in feet, of the sides of right triangle $\triangle ABC$ are as shown in the diagram below, with $x > 0$. What is the cotangent of $\angle A$, in terms of x?

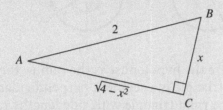

A. $\sqrt{4-x^2}$

B. $\dfrac{2}{x}$

C. $\dfrac{x}{2}$

D. $\dfrac{x}{\sqrt{4-x^2}}$

E. $\dfrac{\sqrt{4-x^2}}{x}$

Unit Circle

The **unit circle** is a circle with a radius of 1 drawn on the center of the (x, y) coordinate plane. Each quarter of the circle lies in one of the four quadrants:

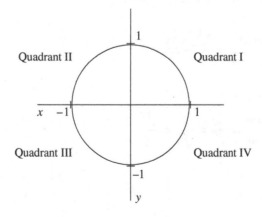

Degrees and Radians

Any radius of the circle creates an angle, measured counterclockwise from the 3:00 position on the *x*-axis. The full circle is 360°, and the angle is known as **theta**, or θ. For example, these drawings show θ equaling 60°, 150°, 240°, and 330°.

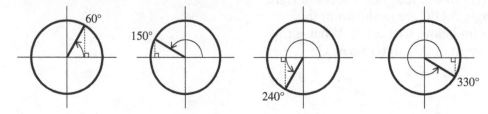

The radius of the circle also creates a right triangle, where the hypotenuse is the radius, the base of the triangle rests on the *x*-axis, and the height of the triangle is a segment perpendicular to the *x*-axis. For example, in this unit circle, θ = 30°, forming a right triangle with side lengths 1, 0.5, and $\frac{\sqrt{3}}{2}$:

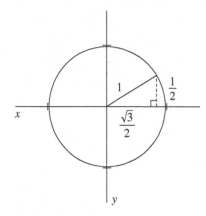

With this right triangle, you can find the sine, cosine, and tangent of θ using *SOH CAH TOA*, where the *opposite* is the height and the *adjacent* is the base. Using the previous example:

- $\sin\theta = \dfrac{\text{opposite}}{\text{hypotenuse}} = \dfrac{\frac{1}{2}}{1} = \dfrac{1}{2}$

- $\cos\theta = \dfrac{\text{adjacent}}{\text{hypotenuse}} = \dfrac{\frac{\sqrt{3}}{2}}{1} = \dfrac{\sqrt{3}}{2}$

- $\tan\theta = \dfrac{\text{opposite}}{\text{adjacent}} = \dfrac{\frac{1}{2}}{\frac{\sqrt{3}}{2}} = \dfrac{1}{\sqrt{3}} = \dfrac{\sqrt{3}}{3}$

Quadrants

In this unit circle, the *xy*-coordinates of the point where the radius intersects the circle are $\left(\frac{\sqrt{3}}{2}, \frac{1}{2}\right)$. When using *SOH CAH TOA*, the opposite and adjacent are $\frac{1}{2}$ and $\frac{\sqrt{3}}{2}$, respectively, which are positive values:

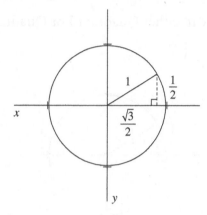

However, the *xy*-coordinates of this point could be negative, as in this example:

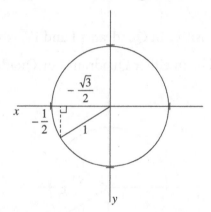

Because the *xy*-coordinates of the point are $\left(-\frac{\sqrt{3}}{2}, -\frac{1}{2}\right)$, the opposite and adjacent are negative, but the hypotenuse is always positive. Use these negative values to find the sine, cosine, and tangent of θ:

- $\sin\theta = \dfrac{\text{opposite}}{\text{hypotenuse}} = \dfrac{-\frac{1}{2}}{1} = -\dfrac{1}{2}$

- $\cos\theta = \dfrac{\text{adjacent}}{\text{hypotenuse}} = \dfrac{-\frac{\sqrt{3}}{2}}{1} = -\dfrac{\sqrt{3}}{2}$

- $\tan\theta = \dfrac{\text{opposite}}{\text{adjacent}} = \dfrac{-\frac{1}{2}}{-\frac{\sqrt{3}}{2}} = \dfrac{1}{\sqrt{3}} = \dfrac{\sqrt{3}}{3}$

In this example, although the sine and cosine are now negative, the tangent stays positive.

Sine, cosine, and tangent can each be positive or negative, based on the quadrant. This is because although the *hypotenuse* always stays positive, the *opposite* and *adjacent* can be positive or negative:

- Sine is always positive in Quadrants I and II, where the *opposite* is positive. If $\sin\theta = \frac{1}{2}$, θ could be in either Quadrant I or Quadrant II:

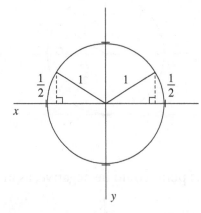

- Cosine is always positive in Quadrants I and IV, where the *adjacent* is positive. If $\cos\theta = \frac{\sqrt{3}}{2}$, θ could be in either Quadrant I or Quadrant IV:

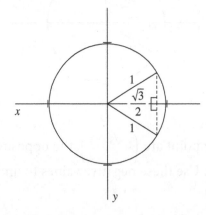

- Tangent is always positive in Quadrants I and III, where the *opposite* and *adjacent* are either both positive or both negative. If tan $\tan\theta = \frac{\sqrt{3}}{3}$, θ could be in either Quadrant I or Quadrant III:

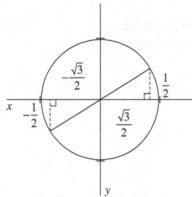

With any sine, cosine, or tangent of an angle, the angle could be in two different quadrants on the unit circle. To discern the position of the angle, you also need to know the quadrant, which the question gives you in terms of π radians.

Degrees and Radians

The unit circle angle can be expressed in either degrees or π radians, where π = 180°. The full circle is 360° or 2π radians:

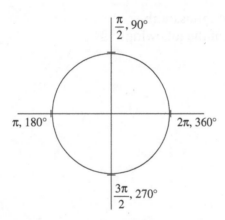

- To convert an angle measure of degrees to radians, multiply the measure by π and divide by 180°. For example, to convert the measure 720° to radians: $\frac{720° \times \pi}{180°} = 4\pi$.

- To convert a measure of radians to degrees, multiply the measure by 180° and divide by π. For example, to convert the measure 3π to degrees: $\frac{3\pi \times 180°}{\pi} = 540°$.

An ACT mathematics test question can use π radians to tell you the quadrant:

- $0 < \theta < \frac{\pi}{2}$ tells you that θ is in Quadrant I.

- $\frac{\pi}{2} < \theta < \pi$ tells you that θ is in Quadrant II.

- $\pi < \theta < \frac{3\pi}{2}$ tells you that θ is in Quadrant III.

- $\frac{3\pi}{2} < \theta < 2\pi$ tells you that θ is in Quadrant IV.

Reporting Category Quiz: Preparing for Higher Mathematics | Geometry

DO YOUR FIGURING HERE.

33. If $\sin\theta = -\frac{3}{5}$ and $\pi < \theta < \frac{3\pi}{2}$, then $\tan\theta = ?$

   F. $-\frac{5}{4}$

   G. $-\frac{3}{4}$

   H. $-\frac{3}{5}$

   J. $\frac{3}{4}$

   K. $\frac{4}{5}$

34. If the value, to the nearest thousandth, of $\cos\theta$ is -0.385, which of the following could be true about θ?

   A. $0 \le \theta < \frac{\pi}{6}$

   B. $\frac{\pi}{6} \le \theta < \frac{\pi}{3}$

   C. $\frac{\pi}{3} \le \theta < \frac{\pi}{2}$

   D. $\frac{\pi}{2} \le \theta < \frac{2\pi}{3}$

   E. $\frac{2\pi}{3} \le \theta \le \pi$

Laws of Sines and Cosines

The laws of sines and cosines apply to all triangles, including non-right triangles.

Law of Sines

The **law of sines** states that given a triangle with angles A, B, and C, and opposite sides a, b, and c, respectively, the ratios of the sine of each angle to its opposite side length are equal:

$$\frac{\sin A}{a} = \frac{\sin B}{b} = \frac{\sin C}{c}$$

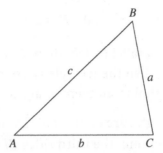

Although the law of sines features three ratios, you usually need to use only two. If one angle is 90°, simplify the ratio by replacing sin 90° with 1, because sin 90° = 1.

Law of Cosines

The **law of cosines** is a function of three side lengths and one angle measure:

$$c^2 = a^2 + b^2 - 2ab\cos C$$

Square root both sides to show the value of c:

$$c = \sqrt{a^2 + b^2 - 2ab\cos C}$$

Note that cos 90° = 0, so when $C = 90°$, as in a right triangle, $2ab\cos C$ goes away, and you're left with the Pythagorean theorem: $c^2 = a^2 + b^2$ or $c = \sqrt{a^2 + b^2}$. Don't worry about memorizing the law of cosines, because the ACT mathematics test question usually provides it for you, and all you do is place the side lengths a and b and the angle measure C from the triangle in the equation.

Chapter 5: Quiz Answers

1. **The correct answer is C.** The angle supplemental to 100° is 80°, which along with the 65° angle form a triangle whose third angle, opposite the $x°$, is 35°.

2. **The correct answer is K.** The shape is a trapezoid, so segments $\overline{AD}$ and $\overline{BC}$ are parallel. If $\angle BAD = 60°$, $\angle ABC = 120°$. The drawing tells you that $\angle DBC = 30°$, so $\angle DBA = 90°$, making $\angle BDA = 30°$. $\angle BDA$ and $\angle CDE$ are supplemental to the angle in question, meaning all three total 180°. You now know that one is 30° while the other is 105°, so the mystery angle is 45°.

3. **The correct answer is C.** If the perimeter is 66 inches and one side is 16 inches, then the other two sides total 50 inches. Find the actual number of inches from the ratio of 2:3 by using the equation:

$$2x + 3x = 50$$
$$x = 10$$
$$2(10) + 3(10) = 50$$
$$20 + 30 = 50$$

4. **The correct answer is H.** If $\overline{AC}$ is parallel to $\overline{DF}$, then $\angle CBF$, which is 35°, is equal to $\angle BFE$, also 35°. If $\overline{BE}$ is congruent to $\overline{BF}$, then the triangle is isosceles, making angles $\angle BFE$ and $\angle BEF$ each 35°. The angle in question is supplementary to $\angle BEF$, so its measure is 145°.

5. **The correct answer is H.** The triangles are congruent: $\overline{DF}$ is congruent to $\overline{EF}$, and they share side $\overline{BF}$, so by the Pythagorean theorem, the third sides $\overline{BD}$ and $\overline{BE}$ are congruent. Therefore the measures of the two smaller angles $\angle DBF$ and $\angle FBE$ are the same, as are the two larger angles, $\angle BFD$ and $\angle FBE$. One small angle, such as $x°$, plus one large angle, such as $y°$, totals 90°.

6. **The correct answer is H.** Find two angle measures where if one were added twice, the three total 180°. Add 40° twice for the correct angle total: $40° + 40° + 100° = 180°$.

7. **The correct answer is H.** This is a 3:4:5 triangle multiplied by 2: $2(3:4:5) = 6:8:10$. You could also use the Pythagorean theorem:

$$a^2 + 8^2 = 10^2$$
$$a^2 + 64 = 100$$
$$a^2 = 36$$
$$a = 6$$

8. **The correct answer is B.** Compare the ratio of the shortest sides to the ratio of the longest sides:

$$\frac{12}{8} = \frac{15}{x}$$
$$\frac{3}{2} = \frac{15}{x}$$
$$3x = 30$$
$$x = 10$$

9. **The correct answer is C.** Draw a right triangle with a base of 10 and hypotenuse of 30, and use the Pythagorean theorem to the height:

$$a^2 + 10^2 = 30^2$$
$$a^2 + 100 = 900$$
$$a^2 = 800$$
$$a = 20\sqrt{2}$$
$$\approx 28.3$$

Note the key word *nearest* in the question.

10. **The correct answer is E.** The side lengths of a 30°-60°-90° triangle are in the ratio $1 : \sqrt{3} : 2$. Note that the side lengths don't have to be in that order.

11. **The correct answer is G.** Each triangle in the corner of the square is a 45°-45°-90° triangle with a side-length ratio of $1 : 1 : \sqrt{2}$. Take triangle AEH: if $\overline{AB} = 12$, then $\overline{AE} = 6$, and hypotenuse $\overline{EH} = 6\sqrt{2}$. The four sides of the square are equal, so the perimeter of $EFGH$ is $24\sqrt{2}$.

12. **The correct answer is E.** Place the coordinates into the distance formula:

$$d = \sqrt{(0-1)^2 + (5-0)^2}$$
$$= \sqrt{(-1)^2 + (5)^2}$$
$$= \sqrt{1 + 25}$$
$$= \sqrt{26}$$

13. **The correct answer is B.** Compare the ratio of the longer side to the ratio of the shorter side:

$$\frac{30}{6} = \frac{x}{4}$$
$$\frac{5}{1} = \frac{x}{4}$$
$$x = 20$$

14. **The correct answer is J.** The perimeter is the sum of all four sides, and the opposite sides are equal. This means two sides measure 150 ft each and two other sides measure 200 ft each: $2(150) + 2(200) = 700$ ft.

15. **The correct answer is E.** The bottom is 26 inches; therefore, the segments of the top also total 26 inches. The segments of the left side total 14 inches, therefore the segments of the right side also total 14 inches: $2(26) + 2(24) = 80$. The 10 on the top and the 6 on the right are extraneous information.

16. **The correct answer is B.** The base is the sum of 3 and 6 at the bottom of the drawing. Multiply this base by the height: $9 \times 4 = 36$.

17. **The correct answer is H.** The diagonal of the rectangle creates a right triangle with side lengths of 54 and 72 meters. You could use the Pythagorean theorem, but this is a 3:4:5 triangle multiplied by 18: $18\,(3:4:5) = 54:72:90$.

18. **The correct answer is C.** If each tile is 4 inches square, then 6 tiles line the 24-inch width and 16 tiles line the 64-inch width. Shannon now has a grid of 6 by 16 tiles: $6 \times 16 = 96$.

19. **The correct answer is B.** Subtract the area of the rectangle from the area of the trapezoid. In square inches, the rectangle is $4 \times 3 = 12$ and the trapezoid is $\left(\frac{4+8}{2}\right)3 = 18$. Subtract these for a difference of 6.

20. **The correct answer is G.** The circumference of a circle can be found with $2\pi r$, so the circumferences of circles with radii 4 and 9 are 8π and 18π, respectively. Set these as a fraction and reduce: $\frac{8\pi}{18\pi} = \frac{4}{9}$.

21. **The correct answer is D.** Isolate the right triangle, where the height is 5, the base is 12, and the hypotenuse is r. You could use the Pythagorean theorem, but this is one of the right triangle ratios with side lengths of 5:12:13.

22. **The correct answer is D.** A circle tangent to the x-axis at 5 and the y-axis at 5 exists in Quadrant I:

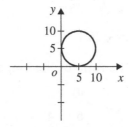

The circle has a center at coordinates $(5, 5)$ and a radius of 5, so its equation is $(x-5)^2 + (y-5)^2 = 25$.

23. **The correct answer is A.** The circle has a center at coordinates $(3, 3)$ and a radius of 3, so its equation is $(x-3)^2 + (y-3)^2 = 9$.

24. **The correct answer is F.** A point reflected across the x-axis has the same x-coordinate but the negative of the y-coordinate. The point (c, d) reflected across the x-axis thus has the coordinates $(c, -d)$.

25. **The correct answer is D.** An image rotated 180° appears upside-down on the opposite side of the graph. Note also that the original graph has an endpoint at coordinates $(0, 0)$, which is

the "anchor" of the rotation; thus, the rotated image not only is upside-down but also has an endpoint at those coordinates.

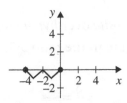

26. **The correct answer is E.** A point with coordinates having opposite signs, such as (−2, 2), is in Quadrant II, and (2, −2) is in Quadrant IV.

27. **The correct answer is B.** This is a rectangular solid with yards as units. You're given the length and width of the football field along with the volume of snow, so use the equation to find the height, which in this case is the depth:

$$(120)(53.5)h = 10,000$$
$$6,420h = 10,000$$
$$h \approx 1.56$$

28. **The correct answer is C.** Place the radius of $1\frac{1}{4}$, or $\frac{5}{4}$, for r in the equation:

$$V = \frac{4}{3}\pi r^3$$
$$= \frac{4}{3}\pi\left(\frac{5}{4}\right)^3$$
$$= \frac{4}{3}\pi\left(\frac{125}{64}\right)$$
$$= \frac{125}{48}\pi$$
$$\approx \frac{125}{48}(3.14)$$
$$\approx 8$$

29. **The correct answer is C.** $\frac{1}{3}$ of a smaller bottle is less than $\frac{1}{3}$ of a larger bottle, so the catsup from the smaller bottle can be added to the larger bottle without filling or overflowing it. The larger bottle would then be more than $\frac{2}{3}$ full, so it couldn't be $\frac{2}{9}$ or $\frac{1}{2}$ full: it could only be $\frac{5}{6}$ full.

30. The correct answer is G. Tangent is *opposite* over *adjacent*. The sides opposite and adjacent to $\angle R$ are r and t, respectively, so $\tan R = \frac{r}{t}$.

31. The correct answer is G. Sine is *opposite* over *hypotenuse*. The sine of $\angle P$ is $\frac{3}{5}$, so the lengths of the base and hypotenuse are in the ratio 3:5. Set this ratio as a fraction equal to the hypotenuse of 16 and base of x:

$$\frac{3}{5} = \frac{x}{16}$$
$$5x = 48$$
$$x = 9.6$$

32. The correct answer is E. Tangent is *opposite* over *adjacent*. The sides opposite and adjacent to $\angle A$ are x and $\sqrt{4-x^2}$, respectively, so $\tan A = \frac{x}{\sqrt{4-x^2}}$. Take the reciprocal for the cotangent: $\cot A = \frac{\sqrt{4-x^2}}{x}$.

33. The correct answer is J. $\pi < \theta < \frac{3\pi}{2}$ places θ in Quadrant III. $\sin\theta = -\frac{3}{5}$ tells you that the ratio of the side length opposite θ to the hypotenuse is 3:5, so the side length adjacent to θ is 4.

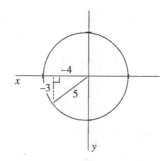

Because these are in Quadrant III, the opposite and adjacent side lengths are negative:

$\tan\theta = \frac{\text{opposite}}{\text{adjacent}} = \frac{-3}{-4} = \frac{3}{4}$.

34. The correct answer is D. If $\cos\theta = -0.385$, then it could be written as $\cos\theta = -\frac{385}{1,000}$ or $\cos\theta = -\frac{2}{5}$. Cosine is *adjacent* over *hypotenuse*, and hypotenuse is always positive, so the adjacent must be negative, placing θ in Quadrant II or III. The answer choices include only Quadrants I and II, so θ is in Quadrant II. Now draw a picture with the adjacent and hypotenuse in the ratio of 2:5:

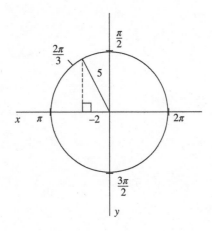

$\frac{2\pi}{3} = 120°$, and θ is between $\frac{\pi}{2}$ and $\frac{2\pi}{3}$.

Chapter 6:
Statistics and Probability

Questions in the **Statistics and Probability** reporting category ask about probabilities of events and interpretation of data distributions, data collection methods, and data relationships. They also ask about averages and medians.

Probability

Probability refers to the likelihood of an event occurring. In its simplest form, it's a fraction with the number of desired outcomes as the numerator and the total possible outcomes as the denominator: $p_e = \frac{\text{number of desired outcomes}}{\text{number of possible outcomes}}$.

> If a box of 9 pens contains 2 red pens, the probability that you pull a red pen is $\frac{2}{9}$.

The probability that something will *not* occur is 1 minus the probability that it does occur.

> The probability that you will not pull a red pen is $1 - \frac{2}{9} = \frac{7}{9}$. This is also true because 7 of the pens aren't red.

The probabilities of one outcome *or* another outcome is the sum of each independent probability.

> If the box has 2 red pens and 3 blue pens, the probability that you pull a red *or* a blue pen is $\frac{2+3}{9} = \frac{5}{9}$.

The probabilities of one outcome *and* another outcome is the product of each independent probability.

> The probability that you pull a red pen today is $\frac{2}{9}$. If you place it back in the box, the
>
> probability that you pull a red pen tomorrow is still $\frac{2}{9}$. The probability that you pull a red
>
> pen on *both* days is $\frac{2}{9} \times \frac{2}{9} = \frac{4}{81}$.

Probability is always a number between 0 and 1. A probability of 0 means that the event will not occur, and a probability of 1 means that the event will definitely occur.

> If a box of 10 sodas contains *only* diet sodas, then the probability that you pull a regular soda
> is $\frac{0}{10}$, or 0.

> From the same box, the probability that you pull a diet soda is $\frac{10}{10}$, or 1.

Reporting Category Quiz: Preparing for Higher Mathematics | Statistics and Probability

DO YOUR FIGURING HERE.

1. If a marble is randomly chosen from a bag that contains exactly 8 red marbles, 6 blue marbles, and 6 white marbles, what is the probability that the marble will NOT be white?

    F. $\frac{3}{4}$

    G. $\frac{3}{5}$

    H. $\frac{4}{5}$

    J. $\frac{3}{10}$

    K. $\frac{7}{10}$

Sets of Numbers

The ACT mathematics test questions can ask for a simple analysis on a **set of numbers**, such as $\{2, 3, 6, 8, 11\}$.

Average/Arithmetic Mean

The **average**, also called the **mean** or **arithmetic mean**, of a set of numbers refers to the sum of the terms divided by the number of terms: $m = \frac{\text{sum of the terms}}{\text{number of terms}}$. For example, to take the average of the 5 numbers $\{2, 3, 6, 8, 11\}$, divide the sum by 5:

$$m = \frac{2+3+6+8+11}{5} = 6$$

The question can provide the average but ask for one of the numbers in the set. For example, the average of $\{2, 6, 17, x\}$ is 8. In this case, set up the equation with x as the missing number and solve for x:

$$\frac{x+2+6+17}{4} = 8$$
$$x+2+6+17 = 32$$
$$x+25 = 32$$
$$x = 7$$

These are examples of averages with one of the numbers missing:

1.   The set of numbers $\{3, 6, 9, 12, x\}$ has an average of 7.

2.   The set of numbers $\{-8, -4, 7, 9, x\}$ has an average of 3.

Results:

1.   5.

   Set up the equation with x as the missing number:

$$\frac{x+3+6+9+12}{5} = 7$$
$$x+3+6+9+12 = 35$$
$$x+30 = 35$$
$$x = 5$$

2.   11.

   Set up the equation with x as the missing number:

$$\frac{x-8-4+7+9}{5} = 3$$
$$x-8-4+7+9 = 15$$
$$x+4 = 15$$
$$x = 11$$

Reporting Category Quiz: Integrating Essential Skills

2. A certain type of notebook costs $2.50 before sales tax is added. When you buy 9 of these notebooks you receive 1 additional notebook free. What is the average cost per notebook for the 10 notebooks before sales tax is added?

   A. $2.78

   B. $2.50

   C. $2.30

   D. $2.25

   E. $2.15

3. Kaya drove 200 miles in 5 hours of actual driving time. By driving an average of 10 miles per hour faster, Kaya could have saved how many hours of actual driving time?

   A. $\dfrac{1}{6}$

   B. $\dfrac{2}{3}$

   C. $\dfrac{7}{10}$

   D. 1

   E. 4

Reporting Category Quiz: Preparing for Higher Mathematics | Statistics and Probability

DO YOUR FIGURING HERE.

4. The following chart shows the current enrollment in all the mathematics classes offered by Eastside High School.

Course title	Section	Period	Enrollment
Pre-Algebra	A	3	23
Algebra I	A	2	24
	B	3	25
	C	4	29
Geometry	A	1	21
	B	2	22
Algebra II	A	4	28
Pre-Calculus	A	6	19

What is the average number of students enrolled per section in Algebra I?

F. 24
G. 25
H. 26
J. 27
K. 29

5. A company earned a profit of $8.0 million each year for 3 consecutive years. For each of the next 2 years the company earned a profit of $9.0 million. For this 5-year period, what was the company's average yearly profit, in millions of dollars?

F. 8.2
G. 8.25
H. 8.4
J. 8.5
K. 8.6

Median and Mode

The **median** of a set of numbers is the middle value in the set. For example, the median of the set {2, 3, 6, 8, 11} is 6. If the numbers are out of order, place them in order before taking the middle number. If there are two middle numbers, such as {3, 6, 8, 11}, take the average of the two middle numbers: $\frac{6+8}{2} = 7$.

The **mode** of a set of numbers is the most commonly occurring value in the set. For example, the mode of {2, 5, 6, 8, 8} is 8. If the set of numbers has two values that occur the most number of times, it is called **bimodal**, meaning it has two modes. The modes of {2, 5, 5, 7, 9, 9} are 5 and 9.

Charts

The ACT mathematics test features a few simple charts in the Statistics and Probability reporting category. The charts appearing in the ACT science test are far more extensive, but the following are the charts you're likely to see in the ACT math test:

- The **column chart** shows dependent results per independent variables:

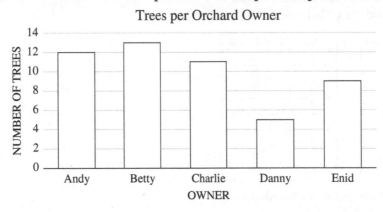

- The **line chart** also shows dependent results per independent variables, but the line chart emphasizes a trend:

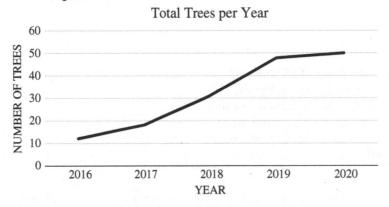

- The **bar chart** is like the column chart, only the *x*- and *y*-axes are reversed:

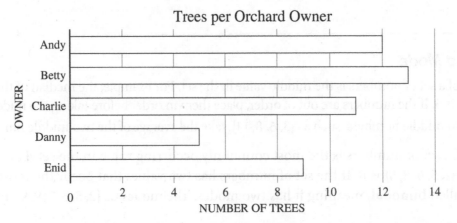

The **pie chart** shows each value as a slice of the pie having either a number or a percent of the total. The entire chart is either the total number of items or 100%:

Trees per Orchard Owner

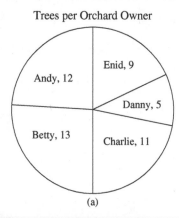

(a)

Trees per Orchard Owner

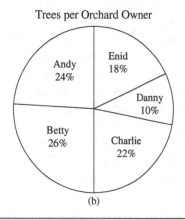

(b)

Reporting Category Quiz: Preparing for Higher Mathematics | Statistics and Probability

DO YOUR FIGURING HERE.

6. The graph below shows the number of cars assembled last year in 4 cities, to the nearest 5,000 cars. According to the graph, what fraction of the cars assembled in all 4 cities were assembled in Coupeville?

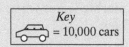

City	Cars assembled
Car Town	🚗🚗🚗🚗
Coupeville	🚗🚗🚙
Truck City	🚗🚗
Sedan Falls	🚗🚙

A. $\frac{1}{5}$

B. $\frac{1}{4}$

C. $\frac{3}{11}$

D. $\frac{3}{10}$

E. $\frac{1}{3}$

(continued)

(continued)

7. Douglas wants to draw a circle graph showing the favorite colors of his friends. When he polled his friends asking each their favorite color, 25% of his friends said red; 30% of his friends said blue; 20% of his friends said green; 10% of his friends said purple; and the remaining friends said colors other than red, blue, green, and purple. The colors other than red, blue, green, and purple will be grouped together in an Other sector. What will be the degree measure of the Other sector?

A. 108°

B. 54°

C. 27°

D. 15°

E. 10°

DO YOUR FIGURING HERE.

Chapter 6: Quiz Answers

1. The correct answer is K. The probability that the marble is not white is 1 minus the probability that it is white. There are 6 white and 20 total marbles:

$$1 - \frac{6}{20} = \frac{14}{20}$$
$$= \frac{7}{10}$$

2. The correct answer is D. Divide the total cost of the notebooks by the number of notebooks:

$$a = \frac{9 \times \$2.50}{10}$$
$$= \frac{\$22.50}{10}$$
$$= \$2.25$$

3. The correct answer is D. First find Kaya's average speed in miles per hour by dividing the total miles driven by the total time:

$$mph = \frac{200}{5}$$
$$= 40$$

Next, increase her speed by 10 miles an hour, and divide the total miles driven by the new speed:

$$h = \frac{200}{40+10}$$
$$= \frac{200}{50}$$
$$= 4$$

If Kaya drove 10 miles per hour faster, she could have made the trip in 4 hours instead of 5, saving 1 hour.

4. **The correct answer is H.** Divide the total number of Algebra I students by the number of sections:

$$m = \frac{24+25+29}{3}$$
$$= \frac{78}{3}$$
$$= 26$$

5. **The correct answer is H.** Divide the total profit by the number of years:

$$m = \frac{8.0+8.0+8.0+9.0+9.0}{5}$$
$$= \frac{42.0}{5}$$
$$= 8.4$$

6. **The correct answer is B.** Place the number of cars assembled in Coupeville over the total number of cars assembled in all 4 cities. Though you could use the car icons to count the actual number of cars, you could also just count the number of icons:

Total car icons: 10

Coupeville car icons: 2.5

$$\frac{2.5}{10} = \frac{1}{4}$$

7. **The correct answer is B.** The total of all the sectors is 100%, which is 360° on the circle graph. First add the percents given and subtract the sum from 100:

$$Other = 100\% - (25 + 30 + 20 + 10)\%$$
$$= 100\% - (85)\%$$
$$= 15\%$$

Next, convert this to a degree measure on the circle graph:

$$\frac{15\%}{100\%} = \frac{x°}{360°}$$
$$\frac{3}{20} = \frac{x}{360}$$
$$20x = 1{,}080$$
$$x = 54$$

7

Chapter 7:
Practice
Questions

Following is a pool of 400 practice ACT mathematics test questions. This includes the practice questions from the text along with additional questions directly from the ACT.

You may use a calculator, but these problems can be solved without one. The questions challenge your ability to understand and work with the math concepts, not crunch numbers.

Answers and explanations are in chapter 8.

1. On level ground, a vertical rod 12 feet tall casts a shadow 4 feet long, and at the same time a nearby vertical flagpole casts a shadow 12 feet long. How many feet tall is the flagpole?

   A. 4
   B. 8
   C. 12
   D. 20
   E. 36

2. Kalino earned 85, 95, 93, and 80 points on the 4 tests, each worth 100 points, given so far this term. How many points must he earn on his fifth test, also worth 100 points, to average 90 points for the 5 tests given this term?

   F. 87
   G. 88
   H. 90
   J. 92
   K. 97

3. If $x = -5$, what is the value of $\frac{x^2 - 1}{x + 1}$?

   A. −6

   B. −4

   C. 4

   D. $5\frac{4}{5}$

   E. 19

DO YOUR FIGURING HERE.

4. Kaya ran $1\frac{2}{5}$ miles on Monday and $2\frac{1}{3}$ miles on Tuesday. What was the total distance, in miles, Kaya ran during those 2 days?

F. $3\frac{2}{15}$

G. $3\frac{3}{8}$

H. $3\frac{2}{5}$

J. $3\frac{7}{15}$

K. $3\frac{11}{15}$

5. Consider the 3 statements below to be true.

All insects that are attracted to honey are ants.
Insect I is not an ant.
Insect J is attracted to honey.

Which of the following statements is necessarily true?

A. Insect I is an ant not attracted to honey.
B. Insect I is an ant attracted to honey.
C. Insect I is attracted to honey.
D. Insect J is not attracted to honey.
E. Insect J is an ant.

6. What is the value of the expression $\sqrt{\dfrac{m}{x-3}}$ when $x = -1$ and $m = -16$?

F. -2
G. 2
H. $2\sqrt{2}$
J. $2i$
K. $2i\sqrt{2}$

7. Tickets for a community theater production cost $6 each when bought in advance and $8 each when bought at the door. The theater group's goal is at least $2,000 in ticket sales for opening night. The theater group sold 142 opening-night tickets in advance. What is the minimum number of tickets they need to sell at the door on opening night to make their goal?

A. 143
B. 144
C. 192
D. 250
E. 357

8. Mark and Juanita own a sandwich shop. They offer 3 kinds of bread, 5 kinds of meat, and 3 kinds of cheese. Each type of sandwich has a combination of exactly 3 ingredients: 1 bread, 1 meat, and 1 cheese. How many types of sandwiches are possible?

F.   11
G.   15
H.   30
J.   45
K.   120

9. If $12(x - 11) = -15$, then $x = ?$

A. $-\dfrac{49}{4}$

B. $-\dfrac{13}{6}$

C. $-\dfrac{5}{4}$

D. $-\dfrac{1}{3}$

E. $\dfrac{39}{4}$

10. In the figure below, A, D, C, and E are collinear. $\overline{AD}$, $\overline{BD}$, and $\overline{BC}$ are all the same length, and the angle measure of $\angle ABD$ is as marked. What is the degree measure of $\angle BCE$?

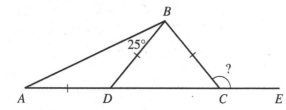

F.   50°
G.   100°
H.   105°
J.   130°
K.   160°

11. If $f(x) = 9x^2 + 5x - 8$, then $f(-2) = ?$

A.   −54
B.   −18
C.   18
D.   36
E.   38

12. What is the least common multiple of 30, 20, and 70 ?

F.   40
G.   42
H.   120
J.   420
K.   42,000

DO YOUR FIGURING HERE.

13. While doing a problem on his calculator, Tom meant to divide a number by 2, but instead he accidentally multiplied the number by 2. Which of the following calculations could Tom then do to the result on the calculator screen to obtain the result he originally wanted?

   A. Subtract the original number
   B. Multiply by 2
   C. Multiply by 4
   D. Divide by 2
   E. Divide by 4

14. The 8-sided figure below is divided into 5 congruent squares. The total area of the 5 squares is 125 square inches. What is the perimeter, in inches, of the figure?

   F. 25
   G. 60
   H. 80
   J. 100
   K. 125

15. Hai has $100 available to buy USB drives to back up data for his business computers. Each USB drive has a price of $8, and Hai will pay a sales tax of 7% of the total price of the USB drives. What is the maximum number of USB drives Hai can buy?

   A. 11
   B. 12
   C. 13
   D. 14
   E. 15

16. A certain computer performs 1.5×10^8 calculations per second. How many seconds would it take this computer to perform 6.0×10^{16} calculations?

   F. 2.5×10^{-9}
   G. 9.0×10^0
   H. 4.0×10^2
   J. 4.0×10^8
   K. 9.0×10^{24}

17. One of the following is an equation of the linear relation shown in the standard (x,y) coordinate plane below. Which equation is it?

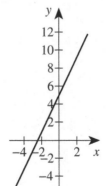

   A. $y = 5x$
   B. $y = 2x$
   C. $y = 5x + 2$
   D. $y = 2x - 5$
   E. $y = 2x + 5$

18. A square is circumscribed about a circle of 7-foot radius, as shown below. What is the area of the square, in square feet?

   F.   49
   G. 56
   H. 98
   J. 49π
   K. 196

DO YOUR FIGURING HERE.

19. Two workers were hired to begin work at the same time. Worker A's contract called for a starting salary of $20,000 with an increase of $800 after each year of employment. Worker B's contract called for a starting salary of $15,200 with an increase of $2,000 after each year of employment. If x represents the number of full years' employment (that is, the number of yearly increases each worker has received), which of the following equations could be solved to determine the number of years until B's yearly salary equals A's yearly salary?

   A. $20,000 + 800x = 15,200 + 2,000x$
   B. $20,000 + 2,000x = 15,200 + 800x$
   C. $(20,000 + 800)x = (15,200 + 2,000)x$
   D. $(2,000 + 800)x = 20,000 - 15,200$
   E. $(2,000 - 800)x = 20,000 + 15,200$

20. A ramp for loading trucks is 13 feet long and covers 12 feet along the level ground, as shown below. How many feet high is the highest point on the ramp?

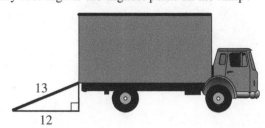

   F. 1

   G. 2

   H. 4

   J. 5

   K. $6\frac{1}{4}$

21. The expression $7(x + 3) - 3(2x - 2)$ is equivalent to:

A. $x + 1$
B. $x + 15$
C. $x + 19$
D. $x + 23$
E. $x + 27$

DO YOUR FIGURING HERE.

22. If 115% of a number is 460, what is 75% of the number?

F. 280
G. 300
H. 320
J. 345
K. 400

23. When $(2x - 3)^2$ is written in the form $ax^2 + bx + c$, where a, b, and c are integers, $a + b + c = ?$

A. -17
B. -5
C. 1
D. 13
E. 25

24. What is the area, in square feet, of the figure below?

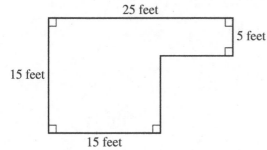

F. 60
G. 80
H. 275
J. 375
K. 450

25. Barb is going to cover a rectangular area 8 feet by 10 feet with rectangular paving blocks that are 4 inches by 8 inches by 2 inches to make a flat patio. What is the minimum number of paving blocks she will need if all the paving blocks will face the same direction?

(Note: Barb will not cut any of the paving blocks.)

A.   80
B.   360
C.   601
D.   960
E.   1,213

DO YOUR FIGURING HERE.

26. What is the slope of the line represented by the equation $6y - 14x = 5$?

F. -14

G. $\dfrac{5}{6}$

H. $\dfrac{7}{3}$

J.   6

K.   14

27. Let m and n be 2 positive integers, such that $m < n$. Which of the following compound inequalities *must* be true?

A. $0 < \sqrt{mn} < m$
B. $1 < \sqrt{mn} < m$
C. $m < \sqrt{mn} < n$
D. $\sqrt{m} < \sqrt{mn} < \sqrt{n}$
E. $\sqrt{m-n} < \sqrt{mn} < \sqrt{m+n}$

28. Two similar triangles have perimeters in the ratio 3:5. The sides of the smaller triangle measure 3 cm, 5 cm, and 7 cm, respectively. What is the perimeter, in centimeters, of the larger triangle?

F.   15
G.   18
H.   20
J.   25
K.   36

DO YOUR FIGURING HERE.

29. Thomas and Jonelle are playing darts in their garage using the board with the point values for each region shown below. The radius of the outside circle is 10 inches, and each of the other circles has a radius 2 inches smaller than the next larger circle. All of the circles have the same center. Thomas has only 1 dart left to throw and needs at least 30 points to win the game. Assuming that his last dart hits at a random point within a single region on the board, what is the percent chance that Thomas will win the game?

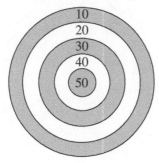

A. 36%

B. 30%

C. 16%

D. 9%

E. $1\frac{1}{2}\%$

30. When asked his age, the algebra teacher said, "If you square my age, then subtract 23 times my age, the result is 50." How old is he?

F. 23
G. 25
H. 27
J. 46
K. 50

31. The distance, d, an accelerating object travels in t seconds can be modeled by the equation $d = \frac{1}{2}at^2$, where a is the acceleration rate, in meters per second per second. If a car accelerates from a stop at the rate of 20 meters per second per second and travels a distance of 80 meters, about how many seconds did the car travel?

A. Between 1 and 2
B. Between 2 and 3
C. Between 3 and 4
D. 4
E. 8

32. Which of the following is the set of all real numbers x such that $x + 3 > x + 5$?

F. The empty set
G. The set containing all real numbers
H. The set containing all negative real numbers
J. The set containing all nonnegative real numbers
K. The set containing only zero

Use the following information to answer questions 33–35.

A survey in a study skills class asked the 20 students enrolled in the class how many hours (rounded to the nearest hour) they had spent studying on the previous evening. The 20 responses are summarized by the histogram below.

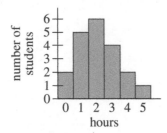

33. What fraction of the students responded that they had spent less than 3 hours studying?

A. $\frac{13}{100}$

B. $\frac{1}{5}$

C. $\frac{3}{10}$

D. $\frac{13}{20}$

E. $\frac{17}{20}$

34. The teacher decides to show the data in a circle graph (pie chart). What should be the measure of the central angle of the sector for 3 hours?

F. 18°
G. 20°
H. 36°
J. 72°
K. 90°

35. To the nearest tenth of an hour, what is the average number of hours for the 20 survey responses?

A. 2.0
B. 2.1
C. 2.3
D. 2.5
E. 3.0

DO YOUR FIGURING HERE.

36. Pentagons have 5 diagonals, as illustrated below.

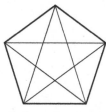

How many diagonals does the octagon below have?

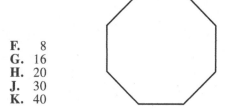

F.   8
G. 16
H. 20
J. 30
K. 40

37. The bottom of the basket of a hot-air balloon is parallel to the level ground. One taut tether line 144 feet long is attached to the center of the bottom of the basket and is anchored to the ground at an angle of 72°, as shown in the figure below. Which of the following expressions gives the distance, in feet, from the center of the bottom of the basket to the ground?

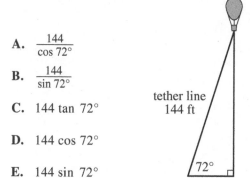

A. $\dfrac{144}{\cos 72°}$

B. $\dfrac{144}{\sin 72°}$

C.   144 tan 72°

D.   144 cos 72°

E.   144 sin 72°

tether line
144 ft

72°

38. The coordinates of the endpoints of $\overline{GH}$, in the standard (x,y) coordinate plane, are $(-8,-3)$ and $(2,3)$. What is the x-coordinate of the midpoint of $\overline{GH}$?

F. −6
G. −3
H.   0
J.   3
K.   5

39. Let $2x + 3y = 4$ and $5x + 6y = 7$. What is the value of $8x + 9y$?

A. -10
B. -1
C. 2
D. 7
E. 10

DO YOUR FIGURING HERE.

40. What are the values of θ, between 0 and 2π, when $\tan \theta = -1$?

F. $\frac{\pi}{4}$ and $\frac{3\pi}{4}$ only

G. $\frac{3\pi}{4}$ and $\frac{5\pi}{4}$ only

H. $\frac{3\pi}{4}$ and $\frac{7\pi}{4}$ only

J. $\frac{5\pi}{4}$ and $\frac{7\pi}{4}$ only

K. $\frac{\pi}{4}$, $\frac{3\pi}{4}$, $\frac{5\pi}{4}$, and $\frac{7\pi}{4}$

41. For the complex number i and an integer x, which of the following is a possible value of i^x ?

A. 0
B. 1
C. 2
D. 3
E. 4

42. A can of soda pop has the shape of a right circular cylinder with an inside height of 6 inches and an inside diameter of 2 inches. When you pour the soda pop from the full can into a cylindrical glass with an inside diameter of 3 inches, about how many inches high is the soda pop in the glass?

(Note: The volume of a right circular cylinder is $\pi r^2 h$.)

F. $2\frac{2}{3}$

G. 4

H. 5

J. $6\frac{2}{3}$

K. 8

43. The height and radius of the right circular cylinder below are given in meters. What is the volume, in cubic meters, of the cylinder?

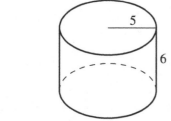

A. 30π
B. 31π
C. 150π
D. 180π
E. 900π

DO YOUR FIGURING HERE.

44. Lines l_1 and l_2 intersect each other and 3 parallel lines, l_3, l_4, and l_5, at the points shown in the figure below. The ratio of the perimeter of $\triangle ABC$ to the perimeter of $\triangle AFG$ is 1:3. The ratio of $\overline{DE}$ to $\overline{FG}$ is 2:3. What is the ratio of $\overline{AC}$ to $\overline{CE}$?

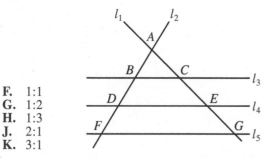

F. 1:1
G. 1:2
H. 1:3
J. 2:1
K. 3:1

45. A rocket lifted off from a launch pad and traveled vertically 30 kilometers, then traveled 40 kilometers at 30° from the vertical, and then traveled 100 kilometers at 45° from the vertical, as shown in the figure below. At that point, the rocket was how many kilometers above the height of the launch pad?

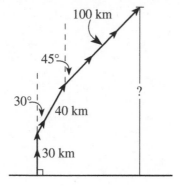

A. 100
B. 170
C. 190
D. $20\sqrt{3} + 50\sqrt{2}$
E. $30 + 20\sqrt{3} + 50\sqrt{2}$

46. Machine A produces 500 springs a day. The number of *defective* springs produced by this machine each day is recorded for 60 days. Based on the distribution given below, what is the expected value of the number of *defective* springs produced by Machine A in any single day?

Number, n, of defective springs produced	Probability that n defective springs are produced in any single day
0	0.70
1	0.20
2	0.05
3	0.05

F. 0.00
G. 0.45
H. 0.70
J. 1.00
K. 1.50

47. The height above the ground, h units, of an object t seconds after being thrown from the top of a building is given by the equation $h = -2t^2 + 10t + 48$. An equivalent factored form of this equation shows that the object:

A. starts at a point 2 units off the ground.
B. reaches a maximum height of 3 units.
C. reaches a maximum height of 8 units.
D. reaches the ground at 3 seconds.
E. reaches the ground at 8 seconds.

48. For all positive values of g and h, which of the following expressions is equivalent to $g^2\sqrt{g^5} \cdot h^2\sqrt[4]{h^5}$?

F. $g^2h^2\sqrt[5]{g^2h^2}$

G. $g^3h\sqrt[4]{g^2h^3}$

H. $g^4h^3\sqrt[4]{g^2h}$

J. $g^4h^4\sqrt{gh}$

K. g^7h^7

49. The value of $\log_5\left(5^{\frac{13}{2}}\right)$ is between which of the following pairs of consecutive integers?

A. 0 and 1
B. 4 and 5
C. 5 and 6
D. 6 and 7
E. 9 and 10

DO YOUR FIGURING HERE.

Use the following information to answer questions 50–52.

A storage facility is currently offering a special rate to customers who sign contracts for 6 months or more. According to this special rate, the first month's rent is $1, and for each month after the first month, customers pay the regular monthly rental rate. The table below shows the storage unit sizes available, the floor dimensions, and the regular monthly rental rate. All the units have the same height.

Size	Floor dimensions, in meters	Regular monthly rental rate
1	2 × 4	$ 30
2	4 × 4	$ 60
3	4 × 8	$100
4	8 × 8	$150
5	8 × 16	$200

50. Daria will sign a contract to rent a Size 3 unit for 12 months at the current special rate. The amount Daria will pay for 12 months at the current special rate represents what percent decrease from the regular rental rate for 12 months?

F. 8.25%
G. 8.33%
H. 8.42%
J. 9.00%
K. 9.09%

51. Size 5 units can be subdivided to form other sizes of units. What is the greatest number of Size 1 units that can be formed from a single Size 5 unit?

A. 2
B. 4
C. 8
D. 10
E. 16

52. Janelle, the owner of the storage facility, is considering building new units that have floor dimensions larger than Size 5 units. She will use the floor area to determine the heating requirements of these larger units. For this calculation, Janelle will use the same relationship between the unit size number and the respective floor area for Sizes 1 through 5. Which of the following expressions gives the floor area, in square meters, of a Size x storage unit?

F. $2^3 \cdot x$
G. 2^{3x}
H. $2^{(2+x)}$
J. $2(x+1)^2$
K. $(x+2)^2$

53. A trigonometric function with equation $y = a \sin(bx + c)$, where a, b, and c are real numbers, is graphed in the standard (x,y) coordinate plane below. The *period* of this function $f(x)$ is the smallest positive number p such that $f(x + p) = f(x)$ for every real number x. One of the following is the period of this function. Which one is it?

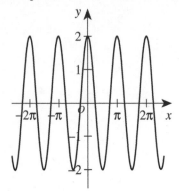

A. $\dfrac{\pi}{2}$

B. π

C. 2π

D. 4π

E. 2

54. The component forms of vectors **u** and **v** are given by $\mathbf{u} = \langle 5,3 \rangle$ and $\mathbf{v} = \langle 2,-7 \rangle$. Given that $2\mathbf{u} + (-3\mathbf{v}) + \mathbf{w} = \mathbf{0}$, what is the component form of **w** ?

F. $\langle -16,\ 15 \rangle$

G. $\langle\ -4,-27 \rangle$

H. $\langle\ \ 3,\ 10 \rangle$

J. $\langle\ \ 4,\ 27 \rangle$

K. $\langle\ 16,-15 \rangle$

55. For how many integers x is the equation $3^{x+1} = 9^{x-2}$ true?

A.   0
B.   1
C.   2
D.   3
E.   An infinite number

56. In $\triangle ABC$ shown below, the length of $\overline{AC}$ and the measure of θ will remain constant. The length of $\overline{AC}$ is 20 inches and the measure of $\angle C$ is equal to θ. Initially, the length of $\overline{BC}$ is 15 inches, and the length of $\overline{BC}$ is the function given by $f(t) = 15 - 2t$, where t is time, in seconds, since the length of $\overline{BC}$ began to decrease. What is the time, t, at which the resulting triangle will have an area that is $\frac{1}{2}$ the area of the original triangle?

(Note: The area of a triangle is $\frac{1}{2}ab \sin x$, where a and b are the lengths of the sides that form the interior angle with measure x.)

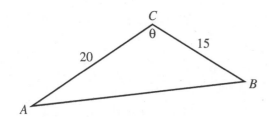

F. 0

G. $\frac{15}{8}$

H. $\frac{15}{4}$

J. $\frac{45}{8}$

K. $\frac{45}{4}$

57. Which of the following expressions gives the number of distinct permutations of the letters in PEOPLE ?

A. 6!

B. 4(4!)

C. $\frac{6!}{4!}$

D. $\frac{6!}{2!}$

E. $\frac{6!}{(2!)(2!)}$

DO YOUR FIGURING HERE.

58. Which of the following expressions is equivalent to $49x^2 + 81$?

    F. $(7x + 9)^2$
    G. $(7x + 9i)^2$
    H. $(7x - 9i)^2$
    J. $(7x - 9)(7x + 9)$
    K. $(7x - 9i)(7x + 9i)$

DO YOUR FIGURING HERE.

59. A bivariate data set of observed values along with a line of best fit for the data set are shown in the standard (x,y) coordinate plane below. The set of 4 residuals for the model is given by $y_i - y(x_i)$, for $i = 1, 2, 3, 4$, where y_i is the observed y-value corresponding to the input x_i, and $\left(x_i, y(x_i)\right)$ is on the line of best fit. What is the absolute value of the largest residual for this model?

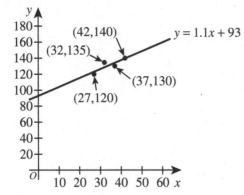

    A. 2.5
    B. 6.8
    C. 15.0
    D. 20.0
    E. 42.0

60. For the first 5 possible values of x, the table below gives the probability, $P(x)$, that a certain factory machine will make x errors on any given workday.

x errors	$P(x)$
0	0.0823
1	0.2185
2	0.2712
3	0.2046
4	0.1238

Which of the following values is closest to the probability that this machine will make at least 1 error on any given workday?

F. 0.2185
G. 0.5996
H. 0.6992
J. 0.8181
K. 0.9177

61. $3x^3 \cdot 2x^2y \cdot 4x^2y$ is equivalent to:

F. $9x^7y^2$

G. $9x^{12}y^2$

H. $24x^7y^2$

J. $24x^{12}y$

K. $24x^{12}y^2$

62. Mr. Dietz is a teacher whose salary is $22,570 for this school year, which has 185 days. In Mr. Dietz's school district, substitute teachers are paid $80 per day. If Mr. Dietz takes a day off without pay and a substitute teacher is paid to teach Mr. Dietz's classes, how much less does the school district pay in salary by paying a substitute teacher instead of paying Mr. Dietz for that day?

A. $42
B. $80
C. $97
D. $105
E. $122

63. So far, a student has earned the following scores on four 100-point tests this grading period: 65, 73, 81, and 82. What score must the student earn on the fifth and last 100-point test of the grading period to earn an average test grade of 80 for the 5 tests?

F. 75
G. 76
H. 78
J. 99
K. The student cannot earn an average of 80.

DO YOUR FIGURING HERE.

64. The oxygen saturation level of a river is found by dividing the amount of dissolved oxygen the river water currently has per liter by the dissolved oxygen capacity per liter of the water and then converting to a percent. If the river currently has 7.3 milligrams of dissolved oxygen per liter of water and the dissolved oxygen capacity is 9.8 milligrams per liter, what is the oxygen saturation level, to the nearest percent?

   A. 34%
   B. 70%
   C. 73%
   D. 74%
   E. 98%

65. A rectangular lot that measures 150 ft by 200 ft is completely fenced. What is the approximate length, in feet, of the fence?

   F. 300
   G. 350
   H. 400
   J. 700
   K. 1,400

66. The expression $a[b + (c - d)]$ is equivalent to:

   A. $ab + ac - ad$
   B. $ab + ac + ad$
   C. $ab + ac - d$
   D. $ab + c + d$
   E. $ab + c - d$

67. If $4x + 3 = 9x - 4$, then $x = ?$

   F. $\dfrac{7}{5}$

   G. $\dfrac{5}{7}$

   H. $\dfrac{7}{13}$

   J. $\dfrac{1}{5}$

   K. $-\dfrac{7}{5}$

68. What 2 numbers should be placed in the blanks below so that the difference between consecutive numbers is the same?

   17,_____,_____,41

   A. 23, 29
   B. 24, 34
   C. 25, 33
   D. 26, 35
   E. 27, 31

69. If x is a real number such that $x^3 = 64$, then $x^2 + \sqrt{x} = ?$

   F. 4
   G. 10
   H. 18
   J. 20
   K. 47

DO YOUR FIGURING HERE.

70. A formula for the volume V of a sphere with radius r is $V = \frac{4}{3}\pi r^3$. If the radius of a spherical rubber ball is $1\frac{1}{4}$ inches, what is its volume to the nearest cubic inch?

A. 5
B. 7
C. 8
D. 16
E. 65

71. If a marble is randomly chosen from a bag that contains exactly 8 red marbles, 6 blue marbles, and 6 white marbles, what is the probability that the marble will NOT be white?

F. $\frac{3}{4}$

G. $\frac{3}{5}$

H. $\frac{4}{5}$

J. $\frac{3}{10}$

K. $\frac{7}{10}$

72. The number of students participating in fall sports at a certain high school is shown by the following matrix.

Tennis	Soccer	Cross-Country	Football
[40	60	80	80]

The athletic director estimates the ratio of the number of sports awards that will be earned to the number of students participating with the following matrix.

$$\begin{matrix} \text{Tennis} \\ \text{Soccer} \\ \text{Cross-Country} \\ \text{Football} \end{matrix} \begin{bmatrix} 0.3 \\ 0.4 \\ 0.2 \\ 0.5 \end{bmatrix}$$

Given these matrices, what is the athletic director's estimate for the number of sports awards that will be earned for these fall sports?

A. 80
B. 88
C. 91
D. 92
E. 99

DO YOUR FIGURING HERE.

Use the following information to answer questions 73–74.

The following chart shows the current enrollment in all the mathematics classes offered by Eastside High School.

Course title	Section	Period	Enrollment
Pre-Algebra	A	3	23
Algebra I	A	2	24
	B	3	25
	C	4	29
Geometry	A	1	21
	B	2	22
Algebra II	A	4	28
Pre-Calculus	A	6	19

73. What is the average number of students enrolled per section in Algebra I?

F. 24
G. 25
H. 26
J. 27
K. 29

74. The school owns 2 classroom sets of 30 calculators each, which students are required to have during their mathematics class. There are 2 calculators from one set and 6 calculators from the other set that are not available for use by the students because these calculators are being repaired. For which of the following class periods, if any, are there NOT enough calculators available for each student to use a school-owned calculator without having to share?

A. Period 2 only
B. Period 3 only
C. Period 4 only
D. Periods 3 and 4 only
E. There are enough calculators for each class period.

DO YOUR FIGURING HERE.

75. What expression must the center cell of the table below contain so that the sums of each row, each column, and each diagonal are equivalent?

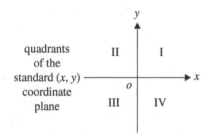

x	$8x$	$-3x$
$-2x$	?	$6x$
$7x$	$-4x$	$3x$

F. $6x$
G. $4x$
H. $2x$
J. $-2x$
K. $-4x$

76. Point A is to be graphed in a quadrant, not on an axis, of the standard (x,y) coordinate plane below.

quadrants
of the
standard (x, y)
coordinate
plane

II   I

III   IV

o

y

x

If the x-coordinate and the y-coordinate of point A are to have opposite signs, then point A *must* be located in:

A. Quadrant II only.
B. Quadrant IV only.
C. Quadrant I or III only.
D. Quadrant I or IV only.
E. Quadrant II or IV only.

77. Kareem has 4 sweaters, 6 shirts, and 3 pairs of slacks. How many distinct outfits, each consisting of a sweater, a shirt, and a pair of slacks, can Kareem select?

F. 13
G. 36
H. 42
J. 72
K. 216

78. At a refinery, 100,000 tons of sand are required to produce each 60,000 barrels of a tarry material. How many tons of sand are required to produce 3,000 barrels of this tarry material?

A. 5,000
B. 18,000
C. 20,000
D. 40,000
E. 50,000

79. If a rectangle measures 54 meters by 72 meters, what is the length, in meters, of the diagonal of the rectangle?

F. 48
G. 63
H. 90
J. 126
K. 252

DO YOUR FIGURING HERE.

80. For all positive integers x, y, and z, which of the following expressions is equivalent to $\frac{x}{y}$?

A. $\frac{x \cdot z}{y \cdot z}$

B. $\frac{x \cdot x}{y \cdot y}$

C. $\frac{y \cdot x}{x \cdot y}$

D. $\frac{x - z}{y - z}$

E. $\frac{x + z}{y + z}$

81. What is the slope-intercept form of $8x - y - 6 = 0$?

F. $y = -8x - 6$
G. $y = -8x + 6$
H. $y = 8x - 6$
J. $y = 8x + 6$
K. $y = 6x - 8$

82. For right triangle $\triangle RST$ shown below, what is tan R?

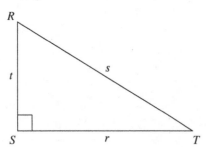

F. $\dfrac{r}{s}$

G. $\dfrac{r}{t}$

H. $\dfrac{t}{r}$

J. $\dfrac{t}{s}$

K. $\dfrac{s}{t}$

83. A chord 24 inches long is 5 inches from the center of a circle, as shown below. What is the radius of the circle, to the nearest tenth of an inch?

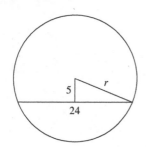

A. 29.0
B. 24.5
C. 16.9
D. 13.0
E. 10.9

84. The length L, in meters, of a spring is given by the equation $L = \frac{2}{3}F + 0.03$, where F is the applied force in newtons. What force, in newtons, must be applied for the spring's length to be 0.18 meters?

F. 0.13
G. 0.15
H. 0.225
J. 0.255
K. 0.27

85. After a snowstorm, city workers removed an estimated 10,000 cubic yards of snow from the downtown area. If this snow were spread in an even layer over the entire rectangular football field shown below, about how many yards deep would the layer of snow be?

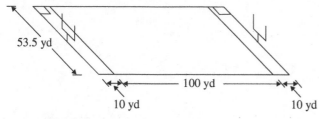

A. Less than 1
B. Between 1 and 2
C. Between 2 and 3
D. Between 3 and 4
E. More than 4

DO YOUR FIGURING HERE.

86. The hypotenuse of the right triangle $\triangle PQR$ shown below is 16 feet long. The sine of $\angle P$ is $\frac{3}{5}$. About how many feet long is $\overline{QR}$?

DO YOUR FIGURING HERE.

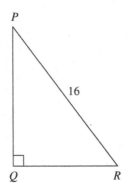

F. 8.0
G. 9.6
H. 12.4
J. 14.3
K. 15.4

87. The graph below shows the number of cars assembled last year in 4 cities, to the nearest 5,000 cars. According to the graph, what fraction of the cars assembled in all 4 cities were assembled in Coupeville?

Key
= 10,000 cars

City	Cars assembled
Car Town	🚗 🚗 🚗 🚗
Coupeville	🚗 🚗 🚙
Truck City	🚗 🚗
Sedan Falls	🚗 🚙

A. $\frac{1}{5}$

B. $\frac{1}{4}$

C. $\frac{3}{11}$

D. $\frac{3}{10}$

E. $\frac{1}{3}$

88. What is the *x*-coordinate of the point in the standard (x,y) coordinate plane at which the 2 lines $y = 2x + 6$ and $y = 3x + 4$ intersect?

   A. 1
   B. 2
   C. 4
   D. 6
   E. 10

89. For all pairs of real numbers *M* and *V* where $M = 3V + 6$, $V = ?$

   F. $\dfrac{M}{3} - 6$

   G. $\dfrac{M}{3} + 6$

   H. $3M - 6$

   J. $\dfrac{M - 6}{3}$

   K. $\dfrac{M + 6}{3}$

90. Parallelogram *ABCD*, with dimensions in inches, is shown in the diagram below. What is the area of the parallelogram, in square inches?

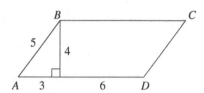

   A. 18
   B. 36
   C. 39
   D. 45
   E. 72

91. If $a = b + 2$, then $(b - a)^4 = ?$

   F. −16
   G. −8
   H. 1
   J. 8
   K. 16

92. The larger of two numbers exceeds twice the smaller number by 8. The sum of twice the larger and 3 times the smaller number is 65. If *x* is the smaller number, which equation below determines the correct value of *x* ?

   F. $3(2x + 8) + 2x = 65$
   G. $3(2x - 8) + 2x = 65$
   H. $(4x + 8) + 3x = 65$
   J. $2(2x + 8) + 3x = 65$
   K. $2(2x - 8) + 3x = 65$

DO YOUR FIGURING HERE.

93. Members of the fire department lean a 30-foot ladder against a building. The side of the building is perpendicular to the level ground so that the base of the ladder is 10 feet away from the base of the building. To the nearest foot, how far up the building does the ladder reach?

    A. 10
    B. 20
    C. 28
    D. 31
    E. 40

94. The ratio of the side lengths for a triangle is exactly 12:14:15. In a second triangle similar to the first, the shortest side is 8 inches long. To the nearest tenth of an inch, what is the length of the longest side of the second triangle?

    A. 11.0
    B. 10.0
    C. 9.3
    D. 6.4
    E. Cannot be determined from the given information

95. In the figure below, *ABCD* is a trapezoid, *E* lies on $\overline{AD}$, and angle measures are as marked. What is the measure of ∠*BDC*?

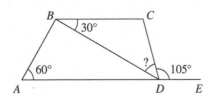

    F. 15°
    G. 25°
    H. 30°
    J. 35°
    K. 45°

96. In the figure shown below, each pair of intersecting line segments meets at a right angle, and all the lengths given are in inches. What is the perimeter, in inches, of the figure?

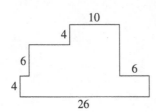

    A. 40
    B. 52
    C. 56
    D. 66
    E. 80

DO YOUR FIGURING HERE.

97. Of the 804 graduating seniors in a certain high school, approximately $\frac{2}{5}$ are going to college and approximately $\frac{1}{4}$ of those going to college are going to a state university. Which of the following is the closest estimate for how many of the graduating seniors are going to a state university?

F. 80
G. 90
H. 160
J. 200
K. 320

98. What is the distance in the standard (x,y) coordinate plane between the points $(1,0)$ and $(0,5)$?

A. 4
B. 6
C. 16
D. 36
E. $\sqrt{26}$

99. The ratio of the radii of two circles is 4:9. What is the ratio of their circumferences?

F. 2:3
G. 4:9
H. 16:81
J. $4:8\pi$
K. $9:18\pi$

100. A circle in the standard (x,y) coordinate plane is tangent to the x-axis at 5 and tangent to the y-axis at 5. Which of the following is an equation of the circle?

A. $x^2 + y = 5$
B. $x^2 + y = 25$
C. $(x-5)^2 + (y-5)^2 = 5$
D. $(x-5)^2 + (y-5)^2 = 25$
E. $(x+5)^2 + (y+5)^2 = 25$

101. Which of the following statements describes the total number of dots in the first n rows of the triangular arrangement illustrated below?

•   1st row
• • •   2nd row
• • • • •   3rd row
• • • • • • •   4th row
• • • • • • • • •   5th row

A. This total is always equal to 25 regardless of the number of rows.
B. This total is equal to twice the number of rows.
C. This total is equal to 5 times the number of rows.
D. This total is equal to the square of the number of rows.
E. There is no consistent relationship between this total and the number of rows.

DO YOUR FIGURING HERE.

102. Douglas wants to draw a circle graph showing the favorite colors of his friends. When he polled his friends asking each their favorite color, 25% of his friends said red; 30% of his friends said blue; 20% of his friends said green; 10% of his friends said purple; and the remaining friends said colors other than red, blue, green, and purple. The colors other than red, blue, green, and purple will be grouped together in an Other sector. What will be the degree measure of the Other sector?

A. 108°
B. 54°
C. 27°
D. 15°
E. 10°

DO YOUR FIGURING HERE.

103. If $\sin\theta = -\frac{3}{5}$ and $\pi < \theta < \frac{3\pi}{2}$, then $\tan\theta = ?$

F. $-\frac{5}{4}$

G. $-\frac{3}{4}$

H. $-\frac{3}{5}$

J. $\frac{3}{4}$

K. $\frac{4}{5}$

104. Which of the following systems of inequalities is represented by the shaded region of the graph below?

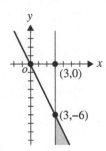

A. $y \le -2x$ and $x \ge 3$
B. $y \le -2x$ or $x \ge 3$
C. $y \ge -2x$ and $x \ge 3$
D. $y \ge -2x$ or $x \ge 3$
E. $y \ge -2x$ and $x \le 3$

DO YOUR FIGURING HERE.

105. If $f(x) = x^2 - 2$, then $f(x+h) = ?$

F. $x^2 + h^2$

G. $x^2 - 2 + h$

H. $x^2 + h^2 - 2$

J. $x^2 + 2xh + h^2$

K. $x^2 + 2xh + h^2 - 2$

106. Which of the following is the graph, in the standard (x,y) coordinate plane, of $y = \frac{2x^2 + x}{x}$?

A.

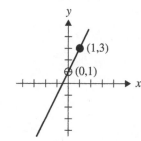

B.

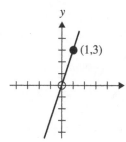

C.

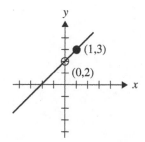

D.

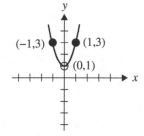

E.

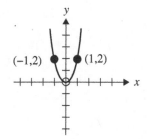

107. A triangle, $\triangle ABC$, is reflected across the x-axis to have the image $\triangle A'B'C'$ in the standard (x,y) coordinate plane; thus, A reflects to A'. The coordinates of point A are (c,d). What are the coordinates of point A'?

F. $(c, -d)$

G. $(-c, d)$

H. $(-c, -d)$

J, (d, c)

K. Cannot be determined from the given information

108. If $x = 2t - 9$ and $y = 5 - t$, which of the following expresses y in terms of x?

A. $y = \dfrac{1-x}{2}$

B. $y = \dfrac{19-x}{2}$

C. $y = 14 - 2x$

D. $y = 5 - x$

E. $y = 1 - x$

DO YOUR FIGURING HERE.

109. What is $\sin\frac{\pi}{12}$ given that $\frac{\pi}{12} = \frac{\pi}{3} - \frac{\pi}{4}$ and that $\sin(\alpha - \beta) = (\sin\alpha)(\cos\beta) - (\cos\alpha)(\sin\beta)$?

(Note: You may use the following table of values.)

θ	$\sin\theta$	$\cos\theta$
$\dfrac{\pi}{6}$	$\dfrac{1}{2}$	$\dfrac{\sqrt{3}}{2}$
$\dfrac{\pi}{4}$	$\dfrac{\sqrt{2}}{2}$	$\dfrac{\sqrt{2}}{2}$
$\dfrac{\pi}{3}$	$\dfrac{\sqrt{3}}{2}$	$\dfrac{1}{2}$

F. $\dfrac{1}{4}$

G. $\dfrac{1}{2}$

H. $\dfrac{\sqrt{3}-2}{4}$

J. $\dfrac{\sqrt{3}-\sqrt{2}}{2}$

K. $\dfrac{\sqrt{6}-\sqrt{2}}{4}$

110. If 12 vases cost $18.00, what is the cost of 1 vase?

   F. $0.67
   G. $1.05
   H. $1.33
   J. $1.50
   K. $1.60

111. Your friend shows you a scale drawing of her apartment. The drawing of the apartment is a rectangle 4 inches by 6 inches. Your friend wants to know the length of the shorter side of the apartment. If she knows that the length of the longer side of the apartment is 30 feet, how many feet long is the shorter side of her apartment?

   A. 9
   B. 20
   C. 24
   D. 30
   E. 45

112. A company earned a profit of $8.0 million each year for 3 consecutive years. For each of the next 2 years the company earned a profit of $9.0 million. For this 5-year period, what was the company's average yearly profit, in millions of dollars?

   F. 8.2
   G. 8.25
   H. 8.4
   J. 8.5
   K. 8.6

113. A company rents moving vans for a rental fee of $25.00 per day with an additional charge of $0.30 per mile that the van is driven. Which of the following expressions represents the cost, in dollars, of renting a van for 1 day and driving it m miles?

   A. $0.30m + 25$
   B. $25m + 30$
   C. $30m + 25$
   D. $25.30m$
   E. $55m$

114. The relationship between temperature in degrees Fahrenheit, F, and temperature in degrees Celsius, C, is expressed by the formula $F = \frac{9}{5}C + 32$. Calvin reads a temperature of 38° on a Celsius thermometer. To the nearest degree, what is the equivalent temperature on a Fahrenheit thermometer?

   F. 36°
   G. 53°
   H. 68°
   J. 70°
   K. 100°

DO YOUR FIGURING HERE.

115. Nick needs to order 500 pens from his supplier. The catalog shows that these pens come in cases of 24 boxes with 10 pens in each box. Nick knows that he may NOT order partial cases. What is the fewest number of cases he should order?

   A. 2
   B. 3
   C. 18
   D. 21
   E. 50

116. When $a + b = 6$, what is the value of

$$2(a+b) + \frac{a+b}{6} + (a+b)^2 - 2?$$

   F. 23
   G. 37
   H. 38
   J. 43
   K. 47

117. The cost of a hamburger and a soft drink together is $2.10. The cost of 2 hamburgers and a soft drink together is $3.50. What is the cost of a soft drink?

   A. $0.50
   B. $0.55
   C. $0.70
   D. $1.05
   E. $1.40

118. Shannon is planning to tile a rectangular kitchen countertop that is 24 inches wide and 64 inches long. She determined that 1 tile will be needed for each 4-inch-by-4-inch region. What is the minimum number of tiles that will be needed to completely cover the countertop to its edges?

   A. 44
   B. 88
   C. 96
   D. 176
   E. 384

119. Which of the following lists gives 2 of the 3 interior angle measurements of a triangle for which the third angle measurement would be equal to 1 of the 2 given measurements?

   F. 20°, 40°
   G. 30°, 60°
   H. 40°, 100°
   J. 45°, 120°
   K. 50°, 60°

120. A triangle with a perimeter of 66 inches has one side that is 16 inches long. The lengths of the other two sides have a ratio of 2:3. What is the length, in inches, of the *longest* side of the triangle?

   A. 16
   B. 20
   C. 30
   D. 40
   E. 50

DO YOUR FIGURING HERE.

121. In the figure below, lines *m* and *n* are parallel, transversals *r* and *s* intersect to form an angle of measure $x°$, and 2 other angle measures are as marked. What is the value of *x*?

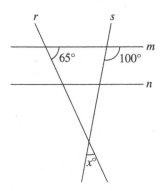

A. 15
B. 25
C. 35
D. 65
E. 80

122. What is the slope of any line parallel to the line $7x + 9y = 6$?

A. -7

B. $-\dfrac{7}{9}$

C. $\dfrac{7}{6}$

D. 6

E. 7

123. A ramp for wheelchair access to the gym has a slope of 5% (that is, the ramp rises 5 feet vertically for every 100 feet of horizontal distance). The entire ramp is built on level ground, and the entrance to the gym is 2 feet above the ground. What is the *horizontal* distance, in feet, between the ends of the ramp?

A. 4
B. 10
C. 40
D. 100
E. 400

124. $(x^2 - 4x + 3) - (3x^2 - 4x - 3)$ is equivalent to:

F. $2x^2 - 6$

G. $2x^2 - 8x$

H. $2x^2 - 8x - 6$

J. $-2x^2 + 6$

K. $-2x^2 - 8x$

DO YOUR FIGURING HERE.

125. Which of the following sets of 3 numbers could be the side lengths, in meters, of a 30°–60°–90° triangle?

A. $1, 1, 1$
B. $1, 1, \sqrt{2}$
C. $1, \sqrt{2}, \sqrt{2}$
D. $1, \sqrt{2}, \sqrt{3}$
E. $1, \sqrt{3}, 2$

DO YOUR FIGURING HERE.

126. Which of the following statements is NOT true about the arithmetic sequence $17, 12, 7, 2, \ldots$?

A. The fifth term is -3.
B. The sum of the first 5 terms is 35.
C. The eighth term is -18.
D. The common difference of consecutive terms is -5.
E. The common ratio of consecutive terms is -5.

127. The normal amount of lead in a certain water supply is 1.5×10^{-5} milligrams per liter. Today, when the water was tested, the lead level found was exactly 100 times as great as the normal level, still well below the Environmental Protection Agency's action level. What concentration of lead, in milligrams per liter, was in the water tested today?

A. 1.5×10^{-105}

B. 1.5×10^{-10}

C. 1.5×10^{-7}

D. 1.5×10^{-3}

E. $1.5 \times 10^{-\frac{5}{2}}$

128. $\left(\dfrac{1}{2}x - y \right)^2 = ?$

A. $\dfrac{1}{4}x^2 + y^2$

B. $\dfrac{1}{4}x^2 - xy + y^2$

C. $\dfrac{1}{2}x^2 - xy + y^2$

D. $x^2 + y^2$

E. $x^2 - xy + y^2$

129. How many prime numbers are there between 30 and 50 ?

    F. 4
    G. 5
    H. 6
    J. 7
    K. 8

DO YOUR FIGURING HERE.

130. The lengths, in feet, of the sides of right triangle $\triangle ABC$ are as shown in the diagram below, with $x > 0$. What is the cotangent of $\angle A$, in terms of x ?

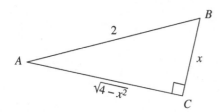

    A. $\sqrt{4 - x^2}$

    B. $\dfrac{2}{x}$

    C. $\dfrac{x}{2}$

    D. $\dfrac{x}{\sqrt{4 - x^2}}$

    E. $\dfrac{\sqrt{4 - x^2}}{x}$

131. The trapezoid below is divided into 2 triangles and 1 rectangle. Lengths are given in inches. What is the combined area, in square inches, of the 2 shaded triangles?

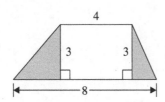

    A. 4
    B. 6
    C. 9
    D. 12
    E. 18

132. In the figure below, *ABCD* is a square and *E*, *F*, *G*, and *H* are the midpoints of its sides. If $\overline{AB}$ = 12 inches, what is the perimeter of *EFGH*, in inches?

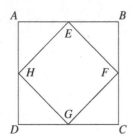

DO YOUR FIGURING HERE.

F. 24

G. $24\sqrt{2}$

H. $36\sqrt{2}$

J. $48\sqrt{2}$

K. 72

133. If the value, to the nearest thousandth, of cos θ is −0.385, which of the following could be true about θ?

A. $0 \le \theta < \frac{\pi}{6}$

B. $\frac{\pi}{6} \le \theta < \frac{\pi}{3}$

C. $\frac{\pi}{3} \le \theta < \frac{\pi}{2}$

D. $\frac{\pi}{2} \le \theta < \frac{2\pi}{3}$

E. $\frac{2\pi}{3} \le \theta \le \pi$

134. Which of the following quadratic equations has solutions $x = 6a$ and $x = -3b$?

F. $x^2 - 18ab = 0$

G. $x^2 - x(3b - 6a) - 18ab = 0$

H. $x^2 - x(3b + 6a) + 18ab = 0$

J. $x^2 + x(3b - 6a) - 18ab = 0$

K. $x^2 + x(3b + 6a) + 18ab = 0$

135. In the standard (x,y) coordinate plane below, the vertices of the square have coordinates (0,0), (6,0), (6,6), and (0,6). Which of the following is an equation of the circle that is inscribed in the square?

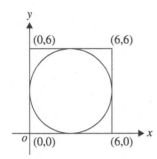

A. $(x-3)^2+(y-3)^2=9$

B. $(x-3)^2+(y-3)^2=3$

C. $(x+3)^2+(y+3)^2=9$

D. $(x+3)^2+(y+3)^2=6$

E. $(x+3)^2+(y+3)^2=3$

136. What is the value of the expression $g \cdot (g + 1)^2$ for $g = 2$?

F. 10

G. 12

H. 18

J. 20

K. 36

137. Company A sells 60 pens for $15.00. Company B sells the same type of pens in packs of 40 for $8.00. Which company's price per pen is cheaper, and what is that price?

A. Company A, at $0.20

B. Company A, at $0.23

C. Company A, at $0.25

D. Company B, at $0.20

E. Company B, at $0.25

138. A ladder is 10 ft long and reaches 8 ft up a wall, as shown below. How many feet is the bottom of the ladder from the base of the wall?

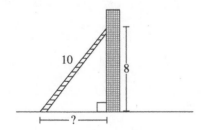

F. 2

G. 3

H. 6

J. $\sqrt{2}$

K. $\sqrt{164}$

DO YOUR FIGURING HERE.

139. A city utility department charges residential customers $2.50 per 1,000 gallons of water and $16.00 per month for trash pickup. Which of the following expressions gives a residential customer's total monthly charges, in dollars, for use of g thousand gallons of water and trash pickup?

   F. $2.50g + 16.00$
   G. $2.50g + 1,016.00$
   H. $16.00g + 2.50$
   J. $18.50\,g$
   K. $2,500.00g + 16.00$

140. What is the value of x that satisfies the equation $2(x + 4) = 5x - 7$?

   A. -1
   B. $\dfrac{1}{3}$
   C. $\dfrac{11}{3}$
   D. 5
   E. $\dfrac{45}{3}$

141. In the figure below, B is on $\overline{AC}$, E is on $\overline{DF}$, $\overline{AC}$ is parallel to $\overline{DF}$, and $\overline{BE}$ is congruent to $\overline{BF}$. What is the measure of $\angle DEB$?

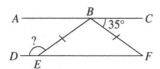

   F. $35°$
   G. $135°$
   H. $145°$
   J. $155°$
   K. $215°$

142. What is the least common denominator when adding the fractions $\dfrac{a}{2}, \dfrac{b}{3}, \dfrac{c}{9}$, and $\dfrac{d}{15}$?

   A. 45
   B. 90
   C. 135
   D. 270
   E. 810

143. Which of the following expressions is equivalent to $3x(x^2y + 2xy^2)$?

   F. $3x^2y + 6xy^2$
   G. $3x^3y + 2xy^2$
   H. $3x^3y + 6x^2y^2$
   J. $5x^4y^3$
   K. $9x^4y^3$

DO YOUR FIGURING HERE.

144. A certain type of notebook costs $2.50 before sales tax is added. When you buy 9 of these notebooks you receive 1 additional notebook free. What is the average cost per notebook for the 10 notebooks before sales tax is added?

  A. $2.78
  B. $2.50
  C. $2.30
  D. $2.25
  E. $2.15

145. For all x, $(3x + 1)^2 = $?

  F. $6x + 2$
  G. $6x^2 + 2$
  H. $9x^2 + 1$
  J. $9x^2 + 3x + 1$
  K. $9x^2 + 6x + 1$

146. On the real number line, what is the midpoint of -5 and 17?

  A. -11
  B. 6
  C. 11
  D. 12
  E. 22

147. If $3\frac{3}{5} = x + 2\frac{2}{3}$, then $x = $

  F. $\dfrac{4}{5}$

  G. $\dfrac{14}{15}$

  H. $1\dfrac{1}{2}$

  J. $1\dfrac{6}{15}$

  K. $6\dfrac{4}{15}$

148. A system of linear equations is shown below.

$$3y = -2x + 8$$
$$3y = 2x + 8$$

Which of the following describes the graph of this system of linear equations in the standard (x, y) coordinate plane?

  A. Two distinct intersecting lines
  B. Two parallel lines with positive slope
  C. Two parallel lines with negative slope
  D. A single line with positive slope
  E. A single line with negative slope

149. Which real number satisfies $(2^x)(4) = 8^3$?

  F. 2
  G. 3
  H. 4
  J. 4.5
  K. 7

DO YOUR FIGURING HERE.

150. The graph shown in the standard (x,y) coordinate plane below is to be rotated in the plane 180° about the origin.

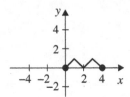

One of the following graphs is the result of this rotation. Which one is it?

A.

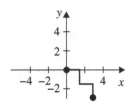

D.

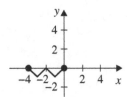

B.

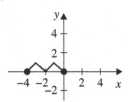

E.

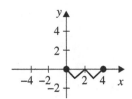

C.

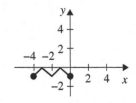

151. On the real number line below, with coordinates as labeled, an object moves according to the following set of instructions: from point P the object moves right to Q, then left to R, then right to S, and finally left until it returns to its original position at P. What is the closest estimate of the total length, in coordinate units, of the movements this object makes?

A. 0
B. 4
C. 12
D. 22
E. 36

152. By definition, the determinant $\begin{vmatrix} a & b \\ c & d \end{vmatrix}$ equals $ad - bc$. What is the value of $\begin{vmatrix} 2x & 3y \\ 5x & 4y \end{vmatrix}$ when $x = -3$ and $y = 2$?

F. −138
G. −42
H. 12
J. 42
K. 138

153. When Angela was cleaning her refrigerator, she found 2 bottles of catsup. Looking at the labels, she noticed that the capacity of the larger bottle was twice the capacity of the smaller bottle. She estimated that the smaller bottle was about $\frac{1}{3}$ full of catsup and the larger bottle was about $\frac{2}{3}$ full of catsup. She poured all the catsup from the smaller bottle into the larger bottle. Then, about how full was the larger bottle?

A. $\frac{2}{9}$ full

B. $\frac{1}{2}$ full

C. $\frac{5}{6}$ full

D. Completely full

E. Overflowing

154. When Jeff starts a math assignment, he spends 5 minutes getting out his book and a sheet of paper, sharpening his pencil, looking up the assignment in his assignment notebook, and turning to the correct page in his book. The equation $t = 10p + 5$ models the time, t minutes, Jeff budgets for a math assignment with p problems. Which of the following statements is necessarily true according to Jeff's model?

    F. He budgets 15 minutes per problem.
    G. He budgets 10 minutes per problem.
    H. He budgets 5 minutes per problem.
    J. He budgets 10 minutes per problem for the hard problems and 5 minutes per problem for the easy problems.
    K. He budgets a 5-minute break after each problem.

DO YOUR FIGURING HERE.

155. Kaya drove 200 miles in 5 hours of actual driving time. By driving an average of 10 miles per hour faster, Kaya could have saved how many hours of actual driving time?

    A. $\dfrac{1}{6}$

    B. $\dfrac{2}{3}$

    C. $\dfrac{7}{10}$

    D. 1

    E. 4

156. If the inequality $|a| > |b|$ is true, then which of the following *must* be true?

    A. $a = b$
    B. $a \neq b$
    C. $a < b$
    D. $a > b$
    E. $a > 0$

157. What is the slope of the line given by the equation $14x - 11y + 16 = 0$?

    F. -11

    G. $-\dfrac{14}{11}$

    H. $-\dfrac{11}{14}$

    J. $\dfrac{14}{11}$

    K. 14

158. In △ABC below, D, E, and F are points on $\overline{AB}$, $\overline{BC}$, and $\overline{AC}$, respectively, and $\overline{DF}$ is congruent to $\overline{EF}$. What is the *sum* of the measures of the angles marked x and y?

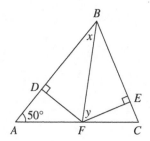

F. 40°
G. 80°
H. 90°
J. 100°
K. 130°

159. Which of the following expressions is equivalent to $(-2x^5y^2)^4$?

A. $-16x^{20}y^8$

B. $-8x^{20}y^8$

C. $-8x^9y^6$

D. $16x^9y^6$

E. $16x^{20}y^8$

160. If $a^2 = 49$ and $b^2 = 64$, which of the following CANNOT be a value of $a + b$?

A. −15
B. −1
C. 1
D. 15
E. 113

161. For each of 3 years, the table below gives the number of games a football team played, the number of running plays they ran, and the total number of yards the team gained on running plays.

Year	Games	Running plays	Total yards gained on running plays
1997	11	397	1,028
1998	11	394	1,417
1999	9	378	1,920

To the nearest tenth of a yard, what is the average number of yards gained per running play in 1998 ?

A. 2.6
B. 2.7
C. 3.6
D. 4.9
E. 5.1

DO YOUR FIGURING HERE.

162. For the polygon below, the lengths of 2 sides are not given. Each angle between adjacent sides measures 90°. What is the polygon's perimeter, in feet?

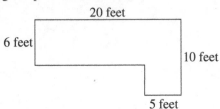

F. 41
G. 52
H. 60
J. 140
K. 200

163. Which of the following inequalities represents the graph shown below on the real number line?

$$\overset{+\ \ \bullet\ \ +\ \ +\ \ +\ \ +\ \ \circ\ \ +\ \ +}{\underset{-3\ -2\ -1\ \ 0\ \ 1\ \ 2\ \ 3\ \ 4\ \ x}{}}$$

A. $-2 \le x \le 2$
B. $-2 \le x < 3$
C. $0 \le x < 3$
D. $2 \le x \le 3$
E. $3 < x \le -2$

164. What is the value of $3 \cdot 2^{x+y}$ when $x = 4$ and $y = -1$?

    F. 216
    G. 96
    H. 47
    J. 24
    K. 18

DO YOUR FIGURING HERE.

165. For integers a and b such that $ab = 8$, which of the following is NOT a possible value of a ?

    A. 2
    B. 1
    C. −4
    D. −6
    E. −8

166. What is the volume, in cubic centimeters, of a cube whose edges each measure 4 centimeters in length?

    F. 12
    G. 16
    H. 24
    J. 64
    K. 96

167. A community center sponsored a 1-day craft show. The center offered 2 sizes of display tables for rent and charged $40 to rent one of the 70 large tables and $25 to rent one of the 50 small tables. Which of the following expressions gives the total amount of money, in dollars, collected from renting all of the small tables and L of the large tables?

    A. $L + 50$
    B. $40L + 1{,}250$
    C. $40L + 2{,}000$
    D. $65L$
    E. $4{,}050L$

168. In the figure below, A, B, and C are collinear, the measure of $\angle ABD$ is $7x°$, and the measure of $\angle CBD$ is $3x°$. What is the measure of $\angle ABD$?

F. 252°
G. 126°
H. 108°
J. 54°
K. 18°

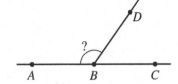

DO YOUR FIGURING HERE.

169. Which of the following is NOT a possible value for a probability?

A. 0.001

B. 0.5

C. $\frac{6}{10}$

D. $\frac{3}{8}$

E. $\frac{34}{31}$

170. For the first several months after the Fiery Red Scooter arrived in toy stores, the rate of sales increased slowly. As this new scooter caught on, however, the rate of sales increased rapidly. After several more months, many people owned a Fiery Red Scooter, and the rate of sales decreased. Which of the following graphs could represent the total number of Fiery Red Scooters sold as a function of time, in months, after the scooter arrived in toy stores?

F.
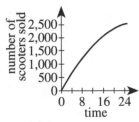

J.
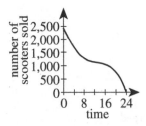

G.
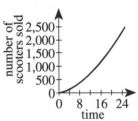

K.
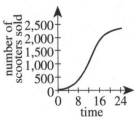

H.
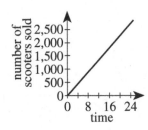

171. For a community service project, members of the junior class at San Carlos High School are going to varnish the rectangular dining room floor of a local nursing home. The floor is 60 feet wide and 80 feet long. Under the assumption that 1 can of varnish covers exactly 250 square feet, what is the minimum number of cans of varnish they will need in order to put 1 coat of varnish on this floor?

    A. 1
    B. 9
    C. 10
    D. 19
    E. 20

DO YOUR FIGURING HERE.

172. Carl is making a scale drawing of his rectangular bedroom floor. The floor is 12 feet wide by 14 feet long. He is using a scale of $\frac{1}{4}$ inch = 1 foot for the scale drawing of the floor. What will be the dimensions, in inches, of Carl's bedroom floor in the scale drawing?

    F. 3 by $3\frac{1}{2}$

    G. 4 by $4\frac{2}{3}$

    H. 6 by 7

    J. 36 by 42

    K. 48 by 56

173. According to a recent survey of students about the juice they each preferred, 20% of the students preferred cranberry juice, 40% preferred orange juice, 20% preferred grapefruit juice, and the remaining students preferred tomato juice. If each student preferred only 1 juice and 250 students preferred tomato juice, how many students were surveyed?

    A.   330
    B.   500
    C.   625
    D. 1,000
    E. 1,250

174. The circumference of each tire on a bicycle is 50 inches. About how many revolutions does one of these bicycle tires make traveling 300 feet (3,600 inches) without slipping?

    F.   6
    G.   18
    H.   72
    J. 300
    K. 864

175. $(4x^2 - 3x + 7) - (-1 + 5x + 2x^2)$ is equivalent to:

A. $2x^2 - 8x + 8$
B. $2x^2 + 2x + 8$
C. $2x^4 + 2x^2 + 6$
D. $6x^2 - 8x + 6$
E. $6x^4 - 8x^2 + 6$

176. A ticket for a movie at the Hazelnut Cinema costs $5.00. Latoya treats her younger brother to a movie at the Hazelnut Cinema. She gives him $\frac{1}{2}$ the money she brought with her, for his ticket and a snack. When he asks to play a video game, she gives him $1.00. That leaves Latoya exactly enough money to buy her own ticket. How much money did Latoya bring with her?

F. $10.00
G. $11.00
H. $12.00
J. $13.00
K. $14.00

177. Mr. Gomez gave his class a test on 20 spelling words. Only one of the following percents is possible as the percent of the 20 words a student spelled correctly. Which one is it?

A. 77%
B. 85%
C. 88%
D. 96%
E. 99%

178. The first 5 terms of a geometric sequence are 0.375, −1.5, 6, −24, and 96. What is the 6th term?

F. −384
G. −126
H. −66
J. 126
K. 384

179. $(2x - 3y)^2$ is equivalent to:

A. $4x^2 - 12xy + 9y^2$
B. $4x^2 - 10xy + 9y^2$
C. $4x^2 - 9y^2$
D. $4x^2 + 9y^2$
E. $4x - 6y$

DO YOUR FIGURING HERE.

180. As shown in the figure below, Mr. Thompson, who is standing at point *A*, needs to determine the distance from point *C* on the ground to point *E* at the top of one of the second-story windows of his house. He places a mirror on the ground at point *B* so that when he looks in the mirror, he can see the top of the window. Mr. Thompson's eye level, at point D, is 6 ft above the ground. He notes that *AB* = 4 ft and *BC* = 14 ft. Approximately how many feet above the ground is the top of the second-story window?

(Note: In △*ABD* and △ *CBE*, ∠*ABD* is congruent to ∠*CBE*.)

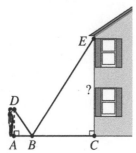

DO YOUR FIGURING HERE.

- **F.** 2
- **G.** 10
- **H.** 16
- **J.** 21
- **K.** 24

181. What is the solution to the equation $7x - (x - 3) = 6$?

- **A.** $-\frac{3}{2}$
- **B.** -2
- **C.** $\frac{1}{2}$
- **D.** $\frac{3}{2}$
- **E.** 2

182. The area of △*XYZ* below is 32 square inches. If $\overline{XZ}$ is 8 inches long, how long is altitude $\overline{YW}$, in inches?

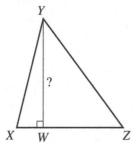

- **F.** 10
- **G.** 8
- **H.** 6
- **J.** 4
- **K.** 2

183. Given $f(x) = 2x^2 - 5x + 7$, what is the value of $f(-10)$?

- A. −243
- B. −143
- C.   157
- D.   257
- E.   457

184. The cheerleading squad wants to purchase new uniforms to wear at the regional championship competition. They decide to sell candy bars for $1.00 each. The squad will receive $0.40 for each of the first 200 candy bars sold. For each of the next 300 sold, the squad will receive $0.50. For each additional candy bar sold, the squad will receive $0.60. How many candy bars must the squad sell to reach their goal of raising $350.00 ?

- F.   350
- G.   584
- H.   667
- J.   700
- K.   875

185. The table below shows the age distribution of the student body at Memorial High School.

Age, in years	14	15	16	17	18
Percent of students	6%	28%	26%	31%	9%

What percent of the students are at least 16 years old?

- A. 34%
- B. 40%
- C. 50%
- D. 60%
- E. 66%

186. What percent of $\frac{2}{3}$ is $\frac{1}{3}$?

- F.   22%
- G.   33%
- H.   50%
- J.   67%
- K. 200%

187. The sign below advertises a sale on coats. What is the sale price of a coat with a regular price of $84.00 ?

SALE	SALE	SALE
	All Coats	
	3/4 off the regular price!	
SALE	SALE	SALE

- A. $ 9.00
- B. $21.00
- C. $42.00
- D. $63.00
- E. $83.25

DO YOUR FIGURING HERE.

188. The ratio of a side of square A to the length of rectangle B is 2:3. The ratio of a side of square A to the width of rectangle B is 2:1. What is the ratio of the area of square A to the area of rectangle B ?

    F. 2:1
    G. 3:1
    H. 3:2
    J. 4:1
    K. 4:3

189. In Intermediate Algebra class, Ms. Schimmack makes the statement "y varies directly as the product of w^2 and x, and inversely as z^3" and asks her students to translate it into an equation. Which of the following equations, with k as the constant of proportionality, is a correct translation of Ms. Schimmack's statement?

    A. $y = \dfrac{kw^2x}{z^3}$

    B. $y = \dfrac{kz^3}{w^2x}$

    C. $y = \dfrac{w^2xz^3}{k}$

    D. $y = \dfrac{z^3}{kw^2x}$

    E. $y = kw^2xz^3$

190. In a certain isosceles triangle, the measure of each of the base angles is twice the measure of the vertex angle. What is the measure, in degrees, of each of the base angles?

    F. $36°$
    G. $60°$
    H. $72°$
    J. $120°$
    K. $144°$

191. For a single production run, when n items are made and sold, a company's profit, P dollars, can be modeled by $P = n^2 - 300n - 100{,}000$. What is the smallest number of items that must be made and sold in order for the company not to lose money on the production run?

    A. 150
    B. 200
    C. 300
    D. 350
    E. 500

DO YOUR FIGURING HERE.

Use the following information to answer questions 192–194.

Mousepads Galore is a company that produces computer mousepads. *Cost* is the total money spent to produce and sell the mousepads, and *revenue* is the total income generated by the sale of the mousepads. The graph below depicts projections for the linear cost function, $C(x)$, and the linear revenue function, $R(x)$.

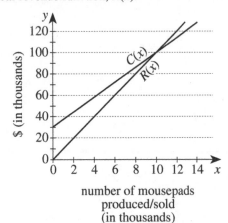

number of mousepads
produced/sold
(in thousands)

192. During the month of April, Mousepads Galore broke even (did not gain or lose any money) when x mousepads were produced and sold. How many mousepads did the company produce and sell during the month of April?

F. 10,000
G. 12,000
H. 14,000
J. 15,000
K. 30,000

193. The cost function shown in the graph for Mousepads Galore has 2 components: a fixed cost, plus a constant production cost per mousepad. Which of the following is the fixed cost?

A. $ 0
B. $ 1,000
C. $ 10,000
D. $ 30,000
E. $100,000

194. Mousepads Galore sells each mousepad at the same price, which is an integer number of dollars. According to the revenue function, what is the price of each of these mousepads?

F. $ 3
G. $ 7
H. $10
J. $12
K. Cannot be determined from the given information

195. Which of the following is a *complete* factorization of the expression $2x + 2xy + 6x^2y$?

  A. $2x(y + 3xy)$
  B. $2x + 2xy(1 + 3x)$
  C. $2x(1 + y + 4xy)$
  D. $1 + y + 3xy$
  E. $2x(1 + y + 3xy)$

DO YOUR FIGURING HERE.

196. Which of the following is an equation of the line that passes through the points $(1, 3)$ and $(-3, -13)$ in the standard (x, y) coordinate plane?

  F. $x + y = 4$
  G. $4x - y = 1$
  H. $5x - y = 2$
  J. $6x - 2y = 8$
  K. $7x - 2y = 5$

197. A square has sides that are the same length as the radius of a circle. If the circle has an area of 36π square units, how many units long is the perimeter of the square?

  A. 18
  B. 24
  C. 36
  D. 72
  E. 324

198. If the following system has a solution, what is the x-coordinate of the solution?

$$3x + 6y = 52$$
$$x + 6y = 24$$

  F. 19
  G. 14
  H. 6
  J. 0
  K. The system has no solution.

Use the following information to answer
questions 199–201.

In the figure below, B and C are on $\overline{HD}$ and G and F are
on $\overline{HE}$. The measurements given are in inches. Both $BGFC$
and $CFED$ are trapezoids. The area, A, of a trapezoid is
given by $A = \frac{1}{2}h(b_1 + b_2)$, where h is the height and b_1 and
b_2 are the lengths of the 2 parallel sides.

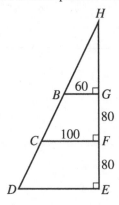

199. What is the area of $BGFC$, in square inches?

   A.   2,500
   B.   5,400
   C.   6,400
   D.   7,000
   E. 12,800

200. What is the length of $\overline{BC}$, in inches?

   F.   90
   G.   100
   H. $\sqrt{4,800}$
   J. $\sqrt{8,000}$
   K. $\sqrt{16,400}$

201. What is the radius, in inches, of the largest circle that can
be drawn so that no point of the circle is outside $CFED$?

   A. 40
   B. 50
   C. 60
   D. 70
   E. 80

202. As shown in the figure below, an escape ramp leading from an emergency exit of an airplane is 35 feet long when fully extended and forms a 15° angle with the level ground.

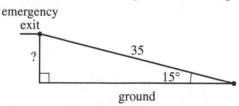

Given the trigonometric approximations in the table below, what is the height above the ground of the emergency exit, rounded to the nearest 0.1 foot?

cos 15°	0.966
sin 15°	0.259
tan 15°	0.268

F. 2.8
G. 7.4
H. 7.7
J. 9.1
K. 9.4

203. There are 10 equally spaced dots marked on a circle. Kim chooses an integer, n, that is greater than 1. Beginning at a randomly chosen dot, Kim goes around the circle clockwise and colors in every nth dot. He continues going around and around the circle coloring in every nth dot, counting each dot whether it is colored in or not, until he has colored in every dot. Which of the following could have been Kim's integer n ?

A. 2
B. 3
C. 4
D. 5
E. 6

204. Consider the exponential equation $y = Ca^t$, where C and a are positive real constants and t is a positive real number. The value of y decreases as the value of t increases if and only if which of the following statements about a is true?

F. $-1 < a$
G. $0 < a$
H. $0 < a < 1$
J. $1 < a < 2$
K. $1 < a$

205. What is the distance, in coordinate units, between the points $P(-2, -1)$ and $Q(1, 3)$ in the standard (x, y) coordinate plane?

A. $\sqrt{5}$
B. $\sqrt{7}$
C. 3
D. 5
E. 7

DO YOUR FIGURING HERE.

206. During their morning jog in the park, Jean stops at a drinking fountain. Sula continues to jog and gets 10 meters ahead of Jean. Sula is jogging at a constant rate of 2 meters per second, and Jean starts jogging at a constant rate of 2.4 meters per second to catch up to Sula. Which of the following equations, when solved for t, gives the number of seconds Jean will take to catch up to Sula?

F. $2t + 10 = 2.4t$

G. $2t - 10 = 2.4t$

H. $\dfrac{10 + 2.4t}{2.4} = 2t$

J. $2t = 10$

K. $2.4t = 10$

207. Which of the following defines the solution set for the system of inequalities below?

$$x \leq 6$$
$$4 + 2x \geq 0$$

A. $x \geq \ -2$

B. $x \leq \ \ \ 6$

C. $-8 \leq x \leq 6$

D. $-2 \leq x \leq 6$

E. $\ \ 2 \leq x \leq 6$

208. At Brookfield High School, 55 seniors are enrolled in the sociology class and 40 seniors are enrolled in the drawing class. Of these seniors, 20 are enrolled in both the sociology class and the drawing class. How many of the 120 seniors enrolled at Brookfield High School are NOT enrolled in either the sociology class or the drawing class?

F.   5

G.   15

H.   20

J.   35

K.   45

209. If two lines in the standard (x, y) coordinate plane are perpendicular and the slope of one of the lines is 3, what is the slope of the other line?

A. -3

B. -1

C. $-\dfrac{1}{3}$

D. $\dfrac{1}{3}$

E.   3

DO YOUR FIGURING HERE.

210. In the standard (x, y) coordinate plane, $(12, 3)$ is half-way between $(2a, a + 3)$ and $(4a, a - 5)$. What is the value of a ?

   F. 0
   G. 2
   H. 3
   J. 4
   K. 6

211. How many 3-letter orderings, where no letter is repeated, can be made using the letters of the word GATORS ?

   A.   3
   B.   6
   C. 27
   D. 120
   E. 216

212. As shown in the (x, y, z) coordinate space below, the cube with vertices A through H has edges that are 1 coordinate unit long. The coordinates of F are $(0,0,0)$, and H is on the positive y-axis. What are the coordinates of D ?

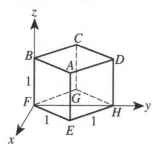

   F. $(0,1,1)$
   G. $(0,\sqrt{2},0)$
   H. $(0, \sqrt{2},1)$
   J. $(0, \sqrt{2},\sqrt{3})$
   K. $(1,1,1)$

213. Whenever x, y, and z are positive real numbers, which of the following expressions is equivalent to $2 \log_3 x + \frac{1}{2}\log_6 y - \log_3 z$?

   A. $\log_3\left(\frac{x^2 y}{z}\right)$
   B. $\log_3\left(\frac{x^2}{z}\right) + \log_6(\sqrt{y})$
   C. $\log_3\left(\frac{z}{x^2}\right) + \log_6\left(\frac{y}{2}\right)$
   D. $\log_3(x - z) + \log_6(\sqrt{y})$
   E. $2 \log_3(x - z) + \log_6\left(\frac{y}{2}\right)$

214. If $2 \leq x \leq 5$ and $-4 < y \leq -3$, what is the maximum value of $|y - 2x|$?

   F. 20
   G. 14
   H. 13
   J. 8
   K. 7

DO YOUR FIGURING HERE.

215. The measure of each interior angle of a regular n-sided polygon is $\frac{(n-2)180°}{n}$. A regular pentagon is shown below. What is the measure of the designated angle?

   A. 108°
   B. 144°
   C. 198°
   D. 252°
   E. 288°

216. Which of the following trigonometric functions has an amplitude of 2 ?

(Note: The *amplitude* of a trigonometric function is $\frac{1}{2}$ the nonnegative difference between the maximum and minimum values of the function.)

   F. $f(x) = 2 \sin x$

   G. $f(x) = 2 \tan x$

   H. $f(x) = \sin\left(\frac{1}{2}x\right)$

   J. $f(x) = \cos 2x$

   K. $f(x) = \frac{1}{2}\cos x$

217. Which of the following is an equivalent expression for r in terms of S and t whenever r, S, and t are all distinct and $S = \frac{rt - 3}{r - t}$?

   A. $\frac{St - 3}{S - t}$

   B. $\frac{S - 3}{S - 1}$

   C. $\frac{S - t}{S - 3}$

   D. $\frac{St - 3}{S + t}$

   E. $\frac{3}{t - S}$

218. In the figure below, lines *l* and *m* are parallel and angle measures are as marked. If it can be determined, what is the value of *x* ?

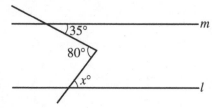

F. 35
G. 45
H. 65
J. 80
K. Cannot be determined from the given information

219. In the triangle below, where the 2 given side lengths are expressed in feet, what is the value of *b* ?

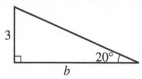

A. 3 cos 20°
B. 3 sin 20°
C. 3 tan 20°
D. 3 sin 70°
E. 3 tan 70°

220. An angle in standard position in the standard (*x*, *y*) coordinate plane has its vertex at the origin and its initial side on the positive *x*-axis. If the measure of an angle in standard position is 1,573°, it has the same terminal side as an angle of each of the following measures EXCEPT:

F. −587°
G. −227°
H. 133°
J. 493°
K. 573°

221. If $m = 4$, $n = -5$, and $p = 9$, what is the value of $mp - mn$?

    A. 16
    B. 31
    C. 41
    D. 56
    E. 81

DO YOUR FIGURING HERE.

222. Vehicle A averages 19 miles per gallon of gasoline, and Vehicle B averages 37 miles per gallon of gasoline. At these rates, how many more gallons of gasoline does Vehicle A need than Vehicle B to make a 1,406-mile trip?

    F. 28
    G. 36
    H. 38
    J. 56
    K. 74

223. If $\frac{x}{y} = \frac{1}{9}$ and $\frac{y}{z} = \frac{9}{8}$, then $\frac{z}{x} = $?

    A. $\frac{1}{648}$

    B. $\frac{1}{8}$

    C. $\frac{8}{81}$

    D. $\frac{81}{8}$

    E. 8

224. If $12(x - 7) = -11$, then $x = $?

F. $-\frac{95}{12}$

G. $-\frac{3}{2}$

H. $-\frac{11}{12}$

J. $-\frac{1}{3}$

K. $\frac{73}{12}$

225. The legs of a right triangle measure 18 m and 24 m, respectively. What is the length, in meters, of its hypotenuse?

A.   21
B.   30
C.   42
D. $\sqrt{252}$
E. $\sqrt{432}$

226. In the school cafeteria, students choose their lunch from 4 sandwiches, 2 soups, 2 salads, and 2 drinks. How many different lunches are possible for a student who chooses exactly 1 sandwich, 1 soup, 1 salad, and 1 drink?

F.   2
G.   4
H. 10
J. 16
K. 32

227. What is $\frac{1}{9}$ of 63% of $6,000 ?

A. $34,020
B. $ 4,200
C. $ 3,402
D. $ 420
E. $ 42

228. DMC Electronics Company builds 2 products: a DVD player and a VCR. Employees of the company can build a maximum of 150 DVD players per week and a maximum of 200 VCRs per week. No more than 250 products can be built per week. In the following inequalities, d represents the number of DVD players and v represents the number of VCRs. Which inequality expresses the constraint on the number of products built per week?

F. $d + v \le 150$
G. $d + v \ge 200$
H. $d + v \le 200$
J. $d + v \ge 250$
K. $d + v \le 250$

DO YOUR FIGURING HERE.

229. In the figure below, $\angle ADC$ measures 50°, $\angle ACB$ measures 65°, and $\angle BAC$ measures 90°. What is the measure of $\angle BAD$?

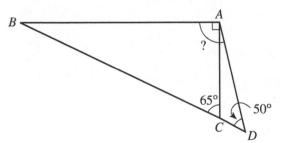

   A. 105°
   B. 115°
   C. 130°
   D. 140°
   E. 155°

230. Which of the following is equivalent to $(2x + 3)(x - 7)$?
   F. $2x^2 - 21$
   G. $2x^2 - 11x - 21$
   H. $2x^2 + 11x - 21$
   J. $2x^2 + 17x - 21$
   K. $2x^2 + 17x + 21$

231. A baker has $4\frac{2}{3}$ cups of sugar in her pantry. Each cake she bakes requires $\frac{1}{2}$ cup sugar. Which of the following is the largest number of whole cakes for which she has enough sugar in her pantry?
   A. 2
   B. 3
   C. 8
   D. 9
   E. 10

232. If $f(x) = 6x^2 + 4x - 11$, then $f(-5) = ?$
   F. −181
   G. −119
   H. 61
   J. 119
   K. 159

233. Which of the following expressions is equivalent to $-x^2 - x$?
   A. $-x(x + 1)$
   B. $-x(x - 1)$
   C. $-x(1 - x)$
   D. $x(x + 1)$
   E. $x(x - 1)$

DO YOUR FIGURING HERE.

234. The student body at Julian High School consists of sophomores, juniors, and seniors only. The ratio of sophomores to juniors to seniors on Julian High School's student council is 2:3:4. There are 15 juniors on the student council. How many students are on the entire student council?

F. 21
G. 24
H. 45
J. 60
K. 135

235. The second term of an arithmetic sequence is −14, and the third term is −34. What is the first term?

(Note: In an arithmetic sequence, consecutive terms differ by the same amount.)

A. $\frac{1}{14}$
B. 6
C. 14
D. 20
E. −20

236. Last year, Tom earned an annual salary of $S from which a total of $D was deducted for taxes and insurance. The balance was Tom's take-home pay. Tom's take-home pay represents what fraction of his annual salary?

F. $\frac{D}{S}$
G. $\frac{S}{D}$
H. $\frac{D-S}{D}$
J. $\frac{D-S}{S}$
K. $\frac{S-D}{S}$

237. Mara is the timer for a road race. She is 200 feet from the starting gun. Using 1,120 feet per second for the speed of sound, which of the following is closest to how many seconds after the starting gun is fired that Mara will hear the starting gun?

A. 0.1
B. 0.2
C. 0.6
D. 0.9
E. 1.3

DO YOUR FIGURING HERE.

238. What is the slope of the line represented by the equation $6y - 18x = 6$?

F. 1
G. 3
H. 6
J. 18
K. −18

239. At a buffet restaurant, the price for dinner for an adult is $6.95 and the price for dinner for a child is $3.95. A group of 8 people went to the restaurant for dinner and paid a total of $46.60, excluding tax and tip. How many adults were in the group?

A. 2
B. 3
C. 4
D. 5
E. 6

240. The graph below shows the distance, d miles, you are from home t hours following the start of a walk. Which of the following statements accurately describes your walk?

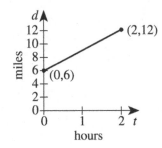

F. You start at home, and after 2 hours are 12 miles from home.
G. You start at home, and after 2 hours are 6 miles from home.
H. You start 12 miles from home, and after 2 hours are home.
J. You start 12 miles from home, and after 2 hours are 6 miles from home.
K. You start 6 miles from home, and after 2 hours are 12 miles from home.

241. In right triangle $\triangle XYZ$ below, $\cos Z = \frac{4}{7}$. Which of the following expressions is equal to $\cos X$?

A. $\frac{7}{4}$

B. $\frac{\sqrt{65}}{4}$

C. $\frac{\sqrt{33}}{4}$

D. $\frac{\sqrt{65}}{7}$

E. $\frac{\sqrt{33}}{7}$

242. For any nonzero value of y, $(y^{-5})^3 = ?$

   F. $\dfrac{1}{y^{15}}$

   G. $\dfrac{1}{y^2}$

   H. y^8

   J. y^{15}

   K. y^{125}

DO YOUR FIGURING HERE.

243. The ratio of the side lengths of 2 similar triangles is 3:5. The smaller triangle has sides that measure 5 centimeters, 7 centimeters, and 9 centimeters. What is the perimeter, in centimeters, of the larger triangle?

   A. $12\frac{3}{5}$

   B. 21

   C. 35

   D. 63

   E. 105

244. Points $R(6,4)$ and $S(-4,5)$ lie in the standard (x, y) coordinate plane. What is the slope of $\overline{RS}$?

   F. $-\dfrac{1}{10}$

   G. $\dfrac{1}{10}$

   H. $-\dfrac{2}{9}$

   J. $\dfrac{2}{9}$

   K. $\dfrac{9}{2}$

245. In the figure below, E is a point on side $\overline{AB}$ of rectangle $ABCD$. The measures given are in inches. What is the area of $\triangle DEC$, in square inches?

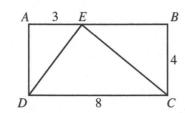

   A. 10
   B. 12
   C. 16
   D. 20
   E. 32

Use the following information to answer questions 246–248.

Fran is planning to fence a 10-foot-by-15-foot rectangular plot of ground to use as a garden. She intends to plant a 1-foot-wide border of flowers along the inside of the entire perimeter. The rectangular section surrounded by this border will be planted with vegetables in 11-foot-long rows parallel to the longer sides.

246. What is the minimum number of feet of fence Fran would need to enclose the garden if there will be a 3-foot-wide opening on one side of the plot for people to walk through?

   F.   22
   G.   25
   H.   47
   J.   50
   K. 150

247. What is the area, in square feet, of the rectangular plot?

   A.   50
   B. 104
   C. 126
   D. 146
   E. 150

248. When Fran plants the vegetables, she wants the center lines of adjacent rows to be at least 10 inches apart. She also wants the center lines of the outermost rows to be at least 10 inches from the inner edge of the flower border. According to these planting restrictions, what is the maximum number of 11-foot-long rows of vegetables that could be planted within this garden plot?

   F.   8
   G.   9
   H. 10
   J. 11
   K. 12

249. If $|x + 9| = 19$, what are the possible values for x ?

   A. −28 and 10
   B. −10 and 10
   C. −10 and 28
   D.   −9 and 9
   E.   10 and 28

250. In the standard (x, y) coordinate plane, $M(9, -8)$ is the midpoint of $\overline{TW}$. If W has coordinates $(3, 1)$, what are the coordinates of T?

F. $(15, -7)$

G. $(15, -17)$

H. $\left(6, -\frac{7}{2}\right)$

J. $(6, -9)$

K. $(6, -15)$

251. If the circumference of a circle is 96π centimeters, what is the radius of the circle, in centimeters?

A. $\sqrt{96}$
B. 24
C. 48
D. 96
E. 192

252. A rectangular tabletop is 14 inches wide and 48 inches long. Which of the following is closest to the length, in inches, of the diagonal of this tabletop?

F. 34
G. 50
H. 55
J. 62
K. 68

253. Rectangle $ABCD$ has vertices in the standard (x, y) coordinate plane at $A(-4, -2)$, $B(-4, 3)$, $C(2, 3)$, and $D(2, -2)$. A translation of rectangle $ABCD$ is a second rectangle, $A'B'C'D'$, with vertices $A'(4, -12)$, $B'(x, y)$, $C'(10, -7)$, and $D'(10, -12)$. What are the coordinates of B'?

A. $(3, -6)$
B. $(4, 3)$
C. $(4, -7)$
D. $(4, -13)$
E. $(6, -5)$

254. The solution set for x of the equation $x^2 + nx - 8 = 0$ is $\{-2, 4\}$. What does n equal?

F. -8
G. -6
H. -2
J. 2
K. 6

DO YOUR FIGURING HERE.

Use the following information to answer questions 255–257.

The Dow Jones Industrial Average (DJIA) is an index of stock values. The chart below gives the DJIA closing values from August 24 through September 30 of a certain year and the change in the closing value from the previous day. A minus sign indicates a *decline* (a closing value less than the previous day's closing value). A plus sign indicates an *advance* (a closing value greater than the previous day's closing value).

Dow Jones Industrial Average Closing Values

Date	Closing value	Change	Date	Closing value	Change
8/24	8,600		9/13	7,945	+150
8/25	8,515	−85	9/14	8,020	+75
8/26	8,160	−355	9/15	8,090	+70
8/27	8,050	−110	9/16	7,870	−220
8/30	7,540	−510	9/17	7,895	+25
8/31	7,825	+285	9/20	7,930	+35
9/01	7,780	−45	9/21	7,900	−30
9/02	7,680	−100	9/22	8,150	+250
9/03	7,640	−40	9/23	8,000	−150
9/07	8,020	+380	9/24	8,025	+25
9/08	7,860	−160	9/27	8,110	+85
9/09	8,045	+185	9/28	8,080	−30
9/10	7,795	−250	9/29	7,845	−235
			9/30	7,630	−215

255. Which of the following is closest to the percent of decrease from the August 24 closing value to the September 30 closing value?

A. 7.9%
B. 8.9%
C. 11.3%
D. 12.7%
E. 88.7%

256. The chart shows 4 more declines than advances. All of the following statements are true. Which one best explains why the decline from the August 24 closing value to the September 30 closing value was relatively large?

F. The greatest change in the chart was a decline.
G. The least change in the chart was an advance.
H. The greatest number of consecutive declines was greater than the greatest number of consecutive advances.
J. The first change was a decline.
K. The average of the declines was much greater than the average of the advances.

257. What is the average closing value for the 5-day period from September 13 through September 17 ?

  A. 7,895
  B. 7,920
  C. 7,964
  D. 7,980
  E. 8,090

DO YOUR FIGURING HERE.

---

258. The angle of elevation from a point on the ground to the top of a building is 37°, as shown below. The point is 75 feet away from the building. Which of the following is closest to the height, in feet, of the building?

(Note: sin 37° ≈ 0.602, cos 37° ≈ 0.799, and tan 37° ≈ 0.754)

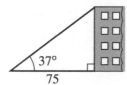

  F.   45
  G. 57
  H. 60
  J.   94
  K. 125

259. For trapezoid *ABCD* shown below, *AB* = 8 m, *DC* = 5 m, and the perimeter is 39 m. What is the area, in square meters, of *ABCD* ?

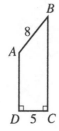

  A. $32\frac{1}{2}$
  B. 52
  C. 65
  D. 130
  E. 260

260. The average distance from Earth to the Sun, which is 9.3×10^7 miles, is about how many times the average distance from Earth to the Moon, which is 2.4×10^5 miles?

    F. 4×10^2

    G. 7×10^2

    H. 4×10^{12}

    J. 1×10^{13}

    K. 2×10^{13}

261. Which of the following operations will produce the largest result when substituted for the blank in the expression $35 \underline{} \left(-\frac{1}{56}\right)$?

    A. Averaged with

    B. Minus

    C. Plus

    D. Divided by

    E. Multiplied by

262. A circle in the standard (x, y) coordinate plane has center $(7,-6)$ and radius 10 coordinate units. Which of the following is an equation of the circle?

    F. $(x + 7)^2 - (y - 6)^2 = 100$

    G. $(x + 7)^2 - (y - 6)^2 = 10$

    H. $(x + 7)^2 + (y - 6)^2 = 10$

    J. $(x - 7)^2 + (y + 6)^2 = 100$

    K. $(x - 7)^2 + (y + 6)^2 = 10$

263. In $\triangle XYZ$, $\overline{XY} \cong \overline{XZ}$ and the measure of $\angle Y$ is $22°$. What is the measure of $\angle X$?

    A. $136°$

    B. $79°$

    C. $68°$

    D. $44°$

    E. $22°$

264. What is the volume, in cubic centimeters, of a cube if the area of 1 square face is 144 square centimeters?

    F. 36

    G. $1,728$

    H. $20,736$

    J. $46,656$

    K. $373,248$

DO YOUR FIGURING HERE.

265. If a number is chosen at random from the set {1, 2, 3, 4, ⋯, 12}, what is the probability that the chosen number is a factor of 12 ?

A. $\frac{1}{3}$

B. $\frac{5}{12}$

C. $\frac{1}{2}$

D. $\frac{5}{6}$

E. 1

266. Jamal invested $1,000 on January 1. At the end of 9 months, during which time Jamal made no withdrawals and no other deposits, the investment has earned $75 in interest. Jamal's $1,000 investment returned an annual percentage yield closest to which of the following percents?

(Note: Interest can be estimated using $I = Prt$, where I is the amount of interest earned; P is the amount of money initially invested; r is the annual percentage yield that the money returned; and t is the time, in years, the money is invested.)

F. 12%
G. 11%
H. 10%
J. 8%
K. 7%

267. Consider the function $f(x) = 2x^2 + x$. What is the value of $f(f(3))$?

A. 75
B. 168
C. 465
D. 885
E. 903

268. What are the possible values of y such that $xy^2 = 54$, $x < 10$, $y < 10$, and x and y are integers?

F. −3, 3
G. 1, 3
H. 1, 9
J. 3
K. 6

DO YOUR FIGURING HERE.

269. Each side of a quadrilateral is 12 cm long. Which 2 of the following *must* also describe this quadrilateral?

      I. Square (sides of equal length and 90° angles)
     II. Rhombus (sides of equal length)
    III. Rectangle (90° angles)
    IV. Parallelogram (opposite sides parallel)

  A. I and II only
  B. I and III only
  C. II and III only
  D. II and IV only
  E. III and IV only

270. The points $(-2,3)$ and $(0,1)$ lie on a straight line. What is the slope-intercept equation of the line?

  F. $y = 2x - 1$
  G. $y = x + 5$
  H. $y = x + 1$
  J. $y = -x + 1$
  K. $y = -2x + 3$

271. Each number on a list containing 100 numbers is divided by 10 to produce a second list containing 100 numbers. Each of the 100 numbers on the second list is decreased by 2 to produce a third list of 100 numbers. The median of the third list is x. Which of the following expressions gives the median of the original list?

  A. $\frac{x}{10} - 2$

  B. $\frac{x}{10}$

  C. $x + 2$

  D. $10x + 2$

  E. $10(x + 2)$

272. Whenever $(x + 4)(x - 3) < 0$, which of the following expressions *always* has a negative value?

  F. $x - 5$
  G. $x - 2$
  H. $x + 5$
  J. $2x$
  K. $x^2 - 1$

DO YOUR FIGURING HERE.

273. Which of the following graphs in the standard (x, y) coordinate plane represents the solution set of the inequality $|x + y| > 1$?

DO YOUR FIGURING HERE.

A.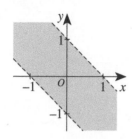

D.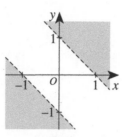

B.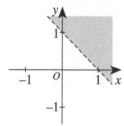

E.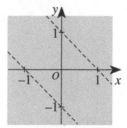

C.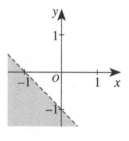

274. The expression $4 \sin x \cos x$ is equivalent to which of the following?

(Note: $\sin(x + y) = \sin x \cos y + \cos x \sin y$)

- **F.** $2 \sin 2x$
- **G.** $2 \cos 2x$
- **H.** $2 \sin 4x$
- **J.** $8 \sin 2x$
- **K.** $8 \cos 2x$

275. The angle at which light strikes a mirror is equal in measure to the angle at which it is reflected. In the hall of the mirrors below, what is the measure of the indicated angle?

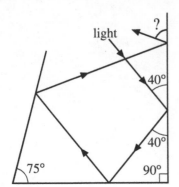

A. 50°
B. 55°
C. 70°
D. 80°
E. 90°

276. Which of the following is the graph of the solution set for $|x - c| \geq 2$?

F.

$c - 2 \quad c \quad c + 2 \qquad x$

G.

$c - 2 \quad c \quad c + 2 \qquad x$

H.

$c - 2 \quad c \quad c + 2 \qquad x$

J.

$c - 2 \quad c \quad c + 2 \qquad x$

K.

$c - 2 \quad c \quad c + 2 \qquad x$

277. Square *ABCD* is shown below in the standard (x, y) coordinate plane. The line $y = ax + 2$ divides the square into 2 congruent regions if $a = $?

A. $\frac{2}{3}$

B. $\frac{1}{6}$

C. $\frac{5}{6}$

D. $\frac{6}{7}$

E. 1

278. If $\log_3 2 = p$ and $\log_3 5 = q$, which of the following expressions is equal to 10 ?

F. 3^{p+q}
G. $3^p + 3^q$
H. 9^{p+q}
J. pq
K. $p + q$

DO YOUR FIGURING HERE.

279. The domain of the function $y(x) = 3 \cos(5x - 4) + 1$ is all real numbers. Which of the following is the range of the function $y(x)$?

A. $-3 \le y(x) \le 3$
B. $-4 \le y(x) \le 3$
C. $-4 \le y(x) \le 2$
D. $-2 \le y(x) \le 4$
E. All real numbers

280. In the figure below, both solids consist of 4 cubes, each 1 unit on a side. In the solid on the right, the 4 cubes form a rectangular prism that is 2 units long, 1 unit wide, and 2 units high. The solid on the left is the result of moving Cube D from its position above Cube C to beside it so that Cubes B, C, and D form a rectangular prism 3 units long, 1 unit wide, and 1 unit high. To the nearest percent, the total surface area of the solid on the right is what percent less than the total surface area of the solid on the left?

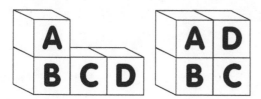

F. 0%
G. 2%
H. 6%
J. 11%
K. 13%

281. What is the value of the expression $(x - 2y)(x + 2y)$ when $x = 4$ and $y = \frac{1}{2}$?

    A. 8
    B. 9
    C. 14
    D. 15
    E. 25

DO YOUR FIGURING HERE.

282. Tyrone wants to score 80% or better on today's 40-point biology test. What is the least number of points that Tyrone must score to achieve 80% ?

    F. 4
    G. 8
    H. 20
    J. 32
    K. 36

283. $(2x - 3)(3x - 4)$ is equivalent to:

    A. x^2
    B. $5x^2 - 12x - 7$
    C. $5x^2 + 12$
    D. $6x^2 - 17x + 12$
    E. $6x^2 + 12$

284. The probability that an event happens is $\frac{2}{9}$. What is the probability that the event does NOT happen?

    F. 0
    G. $\frac{1}{9}$
    H. $\frac{2}{9}$
    J. $\frac{7}{9}$
    K. $\frac{9}{2}$

285. A recipe for 150 servings requires 4.5 liters of sauce. About how many liters of sauce are required for 80 servings?

   A. 2.1
   B. 2.4
   C. 3.0
   D. 8.4
   E. 15.5

286. Pei bought a 36-inch-long candle. It burns at a steady rate of 0.48 inches every hour. Which of the following is a relationship between the length, l, in inches, of the candle and the time, t, in hours, the candle has burned?

   F. $l = 36 - 0.48t$
   G. $l = 36 + 0.48t$
   H. $l = 0.48t$
   J. $l = 35.52t$
   K. $l = 75t$

287. In $\triangle ABC$ below, $AB = BC$, and $\angle ABC$ measures $70°$. What is the measure of $\angle BAC$?

   A. $35°$
   B. $50°$
   C. $55°$
   D. $70°$
   E. $110°$

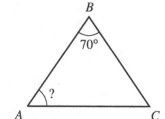

288. You have 4 rectangular regions that you want to cover with cedar chips. One region is 2 feet by 8 feet; another is 1 foot by 4 feet; another is 2 feet by 20 feet; and the last one is 1 foot by 5 feet. If a bag of cedar chips covers 10 square feet, how many bags of cedar chips will you need?

   F. 5
   G. 6
   H. 7
   J. 9
   K. 12

289. A function that is defined by the set of ordered pairs $\{(2, 1), (4, 2), (6, 3)\}$ has domain $\{2, 4, 6\}$. What is the domain of the function defined by the set of ordered pairs $\{(0, 2), (2, 2), (3, -2)\}$?

   A. $\{2\}$
   B. $\{-2, 2\}$
   C. $\{-2, 0, 3\}$
   D. $\{0, 2, 3\}$
   E. $\{-2, 0, 2, 3\}$

DO YOUR FIGURING HERE.

290. Let p and q be statements.

Statement S:	If p, then q.
Converse of S:	If q, then p.
Inverse of S:	If not p, then not q.
Contrapositive of S:	If not q, then not p.

One of the following statements is the converse of the statement "If the lights are on, then the store is open." Which one is it?

F. If the store is open, then the lights are on.
G. If the lights are not on, then the store is not open.
H. If the store is not open, then the lights are not on.
J. The lights are not on.
K. The store is not open.

291. A point with coordinates (a,b) is plotted in the standard (x, y) coordinate plane as shown below. The point is then reflected across the y-axis. Which of the following are the coordinates for the point after the reflection?

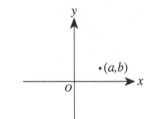

A. $(-a, \ b)$
B. $(\ a, -b)$
C. $(\ b, \ a)$
D. $(-b, \ a)$
E. $(\ b, -a)$

292. What quantity must be added to $4x^2 + x - 5$ to obtain $x^2 + 5x + 1$?

F. $5x^2 + 6x + 6$

G. $5x^2 + 6x - 4$

H. $-3x^2 + 6x + 6$

J. $-3x^2 + 6x - 4$

K. $-3x^2 + 4x + 6$

293. A 5-pound bag of potatoes costs $1.99 at Grocery Garden. A 5-pound bag of the same type of potatoes costs $2.19 at Food Fair. How much cheaper, *per pound*, are the Grocery Garden potatoes than the Food Fair potatoes?

A. $0.02
B. $0.04
C. $0.20
D. $1.00
E. $2.00

294. What is the solution of the equation $12x = -8(10 - x)$?

F. −20

G. $-6\frac{2}{13}$

H. −4

J. $\frac{2}{13}$

K $7\frac{3}{11}$

295. The $414 price a store charges for a small refrigerator consists of the refrigerator's original cost to the store plus a profit of 15%. What was the refrigerator's original cost to the store?

A. $ 54
B. $360
C. $399
D. $429
E. $478

296. In the figure below, $ABCD$ is a square with side length 10 centimeters. The midpoint of $\overline{AB}$ is E. What is the area, in square centimeters, of the shaded region?

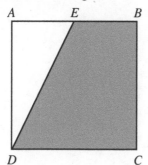

F. 25
G. 50
H. $50\sqrt{5}$
J. 75
K. 100

297. What is the solution to the following system of equations?

$$x + 2y = 12$$
$$x - y = 3$$

	x	y
A.	−6	9
B.	2	5
C.	3	4.5
D.	6	3
E.	18	15

298. If $f(x) = 2x$ and $g(x) = x^2$, what is $f(g(3))$?

F. 6
G. 12
H. 18
J. 36
K. 54

DO YOUR FIGURING HERE.

299. A dinner combination at Nassif's Family Restaurant contains exactly 1 appetizer, 1 main course, and 1 dessert. How many different dinner combinations are possible when choosing from 5 appetizers, 4 main courses, and 5 desserts?

- **A.** 14
- **B.** 40
- **C.** 45
- **D.** 80
- **E.** 100

DO YOUR FIGURING HERE.

300. Which of the following is equivalent to the inequality $-5 + m \le -4 + 2m$?

- **F.** $m \ge -9$
- **G.** $m \ge -3$
- **H.** $m \ge -1$
- **J.** $m \ge -\frac{1}{3}$
- **K.** $m \ge 3$

301. Which of the following lists orders $\frac{1}{3}$, 0.28, $\frac{2}{5}$, $\frac{3}{8}$, 0.37, and $\frac{3}{10}$ from least to greatest?

- **A.** $0.28, \frac{3}{10}, \frac{1}{3}, \frac{3}{8}, 0.37, \frac{2}{5}$
- **B.** $0.28, \frac{3}{10}, \frac{1}{3}, 0.37, \frac{3}{8}, \frac{2}{5}$
- **C.** $0.28, 0.37, \frac{3}{10}, \frac{1}{3}, \frac{3}{8}, \frac{2}{5}$
- **D.** $0.28, \frac{3}{10}, \frac{3}{8}, \frac{2}{5}, \frac{1}{3}, 0.37$
- **E.** $\frac{1}{3}, \frac{2}{5}, \frac{3}{8}, \frac{3}{10}, 0.28, 0.37$

302. Which of the following is equivalent to $(3x^3)^{-2}$?

- **F.** $\frac{1}{9x^6}$
- **G.** $\frac{1}{9x^9}$
- **H.** $\frac{3}{x^6}$
- **J.** $-6x^3$
- **K.** $-9x^6$

303. In the figure below, line a is parallel to line b. The 2 transversals intersect at a point on line a. Which of the following pairs of angles is NOT necessarily congruent?

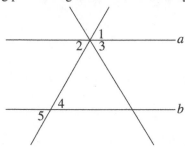

DO YOUR FIGURING HERE.

- **A.** $\angle 1$ and $\angle 4$
- **B.** $\angle 1$ and $\angle 5$
- **C.** $\angle 2$ and $\angle 3$
- **D.** $\angle 2$ and $\angle 4$
- **E.** $\angle 4$ and $\angle 5$

304. If $A = 10^{B+C}$, what is $\log_{10} A$?

- **F.** B
- **G.** $B + C$
- **H.** 10^A
- **J.** $10^B + 10^C$
- **K.** $10^B + C$

305. What is the solution set of the equation $4x^2 - 9 = 0$?

- **A.** $\left\{-\sqrt{2}, \sqrt{2}\right\}$
- **B.** $\left\{-\frac{3}{2}, \frac{3}{2}\right\}$
- **C.** $\left\{-\sqrt{3}, \sqrt{3}\right\}$
- **D.** $\{-2, 2\}$
- **E.** $\left\{\frac{9}{4}\right\}$

306. The given dimensions of the right triangle shown below are in inches. What is the length, in inches, of the hypotenuse of the triangle?

- **F.** $\sqrt{3}$
- **G.** $\sqrt{5}$
- **H.** 2
- **J.** 3
- **K.** 5

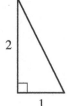

307. Pilar obtained estimates for cleaning her furnace from 2 heating companies. Lehman Heating's estimate was $30 for a service call plus $22 per hour for cleaning the furnace. A-1 Heating's estimate was $35 for a service call plus $20 per hour for cleaning the furnace. If the estimates were the same in both the total amount and the number of hours for cleaning Pilar's furnace, how many hours for cleaning the furnace were reflected in the estimates?

A. 2

B. $2\frac{1}{2}$

C. 3

D. $3\frac{1}{2}$

E. 4

DO YOUR FIGURING HERE.

308. In the standard (x, y) coordinate plane, what is the slope of the line that passes through the points $(-3,5)$ and $(7,3)$?

F. -5

G. -2

H. $-\frac{1}{5}$

J. $\frac{1}{2}$

K. 2

309. If 4 is the first term and 256 is the fourth term of a geometric progression, which of the following is the second term?

A. 8
B. 12
C. 16
D. 32
E. 64

310. The legs of the right triangle below are doubled in length to become the legs of a new right triangle. What is the length, in feet, of the longest side of the new triangle?

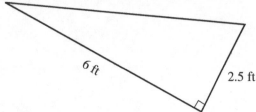

F.   5
G. 12
H. 13
J. 15
K. 17

311. If $3x + a = 9$, then, in terms of a, $x = ?$

   A. $\frac{a}{6}$

   B. $3a$

   C. $3 - a$

   D. $\frac{9 - a}{3}$

   E. $\frac{9 + a}{3}$

DO YOUR FIGURING HERE.

312. As part of one day's training workout, 5 members of a track team ran for exactly 3 minutes each. The 5 runners ran the 5 distances given below, in miles. Which distance corresponds to the fastest speed?

   F. $\frac{3}{5}$

   G. $\frac{3}{8}$

   H. $\frac{5}{8}$

   J. $\frac{7}{9}$

   K. $\frac{11}{16}$

313. Which of the following is an equation for the line passing through $(0, 0)$ and $(4, 3)$ in the standard (x, y) coordinate plane?

   A. $x - y = 1$
   B. $x + y = 7$
   C. $3x - 4y = 0$
   D. $3x + 4y = 25$
   E. $4x + 3y = 25$

314. Points P, Q, R, and S lie on a line in the order given. Point R is the midpoint of $\overline{QS}$, $\overline{PR}$ is 5 cm long, and $\overline{PS}$ is 7 cm long. How many centimeters long is $\overline{QS}$?

   F. 2
   G. 3
   H. 4
   J. 5
   K. 6

315. Which of the following expressions is equivalent to $3x^4 + 6x^2 - 45$?

   A. $(x^2 + 5)(x^2 - 3)$
   B. $(3x^2 - 15)(x^2 + 3)$
   C. $3(x^4 + 6x^2 - 45)$
   D. $3(x^2 - 5)(x^2 + 3)$
   E. $3(x^2 + 5)(x^2 - 3)$

Use the following information to answer
questions 316–318.

A student is working on a social studies project with her
partner. They are drawing local points of interest on a
map that is laid out in a coordinate plane, as shown below,
where the distance between adjacent grid lines is 1 cm and
represents 4 miles.

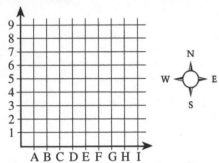

316. The student tells her partner that 2 high schools are to be
$2\frac{1}{2}$ cm apart on the map. About how many miles apart are
these high schools?

   F. 12
   G. 10
   H. 9
   J. 8
   K. 6

317. Two historical landmarks are 24 miles apart. One landmark
is at D-3; the second landmark is due northeast of the first
one. Which one of the following is closest to the second
landmark's location?

   A. E-8
   B. F-6
   C. G-6
   D. H-7
   E. I-4

318. A square park measures $\frac{1}{2}$ mile on each side. What should
be the park's area, in square centimeters, on the map?

   F. $\frac{1}{64}$

   G. $\frac{1}{16}$

   H. $\frac{1}{8}$

   J. 1

   K. 2

319. A quadrilateral has diagonals that do NOT bisect each other. Which of the following types of quadrilaterals could it be?

A. Parallelogram
B. Rectangle
C. Rhombus
D. Square
E. Trapezoid

320. Mary takes 2 medications throughout the day and night. One medication is to be taken every 6 hours and the other is to be taken every 4 hours. If Mary begins taking both medications at 7:00 A.M. and takes both medications on schedule, how many hours later will it be when she next takes both medications at the same time?

F. 6
G. 9
H. 10
J. 12
K. 24

321. The table below contains information about the 1996 season baseball standings for the American League Eastern Division. Which team won the most games away from home in 1996 ?

Team	Wins	Losses	Winning rate	Home win-loss record
New York	92	70	.568	49-31
Baltimore	88	74	.543	43-38
Boston	85	77	.525	47-34
Toronto	74	88	.457	35-46
Detroit	53	109	.327	27-54

A. New York
B. Baltimore
C. Boston
D. Toronto
E. Detroit

322. If 1 is a solution of the equation $x^2 + hx + 10 = 0$, what does h equal?

F. −11
G. −10
H. −1
J. 10
K. 11

DO YOUR FIGURING HERE.

323. Benjamin is flying a kite using 130 feet of string, as shown in the figure below. His string makes an angle of 40° with the level ground. About how many feet above the ground is the kite when the string is taut?

(Note: cos 40° ≈ 0.766
       sin 40° ≈ 0.643
       tan 40° ≈ 0.839)

  A.   80
  B. 100
  C. 110
  D. 170
  E. 200

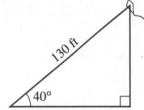

DO YOUR FIGURING HERE.

324. The 5 congruent circles shown in the diagram below have their centers lying on the same diameter of the larger circle. Each circle is tangent to 2 other circles. If the area of each small circle is 4π square units, what is the area, in square units, of the larger circle?

  F. 100π
  G. 50π
  H. 40π
  J. 30.5π
  K. 20π

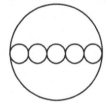

325. Which of the following is equivalent to $\sqrt[3]{27\,r^6}$?

  A. $3r^2$

  B. $3r^3$

  C. $9r^2$

  D. $9r^3$

  E. $729r^2$

326. There is a pattern when adding the cubes of the first c consecutive counting numbers, as illustrated below.

$$1^3 + 2^3 = 9 = (1 + 2)^2$$
$$1^3 + 2^3 + 3^3 = 36 = (1 + 2 + 3)^2$$

Which of the following is an expression for the sum of the cubes of the first c consecutive counting numbers?

  F. $(c + 1)^3$
  G. $(c + 1)^2$
  H. $(1 + 2 + \cdots + c)^c$
  J. $(1 + 2 + \cdots + c)^3$
  K. $(1 + 2 + \cdots + c)^2$

327. The volume of a sphere is $\frac{4}{3}\pi r^3$, where r is the radius of the sphere. The shapes of the planets Uranus and Earth are approximately spheres. The radius of Uranus is about 4 times that of Earth. About how many times the volume of Earth is the volume of Uranus?

   A. 81
   B. 64
   C. 16
   D. 12
   E. 4

DO YOUR FIGURING HERE.

328. The 5 positive integers a, a, a, b, and c have an average of a. What is the value of $\frac{b+c}{2}$?

   F. $\frac{a}{3}$

   G. $\frac{a}{2}$

   H. a

   J. $2a$

   K. $3a$

329. From the top of a 120-foot lighthouse, a small sailboat is sighted on the water 500 feet from the base of the lighthouse, as shown below. The angle of depression, θ, can be found using which of the following equations?

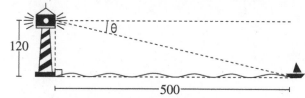

   A. $\cos\theta = \frac{120}{500}$

   B. $\sin\theta = \frac{500}{120}$

   C. $\sin\theta = \frac{120}{500}$

   D. $\tan\theta = \frac{500}{120}$

   E. $\tan\theta = \frac{120}{500}$

330. A rectangle that measures 4 cm by 6 cm is divided into 24 squares with sides 1 cm in length. What is the total number of 1 cm long sides in those 24 squares?

(Note: If 2 squares share a side, the side should be counted only once.)

F. 24
G. 48
H. 58
J. 70
K. 96

331. In the figure below, *A*, *B*, and *C* are the midpoints of the sides of △*PQR*, and *M*, *N*, and *O* are the midpoints of the sides of △*ABC*. The interiors of △*PAB*, △*AQC*, △*BCR*, and △*MNO* are shaded. What fraction of the interior of △*PQR* is shaded?

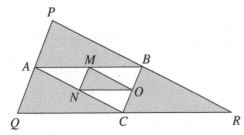

A. $\frac{1}{2}$

B. $\frac{4}{7}$

C. $\frac{5}{8}$

D. $\frac{3}{4}$

E. $\frac{13}{16}$

332. The Malcolm X High School Student Council is planning a spring outdoor carnival. In the figure below, the locations for several planned activities are represented as points *X*, *Y*, *Z*, *P*, and *Q* on the standard (*x*, *y*) coordinate plane, where each coordinate unit represents 1 yard. The ticket booth is to be placed exactly midway between *X* and *Z*. About how many yards will the ticket booth be from *Y* ?

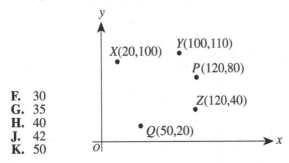

F. 30
G. 35
H. 40
J. 42
K. 50

333. For what value of t does the equation $h = 3t - t^2$ have its maximum value for h ?

   A. $\frac{3}{2}$

   B. 2

   C. $\frac{9}{4}$

   D. 3

   E. $\frac{9}{2}$

334. For all $x > 0$, which of the following is equivalent to $\frac{1}{x+1} + \frac{1}{x}$?

   F. $\frac{1}{x(x+1)}$

   G. $\frac{1}{2x+1}$

   H. $\frac{2}{x(x+1)}$

   J. $\frac{2}{x} + 1$

   K. $\frac{2x+1}{x(x+1)}$

335. The interior angles of a quadrilateral are in the ratio 1:2:3:4. What is the measure of the largest interior angle?

   A. 100°

   B. 108°

   C. 120°

   D. 144°

   E. 160°

336. The 2 legs of a right triangle measure 37 inches and 45 inches, respectively. What is the cosine of the triangle's smallest interior angle?

   F. $\frac{37}{45}$

   G. $\frac{45}{37}$

   H. $\frac{37}{\sqrt{37+45}}$

   J. $\frac{37}{\sqrt{37^2+45^2}}$

   K. $\frac{45}{\sqrt{37^2+45^2}}$

DO YOUR FIGURING HERE.

337. In creating a business plan for a cycle shop that sells both tricycles and bicycles, a business analyst graphed the inventory constraints set by the shop owner, and then shaded the region, shown below, where all of the constraints were met. Which of the following statements defines the shaded region?

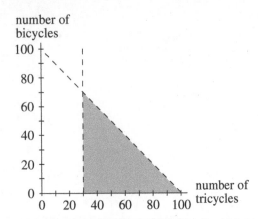

A. The number of tricycles exceeds 30, and the number of bicycles exceeds 30.
B. The number of tricycles exceeds 30, and the number of bicycles is less than the number of tricycles.
C. The number of tricycles is less than 100, and the number of bicycles is less than 100.
D. The number of tricycles and bicycles together exceeds 100, and the number of bicycles is less than 100.
E. The number of tricycles and bicycles together is less than 100, and the number of tricycles exceeds 30.

338. The horizontal line in the graph below shows the distance between a fixed point and an object as a function of elapsed time. The object could be doing which of the following?

    I. Moving in a circle around the fixed point
    II. Moving in a straight line away from the fixed point
    III. Standing still

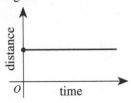

F. I only
G. II only
H. III only
J. I and II only
K. I and III only

339. In trigonometry, an angle of $-\frac{7\pi}{6}$ radians has the same sine and cosine as an angle that has which of the following degree measures?

A. 30°
B. 60°
C. 120°
D. 150°
E. 210°

DO YOUR FIGURING HERE.

340. Which of the following is an equation of the circle with center at (−2,3) and a radius of 5 coordinate units in the standard (x, y) coordinate plane?

F. $x^2 + y^2 + 4x - 6y = 5$
G. $x^2 + y^2 + 4x - 6y = 12$
H. $x^2 + y^2 + 4x - 6y = 25$
J. $x^2 + y^2 - 4x + 6y = 12$
K. $x^2 + y^2 - 4x + 6y = 25$

341. A group of 6 people planned to spend $10.00 each to rent a boat for an outing. At the last minute, 1 person could not go on the outing. The others then paid equally for the boat. How much did each pay?

    A. $ 8.00
    B. $ 8.33
    C. $11.67
    D. $12.00
    E. $20.00

DO YOUR FIGURING HERE.

342. A calculator has a regular price of $58.95 before taxes. It goes on sale at 20% below the regular price. Before taxes are added, what is the sale price of the calculator?

    F. $53.95
    G. $47.16
    H. $38.95
    J. $29.48
    K. $11.79

343. Melissa knows that 30 miles per hour is equivalent to 44 feet per second. If Melissa drives at a speed of 70 miles per hour, which of the following is closest to her speed in feet per second?

    A.   31
    B.   48
    C.   103
    D.   127
    E.   1,027

344. If $r = 5$, $b = 2$, and $g = -3$, what does $(r + b - g)(b + g)$ equal?

    F.   −10
    G.   −4
    H.   4
    J.   9
    K.   10

345. What is the largest value of x for which there exists a real value of y such that $x^2 + y^2 = 256$?

   A. 16
   B. 128
   C. 240
   D. 256
   E. 512

DO YOUR FIGURING HERE.

346. At Riverland Amusement Park, if an individual is not more than 4 feet tall, then that individual cannot ride the roller coaster. If Antoine rode the roller coaster at Riverland Amusement Park today, then which of the following may be logically concluded?

   F. Antoine is at most 3 feet tall.
   G. Antoine is less than 4 feet tall.
   H. Antoine is exactly 4 feet tall.
   J. Antoine is more than 4 feet tall.
   K. Antoine is at least 5 feet tall.

347. The number, N, of students at Hamlet High School who will catch the flu through Week t of school is modeled by the function $N(t) = \dfrac{1,200\,t^2 + 10}{t^2 + 1}$. According to the model, how many students will catch the flu through Week 4 ?

   A. 114
   B. 1,068
   C. 1,130
   D. 1,835
   E. 1,951

348. $3x^5 \cdot 7x^9$ is equivalent to:

   F. $10x^4$
   G. $10x^{14}$
   H. $10x^{45}$
   J. $21x^{14}$
   K. $21x^{45}$

349. A bag contains 5 yellow jellybeans, 4 red jellybeans, and 3 green jellybeans, all of the same shape and size. When 1 jellybean is randomly picked from the bag, what is the probability that it is green?

   A. $\dfrac{1}{12}$
   B. $\dfrac{1}{4}$
   C. $\dfrac{1}{3}$
   D. $\dfrac{5}{12}$
   E. $\dfrac{2}{3}$

350. What is the least common denominator for adding the fractions $\frac{4}{35}$, $\frac{1}{56}$ and $\frac{3}{16}$?

    F.   80
    G.   560
    H. 1,960
    J.   4,480
    K. 31,360

351. Marisa's design for a rectangular stained glass window with 7 triangles is shown below. The 2 white triangles are congruent ($\triangle ABC \cong \triangle DEC$) and will be a different color than the other 5 triangles. The design includes the measures of $\angle CAB$, $\angle ACB$, and $\angle DCE$. What is the measure of $\angle CED$?

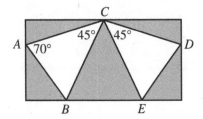

    A.   45°
    B.   65°
    C.   70°
    D. 115°
    E. 135°

352. The expression $\frac{8+\frac{1}{7}}{1+\frac{1}{4}}$ is equal to:

    F. $\frac{38}{5}$

    G. $\frac{855}{7}$

    H. 4

    J. 5

    K. 10

353. The sum of the real numbers x and y is 15. Their difference is 9. What is the value of xy ?

    A.   12
    B.   15
    C.   24
    D.   36
    E. 135

354. Four points, A, B, C, and D, lie on a circle having a circumference of 17 units. B is 6 units counterclockwise from A. C is 2 units clockwise from A. D is 9 units clockwise from A and 8 units counterclockwise from A. What is the order of the points, starting with A and going clockwise around the circle?

    F. A, B, C, D
    G. A, B, D, C
    H. A, C, B, D
    J. A, C, D, B
    K. A, D, C, B

DO YOUR FIGURING HERE.

355. To determine a student's overall test score for the semester, Ms. Rainwater deletes the lowest test score and calculates the average of the remaining test scores. Galen took all 5 tests and earned the following test scores in Ms. Rainwater's class this semester: 81, 83, 88, 92, and 99. What overall test score did Galen earn in Ms. Rainwater's class this semester?

    A. 88.0
    B. 88.6
    C. 90.0
    D. 90.5
    E. 91.0

356. What is the slope-intercept form of $6x - y - 2 = 0$?

    F. $y = -6x + 2$
    G. $y = -6x - 2$
    H. $y = 2x - 6$
    J. $y = 6x + 2$
    K. $y = 6x - 2$

357. What is the sum of the 2 solutions of the equation $x^2 - 3x - 28 = 0$?

    A. 7
    B. 3
    C. 0
    D. −4
    E. −28

358. $|5(-4) + 3(6)| = ?$

    F. −2
    G. 2
    H. 10
    J. 19
    K. 38

359. Tracy is trying to find a wrench to fit a bolt. The $\frac{3}{8}$-inch wrench is too large, and the $\frac{5}{16}$-inch wrench is too small. Which of the following could be the size of the wrench that will fit the bolt exactly?

    A. $\frac{1}{4}$-inch
    B. $\frac{9}{32}$-inch
    C. $\frac{11}{32}$-inch
    D. $\frac{25}{64}$-inch
    E. $\frac{13}{32}$-inch

DO YOUR FIGURING HERE.

360. What is the slope of the line containing the points (3, 8) and (−2, 10) in the standard (*x*, *y*) coordinate plane?

DO YOUR FIGURING HERE.

F. $\frac{1}{18}$

G. $\frac{12}{5}$

H. 18

J. $-\frac{5}{2}$

K. $-\frac{2}{5}$

361. The expression $a + b + c + a + b + c$ is equivalent to:

A. $6abc$

B. $a^2b^2c^2$

C. $6a^2b^2c^2$

D. $a^2 + b^2 + c^2$

E. $2a + 2b + 2c$

362. During a 5-year period, 875 houses were built in Somerville. The graph below shows how many of these houses were built in each of these 5 years. A certain percent of the 875 houses were built in 1993. Which of the following is closest to that percent?

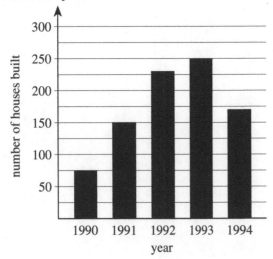

F. 20%

G. 25%

H. 30%

J. 35%

K. 40%

363. How many terms are there between 13 and 37, exclusive of 13 and 37, in the arithmetic sequence below?

$$4, 7, 10, 13, \cdots, 37$$

- **A.** 0
- **B.** 7
- **C.** 8
- **D.** 28
- **E.** 36

DO YOUR FIGURING HERE.

364. For $x^2 \neq 49$, $\dfrac{(x-7)^2}{x^2-49} = ?$

- **F.** $\dfrac{x-7}{x+7}$
- **G.** $\dfrac{1}{x-7}$
- **H.** $\dfrac{1}{x+7}$
- **J.** $-\dfrac{1}{7}$
- **K.** $\dfrac{1}{7}$

365. The sides of one triangle are 12 inches, 14 inches, and 15 inches long, respectively. In a second triangle similar to the first, the shortest side is 8 inches long. To the nearest tenth of an inch, what is the length of the longest side of the second triangle?

- **A.** 6.4
- **B.** 9.3
- **C.** 10.0
- **D.** 11.0
- **E.** 14.4

366. Which of the following is equivalent to $(x + 2)^0$ whenever $x \neq -2$?

- **F.** $x + 2$
- **G.** 0
- **H.** 1
- **J.** 2
- **K.** 3

367. A pentagon has 1 side of length z cm, 2 sides of length $(z + 2)$ cm each, 1 side of length 5 cm, and 1 side of length $3z$ cm. What is the perimeter, in centimeters, of the pentagon?

- **A.** $9z + 6$
- **B.** $6z + 9$
- **C.** $6z + 4$
- **D.** $5z + 9$
- **E.** $5z + 7$

368. A park has the shape and dimensions in blocks given below. A water fountain is located halfway between B and D. If you are at A, the water fountain is:

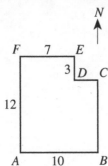

F. $4\frac{1}{2}$ blocks north and 5 blocks east.

G. $4\frac{1}{2}$ blocks north and $8\frac{1}{2}$ blocks east.

H. 6 blocks north and $3\frac{1}{2}$ blocks east.

J. 6 blocks north and 5 blocks east.

K. $7\frac{1}{2}$ blocks north and 9 blocks east.

369. If $a = 2c$ and $b = 6c$, which of the following relationships holds between a and b for each nonzero value of c ?

A. $a = 3b$

B. $a = 2b$

C. $a = b$

D. $a = \frac{1}{6}b$

E. $a = \frac{1}{3}b$

370. For a certain plant, the recommended nighttime temperature range in degrees Fahrenheit is $59° \leq F \leq 68°$. Given the formula $C = \frac{5}{9}(F - 32)$, where C is the temperature in degrees Celsius and F is the temperature in degrees Fahrenheit, what is the corresponding nighttime temperature range in degrees Celsius for the plant?

F.　$0° \leq C \leq 5°$
G.　$5° \leq C \leq 10°$
H.　$10° \leq C \leq 15°$
J.　$15° \leq C \leq 20°$
K.　$20° \leq C \leq 25°$

371. In parallelogram *ABCD* below, the measure of ∠*BCD* is 98° and the measure of ∠*CDB* is 38°. What is the measure of ∠*BDA* ?

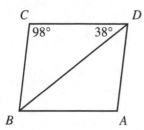

A. 38°
B. 41°
C. 44°
D. 49°
E. 52°

372. All the adjacent line segments in the figure below intersect in right angles. If each segment is 6 units long, what is the area, in square units, of the entire figure?

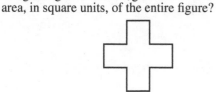

F.   72
G. 120
H. 144
J. 180
K. 324

373. Rhombus *RHOM* is shown in the figure below. If *HR* = 5 m and *HM* = 6 m, then what is the length, in meters, of $\overline{OR}$?

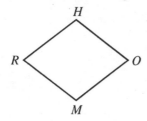

A. 3
B. 4
C. 5
D. 6
E. 8

374. Grid lines are shown at 1-unit intervals in the standard (x, y) coordinate plane below. Some of the 1-by-1 squares are shaded in the grid. What is the least number of additional 1-by-1 squares that must be shaded so the total shaded region will be symmetric about the y-axis?

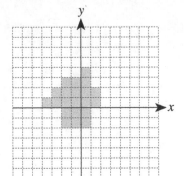

F. 3
G. 5
H. 7
J. 11
K. 22

375. The ratio of the side lengths of a rectangle with an area of 80 square yards is 4:1. Which of the following is closest to the length, in yards, of the *longer* side of the rectangle?

A. 10
B. 16
C. 18
D. 32
E. 40

376. Ms. Luciano's Algebra I class is describing the volume of geometric figures in terms of variables. She draws a rectangular prism that has a length of $(x + 2)$ meters, a width of $(x - 2)$ meters, and a height of $(x + 1)$ meters. Which of the following is an expression for the volume, in cubic meters, of the rectangular prism?

F. $3x - 4$

G. $3x + 1$

H. $x^3 - 4$

J. $x^3 + 2x^2 - 2x - 4$

K. $x^3 + x^2 - 4x - 4$

377. A data set has 15 elements. The 15 elements in a second data set are obtained by multiplying each element in the first data set by 10. The 15 elements in a third data set are obtained by decreasing each element of the second data set by 20. The median of the third data set is 50. What is the median of the first data set?

A. −20
B. 7
C. 50
D. 70
E. 750

378. Jamal sees a tree on the shore directly across a lake and wonders what the distance is across the lake to the tree. He turns 90° to the right and walks in a straight line for 100 meters. Jamal turns to face the tree and finds the angle between his line of sight and his path measures 25°, as shown below. Which of the following is closest to the distance, in meters, from Jamal's initial position to the tree?

(Note: sin 25° ≈ 0.42, cos 25° ≈ 0.91, tan 25° ≈ 0.47)

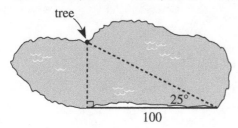

DO YOUR FIGURING HERE.

- **F.** 42
- **G.** 47
- **H.** 91
- **J.** 213
- **K.** 238

379. In the standard (x, y) coordinate plane, a right triangle has vertices at $(-3, 4)$, $(3, 4)$, and $(3, -4)$. What is the length, in coordinate units, of the hypotenuse of this triangle?

- **A.** 3
- **B.** 4
- **C.** 6
- **D.** 8
- **E.** 10

380. Each edge of a cube is 4 inches long. Each edge of a second cube is triple the length of each edge of the first cube. The volume of the second cube is how many cubic inches bigger than the volume of the first cube?

- **F.** 128
- **G.** 512
- **H.** 576
- **J.** 1,664
- **K.** 1,728

381. A particular circle in the standard (x, y) coordinate plane has an equation of $(x - 8)^2 + y^2 = 15$. What are the radius of the circle, in coordinate units, and the coordinates of the center of the circle?

	radius	center
A.	7.5	$(-8, 0)$
B.	7.5	$(8, 0)$
C.	15	$(8, 0)$
D.	$\sqrt{15}$	$(-8, 0)$
E.	$\sqrt{15}$	$(8, 0)$

Use the following information to answer
questions 382–384.

The Springfield City Council is going to create a park
on some unused land the city owns. The park will be a
rectangular region 60 feet by 150 feet with an area of 9,000
square feet. There will be a picnic shelter in the park that
will cover a square region 30 feet by 30 feet with an area
of 900 square feet. The park will be grass, except for the
region where the picnic shelter is.

382. The City Council decides to put fencing around the park.
What is the perimeter, in feet, of the park?

   F. 150
   G. 210
   H. 270
   J. 420
   K. 540

383. The picnic shelter must be at least 10 feet from any edge
of the park. On graph paper with the distance between grid
lines representing 10 feet, a city engineer makes a scale
drawing of the park, as shown below. The region where
the picnic shelter CANNOT be built is shown shaded.
The corners of both the park and the region where the
picnic shelter may be built are at the intersections of grid
lines. The corners of the picnic shelter must also be at the
intersections of grid lines. How many different locations
in the park are possible for the placement of the picnic
shelter?

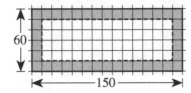

   A. 22
   B. 36
   C. 52
   D. 70
   E. 90

384. The City Council's long-term plan for the park involves
doubling the area of the park. The length and width of
the park will each be extended by d feet. For which of the
following equations is $x = d$ a solution?

   F. $(x + 60)(x + 150) = 2(9,000)$
   G. $(x + 2(60))(x + 2(150)) = 9,000$
   H. $(x + 2(60))(x + 2(150)) = 2(9,000)$
   J. $(2x + 60)(2x + 150) = 2(9,000)$
   K. $2(x + 60)(x + 150) = 9,000$

385. The graphs of $f(x) = \cos x$ and $g(x) = \cos\left(x - \frac{\pi}{4}\right) + 1$ are shown in the standard (x, y) coordinate plane below. After one of the following pairs of transformations is applied to the graph of $f(x)$, the image of the graph of $f(x)$ is the graph of $g(x)$. Which pair is it?

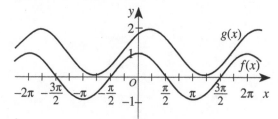

A. Shift $f(x)$ 1 unit left and $\frac{\pi}{4}$ units down.

B. Shift $f(x)$ 1 unit left and $\frac{\pi}{4}$ units up.

C. Shift $f(x)$ 1 unit right and $\frac{\pi}{4}$ units down.

D. Shift $f(x)$ $\frac{\pi}{4}$ units left and 1 unit up.

E. Shift $f(x)$ $\frac{\pi}{4}$ units right and 1 unit up.

386. Let p and q be numbers such that $0 < p < q$. Which of the following inequalities *must* be true for all such p and q ?

F. $p + 1 > q + 1$

G. $\frac{p}{q} > 1$

H. $\frac{1}{q} > \frac{1}{p}$

J. $p^2 > q^2$

K. $-p > -q$

387. If a is 25% of b, then 135% of b is what percent of a ?

A. 160%
B. 210%
C. 337.5%
D. 540%
E. 875%

388. The expression $\sin^2\theta - 4 + \cos^2\theta$ is equivalent to:

F. -5
G. -4
H. -3
J. 3
K. 5

DO YOUR FIGURING HERE.

389. Figure *ABCDEF*, shown in the standard (*x*, *y*) coordinate plane below, has been reflected across a line to figure *A'B'CD'EF'*. Which of the following lines of reflection would best describe this transformation?

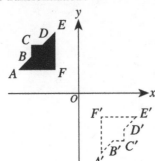

A. *y* = 0
B. *y* = $\frac{1}{2}$
C. *y* = −*x*
D. *x* = 0
E. *x* = *y*

390. What is the length, in inches, of a 144° arc of a circle whose circumference is 60 inches?

F. $\frac{36}{\pi}$
G. 12
H. 24
J. 36
K. 12π

391. A solid, right circular cone is sliced perpendicular to its base through its vertex and the center of its base, as shown below. Which of the following best represents the plane section?

A.

B.

C.

D.

E.

392. If b is a positive number such that $\log_b(\frac{1}{81}) = -4$, then $b = ?$

    F.   3

    G.   9

    H.   85

    J. $\frac{1}{3}$

    K. $\frac{1}{9}$

DO YOUR FIGURING HERE.

393. The graph in the standard (x, y) coordinate plane below is the graph of $y = f(x)$. One of the following graphs is the graph of $y = f(x - 3) + 2$. Which one?

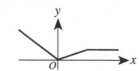

A.

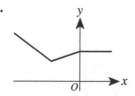

D.

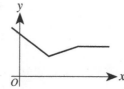

B.

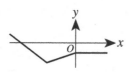

E.

C.

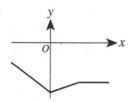

394. In the figure below, parallel lines a and b intersect parallel lines c and d. If it can be determined, what is the sum of the degree measures of $\angle 1$ and $\angle 2$?

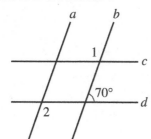

    F.   220°

    G.   180°

    H.   140°

    J.   110°

    K.   Cannot be determined from the given information

Use the following information to answer questions 395–397.

DO YOUR FIGURING HERE.

Consider the set of all points (x, y) that satisfy all 3 of the conditions below:

$$y \geq 0$$
$$y \leq 2x + 4$$
$$y \leq -x + 4$$

The graph of this set is $\triangle ABC$ and its interior, which is shown shaded in the standard (x, y) coordinate plane below. Let this set be the domain of the function $P(x, y) = 4x + 3y$.

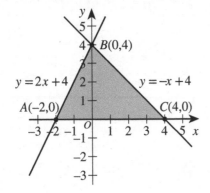

395. What is the maximum value of $P(x, y)$ when x and y satisfy the 3 conditions given?

A. 4
B. 8
C. 12
D. 16
E. 28

396. The quadrants of the standard (x, y) coordinate plane are labeled in the figure below. The domain of $P(x, y)$ contains points in which quadrants?

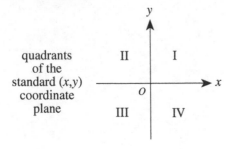

F. I and II only
G. I and III only
H. I and IV only
J. II and III only
K. II and IV only

397. tan $\angle BCA = ?$

   A. 1

   B. $\frac{2}{3}$

   C. $\frac{\sqrt{5}}{3}$

   D. $\frac{3}{\sqrt{5}}$

   E. $\frac{3}{2\sqrt{2}}$

DO YOUR FIGURING HERE.

_____

398. The function $f(x)$ is a cubic polynomial that has the value of 0 when x is 0, 3, and −5. If $f(1) = -24$, which of the following is an expression for $f(x)$?

   F. $x^3 - 25$
   G. $-2x(x-3)(x+5)$
   H. $x(x-3)(x+5)$
   J. $2x(x+3)(x-5)$
   K. $2x(x-3)(x+5)$

399. Water is considered contaminated when the level of zinc in the water reaches 5 parts of zinc per 1 million parts of water. What is this level of zinc contamination written in scientific notation?

   A. 5.0×10^{-9}
   B. 5.0×10^{-7}
   C. 5.0×10^{-6}
   D. 5.0×10^{6}
   E. 5.0×10^{9}

400. Given $a > b$ and $(a - b) > (a^2 - b^2)$, then $(a + b)$ must be:

   F. less than 1.
   G. greater than 1.
   H. greater than a.
   J. greater than $(a - b)$.
   K. equal to $(a - b)$.

Chapter 8: Answers and Explanations

Check your answers with the following answer key. If you missed a question or would like tips on solving it faster, review the answer explanations on the following pages.

Answer Key

1.	E	41.	B	81.	H	121.	C
2.	K	42.	F	82.	G	122.	B
3.	A	43.	C	83.	D	123.	C
4.	K	44.	F	84.	H	124.	J
5.	E	45.	E	85.	B	125.	E
6.	G	46.	G	86.	G	126.	E
7.	B	47.	E	87.	B	127.	D
8.	J	48.	H	88.	B	128.	B
9.	E	49.	D	89.	J	129.	G
10.	J	50.	F	90.	B	130.	E
11.	C	51.	E	91.	K	131.	B
12.	J	52.	H	92.	J	132.	G
13.	E	53.	B	93.	C	133.	D
14.	G	54.	G	94.	B	134.	J
15.	A	55.	B	95.	K	135.	A
16.	J	56.	H	96.	E	136.	H
17.	E	57.	E	97.	F	137.	D
18.	K	58.	K	98.	E	138.	H
19.	A	59.	B	99.	G	139.	F
20.	J	60.	K	100.	D	140.	D
21.	E	61.	H	101.	D	141.	H
22.	G	62.	A	102.	B	142.	B
23.	C	63.	J	103.	J	143.	H
24.	H	64.	D	104.	A	144.	D
25.	B	65.	J	105.	K	145.	K
26.	H	66.	A	106.	A	146.	B
27.	C	67.	F	107.	F	147.	G
28.	J	68.	C	108.	A	148.	A
29.	A	69.	H	109.	K	149.	K
30.	G	70.	C	110.	J	150.	D
31.	B	71.	K	111.	B	151.	E
32.	F	72.	D	112.	H	152.	J
33.	D	73.	H	113.	A	153.	C
34.	J	74.	C	114.	K	154.	G
35.	B	75.	H	115.	B	155.	D
36.	H	76.	E	116.	K	156.	B
37.	E	77.	J	117.	C	157.	J
38.	G	78.	A	118.	C	158.	H
39.	E	79.	H	119.	H	159.	E
40.	H	80.	A	120.	C	160.	E

161.	C	209.	C	257.	C	305.	B	353.	D
162.	H	210.	J	258.	G	306.	G	354.	J
163.	B	211.	D	259.	C	307.	B	355.	D
164.	J	212.	H	260.	F	308.	H	356.	K
165.	D	213.	B	261.	B	309.	C	357.	B
166.	J	214.	G	262.	J	310.	H	358.	G
167.	B	215.	D	263.	A	311.	D	359.	C
168.	G	216.	F	264.	G	312.	J	360.	K
169.	E	217.	A	265.	C	313.	C	361.	E
170.	K	218.	G	266.	H	314.	H	362.	H
171.	E	219.	E	267.	E	315.	E	363.	B
172.	F	220.	K	268.	F	316.	G	364.	F
173.	E	221.	D	269.	D	317.	D	365.	C
174.	H	222.	G	270.	J	318.	F	366.	H
175.	A	223.	E	271.	E	319.	E	367.	B
176.	H	224.	K	272.	F	320.	J	368.	G
177.	B	225.	B	273.	D	321.	B	369.	E
178.	F	226.	K	274.	F	322.	F	370.	J
179.	A	227.	D	275.	C	323.	A	371.	C
180.	J	228.	K	276.	K	324.	F	372.	J
181.	C	229.	A	277.	A	325.	A	373.	E
182.	G	230.	G	278.	F	326.	K	374.	H
183.	D	231.	D	279.	D	327.	B	375.	C
184.	J	232.	J	280.	J	328.	H	376.	K
185.	E	233.	A	281.	D	329.	E	377.	B
186.	H	234.	H	282.	J	330.	H	378.	G
187.	B	235.	B	283.	D	331.	E	379.	E
188.	K	236.	K	284.	J	332.	K	380.	J
189.	A	237.	B	285.	B	333.	A	381.	E
190.	H	238.	G	286.	F	334.	K	382.	J
191.	E	239.	D	287.	C	335.	D	383.	A
192.	F	240.	K	288.	H	336.	K	384.	F
193.	D	241.	E	289.	D	337.	E	385.	E
194.	H	242.	F	290.	F	338.	K	386.	K
195.	E	243.	C	291.	A	339.	D	387.	D
196.	G	244.	F	292.	K	340.	G	388.	H
197.	B	245.	C	293.	B	341.	D	389.	E
198.	G	246.	H	294.	F	342.	G	390.	H
199.	C	247.	E	295.	B	343.	C	391.	B
200.	J	248.	F	296.	J	344.	F	392.	F
201.	A	249.	A	297.	D	345.	A	393.	D
202.	J	250.	G	298.	H	346.	J	394.	F
203.	B	251.	C	299.	E	347.	C	395.	D
204.	H	252.	G	300.	H	348.	J	396.	F
205.	D	253.	C	301.	B	349.	B	397.	A
206.	F	254.	H	302.	F	350.	G	398.	K
207.	D	255.	C	303.	C	351.	B	399.	C
208.	K	256.	K	304.	G	352.	F	400.	F

Explanatory Answers

Question 1. **The correct answer is E.** You may want to make a sketch of this situation in your mind or, better yet, in the space in your test booklet. A sample sketch is shown in the following:

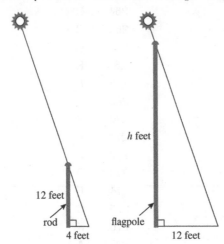

The vertical rod and the vertical flagpole each form a right angle with the level ground, resulting in two right triangles. The smaller right triangle (at left) is composed of the rod, the rod's shadow, and the line of sight of the sun through the top of the rod. The larger right triangle (at right) is composed of the flagpole, the flagpole's shadow, and the line of sight of the sun through the top of the flagpole. Because the angle of elevation of the sun is the same for each triangle, the two triangles are similar by the angle-angle similarity property. Using the ratios of corresponding sides of the similar triangles, the proportion $\frac{12}{h} = \frac{4}{12}$ is solved to find the height of the flagpole, $h = 36$ feet.

Common errors in this problem result from relying on an incorrect mental image or labeling the dimensions on the sketch incorrectly. If you chose **A**, you might have set up and solved the proportion $\frac{h}{12} = \frac{4}{12}$.

Question 2. **The correct answer is K.** If you knew the unknown score, you could check to see that it was correct by adding up all five scores, dividing by 5 to get the average, and checking to see that the result was 90. Let x be the unknown score. Then the sum of all the scores is $85 + 95 + 93 + 80 + x$, and the average is $\frac{85 + 95 + 93 + 80 + x}{5}$. For the average to be 90, that means $\frac{85 + 95 + 93 + 80 + x}{5} = 90$. To solve that equation, you can multiply both sides by 5 to get $85 + 95 + 93 + 80 + x = 450$ and then subtract 353 from both sides to get $x = 97$.

G is closest to the average of the four given scores, $\frac{85 + 95 + 93 + 80}{4} = 88.25$. To raise an average of 88.25 up to 90 would take an increase of about 2 points, but a single new score of 92 (answer choice **J**) would not raise the average much. You can check your answer to see that it is too low: $\frac{85 + 95 + 93 + 80 + 92}{5} = \frac{445}{5} = 89$. You can check any answer choice to see whether it is correct.

Question 3. The correct answer is A. Substituting -5 for x produces a numerator equal to $(-5)^2 - 1 = 25 - 1 = 24$ and a denominator equal to $-5 + 1 = -4$. Therefore, $\frac{x^2 - 1}{x + 1} = \frac{24}{-4} = -6$. The most common wrong answer is **C**, which comes from forgetting the negative sign in the given x-value: $\frac{5^2 - 1}{5 + 1} = \frac{24}{6} = 4$.

Question 4. The correct answer is K. To find the total distance, in miles, Kaya ran, you need the sum of $1\frac{2}{5}$ and $2\frac{1}{3}$. To add mixed numbers together, each fraction must have a common denominator. Because 3 and 5 do not have any common factors besides 1, the least common denominator is 3(5), or 15. To convert $\frac{2}{5}$, you multiply by $\frac{3}{3}$. The result is $\frac{6}{15}$. To convert $\frac{1}{3}$, you multiply by $\frac{5}{5}$. The result is $\frac{5}{15}$. To add $1\frac{6}{15}$ and $2\frac{5}{15}$, you first add 1 and 2 and then $\frac{6}{15} + \frac{5}{15}$. The result is $3\frac{6+5}{15}$, or $3\frac{11}{15}$.

If you chose **F**, you probably added the whole number parts and multiplied the fractions. If you chose **G**, you probably added the whole number parts and added the numerators and the denominators separately: $\frac{2+1}{5+3}$. If you chose **J**, you probably converted $\frac{2}{5}$ to $\frac{2}{15}$ incorrectly and then added $1 + 2$ and $\frac{2}{15} + \frac{5}{15}$.

Question 5. The correct answer is E. Although you could try out various combinations of the given three statements and try to make a conclusion, it might be more straightforward to look at each of the answer choices to see whether it contradicts one of the given three statements or whether it could be deduced from the given three statements.

A and **B** each say that Insect I is an ant. This directly contradicts the second given statement, so **A** and **B** are false.

Consider **C**: if it is true (Insect I is attracted to honey), then the first given statement implies that Insect I is an ant. This contradicts the second given statement, so **C** is false.

D directly contradicts the third given statement, so **D** is false.

For **E**, consider Insect J. The third given statement tells you that Insect J is attracted to honey, and the first given statement tells you that, because all insects attracted to honey are ants, Insect J must be an ant. So **E** must be true.

Question 6. The correct answer is G. You can find the value of this expression by substituting the given values of x and m into the expression and then simplifying: $\sqrt{\frac{-16}{-4}} = \sqrt{4}$.

You may have gotten **F** if you did $\sqrt{\frac{-16}{4}} \Rightarrow -\sqrt{4}$.

You may have gotten **H** if you did $\sqrt{\frac{-16}{-2}} = \sqrt{8}$. You may have gotten **J** if you did $\sqrt{\frac{-16}{4}} = \sqrt{-4}$.

You may have gotten **K** if you did $\sqrt{\frac{-16}{4}} = \sqrt{-4}$.

Question 7. The correct answer is B. The amount collected from the sale of 142 tickets bought in advance is equal to ($6 per ticket)(142 tickets) = $852. The amount collected from the sale of d tickets bought at the door is equal to ($8 per ticket)($d$ tickets) = 8d$. The total amount collected from all ticket sales is $852 + 8d$. To determine the minimum number of tickets to produce $2,000 in ticket sales, you can set up an inequality: $852 + 8d \geq 2,000$. Subtracting 852 from both sides and then dividing by 8 produces the equivalent inequality $d \geq 143.5$. Keep in mind, however, that d must be a whole number of tickets, so you must select the whole number d to satisfy the inequality. This means you must round 143.5 *up* to obtain the correct answer. If you chose **A**, you probably rounded *down* to 143. If you chose **D**, you might have divided 2,000 by 8 without thinking carefully about what the numbers represent. If you chose **C** or **E**, you probably set up the inequality incorrectly.

Question 8. The correct answer is J. For each kind of bread, there are 5 kinds of meat, so that is $3 \cdot 5$ combinations of bread and meat. For each of these 15 combinations of bread and meat, there are 3 kinds of cheese. That makes $15 \cdot 3 = 45$ combinations of bread, meat, and cheese.

The tree diagram on page 200 shows all 45 combinations. It would take a lot of time to list all these cases, but you can imagine what the tree looks like without having to write it all out. You can see that parts of the tree repeat many times, and so you can use multiplication to help you count.

MATHEMATICS • EXPLANATORY ANSWERS

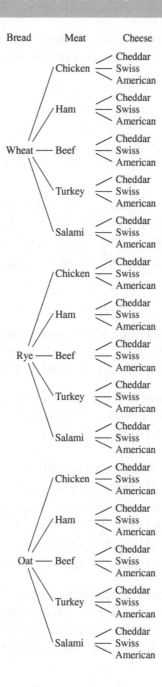

Question 9. The correct answer is E. Use of the distributive property gives the equivalent equation $12x - 132 = -15$. Adding 132 to both sides of the equation results in the equation $12x = 117$, implying that the solution is $x = \frac{117}{12}$, or $\frac{39}{4}$ when reduced to lowest terms. If you distributed 12 to *only* the first term, x, but forgot to distribute 12 to the second term, you probably got an answer of $-\frac{1}{3}$.

MATHEMATICS • EXPLANATORY ANSWERS

Question 10. The correct answer is J. The following figure illustrates the progression of angle measures found in determining the measure of $\angle BCE$.

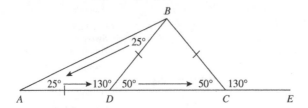

Because $\overline{BD} \cong \overline{AD}, \triangle ABD$ is isosceles, so its base angles are congruent. Therefore, $m\angle BAD = m\angle ABD = 25°$. Because the sum of the angle measures in $\triangle ABD$ must equal 180°, $m\angle ADB = 180° - (25° + 25°) = 130°$. Because $\angle ADB$ and $\angle BDC$ are a linear pair, $m\angle BDC = 180° - 130° = 50°$. Because $\overline{BD} \cong \overline{BC}$, $\triangle DBC$ is isosceles, so *its* base angles are congruent: $m\angle BCD = m\angle BDC = 50°$. Finally, $\angle BCD$ and $\angle BCE$ are a linear pair, so $m\angle BCE = 180° - 50° = 130°$.

Question 11. The correct answer is C. When you substitute −2 for x, you get $9(-2)^2 + 5(-2) - 8 = 9(4) + (-10) - 8 = 18$. If you chose **A**, you probably evaluated $9(-2)^2$ as −36. If you chose **E**, you probably evaluated $5(-2)$ as 10.

Question 12. The correct answer is J. One efficient way to solve this problem numerically is by listing the multiples of the largest of the 3 numbers (70) as a sequence and determining whether or not each succeeding term in the sequence is a multiple of *both* 20 and 30.

70 (multiple of neither)
140 (multiple of 20 only)
210 (multiple of 30 only)
280 (multiple of 20 only)
350 (multiple of neither)
420 (multiple of both 20 and 30)

The first term in the sequence that is a multiple of both 20 and 30 is 420, which is the least common multiple of 20, 30, and 70. You can also find the least common multiple by expressing each of the three numbers as a product of primes (with exponents), listing all bases of exponential expressions shown, and choosing for each base listed the highest-valued exponent shown.

$$30 = 2^1 \times 3^1 \times 5^1$$
$$20 = 2^2 \times 5^1$$
$$70 = 2^1 \times 5^1 \times 7^1$$

The least common multiple is $2^2 \times 3^1 \times 5^1 \times 7^1 = 420$.

Question 13. The correct answer is E. You may want to choose an even integer as Tom's initial number, follow his steps in obtaining the *incorrect* answer, and then determine *what* operation using *what* number is needed to obtain the desired number. For example:

1. Choose the integer 6 as the initial number.

2. When Tom "accidentally multiplies the number by 2," he obtains an incorrect answer of 12.

3. Had Tom correctly divided the initial number by 2, he would have obtained 3 as the answer.

4. To convert his incorrect answer of 12 to the desired answer of 3, he must divide by 4.

You may want to confirm that **E** is the correct answer by choosing a different initial number and repeating the steps.

Question 14. The correct answer is G. The 8-sided figure in the problem consists of 5 congruent squares whose areas total 125 square inches. Therefore, each congruent square has an area of $125 \div 5 = 25$ square inches, so each side of each square is $\sqrt{25} = 5$ inches long. The perimeter of the 8-sided figure is composed of 12 of these sides, each of length 5 inches, as shown in the following figure. Therefore, the 8-sided figure has a perimeter of $12 \times 5 = 60$ inches.

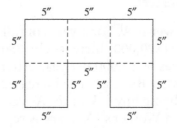

Question 15. The correct answer is A. You can find the total number of USBs Hai can buy by dividing the total cost of \$100 by the cost of 1 USB plus tax for 1 USB, $\$8 \times (1 + 0.07)$: $\frac{100}{1.07(8)}$. You cannot buy a partial USB; therefore, you must round down to 11 whole USBs. You may have gotten **B** if you did $\frac{100}{1.07(8)}$ and rounded up. You may have gotten **C** if you did $\frac{100}{1.08(7)}$ and rounded down. You may have gotten **D** if you did $\frac{100}{1.08(7)}$ and rounded up. You may have gotten **E** if you did $\frac{100 + 8}{7}$ and rounded down.

Question 16. **The correct answer is J.** Because the item gives a unit rate, you can set up a proportional relationship and solve for x: $\frac{1.5 \times 10^8 \text{ calculations}}{1 \text{ second}} = \frac{6.0 \times 10^{16}}{x}$, $x = \frac{6.0 \times 10^{16}}{1.5 \times 10^8}$.
You divide the coefficients and subtract the exponents because the bases are the same in each expression: $4.0 \times 10^{16 - 8} = 4.0 \times 10^8$.

You may have gotten **F** if you did $\frac{1.5 \times 10^8}{6.0 \times 10^{16}} = 0.25 \times 10^{-8}$. You may have gotten **G** if you did $6.0(1.5) \times 10$. You may have gotten **H** if you incorrectly simplified $\frac{6.0 \times 10^{16}}{1.5 \times 10^8}$ to be $4.0 \times 10^{\frac{16}{8}}$. You may have gotten **K** if you did $(1.5 \times 10^8)(6.0 \times 10^{16})$.

Question 17. **The correct answer is E.** Each answer choice is a linear equation in *slope-intercept form*; that is, $y = mx + b$, where the value of m gives the slope of the line and the value of b gives the y-intercept of the line. Only the equation shown in **E** represents a line having a y-intercept ($b = 5$), that matches the value of the y-intercept indicated by the given graph.

Question 18. **The correct answer is K.** To find the area of a square circumscribed about a circle with a radius of 7 feet, you would need to find the side length of the square. Because the diameter of the circle is the distance between 2 opposite sides of the square, the side length of the square is twice the radius, 2(7), or 14 feet. To find the area of the square, you square the side length, 14^2, to get 196 square feet.

If you chose **F**, you probably thought 7 feet was the side length and squared 7 to get 49 square feet. If you chose **J**, you probably used the formula for the area of a circle, πr^2, where r is the radius, to get πr^2, or 49π square feet.

Question 19. **The correct answer is A.** For x years of full years' employment after being hired, Worker A's starting salary ($20,000) increases by $800 per year and Worker B's starting salary ($15,200) increases by $2,000 per year. After x years, Worker A's salary has increased by $800x$ and Worker B's salary has increased by $2,000x$. So, for x years of full years' employment after being hired, Worker A's yearly salary is represented by the expression $20,000 + 800x$ and Worker's B's salary is represented by the expression $15,200 + 2,000x$. These 2 yearly salaries are equal at the value of x for which the equation $20,000 + 800x = 15,200 + 2,000x$ is true.

Question 20. **The correct answer is J.** The figure shows a right triangle with two given side measures. To find the length of the third side, use the Pythagorean theorem:

$$(\text{length of the hypotenuse})^2 = (\text{length of one side of the triangle})^2 + (\text{length of the other side of the triangle})^2$$

In this problem, the 13-foot measure represents the length of the hypotenuse. So the formula gives the equation $13^2 = 12^2 + x^2$, where x feet is the length of the missing side. To find x^2, subtract 12^2 from each side of the equation. The subtraction results in the equivalent equation

$25 = x^2$, resulting in the solution $x = \pm 5$. Because the side length of a triangle must be positive, you can ignore the negative solution. If you chose **F**, you probably took the length of the hypotenuse and subtracted the length of the given leg, without applying the Pythagorean theorem at all. If you chose **G**, you probably *doubled* the lengths, rather than *squaring* them.

Question 21. The correct answer is E. To simplify this expression, use the distributive property: $7(x + 3) - 3(2x - 2) = 7x + (7)(3) + (-3)(2x) + (-3)(-2) = 7x + 21 + (-6x) + 6$. Then combine like terms to obtain $x + 27$. If you chose **B**, perhaps you forgot that $a - b = a + (-b)$, and so you distributed 3 rather than –3 to the –2 term in $(2x - 2)$. If you chose **A**, perhaps you forgot to distribute the 7 and the –3 to the second term in each set of grouping symbols, setting $7(x + 3)$ equal to $7x + 3$ and $-3(2x - 2)$ equal to $-6x - 2$.

Question 22. The correct answer is G. To find 75% of a number, n, for which 115% of n is 460, you first set up an equation to find n using the fact that 115% of n is 460, or $1.15n = 460$. After dividing by 1.15, you find $n = 400$. Then, 75% of 400 is $400(0.75)$, or 300.

If you chose **J**, you probably found 75% of 460 as $460(0.75)$, or 345. If you chose **K**, you probably found n using the equation $1.15n = 460$ by dividing by 1.15 and getting 400.

Question 23. The correct answer is C. This problem tests your knowledge of how to square a binomial. The expression $(2x - 3)^2$ can be expanded into the $ax^2 + bx + c$ form using the distributive property as shown in the following:

$$(2x - 3)^2 = (2x - 3)(2x - 3) = (2x)(2x) + (2x)(-3) + (-3)(2x) + (-3)(-3)$$
$$= 4x^2 - 6x - 6x + 9 = 4x^2 - 12x + 9$$

When the coefficients of $4x^2 - 12x + 9$ are matched with the coefficients of $ax^2 + bx + c$, you can see that $a = 4$, $b = -12$, and $c = 9$, and that $a + b + c = 4 + (-12) + 9 = 1$.

When you square a binomial, you must multiply two binomial expressions using the distributive property. Common errors result from reasoning that $(2x - 3)^2$ is equivalent to $(2x)^2 + (-3)^2$ or $(2x)^2 - (3)^2$, resulting in **B** or **D**.

Question 24. The correct answer is H. Two common approaches are often used in solving this problem.

In the first approach, the polygon can be divided into a 15 ft by 15 ft square and a 10 ft by 5 ft rectangle (see the following Figure 1). The area of the polygon is equal to the sum of the areas of the rectangle and the square: $(15)(15) + (10)(5) = 275$ square feet.

In the second approach, you take the rectangle formed by the 15 ft and 25 ft sides of the polygon and "cut away" a 10 ft by 10 ft square (see the following Figure 2). In this case, the area of the polygon is equal to the difference of the areas of the rectangle and the square: $(15)(25) - (10)(10) = 275$ square feet.

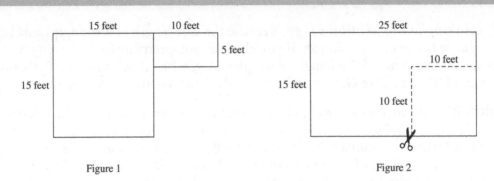

Figure 1   Figure 2

Question 25. The correct answer is B. The way to use the minimum number of blocks is to have a side of the block with the largest area face upward. That is the side that is 4″ by 8″. The 4″ width of the blocks will fit 3 to each foot. The 8″ length of the blocks will fit 3 to each 2 feet. The blocks could be arranged as shown, with 24 block widths in one direction and 15 block lengths in the other direction. That makes $15 \cdot 24 = 360$ blocks. The blocks could be arranged in different patterns, but the top area of all the blocks has to equal the $(8)(10) = 80$-square-foot area Barb is covering.

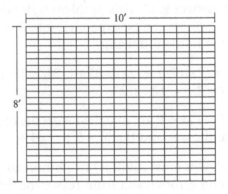

An alternate way to work this problem is to calculate the total area, 80 square feet, and divide by the largest area a single block can cover, 32 square inches. The area to be covered is $(8)(12) = 96$ inches in one direction and $(10)(12) = 120$ inches in the other direction, which makes the total area $(96)(120) = 11,520$ square inches. If you divide this by the area of a single block, 32 square inches, you will get $\frac{11,520}{32} = 360$ blocks.

If you got answer **A**, you may have calculated the area of the patio in square feet.

Question 26. The correct answer is H. To find the slope, you can manipulate the equation $6y - 14x = 5$ algebraically in order to find its equivalent equation expressed in *slope-intercept form*, which is $y = mx + b$, where m is the slope and b is the y-intercept. The manipulations are shown in the following:

$$6y - 14x = 5 \Rightarrow 6y = 14x + 5 \Rightarrow y = \frac{14}{6}x + \frac{5}{6}$$

The slope of the line equals $\frac{14}{6}$, or $\frac{7}{3}$ when reduced to lowest terms.

Question 27. The correct answer is C. First we will show that $m < \sqrt{mn}$:

Because m and n are positive integers such that $m < n$, $n = m + k$ where k is a positive integer and $m \geq 1$. For this reason, we know $\sqrt{mn} = \sqrt{m(m+k)} = \sqrt{m^2 + km}$. Because the square root function increases as its input increases and $m^2 + km > m^2$, $\sqrt{m^2 + km} > \sqrt{m^2}$, and $\sqrt{m^2} = m$. Thus, $\sqrt{mn} > m$.

Then, we will show that $\sqrt{mn} < n$ by a similar argument:

Start by solving $n = m + k$ for m: $n - k = m$. Then write $\sqrt{mn} = \sqrt{(n-k)n} = \sqrt{n^2 - kn}$. Because $n^2 - kn < n^2$, $\sqrt{(n-k)n} < \sqrt{n^2}$, and $\sqrt{n^2} = n$. Thus, $\sqrt{mn} < n$.

We have shown $m < \sqrt{mn}$ and $\sqrt{mn} < n$; thus, $m < \sqrt{mn} < n$.

If you chose **A** or **B**, you might have not realized that $\sqrt{mn}$ must be larger than m. Notice that for $m = 1$ and $n = 4$, $\sqrt{1(4)} > 1$ because $2 > 1$. If you chose **D**, you might have not considered cases such as when $m = 1$ and $n = 2$. Notice that for this case $\sqrt{mn} = \sqrt{n}$; thus, $\sqrt{mn} < \sqrt{n}$ is false. If you chose **E**, you might have not considered cases such as when $m = 3$ and $n = 4$. Notice that for this case $\sqrt{mn} > \sqrt{m+n}$ because $\sqrt{12} > \sqrt{7}$; thus, $\sqrt{mn} < \sqrt{m+n}$ is false.

Question 28. The correct answer is J. Similar triangles are triangles whose corresponding sides are proportional. The solution, x, is found by setting up the following proportion:

$$\frac{\text{the perimeter of the smaller triangle}}{\text{the perimeter of the larger triangle}} = \frac{3}{5} = \frac{(3 + 5 + 7)\text{ cm}}{x\text{ cm}}$$

To solve $\frac{3}{5} = \frac{15}{x}$ for x, cross-multiply to obtain the equivalent equation $3x = 75$, and divide by 3 to obtain $x = 25$.

Question 29. The correct answer is A. The area of the whole board is $\pi r^2 = \pi \cdot 10^2 = 100\pi$ square inches. The radius of the outside of the 20 ring is $10 - 2 = 8$ inches. The radius of the outside of the 30 ring is $8 - 2 = 6$ inches, so the area of

MATHEMATICS • EXPLANATORY ANSWERS

the circle that includes 30, 40, and 50 points is $\pi \cdot 6^2 = 36\pi$ square inches. If a dart hits at a random spot on the board, the chance of it hitting in a certain region is proportional to the area of that region. So, the percent chance of hitting inside a region that is worth at least 30 points is $\frac{36\pi}{100\pi} \cdot 100\% = 36\%$.

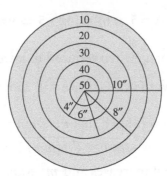

C is the percent chance of getting *more* than 30 points, using the 4-inch radius of the inside of the 30 ring.

Question 30. The correct answer is G. You can use translation skills to set up an algebraic equation that, when solved, yields the solution to the problem.

1. Let the variable a represent the teacher's age.

2. "If you *square* my age" translates into "a^2."

3. "23 *times* my age" translates into "$23a$."

4. "then *subtract* 23 times my age" translates into "$a^2 - 23a$." Because the words *than* and *from* do not appear in the sentence, the order of the terms "a^2" and "$23a$" is NOT reversed when translated into mathematical language.

5. "the result is 50" translates into "$= 50$."

Therefore, the translation gives the equation $a^2 - 23a = 50$, which you may solve by subtracting 50 from both sides and factoring.

The equation $a^2 - 23a - 50 = 0$ is true, provided that $(a + 2)(a - 25) = 0$, which happens if $a = -2$ (but age cannot be negative) or $a = 25$.

Question 31. The correct answer is B. "If a car accelerates from a stop at the *rate* of 20 meters per second per second" implies that $a = 20$, and "travels a *distance* of 80 meters" implies that $d = 80$. Substituting these values into the equation $d = \frac{1}{2}at^2$ gives the equation $80 = \frac{1}{2}(20)t^2$ or, equivalently, $80 = 10t^2$, or $8 = t^2$. Therefore, $t = \sqrt{8} \approx 2.8$ seconds.

Question 32. **The correct answer is F.** To find the real numbers x such that $x + 3 > x + 5$, you would subtract x and 3 from both sides. The result is $0 > 2$, but that inequality is never true, so there is no solution for x. It is the empty set.

If you chose **G**, you probably switched the inequality and got $0 < 2$ after you subtracted x and 3 from both sides. If you chose **H**, you probably got $0 > 2$ and then thought that a negative value for x would change the inequality.

Question 33. **The correct answer is D.** You must first determine from the frequency bar graph the number of students in the class responding that they spent 0, 1, or 2 hours studying on the previous evening. The bars in the graph indicate that 2 students studied 0 hours, 5 students studied 1 hour, and 6 students studied 2 hours. Therefore, the fraction of students in the class that responded they had spent less than 3 hours studying is equal to $\dfrac{\text{the number of students studying less than 3 hours}}{\text{the number of students in the class}} = \dfrac{2+5+6}{20} = \dfrac{13}{20}$.

If you chose **B** (the most common incorrect answer), perhaps you overlooked the phrase "less than" and selected the number of students studying exactly 3 hours as the numerator, obtaining the fraction $\dfrac{4}{20}$, or $\dfrac{1}{5}$.

Question 34. **The correct answer is J.** In the following figure, the shaded sector represents the 3-hour group:

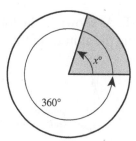

For this circle graph, the ratio $\dfrac{\text{the area of the shaded sector}}{\text{the area of the circle}}$ is equivalent to the ratio $\dfrac{\text{the number of students in the 3-hour group}}{\text{the number of students in the class}}$. These ratios, in turn, are equivalent to the ratio $\dfrac{\text{the measure of the central angle of the sector representing the 3-hour group}}{\text{the measure of the angle covered by 1 complete circle}}$. Letting the numerator of this last ratio equal $x°$, and using the fact that the denominator of this ratio is $360°$, you obtain the proportions $\dfrac{4}{20} = \dfrac{\text{the number of students studying 3 hours}}{\text{the number of students in the class}} = \dfrac{x°}{360°}$, so $x = 72$.

Question 35. **The correct answer is B.** Because this frequency bar graph gives the number of times each response was given, the frequency bar graph was constructed from the following 20 data values:

$$0, 0, 1, 1, 1, 1, 1, 2, 2, 2, 2, 2, 2, 3, 3, 3, 3, 4, 4, 5$$

The average number of hours for the 20 responses is equal to the average of the data values, which is defined to be $\frac{\text{the sum of the data values}}{\text{the number of data values}}$.

This is equal to $\frac{0+0+1+1+1+1+1+2+2+2+2+2+2+3+3+3+3+4+4+5}{20}$, or, equivalently, $\frac{2(0)+5(1)+6(2)+4(3)+2(4)+1(5)}{20} = \frac{42}{20} = 2.1$.

Question 36. **The correct answer is H.** To find the number of diagonals the octagon has, you would label the 8 vertices as endpoints. Those segments (which are the diagonals) are $\overline{AC}, \overline{AD}, \overline{AE}, \overline{AF}, \overline{AG}, \overline{BD}, \overline{BE}, \overline{BF}, \overline{BG}, \overline{BH}, \overline{CE}, \overline{CF}, \overline{CG}, \overline{CH}, \overline{DF}, \overline{DG}, \overline{DH}, \overline{EG}, \overline{EH}$, and $\overline{FH}$. There are 20 diagonals.

If you chose **F**, you probably just found the number of vertices in an octagon. If you chose **G**, you probably just multiplied the number of vertices by the number of endpoints of a diagonal, 8(s), or 16.

Question 37. **The correct answer is E.** As shown in the following figure, the tether line, the level ground, and a line segment representing the altitude of the bottom of the basket form a right triangle.

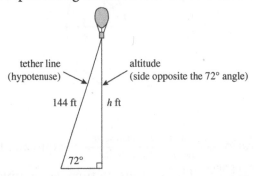

Let the length of the altitude equal h feet. You can use a trigonometric ratio to find h. The tether line forms the hypotenuse of the right triangle, and the line segment representing the altitude is the side opposite the 72° angle. Therefore, the trigonometric ratio to be used with respect to the 72° angle is the sine ratio, which gives the following equation:

$$\sin 72° = \frac{\text{the length of the side opposite the 72° angle}}{\text{the length of the hypotenuse}} = \frac{h}{144}$$

Multiplying both sides of the equation $\frac{h}{144} = \sin 72°$ by 144 yields the value of h, which is 144 sin 72°.

Question 38. **The correct answer is G.** The midpoint of a line segment is the point halfway between the two endpoints of the line segment. A formula for finding the midpoint (x_m, y_m) of two points (x_1, y_1) and (x_2, y_2) in the standard (x,y) coordinate plane is $(x_m, y_m) = \left(\frac{x_1 + x_2}{2}, \frac{y_1 + y_2}{2} \right)$. The x-coordinate of the midpoint, x_m, is the *average* of the x-coordinates of the endpoints of the line segment. In the case of $\overline{GH}$,

$$x_m = \left(\frac{x_1 + x_2}{2} = \frac{-8 + 2}{2} \right) = -3.$$

Question 39. **The correct answer is E.** To determine the value of $8x + 9y$, find the solution (x,y) to the system of two equations given in the problem. This system can be solved using an elimination method. First, determine which of the two variables would be easiest to eliminate. For this system, eliminating the y-variable would be easier. In order to eliminate the y-variable, the y-coefficients in each equation (or equivalent equation) must be opposite numbers (-6 and 6 would be the best choice). Therefore, all terms in the upper equation should be multiplied by -2 (Step 1 following) to form an equivalent equation with -6 as the y-coefficient. Now the two equations have y-coefficients of -6 and 6, respectively, so adding the equations will eliminate the y-variable (Step 2 following).

$$
\begin{array}{ccccc}
 & & \textbf{Step 1} & & \textbf{Step 2} \\
2x + 3y = 4 & & -2(2x + 3y) = -2(4) & & -4x - 6y = -8 \\
5x + 6y = 7 & \Rightarrow & 5x + 6y = 7 & \Rightarrow & \underline{5x + 6y = 7} \\
 & & & & x = -1
\end{array}
$$

Substituting into either of the two initial equations produces an equation that can be solved for y; for example, letting $x = -1$ in $2x + 3y = 4$ gives $2(-1) + 3y = 4$. Solving for y, $-2 + 3y = 4$, so $3y = 6$. Therefore, $y = 2$.

Substituting $x = -1$ and $y = 2$ into $8x + 9y$ yields $8(-1) + 9(2) = -8 + 18 = 10$.

Question 40. **The correct answer is H.** If we draw θ in standard position and its terminal side intersects the unit circle at (x,y), then $\tan \theta = \frac{y}{x}$. Because we want to solve $\tan \theta = -1$, we want the ratio $\frac{y}{x} = -1$. This only happens when $\theta = \frac{3\pi}{4}$ or $\theta = \frac{7\pi}{4}$. Recall that $\tan \theta < 0$ only when the terminal side of θ is in Quadrants II or IV.

You may have gotten **K** if you solved $\tan \theta = \pm 1$. You may have gotten **F** if you thought the tangent of an angle was negative when its terminal side was in Quadrants I and II. You may have gotten **G** if you thought the tangent of an angle was negative when its terminal side was in Quadrants II and III. You may have gotten **J** if you thought the tangent of an angle was negative when its terminal side was in Quadrants III and IV.

Question 41. The correct answer is B. By definition, $i^2 = -1$, so $i^4 = (i^2)^2 = (-1)^2 = 1$. Therefore, $i^x = 1$ for $x = 4$, so 1 is a possible value of i^x when x is an integer. More generally, when x is an integer, the only values of i^x possible are i, -1, $-i$, and 1, as shown in the following table:

...	i^{-3}	i^{-2}	i^{-1}	i^0	i^1	i^2	i^3	i^4	i^5	i^6	i^7	i^8	i^9	i^{10}	i^{11}	i^{12}	...
...	i	-1	$-i$	1	i	-1	$-i$	1	i	-1	$-i$	1	i	-1	$-i$	1	...

This rules out **A, C, D,** and **E.**

Question 42. The correct answer is F. Because the diameter of the can is 2 inches and the diameter of the glass is 3 inches, the radius of the can is 1 inch and the radius of the glass is 1.5 inches. Therefore, using $\pi r^2 h$, the volume of the can is $\pi(1^2)(6)$, or 6π, and the volume of the glass is $\pi(1.5^2)h$, or $2.25\pi h$. Because the volume of the soda pop can and the volume of the glass are equal, $6\pi = 2.25\pi h$. Solving for h gives us $h = 2\frac{2}{3}$.

You may have gotten **G** if you thought that height and diameter were directly proportional: $2(6) = 3h$. You may have gotten **H** if you thought that because the radius increased by 1 inch, then the height should decrease by 1 inch. You may have gotten **J** if you added all the values in the stem. You may have gotten **K** if you did $\frac{6\pi}{\frac{3}{4}\pi}$.

Question 43. The correct answer is C. The volume in cubic meters, V, of a right circular cylinder of radius r meters and height h meters is given by the formula $V = \pi r^2 h$. For the cylinder in this problem, $r = 5$ and $h = 6$. Therefore, $V = \pi(5^2)(6) = 150\pi$ cubic meters.

Question 44. The correct answer is F. The three triangles in the given figure ($\triangle ABC$, $\triangle ADE$, and $\triangle AFG$) can be shown to be similar by use of the angle-angle similarity property.

Because $\triangle ABC \sim \triangle AFG$, the statement "The ratio of the perimeter of $\triangle ABC$ to the perimeter of $\triangle AFG$ is 1:3" implies that the ratio of AC to AG is 1:3. So if $AC = 1$ unit, then $AG = 3$ units (see the following Figure 1).

Because $\triangle ADE \sim \triangle AFG$, the statement "The ratio of DE to FG is 2:3" implies that the ratio of AE to AG is 2:3. So if $AG = 3$ units, then $AE = 2$ units (see the following Figure 2).

This means that $AE = 2$ units when $AC = 1$ unit, implying that $CE = 1$ unit (see the following Figure 3). Therefore, the ratio of AC to CE is 1:1.

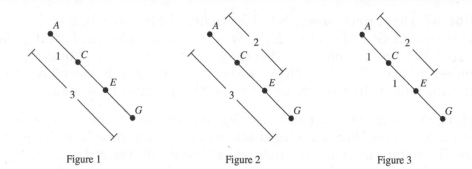

Figure 1   Figure 2   Figure 3

Question 45. The correct answer is E. The following Figure 1 shows the first phase, when the rocket traveled vertically for 30 kilometers.

Figure 2 shows the second phase, when the rocket traveled 40 km at 30° from the vertical. The three distances shown in Figure 2 are in the ratio $1:\sqrt{3}:2$, a characteristic of 30°-60°-90° triangles. The vertical distance covered in the second phase is $20\sqrt{3}$ km.

Figure 3 shows the third phase, when the rocket traveled 100 km at 45° from the vertical. The three distances shown in Figure 3 are in the ratio $1:1:\sqrt{2}$, a characteristic of 45°-45°-90° triangles. The vertical distance covered in the third phase is $50\sqrt{2}$ km.

Taking the sum of the vertical distances covered by each of the three phases gives the vertical distance of the rocket above the launch pad after the third phase.

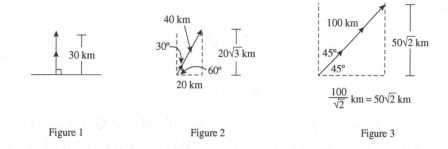

Figure 1   Figure 2   Figure 3

Question 46. The correct answer is G. Let X be a random variable that can take on all and only the values of $x_1, x_2, x_3, \cdots x_n$. The expected value of X is defined by $EV(X) = x_1 p_1 + x_2 p_2 + \cdots + x_n p_n$, where, for $k = 1, 2, 3, \cdots n$, X takes the value of x_k with a probability of p_k. Using this formula, we see $EV(n) = 0(0.70) + 1(0.20) + 2(0.05) + 3(0.05) = 0.45$, **G.** If you chose either **F** or **H**, you probably did not recall the definition of the expected value of a random variable. If you chose **J**, you added the probabilities of the four possible values of n. If you chose **K**, you found the mean of the four possible values of n. In all four of these incorrect cases, please see the previously given definition of expected value.

Question 47. The correct answer is E. We can find the factored form of the equation by first factoring out a GCF of –2, $h = -2(t^2 - 5t - 24)$, and then further factoring the quadratic to $h = -2(t + 3)(t - 8)$. The object reaches the ground when $h = 0$ and time is positive. By the zero product property, $0 = -2(t + 3)(t - 8)$ when $t = -3$ or $t = 8$. Because 8 is the positive value of t that is the solution to $h = 0$, the object will hit the ground at 8 seconds.

If you chose **D**, you might have picked the negative value of t in the solution to $0 = -2(t + 3)(t - 8)$ and then taken the absolute value. If you chose **B** or **C**, you might have confused the factored form of a quadratic equation with the vertex form. This equation can be written as $h = -2(x - 2.5)^2 + 60.5$, so the maximum height is 60.5 units. If you chose **A**, you might have not realized that the starting point is the value of h when $t = 0$, which is 48.

Question 48. The correct answer is H. Rewrite the values in the radicand as exponents, and then simplify.

$$g^2\sqrt{g^5} \cdot h^2\sqrt[4]{h^5}$$

$$g^2 g^{\frac{5}{2}} \cdot h^2 h^{\frac{5}{4}}$$

$$g^{2+\frac{5}{2}} \cdot h^{2+\frac{5}{4}}$$

$$g^{\frac{9}{2}} \cdot h^{\frac{13}{4}}$$

$$g^{4\frac{1}{2}} \cdot h^{3\frac{1}{4}}$$

$$g^4 h^3 \sqrt[4]{g^2 h}$$

You probably got **F** if you did $g^{2+\frac{2}{5}} \cdot h^{2+\frac{2}{5}}$. You probably got **G** if you did $g^{\frac{2+5}{2}} \cdot h^{\frac{2+5}{4}}$. You probably got **J** if you did $g^{2+\frac{5}{2}} \cdot h^{2+\frac{5}{2}}$. You probably got **K** if you did $g^{2+5} \cdot h^{2+5}$.

Question 49. The correct answer is D. The value of $\log_5(5^{\frac{13}{2}})$ is found by solving the equation $\log_5(5^{\frac{13}{2}}) = x$. By definition of logarithm to the base 5, this equation is equivalent to the equation $5^x = 5^{\frac{13}{2}}$. The equation $5^x = 5^{\frac{13}{2}}$ is equivalent to the equation $x = \frac{13}{2}$, whose value is between 6 and 7.

Question 50. The correct answer is F. We need to find the percent decrease, which is found by using the formula for percent change.

$$\text{percent change} = \frac{|\text{original cost} - \text{new cost}|}{\text{original cost}} \times 100$$

The Size 3 unit is $100 per month, and the special rate is $1 for the first month. The original cost would have been 12(100), but because there is a special rate of $1 for the first month, Daria only needs to pay the original monthly fee for 11 months, 11(100) + 1. Use the formula to find the percent decrease.

$$\frac{|12(100) - (11(100) + 1)|}{12(100)} \times 100 = \frac{|99|}{12(100)} \times 100$$

You may have gotten **G** if you did $\frac{100}{12(100)} \times 100$. You may have gotten **H** if you did $\frac{100 + 1}{12(100) - 1} \times 100$. You may have gotten **J** if you did $\frac{100 - 1}{11(100)} \times 100$. You may have gotten **K** if you did $\frac{100}{11(100)} \times 100$.

Question 51. **The correct answer is E.** The Size 5 unit is 8 × 16, and the Size 1 unit is 2 × 4. One way to solve is to divide the width by width and length by length, if width × length. We can see that the Size 1 unit's width of 2 can fit into the Size 5 unit's width of 8 four times, or $\frac{8}{2}$. Similarly, we see that Size 1 unit's length of 4 can fit into Size 5 unit's length of 16 four times, or $\frac{16}{4}$. Because we are dealing with area, we multiply $\frac{8}{2} \left(\frac{16}{4} \right)$, or 4 × 4, to get the maximum number of Size 1 units into Size 5 units. A drawing would also help you see this answer. A possible drawing:

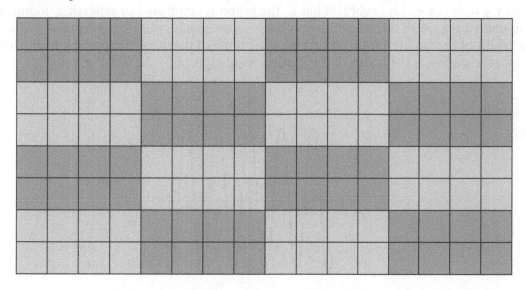

You may have gotten **A** if you divided length from the Size 1 unit and width from the Size 5 unit as $\frac{8}{4}$. You may have gotten **B** if you divided only the widths as $\frac{8}{2}$. You may have gotten **C** if you did $\frac{8}{2} + \frac{16}{4}$. You may have gotten **D** if you did $\frac{16}{2} + \frac{8}{4}$.

Question 52. The correct answer is H. $x =$ unit size number. The relationship between the unit size number and the area of each unit is as follows:

x	Area	Pattern
1	8	8×2^0
2	16	8×2^1
3	32	8×2^2
4	64	8×2^3
5	128	8×2^4

Notice as the unit size number increases, the area increases exponentially. The pattern is shown in the table.

The expression that summarizes this pattern is $8 \times 2^{(x-1)}$ or $2^3 \times 2^{(x-1)}$. Using properties of exponents, the simplest form is $2^{(2+x)}$. You may have gotten **F** if you thought the pattern was $8 \times$ unit size number. You may have gotten **G**, **J**, or **K** if you did not understand the pattern.

Question 53. The correct answer is B. The graph of any trigonometric function of the form $y = a \sin(bx + c)$ is cyclical. That is, the graph is composed of repeating, identical *cycles*. The shaded region in the following graph shows one such cycle. The *period* of the function is the width of the smallest interval of x on which one of these cycles appears. In the following graph, the period is the width of the shaded region, given by $2\pi - \pi = \pi$.

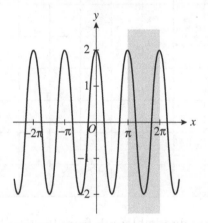

The period of $y = \sin x$ is 2π, which is **C**, the most common incorrect answer. If you chose **E**, you may have confused *period* with *amplitude*.

Question 54. The correct answer is G. The component form of w can be found by adding the opposite of the scalar horizontal components together and the opposite of the scalar vertical components together: $-2\langle 5,3\rangle + 3\langle 2,-7\rangle = \langle -10+6,-6-21\rangle$.
If you got **F**, you may have done $-2\langle 5,3\rangle - 3\langle 2,-7\rangle = \langle -10-6,-6+21\rangle$.
If you got **H**, you may have done $\langle 5,3\rangle - \langle 2,-7\rangle = \langle 5-2,3+7\rangle$.
If you got **J**, you may have done $2\langle 5,3\rangle - 3\langle 2,-7\rangle = \langle 10-6,6+21\rangle$.
If you got **K**, you may have done $2\langle 5,3\rangle + 3\langle 2,-7\rangle = \langle 10+6,6-21\rangle$.

Question 55. The correct answer is B. We can rewrite the bases as powers of a common base. The common base here is 3, because $3^1 = 3$, and $3^2 = 9$.

$$3^{x+1} = 3^{2(x-2)}$$
$$3^{x+1} = 3^{2x-4}$$
$$x+1 = 2x-4$$
$$x = 5$$

This is the one and only solution that makes the equation true.

If you chose **A**, you may have set the exponents equal to each other before finding a common base and found there was no solution, OR you may have not found a common base and tried instead to solve for x. If you chose **C**, you may have rewritten 9 as 3^2 and misinterpreted the squared for two solutions. If you chose **D**, you may have done $\frac{9}{3}$. If you chose **E**, you thought the exponential equation had an infinite number of solutions.

Question 56. The correct answer is H. The area of the original triangle is $\frac{1}{2}(20)(15)\sin\theta$. The area of the resulting triangle is $\frac{1}{2}(20)(15-2t)\sin\theta$. To find the time, t, when the resulting triangle has an area that is $\frac{1}{2}$ the area of the original triangle, you need to set the area of the resulting triangle equal to $\frac{1}{2}$ the area of the original triangle and solve for t:

$$\tfrac{1}{2}(20)(15-2t)\sin\theta = \tfrac{1}{2}\left(\tfrac{1}{2}(20)(15)\sin\theta\right)$$

$$\Leftrightarrow (20)(15-2t)\sin\theta = \tfrac{1}{2}(20)(15)\sin\theta$$

$$\Leftrightarrow (15-2t)\sin\theta = \tfrac{1}{2}(15)\sin\theta$$

$$\Leftrightarrow 15-2t = \tfrac{1}{2}(15)$$

$$\Leftrightarrow 30-4t = 15$$

$$\Leftrightarrow -4t = -15$$

$$\Leftrightarrow t = \tfrac{15}{4}$$

If you chose **F**, you might have incorrectly set the area of the original triangle equal to the area of the resulting triangle and solved for t: $\frac{1}{2}(20)(15)\sin\theta = \frac{1}{2}(20)(15-2t)\sin\theta$. If you chose **G**, **J**, or **K**, you might have set up the problem correctly but made a mistake in your algebra. For **G**, you might not have distributed the four correctly:

$$\frac{1}{2}(20)(15-2t)\sin\theta = \frac{1}{2}\left(\frac{1}{2}(20)(15)\sin\theta\right)$$

$$\Leftrightarrow \frac{1}{2}(15-2t) = \frac{1}{4}(15)$$

$$\Leftrightarrow 4\left(\frac{1}{2}(15-2t)\right) = 4\left(\frac{1}{4}(15)\right)$$

$$\Leftrightarrow 2(15)-8t = 15$$

For **J**, you might have dropped the $\frac{1}{2}$ in the area of the original triangle:

$$\frac{1}{2}(20)(15-2t)\sin\theta = \frac{1}{2}\left(\frac{1}{2}(20)(15)\sin\theta\right)$$

$$\Leftrightarrow (15-2t) = \frac{1}{4}(15)$$

For **K**, you might have thought $\frac{1}{2}\cdot\frac{1}{2}$ canceled out, incorrectly distributed the $\frac{1}{2}$ in the area of the resulting triangle, and then dropped the negative:

$$\frac{1}{2}(20)(15-2t)\sin\theta = \frac{1}{2}\left(\frac{1}{2}(20)(15)\sin\theta\right)$$

$$\Leftrightarrow \frac{1}{2}(15-2t) = 15$$

$$\Leftrightarrow \frac{1}{2}(15)-2t = 30$$

$$\Leftrightarrow 15-4t = 60$$

$$\Leftrightarrow 4t = 45$$

Question 57. The correct answer is E. Distinct permutations are permutations without repetition. We want to find how many unique orderings there are of the letters PEOPLE. The number of ways to order 6 different letters would be 6!. Because the P and the E are repeated twice, we must divide by 2! to account for the repeated P and again by 2! to account for the repeated E. Thus we get $\frac{6!}{(2!)(2!)}$.

If you got **A** you probably didn't account for letters P and E that cannot be repeated. If you got **B** you probably didn't understand distinct permutations. If you got **C** you probably considered the 6 letters in the word and 4 different letters in the word. If you got **D** you probably considered the 6 different letters in the word and that only 1 letter repeated.

Question 58. The correct answer is K. Complex conjugate pairs can be written in the form $(a + bi)(a - bi)$, which when simplified equals $a^2 - b^2i^2 = a^2 + b^2$.

The value of $i^2 = -1$; therefore, when $(7x - 9i)(7x + 9i)$ is simplified, it equals $49x^2 - 81i^2 = 49x^2 - 81(-1) = 49x^2 + 81$. You may have gotten **F** if you took the square root of $49x^2$ and 81. Notice that $(7x + 9)^2 = 49x^2 + 126x + 81$. You may have gotten **G** or **H** if you forgot that a complex conjugate pair consists of one expression with an addition and its conjugate pair has subtraction. You may have gotten **J** if you forgot the i in the conjugate pairs.

Question 59. The correct answer is B. Given an input x_i, the absolute value of the residual gives the vertical distance between the observed y_i-value and the $y(x_i)$-value predicted by the line of best fit. By inspecting the graph, the ordered pair (32, 135) appears to have the greatest vertical distance from the line of best fit. The absolute value of this residual is given by $|135 - y(32)| = |135 - (1.1(32) + 93)| = |135 - 128.2| = 6.8$. The remaining residuals are $|120 - y(27)| = |127 - (1.1(27) + 93)| = 2.7$, $|140 - y(42)| = |140 - (1.1(42) + 93)| = 0.8$, and $|130 - y(37)| = |130 - (1.1(37) + 93)| = 3.7$. If you chose **A**, you may have chosen the correct ordered pair (32, 135) but incorrectly computed the absolute value by adding 32 and 93 before multiplying by 1.1. If you chose **C**, you probably computed the difference in the 2 y_i-values 135 and 120. If you chose **D**, you may have incorrectly thought that the residual is the absolute value of the difference in the largest and smallest y_i-values, 140 and 120. If you chose **E**, you may have correctly identified the point farthest from the line but computed the vertical distance between 135 and the y-intercept of the line, 93.

Question 60. The correct answer is K. Making at least 1 error on any given day and making no errors are complementary events. Hence,

$$P(x \geq 1) = 1 - P(x = 0)$$
$$\Leftrightarrow P(x \geq 1) = 1 - 0.0823$$
$$\Leftrightarrow P(x \geq 1) = 0.9177$$

If you chose **F**, you might have thought that the probability of *at least* 1 error is the same as the probability of *exactly* 1 error, $P(1)$. If you chose **G** or **J**, you might have thought that the table shows the probabilities for making any number of errors possible on a given day and not realized that it only shows the probabilities for making 0–4 errors. For **G**, you might have thought that the probability of at least 1 error is the same as the sum of the probabilities of 2–4 errors, $P(2) + P(3) + P(4)$. For **J**, you might have thought that the probability of at least 1 error is the same as the sum of the probabilities of 1–4 errors, $P(1) + P(2) + P(3) + P(4)$. If you chose **H**, you might have thought that the probability of making at least 1 error is equal to the complement of the sum of the probability of 1 error and the probability of no errors, $1 - (P(1) + P(0)) = 1 - P(1) - P(0)$.

Question 61. The correct answer is H. To find an equivalent expression, you can multiply the constants $(3 \cdot 2 \cdot 4)$, combine the x terms $(x^3 x^2 x^2 => x^{3+2+2} => x^7$, because when you have a common base you use the base and add the exponents), and combine the y terms $(y \cdot y => y^1 y^1 => y^{1+1} => y^2)$. The result is $24x^7 y^2$.

K is the most common incorrect answer and comes from multiplying the exponents on the x terms instead of adding. If you chose **F**, you probably added the constants instead of multiplying. If you chose **G**, you could have added the constants and multiplied the exponents on the x terms instead of adding. If you chose **J**, you possibly multiplied the exponents on the x terms and y terms instead of adding.

Question 62. The correct answer is A. To find Mr. Dietz's pay per day, you can divide his salary, $22,570, by the number of days he works, 185. His pay per day is $\frac{22.570}{185}$, or $122. When Mr. Dietz takes a day off without pay and the school pays a substitute $80, the school district saves the difference in these amounts, $122 - 80$, or $42.

If you chose **B**, you probably just picked a number from the problem. If you got **E**, you probably found Mr. Dietz's pay per day and stopped.

Question 63. The correct answer is J. To find what the student needs to score on the fifth 100-point test to average a score of 80, you need to find the point total for the student so far by adding 65, 73, 81, and 82. That sum is 301. Averaging 80 points on 5 tests means the student must earn 400 points $(80 \cdot 5)$. The score needed on the last test is the difference, $400 - 301$, or 99.

F is the average of the 4 scores, rounded to the nearest whole point. If you chose **H**, you probably took the average of 65, 73, 81, and 82, averaged that average with 80, and rounded to the nearest whole point. If you chose **K**, you possibly thought you needed $5(100)$, or 500, points total, and this total is not possible when adding a number 100 or less to 301.

Question 64. The correct answer is D. To find the oxygen saturation loss, you divide the current number of milligrams of dissolved oxygen per liter of water by the dissolved oxygen capacity in milligrams per liter of water, or $\frac{7.3}{9.8}$. Then, you approximate that fraction as a decimal, 0.7449, then convert to a percent, 74.49%, and round to 74%.

If you chose **A**, you probably divided 9.8 by 7.3, subtracted 1, converted to a percent, and rounded to the nearest whole percent. If you chose **B**, you probably rounded to the nearest 10%, that is, 74.49% to 70%. If you chose **C**, you probably just used numbers from the problem.

Question 65. The correct answer is J. To find the length of fence needed to fence a rectangular lot 150 ft by 200 ft, you need to find the perimeter. The formula for the perimeter of a rectangle is 2 times the sum of the length and width, or $P = 2(l + w) = 2(150 + 200) = 2(350) = 700$.

If you chose **G**, you probably added the dimensions, but didn't double the sum. If you chose **F** or **H**, you possibly used only one dimension and doubled it.

Question 66. The correct answer is A. To find an equivalent expression, multiply a by $b + c - d$. This results in $a(b) + a(c) + a(-d)$, or $ab + ac - ad$.

If you chose **E**, you probably forgot to distribute the a to c and d.

Question 67. The correct answer is F. To solve for x in the equation $4x + 3 = 9x - 4$, you could subtract $4x$ and add 4 to both sides. That results in the equation $7 = 5x$. Then, dividing both sides by 5, the result is $\frac{7}{5} = x$.

If you chose **G**, you probably got to $7 = 5x$ and then divided 5 by 7. If you chose **H**, you probably added $4x$ to $9x$, resulting in $7 = 13x$, and then divided by 13. If you chose **J**, you might have combined the 3 and -4 and somehow got 1, then got to $1 = 5x$ and divided both sides by 5.

Question 68. The correct answer is C. These 4 numbers will be an arithmetic sequence. In an arithmetic sequence, each pair of successive terms differs by the same amount. To find the difference, you can define d as that difference and let 17 be the first term and 41 be the fourth term. By definition, the second term is $17 + d$ and the third term is $(17 + d) + d$. The fourth term, 41, can also be written as $(17 + d + d) + d$. Using that expression you obtain the equation $41 = 17 + d + d + d$, or $41 = 17 + 3d$. After subtracting 17 from both sides, you can then divide by 3, resulting in $8 = d$. The difference is 8. Then, the second term is $17 + 8$, or 25. The third term is $17 + 8 + 8$, or 33.

If you chose **A**, you probably reasoned that because 41 is the fourth term, the relationship is $4d = 24$ (rather than $3d = 24$) and so the difference is 6. If you chose **B**, you probably added 7 to the first term and subtracted 7 from the fourth term. If you chose **E**, you probably added 10 to the first term and subtracted 10 from the fourth term.

Question 69. The correct answer is H. To find what $x^2 + \sqrt{x}$ equals, you need to solve $x^3 = 64$ for x. The solution is $\sqrt[3]{64}$, which is 4. Then, substituting into the original expression, you get $4^2 + \sqrt{4}$. This expression simplifies to $16 + 2$, or 18.

If you chose **F**, you probably solved $x^3 = 64$ for x and stopped. If you chose **G**, you could have gotten $x = 4$, used $4(2)$ for 4^2, and added $4(2)$ and 2 to get 10. If you chose **J**, possibly you got $x = 4$ and then simplified $\sqrt{4}$ to be 4.

Question 70. The correct answer is C. To find the volume, you substitute $\frac{5}{4}$ for r in the equation $V = \frac{4}{3}\pi r^3$. This yields $\frac{4}{3}\pi\left(\frac{5}{4}\right)^3$, or $\frac{125\pi}{48}$. This expression is about 8.18, or 8 to the nearest cubic inch.

If you chose **A**, you might have substituted to get $\frac{4}{3}\pi\left(\frac{5}{4}\right)$, yielding $\frac{20}{12}\pi$, which is about 5. If you chose **B**, you probably substituted to get $\frac{4}{3}\pi\left(\frac{5}{4}\right)\left(\frac{5}{4}\right)$, yielding $\frac{25}{12}\pi$, or about 7. If you chose **D**, you probably substituted to get $\frac{4}{3}\pi\left(\frac{5}{4}\right)(3)$, yielding 5π, or about 16.

MATHEMATICS • EXPLANATORY ANSWERS

Question 71. The correct answer is K. The probability that the marble chosen will not be white when 8 marbles are red, 6 are blue, and 6 are white is the number of favorable outcomes divided by the total number of possible outcomes. The number of *favorable* outcomes is 14 because there are 8 red marbles and 6 blue marbles—a total of 14 marbles. The total number of *possible* outcomes is $8 + 6 + 6 = 20$, the total number of marbles. Thus, the probability of the marble NOT being white is $\frac{8+6}{8+6+6} = \frac{14}{20} = \frac{7}{10}$.

If you chose **G**, you probably added the number of blue marbles and the number of white marbles and divided by the total number of marbles: $\frac{6+6}{20} = \frac{12}{20} = \frac{3}{5}$. If you chose **H**, you probably found $\frac{8+8}{8+6+6} = \frac{16}{20} = \frac{4}{5}$. If you chose **J**, you probably found the probability of choosing a white marble: $\frac{6}{8+6+6} = \frac{6}{20} = \frac{3}{10}$.

Question 72. The correct answer is D. To find the number of sports awards earned, the number of participants in each sport is multiplied by the ratio for that sport and then the 4 products are added. This is a matrix multiplication.

$$[40 \quad 60 \quad 80 \quad 80] \begin{bmatrix} 0.3 \\ 0.4 \\ 0.2 \\ 0.5 \end{bmatrix} = 40(0.3) + 60(0.4) + 80(0.2) + 80(0.5) = 12 + 24 + 16 + 40 = 92$$

If you chose **B**, you probably reversed the order on the first matrix to get $80(0.3) + 80(0.4) + 60(0.2) + 40(0.5) = 24 + 32 + 12 + 20 = 88$. If you chose **C**, you probably totaled the number of athletes and multiplied it by the average of the ratios, $260(0.35)$, which is 91.

Question 73. The correct answer is H. To find the average number of students enrolled per section of Algebra I, you add up the students in all the sections and divide by the number of sections. Thus, you add $24 + 25 + 29$ and get 78, then divide by 3. This results in an average of 26 students enrolled per section in Algebra I.

If you chose **G**, you could have found the median (or middle number) of 24, 25, and 29. Sometimes, *average* can mean the median or the mode. For this test, the directions say that, unless otherwise stated, "The word *average* indicates arithmetic mean." If you chose **J**, you likely found the average of 25 and 29.

Question 74. The correct answer is C. The total number of calculators available is $30 - 2 + 30 - 6 = 52$. To find the class periods for which there are not enough school calculators, find the total needed for each period, as given in the table below.

Period	1	2	3	4	6
Calculators needed	21	46	48	57	19

The only entry in the table more than 52 is 57 for Period 4.

If you chose **D**, you possibly looked at the Algebra I rows in the table and saw that Section B and Section C could not both be covered by the available calculators, and these sections are in Period 3 and Period 4. If you chose **E**, you probably used 60 for the available number of calculators and did not take into account the 8 calculators that are being repaired and are unavailable.

Question 75. **The correct answer is H.** Because the sum of each row is equivalent, the sum of Row 1 is the same as the sum of Row 2.

Row 1 : $\qquad x + 8x + (-3x) => 6x$

Row 2 : $\qquad -2x + ? + 6x => 4x + ?$

The question mark must represent $2x$. You could have done this with other rows, columns, or diagonals.

If you chose **G**, you probably just added the first and last entries in either Row 2, Column 2, or one of the diagonals. If you chose **K**, you may have thought that each sum must be 0 and found that $-4x$ would make the sums of Row 2, of Column 2, and of both diagonals 0.

Question 76. **The correct answer is E.** The x-coordinate is positive if A is to the right of the y-axis. The y-coordinate is positive if A is above the x-axis. The table below shows the sign of x and the sign of y in the four quadrants.

	Sign of:	
Quadrant	x	y
I	+	+
II	−	+
III	−	−
IV	+	−

Thus, the signs are opposite in Quadrants II and IV only.

If you chose **C** or **D**, you probably got confused about where x and y are positive and negative or about the order of the quadrants.

Question 77. **The correct answer is J.** To find the number of distinct outfits that Kareem can select from 4 sweaters, 6 shirts, and 3 pairs of slacks, multiply the numbers of the 3 different clothing pieces together. Thus, there are $4(6)(3)$, or 72, distinct outfits that Kareem can select. The figure below shows that for each sweater, there are 6 shirts, and for each shirt, there are 3 pairs of slacks.

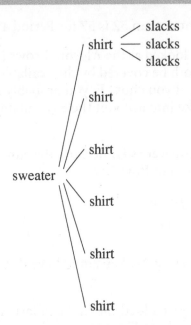

If you chose **F**, you probably added the 3 numbers together, getting $4 + 6 + 3 = 13$.

Question 78. The correct answer is A. To find the number of tons of sand needed to produce 3,000 barrels of a tarry material that requires 100,000 tons of sand for 60,000 barrels, you can set up a proportion with ratios of tons of sand to barrels of tarry material, such as $\frac{100,000}{60,000} = \frac{\text{tons of sand}}{3,000}$, which results in 5,000 tons of sand.

If you chose **B**, you probably calculated $\frac{60,000(30,000)}{100,000}$.

Question 79. The correct answer is H. The following figure shows the rectangle and a diagonal. To find the length of the diagonal, you could use the Pythagorean theorem because the sides of the rectangle are the legs of a right triangle and the diagonal of the rectangle is the hypotenuse of the right triangle. Then $h^2 = 72^2 + 54^2 => h = 90$.

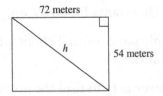

72 meters

h

54 meters

G is the average of 54 and 72. If you chose **J**, you probably added 54 and 72.

Question 80. The correct answer is A. To find an equivalent expression for $\frac{x}{y}$, you must either multiply or divide both the numerator and the denominator by the same value. Multiplying $\frac{x}{y}$ by $\frac{z}{z}$ yields $\frac{x \cdot z}{y \cdot z}$.

If you chose **B**, you probably thought you could multiply by the expression and obtain an equivalent expression, but if $\frac{x}{y}=\frac{2}{3}$, then $\frac{x^2}{y^2}=\frac{4}{9}\neq\frac{2}{3}$. If you chose C, you probably thought you could multiply by the reciprocal and obtain an equivalent expression, but if $\frac{x}{y}=\frac{2}{3}$, then $\frac{x\cdot y}{y\cdot x}=\frac{2\cdot 3}{3\cdot 2}=1\neq\frac{2}{3}$. If you chose **E**, you probably thought you could add the same number to both the numerator and the denominator and obtain an equivalent expression, but if $\frac{x}{y}=\frac{2}{3}$, and $z=2$ then $\frac{x+2}{y+2}=\frac{2+2}{3+2}=\frac{4}{5}\neq\frac{2}{3}$.

Question 81. The correct answer is H. To find the slope-intercept form of the equation $8x-y-6=0$, you could first add 6 and subtract $8x$ from both sides of the equation to get $-y=-8x+6$. Then, multiply by -1 to get $y=8x-6$.

If you chose **F**, you probably forgot to switch the sign on $8x$ when you multiplied by -1. If you chose **G**, you probably just dropped the sign on $-y$. If you chose **J**, you probably forgot to multiply 6 by -1 in the last step.

Question 82. The correct answer is G. To find tan R in ΔRST, take the ratio of the length of the opposite leg to the length of the adjacent leg, or ST to RS, or r to t, or $\frac{r}{t}$.

F is sin R, **H** is cot R, **J** is cos R, and **K** is sec R. If you did not get the correct answer, it would be wise to review trigonometric ratios in a right triangle.

Question 83. The correct answer is D. To find the radius, you can use the right triangle shown on the diagram. Half the length of the chord is 12 inches, which is the length of one leg. The other leg is 5 inches long, and the hypotenuse is r inches long. (This is a right triangle because the distance between a point and a line must be measured perpendicular to the line.) Using the Pythagorean theorem $r^2=12^2+5^2 => r^2=169 => r=13$ inches.

A is $24+5$, which is clearly much longer than the radius. If you chose **B**, you probably used 24 and 5 for the leg lengths and got $r=\sqrt{601}$, which is about $r=24.5$ inches. Choice **C** is closest to $5+12$. Going along the radius line must be shorter than going along the 2 legs of the triangle.

Question 84. The correct answer is H. To find the force F (in newtons) corresponding to a spring length, L, of 0.18 meters when the relationship is given by the equation $L=\frac{2}{3}F+0.03$, you would substitute 0.18 for L to get $0.18=\frac{2}{3}F+0.03$. After subtracting 0.03 from both sides, you'd get $0.15=\frac{2}{3}F$. Then, after multiplying by $\frac{3}{2}$, you'd get $0.225=F$.

G is the result of replacing F by 0.18 and solving for L. If you chose **J**, possibly you got $0.225=F$ and added 0.03.

Question 85. **The correct answer is B.** To find the uniform depth the 10,000 cubic yards of snow would be on the rectangular football field with dimensions 120 yards by 53.5 yards, you would substitute in the formula for volume, V, of a rectangular prism with the height h, length l, and width w, which is $V = lwh$. After substituting you should have $10,000 = 120(53.5)(h)$, or $10,000 = 6,420h$. Thus, $h = \frac{10,000}{6,420}$, or about 1.558. And 1.558 is between 1 and 2. If you chose **A**, you probably took $\frac{6,420}{10,000}$ and got 0.642, which is less than 1. If you chose **C** or **D**, you probably used the wrong dimensions or made a mistake in calculations.

Question 86. **The correct answer is G.** To find the length of $\overline{QR}$ in $\triangle PQR$, where $\overline{PR}$ is 16 feet long and $\sin \angle P = \frac{3}{5}$, use the definition of sine: the ratio of the length of the opposite side to the length of the hypotenuse. In $\triangle PQR$, $\sin \angle P = \frac{QR}{PR}$. After substituting for $\sin \angle P$, and PR, the length of the hypotenuse, you obtain $\frac{3}{5} = \frac{QR}{16} => 5 \cdot QR = 48 => QR = 9.6$ feet.

F is $\frac{1}{2}$ of PR. If you chose **H**, you probably found $\cos \angle P = 0.8$ and then multiplied 16(0.8) to get 12.4.

Question 87. **The correct answer is B.** To find the fraction of cars assembled in Coupeville, you would divide the number assembled in Coupeville by the total number assembled. The following table shows the conversion of car symbols to numbers for the 4 cities and the total.

City	Number of Cars Assembled
Car Town	40,000
Coupeville	25,000
Truck City	20,000
Sedan Falls	15,000
All	100,000

The fraction assembled in Coupeville is $\frac{25,000}{100,000}$, or $\frac{1}{4}$.

If you chose **A**, you probably found the fraction for Truck City, $\frac{20,000}{100,000}$, or $\frac{1}{5}$. If you chose **C**, you may have thought a half car represented 10,000, so your fraction was $\frac{30,000}{110,000}$, or $\frac{3}{11}$. If you chose **D**, you probably used the fraction $\frac{30,000}{100,000}$, or $\frac{3}{10}$. If you chose **E**, you probably used the number in Coupeville divided by the total number from the other 3 cities, $\frac{25,000}{75,000}$, or $\frac{1}{3}$.

Question 88. The correct answer is B. To find the x-coordinate where the 2 lines $y = 2x + 6$ and $y = 3x + 4$ intersect, you could substitute $y = 2x + 6$ into $y = 3x + 4$ to get $2x + 6 = 3x + 4$. Subtracting $2x$ and 4 from both sides results in the equation $2 = x$.

Another strategy is to graph the equations and estimate the coordinates of the intersection point.

If you chose **C**, you probably used the constant from the second equation. If you chose **D**, you probably used the constant from the first equation. If you chose **E**, you probably found the y-coordinate instead of the x-coordinate.

Question 89. The correct answer is J. To solve the equation $M = 3V + 6$ for V, you could subtract 6 from both sides to get $M - 6 = 3V$, and then divide by 3 on both sides to get $\frac{M-6}{3} = V$.

If you chose **F**, you did not divide the 6 by 3. If you chose **G**, you might have moved the 6 from the right side to the left and also forgotten to divide it by 3. If you chose **H**, you possibly transferred the 3 from the V to the M. If you chose **K**, you probably made a sign error.

Question 90. The correct answer is B. The area is bh for a parallelogram with base b and corresponding height h. For parallelogram $ABCD$, base $\overline{AD}$ is $3 + 6$, or 9 inches long, and the corresponding height is 4 inches. So the area is $9(4)$, or 36 square inches.

The most common wrong answer is **D**, which comes from multiplying the two side lengths: $(3 + 6)(5) = 9(5) = 45$.

Question 91. The correct answer is K. To find $(b - a)^4$ given $a = b + 2$, you could solve the equation for $b - a$. By subtracting a and 2 from both sides, you get $-2 = b - a$. Substituting -2 for $b - a$ in $(b - a)^4$ yields $(-2)^4$, or 16.

If you got stuck working this one, you could try choosing a specific value *for b*, say $b = 3$. Then a must be $3 + 2 = 5$. And $(b - a)^4 = (3 - 5)^4 = (-2)^4 = 16$.

If you chose **F**, you probably got -2 for $b - a$ but then replaced $(-2)^4$ by -2^4 or -16. Be careful $(-2)^4 = (-2)(-2)(-2)(-2) = 16$, but $-2^4 = -(2 \cdot 2 \cdot 2 \cdot 2) = -16$.

If you chose **H**, you probably got $b - a = 1$ or $b - a = -1$, and either $(1)^4$ or $(-1)^4$ is 1. Choices **G** and **J** come from calculating 2^4 as $2 \cdot 4$ and, for **G**, making a minus sign mistake.

Because $(b - a)^4$ is an even power of the number $(b - a)$, you can eliminate any negative numbers (**F** and **G**). This kind of observation can help you catch mistakes even when your problem is not multiple-choice.

Question 92. **The correct answer is J.** One strategy for solving this problem is to find equations.

You can let y be the larger number and obtain the equation $y = 2x + 8$ from the first sentence.

The second sentence says that $2y + 3x = 65 \Rightarrow 2(2x + 8) + 3x \Rightarrow 65$.

If you chose **F**, you probably took 3 times the larger number and added it to twice the smaller number to get 65, rather than the other way around. If you chose **G**, you probably defined y as $y = 2x - 8$ and then also made the same error as in **F**. Choice **H** can come from distributing the 2 in $2(2x + 8)$ as $2(2x) + 8$ and doing everything else correctly.

Question 93. **The correct answer is C.** To find out how far a 30-foot ladder 10 feet away from the base of a building reaches tip the building, you can use the Pythagorean theorem. Let the length of the ladder be the hypotenuse, and let the legs be the distances away from the base of the building and from the ground to the top of the ladder along the building (see the figure below).

This gives the equation $30^2 = 10^2 + d^2$, where d is the distance the ladder reaches up the building.

Simplifying, you get $900 = 100 + d^2 \Rightarrow 800 = d^2 \Rightarrow d$ is about 28 feet.

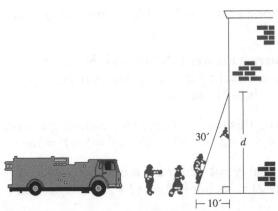

B comes from subtracting 10 from 30 or "simplifying" $\sqrt{900} - 100$ to $\sqrt{900} - \sqrt{100}$.

Question 94. **The correct answer is B.** It might be good to sketch a picture, something like the diagram below. To find the length of the longest side of the second triangle, you can use the ratios of corresponding sides of each triangle. For example, $\frac{12}{8} = \frac{15}{x}$, where x is the length of the longest side of the second triangle. After cross multiplying, you get $12x = 120$. Then, you divide by 12 to get $x = 10$ inches.

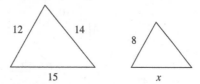

If you chose **A**, you probably noticed that the first triangle's longest side is 3 units longer than its shortest side. If this same relation held in the second triangle, its longest side would be $8 + 3 = 11$. This additive relation does not hold. If you chose **E**, you may have thought you needed the length of the middle side of the second triangle to solve the problem.

Question 95. The correct answer is K. To find the measure of $\angle BDC$ in the figure below, it is helpful to recognize that $\overline{AD}$ and $\overline{BC}$ are parallel and are connected by transversal $\overline{BD}$. Then $\angle CBD$ and $\angle ADB$ are alternate interior angles and so each measures 30°. (Go ahead and write in "30°" for $\angle ADB$ on the figure.)

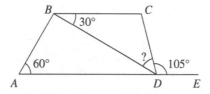

By definition, $\angle ADE$ is a straight angle and has a measure of 180°. Because $\angle ADE$ is made up of $\angle ADB$, $\angle BDC$, and $\angle CDE$, you know that the measures of those 3 angles add up to 180°. You might write this, using m to represent *measure*, as $m\angle ADB + m\angle BDC + m\angle CDE = 180°$.

Substituting the measures you know gives $30° + m\angle BDC + 105° = 180° => m\angle BDC + 135° = 180° => m\angle BDC = 45°$.

If you chose **H**, you might have thought $\angle BDC$ is isosceles. If you chose **J**, you possibly estimated the measure of $\angle BDC$ or made a subtraction error.

Question 96. The correct answer is E. This figure has 10 sides, but lengths are given for only 6 of the sides. Those lengths add up to $4 + 6 + 4 + 10 + 6 + 26 = 56$ inches. The perimeter is longer than this because of the missing 4 sides.

Then you should find the lengths of the missing sides, right? The following figure focuses on the vertical sides. The vertical sides that face left have lengths 4, 6, and 4. The lengths of the sides that face right are unknown. But, the vertical distance that the left-facing sides cover is the same as the vertical distance that the right-facing sides cover.

MATHEMATICS • EXPLANATORY ANSWERS

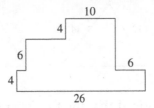

So, since the total length of the left-facing sides is 4 + 6 + 4 = 14 inches, the total length of the right-facing sides is also 14 inches.

Finding the lengths of the horizontal sides (see the figure below) is a similar process. The horizontal distance covered by the top-facing sides must be 26 inches because that's what's covered by the bottom-facing sides.

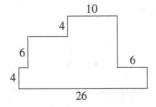

This makes the perimeter the sum of the lengths of the left-facing, right-facing, top-facing, and bottom-facing sides, which is 14 + 14 + 26 + 26 = 80 inches. You can't know the length of each side, but you can find the perimeter.

If you chose **C**, you probably just found the sum of the side lengths shown: 4 + 6 + 4 + 10 + 6 + 26 = 56. If you chose **D**, you may have left out the right-facing sides, or you may have estimated the lengths of the 4 missing sides and been too low. Estimation is a reasonable strategy for this question.

Question 97. The correct answer is F. To find out how many of the 804 seniors in a certain high school are going to a state university when approximately $\frac{2}{5}$ of the seniors are going to college, and when $\frac{1}{4}$ of those going to college are going to a state university, you could first find how many of the 804 seniors are going to college. This is $\frac{2}{5}(804)$, or almost 322 seniors. Then, find the number of those 322 seniors going to college who are going to a state university, which is $\frac{1}{4}(322)$, or about 80 seniors that are going to a state university.

J is closest to $\frac{1}{4}$ of 804.

Question 98. The correct answer is E. To find the distance between 2 points in the standard (x,y) coordinate plane, you can use the distance formula, $\sqrt{(x_2 - x_1)^2 + (y_2 - y_1)^2}$. So the distance is $\sqrt{(5-0)^2 + (0-1)^2} \Rightarrow \sqrt{5^2 + 1^2} \Rightarrow \sqrt{26}$ coordinate units.

A can come from mixing x and y coordinates: $\sqrt{(5-1)^2 + (0-0)^2}$. If you chose **B**, you probably added $1 + 5$ or simplified the radical expression incorrectly.

Question 99. The correct answer is G. To find the ratio of the circumferences of 2 circles for which the ratio of their radii is 4:9, you would recognize that both circumference and radius are one-dimensional attributes of a circle. Because of that, the ratios should be the same, 4:9. Another way is to use the ratio of the radii and let $4x$ be the radius of the first circle and $9x$ be the radius of the second circle. Then, the circumferences would be $2\pi(4x)$ and $2\pi(9x)$, respectively. Setting them in a ratio, you get $8\pi x : 18\pi x$, which simplifies to 4:9.

If you chose **F**, you probably thought that you should take the ratio of the square roots, $\sqrt{4} : \sqrt{9}$, or 2:3. If you chose **H**, you probably thought that you should take the ratio of the squares, $4^2 : 9^2$, or 16:81 (which is the ratio of the circles' areas).

Question 100. The correct answer is D. You may want to have a picture of this situation in your mind, or even sketch it out in the space in your test booklet. Your picture might look something like this.

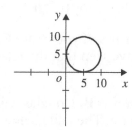

One way to find an equation for a circle is to know the coordinates of the center, (h,k), and the radius, r. Then, an equation is $(x - h)^2 + (y - k)^2 = r^2$. For this circle, the center is at $(5,5)$ and the radius is 5. (It's fairly easy to see that. If you needed to prove those are exactly right, you could use symmetry or you could use the fact that a tangent line is perpendicular to the radius that goes through the point of tangency.) Given center $(5,5)$ and radius 5, the circle has equation $(x - 5)^2 + (y - 5)^2 = 5^2$.

Another way to solve this problem is to find the coordinates of points on the circle and see which equation(s) each point satisfies. The points $(0,5)$, $(5,0)$, $(5,10)$, and $(10,5)$ are all on the circle. Testing these points in all the equations would probably take longer than the first method, but testing the points in the equation you think is correct would be a good check of your answer.

B is a circle centered at (0,0) instead of (5,5). If you chose **C**, you probably forgot to square the radius on the right side of the equation. If you chose **E**, you likely used $(x + h)$ and $(y + k)$ in the equation. Testing (10,5) would have helped you eliminate these incorrect answers.

Question 101. The correct answer is D. You want to find which statement describes the total number of dots in the first n rows of the figure below.

You could make a table like the one below, showing the number of rows and the total number of dots.

Number of rows	1	2	3	4	5
Total number of dots	1	4	9	16	25

You would probably recognize that the total number of dots is the square of the number of rows. This seems like a consistent relationship (it works for all 5 columns in your table). You can rule out **A** because the total is not always 25. For **B**, the total would have to go 2, 4, 6, 8, 10. For **C**, the total would need to be 5, 10, 15, 20, 25.

B works for the total of the first 2 rows. If you chose **C**, that works for the total of the first 5 rows. If you chose **E**, you might have seen that the relationship was not linear and viewed this as inconsistent.

Question 102. The correct answer is B. Douglas will count any color other than red, blue, green, and purple in the Other sector. The table below gives percentages of friends who picked red, blue, green, and purple.

Color	Red	Blue	Green	Purple	Other
Percentage	25%	30%	20%	10%	

The 4 known percentages add up to 85%. That leaves 15% for the Other sector. That means 15% of the 360° in the circle belong in the Other sector. This is $(0.15)(360°) = 54°$.

C is 15% of 180° rather than of 360°. If you chose **D**, you probably found the correct percent for the Other sector and then just labeled it degrees.

Question 103. The correct answer is J. One way to find tan θ, given that $\sin\theta = -\frac{3}{5}$ and $\pi < \theta < \frac{3\pi}{2}$, is to first find cos θ, then find $\frac{\sin\theta}{\cos\theta}$ (which is equivalent to tan θ). To find cos θ, use the facts that cos θ < 0 in Quadrant III and that $\sin^2\theta + \cos^2\theta = 1$. Substituting, you get $\left(-\frac{3}{5}\right)^2 + \cos^2\theta = 1$, or $\frac{9}{25} + \cos^2\theta = 1$. After subtracting $\frac{9}{25}$, you get $\cos^2\theta = \frac{16}{25}$. After taking the square root of both sides, you get $\cos^2\theta = \pm\frac{4}{5}$. Because $\cos\theta < 0$, $\cos\theta = -\frac{4}{5}$. Substituting into $\frac{\sin\theta}{\cos\theta}$ gives you $\frac{-\frac{3}{5}}{-\frac{4}{5}}$, which simplifies to $\frac{3}{4}$.

Another way you could do this problem is to construct an angle in Quadrant III with $\sin\theta = -\frac{3}{5}$. (Recall that sine is the ratio of opposite to hypotenuse.) Such an angle is shown below.

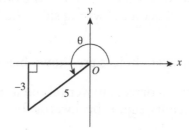

By the Pythagorean theorem, the missing side of the right triangle is 4 coordinate units long, and the directed distance along the side is −4. The figure below shows this.

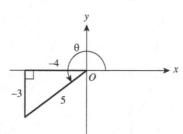

From this right triangle, knowing that tangent is $\frac{\text{opposite}}{\text{adjacent}}$ you can get $\tan\theta = \frac{-3}{-4} = \frac{3}{4}$.

G comes from using $\frac{4}{5}$ for cos θ instead of $-\frac{4}{5}$ If you chose **H**, you might have mixed up the definition of sine or tangent in the right triangle.

Question 104. The correct answer is A. To find the system of inequalities represented by the shaded region of the graph below,

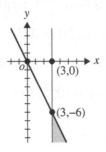

you could first find the equations of the line through (0,0) and (3,–6) and the line through (3,0) and (3,–6). Those are $y = -2x$ and $x = 3$. It is clear from the graph that the inequality that represents the shaded side of $x = 3$ is $x \geq 3$. For the other line, if you test (3,0), you find it satisfies $y > -2x$. Because (3,0) is on the wrong side (the unshaded side) of $y = -2x$, the correct inequality is $y \leq -2x$.

The graphs of the incorrect answer choices are shown below.

Choice **C** is the most common incorrect answer (about as many people choose this as choose the correct answer). The inequality sign is backwards for the line $y = -2x$.

Choice **B** differs from the correct answer only in the "or" connector. The graph of **B** includes points that satisfy one of the inequalities but not necessarily the other inequality, while the "and" connector means the graph can only include points that satisfy both inequalities.

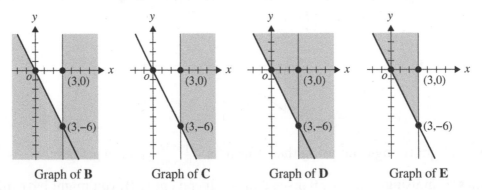

Graph of **B**   Graph of **C**   Graph of **D**   Graph of **E**

Question 105. The correct answer is K. To find $f(x + h)$ when $f(x) = x^2 - 2$, you would substitute $(x + h)$ for x in $f(x) = x^2 - 2$. The result is $(x + h)^2 - 2$. Multiplying out $(x + h)^2$ yields $x^2 + xh + xh + h^2$, or $x^2 + 2xh + h^2$. Then add -2 to the result.

If you chose **G**, you interpreted $f(x + h)$ as $f(x) + h$. If you chose **H**, you replaced $(x + h)^2$ with $x^2 + h^2$. If you chose **J**, you found $(x + h)^2$.

Question 106. The correct answer is A. It might be surprising to see that the graph of this complicated function looks almost like a line. The equation $y = \frac{2x^2 + x}{x}$ can be written as $y = \frac{x(2x+1)}{x}$. This is equivalent to $y = 2x + 1$ except when $x = 0$. When $x = 0$, the original equation is undefined. So the correct graph is $y = 2x + 1$ with a point removed where $x = 0$. If you noticed that the function was undefined when $x = 0$, you may have thought the open dot belonged at $(0,0)$. That leaves **B** as the only answer choice that also goes through $(1,3)$.

Choice **C** is the only one that involves $(0,2)$, and you may have gotten this by substituting $x = 0$ to get $y = \frac{2(0^2) + 0}{0}$, and decided all the zeros could be dropped to yield $y = 2$.

If you chose **D,** you may have "cancelled" x's as $y = \frac{2(x^2) + \cancel{x}}{\cancel{x}}$ to get $y = 2x^2 + 1$. You could have eliminated this answer by testing $(-1,3)$ in the original equation, but testing $(1,3)$ would not have been enough.

Choice **E** can come from "cancelling" x's as $y = \frac{2x^2 + \cancel{x}}{\cancel{x}}$ to get $y = 2x^2$. You could have eliminated this answer by testing $(1,2)$ in the original equation.

Question 107. The correct answer is F. To find the coordinates of vertex A after it is reflected across the x-axis, notice that a reflection across the x-axis does not change the x-coordinate but does change the sign of the y-coordinate. You might sketch or imagine a figure like the one below. Thus, the reflection of $A(c,d)$ across the x-axis is $A'(c, -d)$.

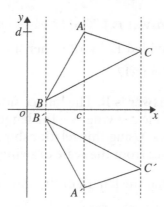

G gives A reflected across the y-axis. **H** gives A reflected across $(0,0)$. **J** gives A reflected over the line $y = x$ and is the most common answer.

Question 108. **The correct answer is A.** To obtain an expression for y in terms of x when $x = 2t - 9$ and $y = 5 - t$, you can first solve $x = 2t - 9$ for t by adding 9 to both sides to get $x + 9 = 2t$. Then, divide both sides by 2 to get $\frac{x+9}{2} = t$. Substitute that expression for t into $y = 5 - t$ to get $y = 5 - \frac{x+9}{2}$. To simplify the right side, rewrite 5 as $\frac{10}{2}$ and then combine the 2 fractions together to get $y = \frac{10-(x+9)}{2}$. You can then distribute and combine like terms to get $y = \frac{1-x}{2}$.

If you chose **B**, you probably got $y = \frac{10-(x+9)}{2}$ and simplified it to $y = \frac{19-x}{2}$. If you chose **C**, you may have substituted $2x - 9$ for t in $y = 5 - t$, which results in $y = 5 - (2x - 9)$. After distributing, this would be $y = 5 - 2x + 9$, or $y = 14 - 2x$.

Question 109. **The correct answer is K.** To find $\sin\frac{\pi}{12}$ using $\sin(\alpha - \beta) = (\sin\alpha)(\cos\beta) - (\cos\alpha)(\sin\beta)$ given that $\frac{\pi}{12} = \frac{\pi}{3} - \frac{\pi}{4}$, you can first substitute $\frac{\pi}{3}$ for α, and $\frac{\pi}{4}$ for β and get $\sin\frac{\pi}{12} = \sin\left(\frac{\pi}{3} - \frac{\pi}{4}\right) = \left(\sin\frac{\pi}{3}\right)\left(\cos\frac{\pi}{4}\right) - \left(\cos\frac{\pi}{3}\right)\left(\sin\frac{\pi}{4}\right)$. Using the table of values to substitute in that equation, you get $\sin\frac{\pi}{12} = \left(\frac{\sqrt{3}}{2}\right)\left(\frac{\sqrt{2}}{2}\right) - \left(\frac{1}{2}\right)\left(\frac{\sqrt{2}}{2}\right) = \frac{\sqrt{6}}{4} - \frac{\sqrt{2}}{4} = \frac{\sqrt{6}-\sqrt{2}}{4}$.

H comes from calculating $\left(\frac{\sqrt{3}}{2}\right)\left(\frac{1}{2}\right) - \left(\frac{\sqrt{2}}{2}\right)\left(\frac{\sqrt{2}}{2}\right)$, which is $\left(\sin\frac{\pi}{3}\right)\left(\cos\frac{\pi}{3}\right) - \left(\sin\frac{\pi}{4}\right)\left(\cos\frac{\pi}{4}\right)$. If you chose **J**, you probably just used $\sin\frac{\pi}{3} - \sin\frac{\pi}{4}$.

Question 110. **The correct answer is J.** The 12 vases cost \$18, so each vase costs $\frac{\$18}{12} = \$1.50$. If you chose **F**, you probably divided 12 by 18 rather than 18 by 12. If vases cost \$0.67 each, then 12 vases would cost less than \$12.

Question 111. **The correct answer is B.** The longer side of the apartment is 30 feet long, and it is 6 inches long on the scale drawing. So, the length of the room, in feet, is 5 times the length on the drawing, in inches. Using this relationship, the length of the shorter side of the apartment is 5 times the 4 inches from the scale drawing. This is 20 feet.

Alternately, you could notice that the length of the shorter side is $\frac{2}{3}$ the length of the longer side on the drawing and so the length of the shorter side of the room is $\frac{2}{3}$ of 30 feet, which is 20 feet.

These solutions are equivalent to using a proportion such as $\frac{6\,in}{30\,ft} = \frac{4\,in}{x\,ft}$ and solving $x = \frac{4 \cdot 30}{6} = 4 \cdot 5 = 20$ feet.

Question 112. The correct answer is H. The total profit for the 5 years was, in millions, $8 + $8 + $8 + $9 + $9 = $42. Then the average profit, in millions, was $\frac{\$42}{5} = \$8.4$.

The most common wrong answer was **J**, which is the average of 8 and 9. Because there were more years with a profit of $8 million than with $9 million, the average for the 5 years must be closer to $8 million than to $9 million.

Question 113. The correct answer is A. If the van were driven for 20 miles, the cost for those miles would be $0.30 • 20 = $6. Then the daily charge of $25 would have to be added in, for a total of $31. Similarly, if the van were driven for m miles, the cost for those miles would be $0.30m$ dollars, and the daily charge would make the total $0.30m + 25$ dollars.

C comes from treating the 30 cents like it was 30 dollars.

Question 114. The correct answer is K. This problem can be solved by substituting the Celsius temperature ($C = 38$) into the formula and solving for F. The substitution step gives $F = \frac{9}{5}(38) + 32$, which can be solved as follows: $F = \frac{9}{5}(38) + 32 => F = 100.4$. It is appropriate to round this to the nearest degree Fahrenheit because the precision of the Celsius temperature was only to the nearest degree Celsius.

If you chose **J**, you may have added 38 + 32 and missed the $\frac{9}{5}$. An answer of **H** might come from calculating $\frac{9}{5}(38)$ correctly and forgetting to add 32.

Question 115. The correct answer is B. Nick can only order whole cases, which contain 24 boxes of pens with 10 pens per box, for a total of 24 • 10 = 240 pens per case. An order of 2 cases would be 480 pens, which falls short of the desired 500 pens. To get 500 pens from his supplier, Nick needs to order 3 cases, and he will get 720 pens.

If you got answer **A**, you may have correctly divided 500 by 240 to get approximately 2.08 cases, but you may have rounded that to the nearest integer, which does not give the correct answer in this context. Answer **E** represents the number of boxes (not cases) of pens needed if Nick could order any whole number of boxes.

Question 116. The correct answer is K. When $a + b = 6$, then $2(a+b) + \frac{a+b}{6} + (a+b)^2 - 2$ becomes $2(6) + \frac{6}{6} + (6)^2 - 2$, which simplifies to $12 + 1 + 36 - 2 = 47$.

Question 117. The correct answer is C. If you bought 1 hamburger and 1 soft drink, it would cost $2.10. If you bought 1 hamburger more, your order would cost $3.50. So, the cost of the additional hamburger was $3.50 − $2.10 = $1.40. Because 1 hamburger and 1 soft drink cost $2.10, a soft drink must cost $2.10 − $1.40 = $0.70.

Alternatively, you could set up two equations with two unknowns. Let h dollars be the cost of each hamburger and s dollars be the cost of each soft drink. Then $h + s = 2.10$ and $2h + s = 3.50$. Subtraction gives:

$$2h+s=3.50$$
$$\underline{-(h+s=2.10)}$$
$$h\qquad=1.40$$

And then, substituting 1.40 for h in $h + s = 2.10$ gives $s = 2.10 - 1.40 = 0.70$.

The most common wrong answer is **E**, which is the correct cost of a hamburger. However, the question asks for the cost of a soft drink. Answer choice D is half of $2.10, which would only be correct if a soft drink cost the same as a hamburger.

Question 118. **The correct answer is C.** There would be 6 tiles along the 24" side (6 • 4" = 24"). There would be 16 tiles along the 64" side (16 • 4" = 64"). Then, 6 • 16 = 96 tiles are needed to completely cover the rectangular countertop:

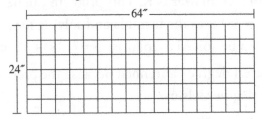

An alternate solution is to figure the area of the countertop in square inches, 24 • 64, which is 1,536 square inches. Then, divide that by the area of a tile, which is 16 square inches. The result is 96, which is the number of tiles needed. The tiles cover the area without being cut because the side lengths of the countertop are divisible by the side length of a tile.

The most common wrong answer is **E**, which comes from correctly calculating the area of the countertop (1,536 square inches), but dividing by the length of the side of the square (4 inches) rather than by 4 • 4 square inches. If you chose **A** or **B**, you may have confused perimeter and area.

Question 119. **The correct answer is H.** If the answer choices give 2 of the 3 interior angle measures in a triangle, then the third angle measure is 180° minus the sum of the given angle measures. The chart below shows this calculation.

	1st angle	2nd angle	Sum of 1st + 2nd angles	3rd angle (180° – Sum of 1st + 2nd angles)
F.	20°	40°	60°	120°
G.	30°	60°	90°	90°
H.	40°	100°	140°	40°
J.	45°	120°	165°	15°
K.	50°	60°	110°	70°

The only place where the third angle has measure equal to one of the first two angles is in **H**, where there are two 40° angles.

Question 120. The correct answer is C. The perimeter of the triangle, 66 inches, is the length of the three sides added together. Because one side is 16 inches long, the lengths of the other two sides added together must be 66 − 16 = 50 inches. The ratio of the lengths of these two sides is 2:3. This ratio denotes 2 parts for the first side, 3 parts for the second side, and therefore 5 parts altogether. Because there are 50 inches altogether, and this must make up the 5 parts, each part is 10 inches long. That makes one side 2 parts, or 20 inches long, and the other side 3 parts, or 30 inches long. So the longest side of the triangle is 30 inches long.

B is the length of another side of the triangle, but not the longest side.

Question 121. The correct answer is C. In the following figure, the angles with measure $a°$ and 100° form a straight angle along line m. This means $a° + 100° = 180°$, or $a° = 80°$. Now, you know two of the three angles in the larger triangle. The sum of all three must be 180°. So, $80° + b° + 65° = 180°$, which means that $b° = 35°$. The angle measure $b°$ is equal to angle measure $x°$ because vertical angles have the same measure. So, $x° = 35°$.

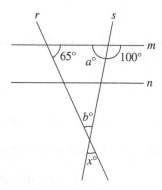

If you chose **A**, you may have calculated 180° − (65° + 100°). These three given angle measures, $x°$, 65°, and 100°, do not need to add to 180°. They are not the measures of the three interior angles in the *same* triangle.

Question 122. The correct answer is B. Parallel lines have the same slope, so any line parallel to this line has the same slope as this line. To find the slope of this line, you could put it into slope-intercept form, and then the slope is the coefficient of x. $7x + 9y = 6 \Rightarrow 9y = -7x + 6 \Rightarrow y = -\frac{7}{9x} = \frac{6}{9}$, and so the slope is $-\frac{7}{9}$.

If you chose **E**, you probably knew that the slope is the coefficient of x, but that only is true when the equation is in slope-intercept form. If you chose **A**, you may have gotten the equation into the form $9y = -7x + 6$ and then read off the coefficient of x. You didn't quite have it in slope-intercept form. If you chose **C**, you may have made a mistake putting the equation in slope-intercept form. Answer choice **D** could be reading off the constant 6 from the original equation.

Question 123. **The correct answer is C.** The figure below shows the ramp.

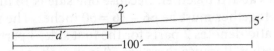

The slope is given as rising 5 feet for every 100 feet of horizontal run. The ramp's rise is 2 feet, and the horizontal run is unknown. Let the horizontal run be represented as d. Then there is a proportion $\frac{2}{d} = \frac{5}{100}$. Its solution is $d = \frac{2 \cdot 100}{5} = 40$ feet.

If you chose **A**, you might have simplified 5% to 0.5. Then the proportion $\frac{2}{d} = 0.5$ has the solution 4 feet. The most common incorrect choice was **B**, which happens when the run is 5 times the rise. This gives a reasonable-looking ramp. However, the slope of such a ramp is $\frac{1}{5}$. The required slope is $\frac{1}{20}$.

Question 124. **The correct answer is J.** A quick scan of the answer choices should give you a clue that combining like terms is in order.

$$(x^2 - 4x + 3) - (3x^2 - 4x - 3)$$
$$= (x^2 - 4x + 3) + (-3x^2 + 4x + 3) \quad \text{subtracting is adding the opposite}$$
$$= (x^2 + (-3x^2)) + (-4x + 4x) + (3 + 3) \quad \text{reordering terms}$$
$$= -2x^2 + 0x + 6 \quad \text{combining like terms}$$

If you chose **K**, you probably subtracted the $3x^2$ but *added* the $-4x$ and the -3. The solution above took care of this explicitly on the second line. The other incorrect answers result from various combinations of errors with minus signs.

Question 125. **The correct answer is E.** The side lengths of a 30°–60°–90° triangle are in the ratio $1 : \sqrt{3} : 2$. If you didn't remember this, you could view a 30°–60°–90° triangle as half of an equilateral triangle, as shown below.

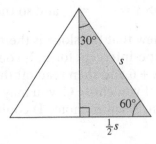

For the shaded triangle, you know that the base is half as long as the hypotenuse, because the base of the equilateral triangle is the same length as the other sides of the equilateral triangle.

If the hypotenuse is s units long and the base is $\frac{1}{2}s$, then the Pythagorean theorem gives the

height as $\sqrt{s^2 + \left(\frac{s}{2}\right)^2} = \sqrt{s^2 + \frac{s^2}{2^2}} = \sqrt{\frac{4s^2}{4} + \frac{s^2}{4}} = \sqrt{\frac{3s^2}{4}} = \sqrt{3\frac{s^2}{4}} = \sqrt{3}\sqrt{\frac{s^2}{4}} = \sqrt{3}\frac{s}{2} = \frac{\sqrt{3}}{2}s$.

This shows that ratios are $\frac{1}{2} : \frac{\sqrt{3}}{2} : 1$, which are equivalent to those given above, $1 : \sqrt{3} : 2$.

(Obviously, it's quicker to know the ratios than to try to derive them each time you need them, but don't give up if you can't remember something; try to find it a different way.) You could also use trigonometry to derive the side length ratios in a 30°–60°–90° triangle.

If you chose **B**, you might have been thinking of a 45°–45°–90° triangle, which has this ratio of side lengths. If you chose **D**, you may have reasoned that because the angle measures are in the ratio 1:2:3, maybe the side lengths are in the ratio $\sqrt{1} : \sqrt{2} : \sqrt{3}$. This is a right triangle (it satisfies the Pythagorean theorem), but the angles are closer to 35°–55°–90°. The triangles in **A** and **C** are not right triangles. You could have eliminated them because they do not satisfy the Pythagorean theorem. For **A**, $\sqrt{1^2 + 1^2} = \sqrt{2} \neq 1$. For **C**, $\sqrt{1^2 + (\sqrt{2})^2} = \sqrt{1+2} \neq \sqrt{2}$.

Question 126. The correct answer is E. This sequence decreases by 17 – 12 = 5 each term. Here are some more terms:

Term#	1	2	3	4	5	6	7	8	9
Value	17	12	7	2	–3	–8	–13	–18	–23

Each of **A**–**D** can be verified from the chart. The common difference for **D** is defined so that it is positive if the sequence is increasing and negative if the sequence is decreasing. In symbols, if the sequence is represented by terms $a_1, a_2, a_3, \cdots$, then the difference between two terms is $a_{i+1} - a_i$, for all i. If this difference is constant for all i, then it is called the *common difference* and the sequence is called *arithmetic*.

That leaves only **E** that could be false. The ratio of consecutive terms is defined by $\frac{a_{i+1}}{a_i}$ for all i.

For the first two terms, the ratio is $\frac{12}{17}$, which is a bit more than 0.70. For the second and third

terms, the ratio is $\frac{7}{12}$, which is a bit less than 0.59. That means the ratios are not equal for all

terms, and so there is no common ratio. That means **E** is false.

The most common incorrect answer is **B**. If you chose this, perhaps you reasoned that, because the sum of the first 4 terms is 38, the sum of the first 5 terms cannot be anything less. Writing out more terms makes it clear that this can be so. Or, you may have made an arithmetic mistake finding the fifth term and so arrived at the wrong sum. If you chose **C** and had the correct sum for the first 5 terms, then perhaps you made an arithmetic mistake subtracting 5 for each term, or you miscounted terms. If you have a different sum for **B** and also have a different eighth term than **C**, you know that there is something amiss in your work and you should go back and try to find your mistake if there is time.

If you chose **D**, perhaps you did not understand the concepts of common difference and common ratio.

Question 127. The correct answer is D. The normal amount of lead is 1.5×10^{-5} milligrams per liter. This can be written as 0.000015 milligrams per liter. Today's level, 100 times the normal amount, is $100(1.5 \times 10^{-5}) = 1.5 \times 10^{-5} \times 10^2 = 1.5 \times 10^{-5+2} = 1.5 \times 10^{-3}$ milligrams per liter. This can be written as 0.0015 milligrams per liter. This is larger than the normal amount.

If you chose **A**, you likely added −100 to the exponent. This answer is 0.00000000…0000000015 milligrams per liter, where there are 104 zeros between the decimal point and the "15." This is smaller than the normal amount. If you chose **B**, you possibly multiplied the exponent 2 from 10^2 by the exponent −5 from the normal amount. This is 0.00000000015 milligrams per liter, which is smaller than the normal amount. If you chose **C**, you could have subtracted the exponent 2 from the exponent −5 in the normal amount. This gives 0.00000015 milligrams per liter, which is smaller than the normal amount.

Question 128. The correct answer is B. This problem is in the general form $(a + b)^2$, which is equivalent to $a^2 + 2ab + b^2$ by the following derivation.

$$(a+b)^2 = (a+b)(a+b) = a \cdot a + a \cdot b + b \cdot a + b \cdot b = a^2 + 2ab + b^2$$

If $a = \frac{1}{2}x$ and $b = -y$, then $(a+b)^2 = \left(\frac{1}{2}x - y\right)^2$. This is equivalent to

$$a^2 + 2ab + b^2 = \left(\frac{1}{2}x\right)^2 + 2\left(\frac{1}{2}x\right)(-y) + (-y)^2 = \frac{1}{4}x^2 - xy + y^2 \cdot$$

If you chose **A**, you probably squared the first term and squared the second term. This is the stereotypical error, and it's something that college math teachers (and high school math teachers) want you to know not to do. Something that might help you remember is to have a concrete example: $(1 + 3)^2 = 4^2 = 16$, but $1^2 + 3^2 = 1 + 9 = 10$.

If you chose **C**, you probably did everything correctly except remembering to square the $\frac{1}{2}$ to get $\frac{1}{4}$.

Question 129. The correct answer is G. One way to solve this problem is to list out all the numbers in this range that you think might be prime, then check to see if any of them factor. You probably know that you don't have to check the even numbers. That leaves the following list:

31 33 35 37 39 41 43 45 47 49

If one of these does factor, it will have a prime factor of at most $\sqrt{49}$, which is 7. You have already eliminated all multiples of 2. If you eliminate all multiples of 3, 5, and 7, anything left on the list is a prime number. The multiples of 3 on the list are 33, 39, and 45. You can eliminate 35 because it is a multiple of 5. You can eliminate 49 because it is a multiple of 7. Then all the numbers remaining, namely 31, 37, 41, 43, and 47, are prime numbers.

If you chose **H**, you must have counted a number as prime that really isn't prime. You might want to figure out which one that was. People who miss this problem tend to count extra numbers as primes.

Question 130. **The correct answer is E.** The cotangent of $\angle A$ in this right triangle is the length of the leg adjacent to the angle divided by the length of the leg opposite the angle. That ratio is $\frac{\sqrt{4-x^2}}{x}$.

If you chose **D**, you chose the tangent of the angle. Answer choice **C** represents the sine of the angle. Answer choice **B** is the cosecant of the angle. If you want to get problems like this correct, you need to have a way to keep the trig functions straight.

Question 131. **The correct answer is B.** The area of the trapezoid is $\frac{1}{2}(b_1 + b_2)h = \frac{1}{2}(8 + 4)3 = 6 \cdot 3 = 18$ square inches. The area of the unshaded rectangle is $4 \cdot 3 = 12$ square inches. The triangles and the rectangle together form the trapezoid, so the area of the trapezoid minus the area of the rectangle is the area of the triangles. And this area is $18 - 12 = 6$ square inches. Another way to solve this problem is to slide the two shaded triangles together and calculate the area of the new triangle. From the original figure, notice that the combined base of the triangles is the amount left over from the trapezoid's bottom base when the width of the rectangle is removed. That is $8 - 4 = 4$ inches. The figure below shows the combined triangles. Their combined area is $\frac{1}{2}bh = \frac{1}{2}(4)(3) = 6$ square inches.

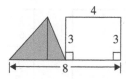

The most common incorrect answer is **D**, which could come up in a variety of ways. Many students have trouble finding the area of trapezoids and resort to calculating bh as if the trapezoid were a rectangle or parallelogram. The figure below shows the trapezoid inside a rectangle with base 8 inches and height 3 inches. The rectangle has area bh, which is clearly larger than the area of the trapezoid.

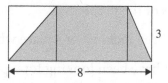

If you chose **E**, perhaps you calculated the area of the trapezoid and stopped. Perhaps you thought the problem was asking for the area of the triangles combined with the area of the rectangle, but it asks for the combined area of the triangles only. The triangle on the left looks like it is half of a square. If so, it has a base of 3 inches and a height of 3 inches and then area $\frac{1}{2}(3)(3) = \frac{9}{2}$ square inches. If the other triangle has the same area, the combined area of the triangles is $\frac{9}{2} + \frac{9}{2} = 9$ square inches. Perhaps you reasoned this way if you chose **C**.

Question 132. The correct answer is G. Each of the corner triangles are right triangles because they share an angle with the square. Both legs of these right triangles are 6 inches long because they are half the length of the side of the square. So, the hypotenuse of each of these triangles is $\sqrt{6^2 + 6^2} = 6\sqrt{1^2 + 1^2} = 6\sqrt{2}$ inches. The perimeter of $EFGH$ is made up of 4 of these hypotenuses, so the perimeter of $EFGH$ is $4 \cdot 6\sqrt{2} = 24\sqrt{2}$ inches.

You could have used the ratio of sides in an isosceles right triangle, rather than the Pythagorean theorem, to get the hypotenuse of the corner triangles. The basic flow of the solution is the same.

If you chose **F**, perhaps you noticed that the area of $EFGH$ is half the area of $ABCD$. That's a good observation. That does not mean, though, that the perimeter of $EFGH$ is half the perimeter of $ABCD$. If that were true, then each side of $EFGH$ would be 6 inches long, and the corner triangles would have 3 sides of length 6 inches. The triangle must then be equilateral and have a right angle. That can't happen. (The perimeter of a figure that is geometrically similar to the original and has area in the ratio 2:1 has perimeter in the ratio $\sqrt{2}$:1.)

Question 133. The correct answer is D. The table below shows the value of the cosine function at values of θ that are the endpoints of the intervals from each of the answer choices.

θ	0	$\frac{\pi}{6}$	$\frac{\pi}{3}$	$\frac{\pi}{2}$	$\frac{2\pi}{3}$	π
$\cos \theta$	1	$\frac{\sqrt{3}}{\pi}$	$\frac{1}{2}$	0	$-\frac{1}{2}$	-1
approximation of $\cos \theta$	1	0.866	0.5	0	-0.5	-1

The value -0.385 is between 0 and -0.5, which is saying that the value of $\cos \theta$ is between $\cos \frac{\pi}{2}$ and $\cos \frac{2\pi}{3}$. Because $\cos \theta$ is continuous, that means there is a value of θ between $\frac{\pi}{2}$ and $\frac{2\pi}{3}$ that satisfies the conditions of the problem.

If you chose **C**, you might have been looking for a place where $\cos \theta = +0.385$ rather than -0.385.

If you chose **A** or **E**, you might have been looking for a place where $\sin \theta = 0.385$.

Question 134. The correct answer is J. The equation $(x - 6a)(x + 3b) = 0$ has these two solutions. (You can check this by substituting $6a$ in for x and substituting $-3b$ in for x.) Multiplying out this equation gives $x^2 + (-6a + 3b)x + (-6a)(3b) = 0$, which is the same as $x^2 + (-6a + 3b)x - 18ab = 0$.

If you chose **F**, you may have gotten the initial equation right, $(x - 6a)(x + 3b) = 0$, but then multiplied incorrectly to get $(x)(x) + (-6a)(3a) + 0$.

Most of the other incorrect answers could be due to mistakes with negative signs. **G** comes from the initial equation $(x + 6a)(x - 3b) = 0$, where the signs are opposite what they should be. (If you substitute $6a$ in for x, you will not get zero on the left side of the equation.) If you chose **H**, you may have started with the equation $(x - 6a)(x - 3b) = 0$.

Question 135. The correct answer is A. The midpoints of the sides of the square are on the circle. These points have coordinates (0,3), (3,6), (6,3), and (3,0). The first point, (0,3), satisfies **A**, but none of the other equations. Alternately, because the circle centered at (h,k) with radius r has the equation $(x-h)^2 +(y-k)^2 = r^2$, you can find the equation by finding the center and radius. From the diagram, you can see that the center of the circle is the same as the center of the square, which is (3,3). Also, the radius of the circle is the distance from (0,3) to (3,3), which is 3 coordinate units. So $(x-3)^2 +(y-3)^2 = 3^2$ is an equation of the circle.

One common mistake is to remember the equation of the circle incorrectly, with plus signs where there should be minus signs (**C**). Another common mistake is to not square the radius on the right side of the equation (**B**). Or, some people do both of these things (**E**). If you chose **D**, you may have used the diameter on the right side of the equation, or you may have used the largest coordinate from the figure (and used plus signs instead of minus).

Question 136. The correct answer is H. When $g = 2$, the value of $g \cdot (g + 1)^2$ is $2 \cdot (2 + 1)^2 = 2 \cdot (3)^2 = 2 \cdot 9 = 18$.

If you chose **F**, you might have thought of $(g + 1)^2$ as equivalent to the alternate expression $g^2 + 1^2$. But, when $g = 2$, the original has the value $(2 + 1)^2 = (3)^2 = 9$, while the alternate has the value $2^2 + 1^2 = 5$.

Question 137. The correct answer is D. Company A sells at \$15 for 60 pens, which is $\frac{\$15}{60}$ per pen. That reduces to $\frac{\$1}{4}$, or \$0.25 per pen. Company B sells at \$8 for 40 pens, which is $\frac{\$8}{40} = \frac{\$1}{5} = \$0.20$ per pen. Company B is a nickel cheaper.

If you chose **A**, you possibly found the minimum cost correctly but identified it with the wrong company. Choice **C** is the average for Company A.

Question 138. The correct answer is H. The Pythagorean theorem applies here, so that $a^2 + 8^2 = 10^2$, where a is the distance from the base of the ladder to the wall, in feet. That means $a^2 = 10^2 - 8^2 = 36$ and then $a = 6$.

K comes from adding $10^2 + 8^2$, which is 164. If you had noticed that the longest side of the triangle is 10 feet long, and $\sqrt{164}$ is more than 10, you could have eliminated this answer choice. **F** (2 feet) cannot be true. If it were, the path along the two shorter sides of the triangle (ground and wall) would be the same length as a path along the longest side of the triangle (ladder). This is impossible because the shortest path between points must go along a straight line, not over and then up.

Question 139. The correct answer is F. Each 1,000 gallons of water cost $2.50, so g of these "1,000 gallons of water" cost $g \bullet (\$2.50)$. On top of this, there is a $16 charge that is added for trash pickup. The result is $\$2.50g + \$16$.

Answer choice **K** represents a cost of $2.50 per gallon rather than per 1,000 gallons.

Question 140. The correct answer is D. The left side of the equation, $2(x + 4)$, can be written as $2x + 8$. Then, the equation becomes $2x + 8 = 5x - 7$. One way to solve this is to first add 7 to both sides (resulting in $2x + 15 = 5x$) and then subtracting $2x$ from both sides (resulting in $15 = 3x$). Dividing both sides by 3 gives the result $5 = x$.

It's a good idea to check this answer: does $2(5 + 4)$ equal $5(5) - 7$? The left simplifies to $2(9)$, which is 18. The right side simplifies to $25 - 7$, which is also 18. Yes!

Some students will write $2(x + 4)$ as $2x + 4$, but it isn't. That mistake would lead to answer choice **C**. Note that $2(x + 4)$ is two $(x + 4)$s added together, or $x + 4 + x + 4$.

Question 141. The correct answer is H. BF is a transversal between the two parallel lines. Therefore, because $\angle CBF$ and $\angle BFE$ are alternate interior angles, their measures are equal, and so $f°$ in the figure below is 35°. You can also see that ΔBEF is isosceles, which makes the base angles equal in measure, so $e°$ is also 35°. The angle the problem asks you to find is the supplement of $\angle BEF$, which makes its measure $180° - 35°$, or 145°.

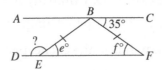

Question 142. The correct answer is B. The least common denominator is the smallest positive multiple of 2, 3, 9, and 15. These four numbers can be written in prime-power form as 2, 3, 3^2, and $3 \bullet 5$. The least common denominator must have all of these as factors. The number $2 \bullet 3^2 \bullet 5$ is divisible by 2, by 3, by 3^2, and by $3 \bullet 5$, and it has no extra prime factors so it is the smallest of all the common multiples. $2 \bullet 3^2 \bullet 5 = 2 \bullet 9 \bullet 5 = 10 \bullet 9 = 90$.

The most common incorrect answer is **A**, which is divisible by 15, by 9, and by 3, but not by 2.

Question 143. The correct answer is H. $3x(x^2y + 2xy^2) = 3x \cdot x^2y + 3x \cdot 2xy^2 = 3x^3y + 6x^2y^2$.

F is $3(x^2y + 2xy^2)$, dropping the x multiplier in $3x$. If you chose **G**, you probably correctly multiplied $3x$ and x^2y but forgot to multiply $3x$ by $2xy^2$.

Question 144. **The correct answer is D.** The 10 notebooks would cost 9($2.50), which is $22.50. The average price for one of the 10 notebooks would be $\frac{\$22.50}{10}$, which is $2.25.

$2.50 $2.50 $2.50 $2.50 $2.50 $2.50 $2.50 $2.50 $2.50 free

If you chose **B**, you may not have understood that notebook 10 was free, so you only had to pay for 9 notebooks.

Question 145. **The correct answer is K.** $(3x + 1)^2 = (3x + 1)(3x + 1)$ because that's what the power 2 means. There are several methods for continuing from this point, such as FOIL (first, outer, inner, last). The solution shown below uses the distributive property.

$$(3x+1)(3x+1) = 3x(3x+1) + 1(3x+1) = 3x(3x) + 3x(1) + 3x + 1 = 9x^2 + 6x + 1$$

It is fairly common for students to think that $(3x + 1)^2$ and $(3x)^2 + (1)^2$ are equivalent, but they're not. If you chose **H**, you may have made this mistake. Understanding why this is a mistake can help you understand other parts of algebra and not make similar mistakes. If you let $x = 1$, then $(3x + 1)^2 = 16$ but $(3x)^2 + (1)^2 = 10$. It makes a difference whether you add first and then square, or whether you square first and then add.

Question 146. **The correct answer is B.** Here's one where drawing a picture might help you avoid some mistakes.

$$\underset{-5 \qquad\quad 0 \qquad\qquad\qquad\qquad\qquad 17}{\text{+++++++++++++++++++++++++++++++++++++++}}$$

The points with coordinates −5 and 17 are 22 units apart. If you go up by 11 units from −5, you should get to the same place as if you go down by 11 units from 17. This is 6.

If you chose C, you may have calculated $\frac{17-(-5)}{2}$. This represents the distance from the midpoint to an endpoint. This expression is very similar to the average of the two coordinates, $\frac{17+(-5)}{2}$ (notice the plus sign), which is the coordinate of the midpoint. That's why drawing a picture is a good idea.

Question 147. **The correct answer is G.**

$$3\tfrac{3}{5} = x + 2\tfrac{2}{3} \Rightarrow x = 3\tfrac{3}{5} - 2\tfrac{2}{3} = (3-2) + \left(\tfrac{3}{5} - \tfrac{2}{3}\right) = 1 + \left(\tfrac{9}{15} - \tfrac{10}{15}\right) = 1 + \left(-\tfrac{1}{15}\right) = \tfrac{14}{15}.$$

The most common wrong answer is **H**, which happens when someone tries to reduce $\left(\tfrac{3}{5} - \tfrac{2}{3}\right)$ to $\frac{(3-2)}{(5-3)}$.

MATHEMATICS • EXPLANATORY ANSWERS

Question 148. The correct answer is A. Although you could deduce some things from the way the equations are given, you might be more comfortable with the equations in slope-intercept form. The system would then be:

$$y = -\frac{2}{3}x + \frac{8}{3}$$
$$y = \frac{2}{3}x + \frac{8}{3}$$

The slopes of the two lines are different (the first is $\frac{2}{3}$, the second $-\frac{2}{3}$). That, by itself, means **A** is correct. The graph below shows what this system looks like. You can see that none of the other answer choices is correct.

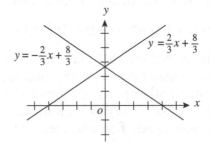

Question 149. The correct answer is K. Properties of exponents make this straightforward to solve. All of the *bases* (2, 4, and 8) are powers of 2. The equation can be rewritten as $(2^x)(2^2) = (2^3)^3$. Properties of exponents lead to the equation $2^{x+2} = 2^{3\cdot3}$, which simplifies to $2^{x+2} = 2^9$. If the two exponents are the same, then the left and right sides are equal. This happens when $x + 2 = 9$, which is when $x = 7$.

You can check this answer (or whatever answer you got). When $x = 7$, the left side of the equation is $(2^7)(4)$, which simplifies to $(128)(4)$, and then to 512. The right side is 8^3, which is also 512.

The most common wrong answer for this problem is **G**, which happens when people combine $(2^x)(4)$ and get (8^x). These are not equivalent (check $x = 2$). Another common mistake is to write $(2^3)^3$ as 2^6, which leads to **H**.

Question 150. The correct answer is D. A rotation of 180° goes halfway around a circle. The graph below illustrates this rotation. Because it is halfway, it does not matter whether you rotate clockwise or counterclockwise.

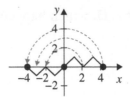

The most common incorrect answer is **B**, which is a reflection across the y-axis. Several of the points on this graph are correct for the rotation, but not all of them.

Question 151. The correct answer is E. To go from P to Q is 9 units. From Q to R is 6 units. From R to S is 9 units. From S back to P is 12 units. The total length is $9 + 6 + 9 + 12 = 36$ units.

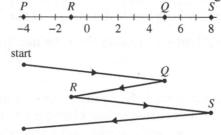

Question 152. The correct answer is J. The determinant $\begin{vmatrix} 2x & 3y \\ 5x & 4y \end{vmatrix}$ has the value $(2x)(4y) - (3y)(5x)$, which simplifies to $8xy - 15xy = -7xy$. When $x = -3$ and $y = 2$, the value of the expression is $-7(-3)(2) = 42$.

Another approach is to substitute $x = -3$ and $y = 2$ first, giving the determinant $\begin{vmatrix} -6 & 6 \\ -15 & 8 \end{vmatrix}$, which has the value $(-6)(8) - (6)(-15) = (-48) - (-90) = -48 + 90 = 42$.

If you got answer **G**, you probably made a mistake with a minus sign. If you got answers **F** or **K**, you probably used the second approach and made an error with a minus sign.

Question 153. The correct answer is C. Let the capacity of the larger bottle be B ounces. Then, the capacity of the smaller bottle is $\frac{1}{2}B$ ounces. The larger bottle starts with $\frac{2}{3}B$ ounces of catsup. The smaller bottle starts with $\frac{1}{3}\left(\frac{1}{2}B\right) = \frac{1}{6}B$ ounces of catsup. When this catsup is poured into the larger bottle (when you pour, be sure to get it all out of the smaller bottle), the larger bottle now contains $\frac{2}{3}B + \frac{1}{6}B$ ounces of catsup, which is $\frac{5}{6}B$ ounces of catsup. This means the bottle is $\frac{5}{6}$ full.

If you find it hard to follow the steps with the abstract "B ounces" for the larger bottle's capacity, try thinking of a particular size of bottle, say a 12-ounce bottle. Then the smaller bottle's capacity is 6 ounces. The larger bottle contains $\frac{2}{3}(12) = 8$ ounces of catsup. The smaller bottle contains $\frac{1}{3}(6)=2$ ounces of catsup. When poured together, the larger bottle would now contain 10 ounces of catsup, which is $\frac{10}{12}=\frac{5}{6}$ of its capacity.

The most common wrong answer is **D**. If one catsup bottle is $\frac{2}{3}$ full and another is $\frac{1}{3}$ full, then together they would be a whole bottle of catsup—if the bottles were the same size. Because the $\frac{1}{3}$ of the smaller bottle is smaller than the missing $\frac{1}{3}$ of the larger bottle, the larger bottle won't be full.

Question 154. **The correct answer is G.** In the given equation, $t = 10p + 5$, the 10 represents the number of minutes that the time changes when the number of problems increases by 1. That's the slope. So, Jeff is budgeting 10 minutes per problem. The 5 minutes for getting set up is not budgeted on a per-problem basis.

For 1 problem, the total time budgeted is $10(1) + 5 = 15$ minutes. This may lead you to believe that **F** is the correct answer, but consider an assignment with 2 problems. Using the given equation, that would be budgeted at $10(2) + 5 = 25$ minutes. Using **F**, it would be budgeted at 30 minutes. Some of the other answer choices could be true, but they do not have to be true. For example, Jeff could budget a 5-minute break after each problem, which would fit into the 10 minutes he budgets per problem. But, he would not have to schedule any breaks between problems, or he could schedule 2-minute breaks.

Question 155. **The correct answer is D.** Because Kaya drove 200 miles in 5 hours, she was averaging $\frac{200}{5}=40$ miles per hour. If she drove 10 miles per hour faster, that would be 50 miles per hour. To complete the 200 miles at 50 miles per hour would take a driving time of $\frac{200}{50} = 4$ hours. That's a savings of 1 hour.

The most common wrong answer was **E**, which is the number of hours the faster trip would take. That isn't what the question asks for.

Question 156. **The correct answer is B.** If $a = b$, then $|a| = |b|$. (This is a property of a *function*, that if you start with the same number then you will get the same result. Absolute value is a function.) This shows that **A** is false, and it also shows that **B** must be true.

You can eliminate **C** by checking $a = 2$ and $b = 1$. You can eliminate **D** and **E** by checking $a = -2$ and $b = 1$. The most common wrong answer is **D**.

Question 157. **The correct answer is J.** One way to solve this is to put the equation into slope-intercept form (solve for y). This can be accomplished as follows:

$14x - 11y + 16 = 0 => -11y = -14x - 16 => y = \frac{14}{11}x + \frac{16}{11}$. The slope is the coefficient of x, which is $\frac{14}{11}$. The most common errors are making a sign mistake (**G**) or getting the fraction upside down (**H**).

Question 158. **The correct answer is H.** $\triangle DFB$ and $\triangle EFB$ are congruent, which can be seen by using side-side-side congruence and the following steps. First, $DF \cong EF$ is given. Second, the triangles share a common side, FB, so certainly $FB \cong FB$. And, the third sides are congruent ($DB \cong EB$) because the length of the third side in each triangle is determined from the other two sides by the Pythagorean theorem—the calculation is the same in both cases.

Because $\triangle DFB$ and $\triangle CFB$ are congruent, $\angle DFB$ is congruent to $\angle EFB$. Then, the three angles within $\triangle DFB$ are a right angle, $\angle x$, and an angle congruent to $\angle y$. That means that the measures of the angles add up to 180°, and so the measures of $\angle x$ and $\angle y$ add up to 90°. It really didn't matter that the given angle at A measured 50°. You can't tell the measure of $\angle x$ or $\angle y$, but you can find the sum.

Question 159. **The correct answer is E.** $(-2x^5y^2)^4 = (-2)^4(x^5)^4(y^2)^4 = 16x^{5 \cdot 4}y^{2 \cdot 4} = 16x^{20}y^8$

If you chose **D**, you likely wrote $(x^5)^4$ as x^{5+4} and $(y^2)^4$ as y^{2+4}. If you chose **A**, you likely multiplied exponents properly but wrote $(-2)^4$ as -16 when it is really $(-2)(-2)(-2)(-2) = +16$.

Question 160. **The correct answer is E.** Because the only real numbers that satisfy $a^2 = 49$ are 7 and −7, and the only real numbers that satisfy $b^2 = 64$ are 8 and −8, the only possibilities for $a + b$ are $7 + 8$, $7 + (-8)$, $-7 + 8$, and $-7 + (-8)$. These possibilities are 15, −1, 1, and −15. The only answer choice left is 113.

Question 161. **The correct answer is C.** The average yards gained per running play in 1998 is the total number of yards in 1998 divided by the number of plays in 1998. This is equal to

$$\frac{1417 \text{ yards in 1998}}{394 \text{ running plays in 1998}} \approx 3.5964 \text{ or } 3.6 \text{ when rounded to the nearest tenth.}$$

If you picked **A**, you may have used the values from 1997 instead of 1998. If you picked **B**, you may have used the 1,028 yards gained in 1997 and divided by the 378 running plays in 1999. If you picked **D**, you may have used the 1,920 yards gained from 1999 and divided by the 394 running plays in 1998. If you picked **E**, you may have used the values from 1999 instead of 1998.

Question 162. **The correct answer is H.** This geometric figure has six sides, but we are only given the length of four of those sides. A way to find the perimeter is to move two of the sides to form a rectangle, which will have the same perimeter.

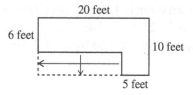

The bottom of the new rectangle is 20 feet long, and the left side is 10 feet long. So, the perimeter can be found by adding lengths (going clockwise), $20 + 10 + 20 + 10 = 60$ feet, or using the perimeter formula $P = 2A + 2B$ resulting in $2(20) + 2(10) = 60$ feet.

An alternate method is to deduce that the unknown vertical length is 4 feet by finding the difference between the right and left lengths: $10 - 6 = 4$ feet. The same process can be repeated to find the unknown horizontal length: $20 - 5 = 15$ feet. Then the perimeter (going clockwise) is $20 + 10 + 5 + 4 + 15 + 6 = 60$ feet.

If you picked **F**, you added the given lengths but may have forgotten to calculate and add the unknown lengths. If you picked **G**, you may have divided the polygon into two rectangles with one having sides of 6 and 20 feet and then stopped before adding the remaining lengths. If you picked **J**, you may have found the area of the figure rather than its perimeter. If you picked **K**, you may have extended the sides to form the 10 by 20 feet rectangle and mistakenly used the area formula rather than the perimeter formula.

Question 163. The correct answer is B. When graphing an inequality on a number line the $<$ and $>$ signs indicate the value is marked with an open circle while the $\leq$ and $\geq$ signs indicate the value is marked with a closed circle. The compound inequality can be understood as two inequalities: $-2 \leq x$ AND $x < 3$. The AND of the compound inequality limits the range to the overlap of values.

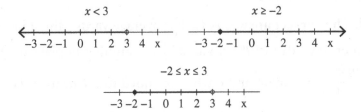

If you picked **A**, you may have identified that the closed circle on -2 is correctly represented on the left side of the inequality and stopped without evaluating the right side of the inequality. If you picked **C**, you may have identified the open circle on 3 is correctly represented on the right side of the inequality and stopped without evaluating the left side of the inequality. If you picked **D**, you may have dropped the negative in front of the -2 value in the number line and mistakenly used a $\leq$ sign for an open circle at 3. If you picked **E**, you may have identified the values from the number line but reversed their position in the inequality without reversing the signs.

Question 164. The correct answer is J. To resolve the expression, we need to substitute the x and y values, resulting in $3 \cdot 2^{4+(-1)}$. Using the proper order of operations, the exponent values are added before being applied to the base of 2, resulting in $3 \cdot 2^3$ becoming $3 \cdot 8 = 24$

If you picked **F**, you may have done an incorrect order of operation by multiplying $3 \cdot 2$ before applying the exponent. If you picked **G**, you may have dropped the negative when substituting the y and had an exponent of 5. If you picked **H**, you may have had a calculator entry error. Rather than the sum of x and y being in the exponent, the y was incorrectly applied at the end of the expression forming $3 \cdot 2^x + y$. If you picked **K**, you may have multiplied the quantity of $(x + y)$ rather than making it an exponent, resulting in $3 \cdot 2 \cdot (4 + (-1)) = 3 \cdot 2 \cdot 3 = 18$.

Question 165. **The correct answer is D.** For the equation $ab = 8$ where a and b are integers, the values of a and b must be positive or negative factors of 8, which are 1, 2, 4, 8 and $-1, -2, -4, -8$. If $a = -6$, the value of b would need to be $-1\frac{1}{3}$, which is not an integer value and thus is NOT a possible solution.

If you picked **A**, you may have missed the NOT portion of the question and, instead, found a value that is possible. If you picked **B**, you may have forgotten to include 1 and 8 as factors of 8. If you picked **C** or **E**, you may not have realized that the value of a can be negative if the value of b is also a negative, thus making both answer choices possible values.

Question 166. **The correct answer is J.** The volume of a cube is s^3 where s is the length of one of the sides. This would mean the volume is $4^3 = 64$.

If you picked **F**, you may have multiplied $4 \cdot 3$ rather than making 3 an exponent, or you may have used $L + W + H$ as the formula for volume instead of $L \cdot W \cdot H$. If you picked **G**, you may have calculated the area of a square rather than the volume of a cube. If you picked **H**, you may have attempted to use the perimeter formula $P = 2(A) + 2(B)$ but applied it in 3 dimensions by adding $3(A) + 3(B) = 3(4) + 3(4) = 24$. If you picked **K**, you may have found the surface area by multiplying the 6 faces of the cube times the area of a single face: $6(4 \cdot 4)$.

Question 167. **The correct answer is B.** The community center had 70 tables at $40 each and 50 tables at $25 each. Renting all the small tables would amount to $50 \cdot \$25 = \$1,250$ and renting L number of large tables at $40 each would amount to $40 \cdot L$. Therefore, the sum of large and small tables would be $40L + 1,250$. If you picked **A**, you may not have calculated the rental cost of the tables for each size and only calculated the number of tables rented. If you picked **C**, you may have applied the $40 rental cost to both the large and small tables. If you picked **D**, you may have added the costs of the two tables together and then multiplied by the L number of large tables rented. If you picked **E**, you may have calculated what the total cost of renting all large and small tables would be and then applied that value to the variable L.

Question 168. **The correct answer is G.** Because the base is a straight line, these two angle measures are supplementary and add up to $180°$. This can be represented as $7x° + 3x° = 180°$. Solving for x gives $10x° = 180°$, then $x° = 18°$. This makes $\angle ABD = 7(18°) = 126°$.

If you picked **F**, you may have used $360°$ as the measure of the straight line rather than $180°$. If you picked **H**, you may have used the value of $360°$ for the straight line. Then when you solved for x you may have plugged that value in for $\angle CBD = 3x°$. If you picked **J**, you solved for x correctly but may have plugged that value in for $\angle CBD = 3x°$. If you picked **K**, you may have just stopped as soon as you found the value of x rather than plugging the value of x into the given angle measure of $\angle ABD$.

Question 169. **The correct answer is E.** In probability, the sum of all possible events is equal to 100% or simply 1.00. The probability of a single event cannot be more than 1; therefore, if any of the answer choices are above 1, they can NOT be a possible value. $\frac{34}{31} \approx 1.097$ and is greater than 1, so it is NOT a possible value. Answer choices **A–D** are all less than or equal to 1, so they are possible probability values.

Question 170. **The correct answer is K.** The rate of toy sales increasing slowly would imply that the slope was positive but with a shallow incline. As the rate increased, the slope would also increase, and the incline would become steep. Finally, the rate of sales decreasing does not imply that the slope becomes negative; rather, it indicates the steep slope is becoming shallow because sales are still occurring but at a reduced rate. The graph that matches these conditions has the first and last segment with a shallow incline and a middle segment with a steep incline.

If you picked **F**, you may have missed the initial shallow incline. If you picked **G**, you may have missed the decreased rate at the end. If you picked **H**, you selected the graph in which the rate was constant and had no rate changes. If you picked **J**, you may have rotated the graph and did the time increasing slowly, rapidly increasing, and slowly increasing rather than increasing sales.

Question 171. **The correct answer is E.** To determine the minimum number of cans needed to varnish the floor, the total area of the floor that needs varnish should be determined, which is $60 \cdot 80 = 4800$ *square feet*. One can of varnish can cover 250 *square feet*. Then divide the total area by the area per can to determine the number of cans needed $\frac{4800 \ sq.ft.}{\frac{250 \ sq.ft.}{1 \ can}} = 19.2 \ cans$. To complete the varnish project, 20 cans would be needed.

If you picked **A**, you may have added the length and width of the floor to determine its area and found that $60 + 80 = 140$, which is less than 250, so 1 can would cover the floor. If you picked **D**, you may have rounded the 19.2 down to 19, forgetting to add an extra can for the area 19 cans won't cover.

Question 172. **The correct answer is F.** The given scale for the drawing is $\frac{1}{4}$ *inch* $= 1$ *foot*. The given width of the floor is 12 feet. One way to solve this is to multiply our scale conversion by 12 to get $12\left(\frac{1}{4} \ inch\right) = 12(1 \ foot)$, which equals 3 *inches* $= 12$ *feet*. The length of the floor is 14, resulting in $14\left(\frac{1}{4}\ inch\right) = 14(1\ foot)$, which is $3\frac{1}{2}\ inches = 14\ feet$. Therefore, a 12 by 14-foot room would scale to a 3 by $3\frac{1}{2}$ inch room.

We could also solve this problem by setting up a proportion:

$$\frac{\frac{1}{4}\ inch}{1\ foot} = \frac{x\ inches}{12\ feet} \Rightarrow x = 3$$

$$\frac{\frac{1}{4}\ inch}{1\ foot} = \frac{y\ inches}{14\ feet} \Rightarrow y = 3\frac{1}{2}$$

If you picked **G,** you may have taken the length of the room and divided by the scale value of $\frac{1}{4}$ instead of multiplying, and then you may have attempted to convert from inches to feet by dividing by 12. If you picked **H,** you may have mistakenly used a scale value of $\frac{1}{2}$ instead of $\frac{1}{4}$. If you picked **J,** you may have converted the feet into inches by multiplying by 12 and then multiplied by $\frac{1}{4}$ for the scale conversion. If you picked **K,** you may have taken the length of the room and divided by the scale value of $\frac{1}{4}$ instead of multiplying.

Question 173. The correct answer is E. Since each surveyed person prefers only 1 juice each, the sum of the percentages must equal 100%. The sum of the given percentages that prefer cranberry, orange, and grapefruit is 20% + 40% + 20% = 80%. To find the students that prefer tomato juice calculate 100% − 80% = 20%. Since it is given that 250 students prefer tomato juice, we can create an equation to find the total number surveyed: 20% · x = 250 where x is the total number surveyed. Thus, $x = \frac{250}{20\%} \Rightarrow 1250$ students.

If you picked **A,** you may have added the percentages of the other juices to the number of students preferring tomato juice: 250 + 20 + 40 + 20. If you picked **B,** you may have just doubled the number that preferred tomato juice. If you picked **C,** you may have divided by the percent of students preferring orange juice $x = \frac{250}{40\%} \Rightarrow 625$. If you picked **D,** you may have divided by 25% or $\frac{1}{4}$, assuming all 4 options have an equal percentage, resulting in $x = \frac{250}{\frac{1}{4}} \Rightarrow 1,000$.

Question 174. The correct answer is H. The circumference of the tire is also the distance it will travel per revolution, thus 1 revolution = 50 inches. To properly solve, we must use the common unit measure of inches instead of feet. Then, to find the number of revolutions to travel 3600 inches, we could set up the proportion $\frac{50\ inches}{1\ revolution} = \frac{3600\ inches}{x\ revolutions}$ then cross-multiply and solve: $x \cdot 50 = 3600 \Rightarrow x = \frac{3600}{50} \Rightarrow x = 72$

It is also possible to set it up as a rate equation of $D = R \cdot T$ where R would be the rate of distance per 1 revolution, T is the number of times it revolves, and D is the distance: $50 \cdot T = 3600 \Rightarrow T = \frac{3600}{50} \Rightarrow T = 72$.

If you picked **F**, you may have divided the distance in feet by the circumference in inches $\frac{300}{50} = 6$. If you picked **G**, you may have assumed that distance traveled to be the diameter of $\frac{50}{\pi}$ and used the travel distance in feet to get $300 \div \frac{50}{\pi} \approx 18$. If you picked **J**, you may have assumed that the circumference was 1 foot and solved $\frac{300 \, feet}{1 \, foot} = 300$. If you picked **K**, you may have calculated 72 correctly but then multiplied by 12, thinking a conversion to inches was needed: $\frac{3600}{50} \cdot 12 = 864$.

Question 175. The correct answer is A. To simplify this expression, use the distributive property to eliminate the negative: $(4x^2 - 3x + 7) - (-1 + 5x + 2x^2) = (4x^2 - 3x + 7) + [(-1)(-1) + (-1)(5x) + (-1)(2x^2)] = 4x^2 - 3x + 7 + 1 + (-5x) + (-2x^2)$. Then combine like terms to obtain $2x^2 - 8x + 8$.

If you picked **B**, you may have incorrectly combined the $-3x$ and $5x$ values by either distributing the -1 to get $-5x$ but still subtracting from $-3x$, resulting in $-3x - (-5x)$ or by not correctly distributing the -1 to the $5x$. If you picked **C**, you may have only applied the distribution of -1 to the $2x^2$ value and when you combined like terms you added the exponents together. If you picked **D**, you may have only applied the distribution of -1 to the $5x$ value. If you picked **E**, you may have only applied the distribution of -1 to the $5x$ value and when you combined like terms, you added the exponents together.

Question 176. The correct answer is H. If Latoya's total amount of money was x, then she and her brother would each have $\frac{1}{2}x$ after she split the money. When Latoya gave her brother $1.00, that leaves her with $\frac{1}{2}x - 1$ and her brother with $\frac{1}{2}x + 1$. Since she has exactly enough for a movie which costs $5.00, the resulting equation would be $\frac{1}{2}x - 1 = 5$ which resolves to $\frac{1}{2}x = 6 \Rightarrow x = \$12$.

If you picked **F**, you may have just accounted for the $5 ticket price and added the ticket price for Latoya and her brother without adding the cost of the snacks. If you picked **G**, you may have determined that a movie and snack was $6 but subtracted the extra dollar that Latoya gave her brother for the video game, making the total $6 + $6 - $1 = $11. If you picked **J**, you may have determined that a movie and snack was $6 but added the extra dollar that Latoya gave her brother for the video game, making the total $6 + $6 + $1 = $13. If you picked **K**, you may have determined that a movie and snack was $6 but added the extra dollar Latoya gave her brother and doubled that value because it was originally split between them: $2(\$6 + \$1) = \$14.00$.

Question 177. The correct answer is B. The spelling test consisted of 20 words and each word is either spelled correctly or it isn't. Therefore, all possible scores must be integer values out of 20.

MATHEMATICS • EXPLANATORY ANSWERS

Score	Percent
20/20	100%
19/20	95%
18/20	90%
17/20	85%
16/20	80%
15/20	75%

Of the possible percentages, only **B** appears in the list. If you picked **A, C, D,** or **E,** you may not have understood that possible scores needed to be integers.

Question 178. **The correct answer is F.** A geometric sequence is defined as having a common ratio, which is found with $\frac{a_{n+1}}{a_n}$ where a_n and a_{n+1} represent consecutive values in the sequence. This sequence has a ratio of $\frac{-1.5}{0.375} = -4$. The first 5 terms are given, so to find the 6th term we multiple the 5th term times the common ratio: $96 \cdot -4 = -384$.

Another approach relies on accurately remembering the following formula for the nth term in a geometric sequence: $a_n = a_1 * r^{(n-1)}$, where a_1 is the first term in the series, r is the common ratio, and n is the number of terms. Plugging in known values we get $a_n = a_1 \cdot r^{(n-1)} \Rightarrow 0.375 \cdot (-4)^{(6-1)} \Rightarrow 0.375 \cdot (-4)^{(5)} \Rightarrow 0.375 \cdot -1024 = -384$.

If you picked **G,** you may have calculated a common difference rather than a common ratio and used $6 - (-24) = 30$ as your common difference. Then you may have added that common difference to 96 like an arithmetic sequence but maintained the pattern of positive and negative values. If you picked **H,** you may have calculated a common difference rather than a common ratio and used $-24 - 6 = -30$ for the common difference. Then you may have added that common difference to 96 like an arithmetic sequence but maintained the pattern of positive and negative values. If you picked **J,** you may have calculated a common difference rather than a common ratio and used $6 - (-24) = 30$ as the common difference, then added that common difference to 96 like an arithmetic sequence. If you picked **K,** you may have forgotten the negative sign in the common ratio when doing your calculation.

Question 179. **The correct answer is A.** To find the expanded form of $(2x - 3y)^2$, we could use the square binomial formula: $(a + b)^2 = a^2 + 2ab + b^2$. Using this formula, we would have $(2x - 3y)^2 = (2x)^2 + 2(2x)(-3y) + (-3y)^2 = 4x^2 - 12xy + 9y^2$.

Another approach would be to perform binomial multiplication using the FOIL method of adding the products of the First, Outer, Inner, and Last terms. The expression $(2x - 3y)^2$ can be (rewritten as $(2x - 3y) \cdot (2x - 3y)$. By using the FOIL method, we would get $(2x)(2x) + (2x)(-3y) + (-3y)(2x) + (-3y)(-3y) = 4x^2 - 6xy - 6xy + 9y^2 = 4x^2 - 12xy + 9y^2$.

If you picked **B,** you may have calculated $2(a + b)$ for the middle value, improperly combining unlike terms. If you picked **C,** you may have calculated $(2x)^2 - (3y)^2$. If you picked **D,** you may have calculated $(2x)^2 + (-3y)^2$. If you picked **E,** you may have multiplied by 2 rather than squaring.

Question 180. The correct answer is J. Because $\angle ABD$ and $\angle CBE$ are defined as congruent and the two triangles have a common right angle, $\triangle ABD$ and $\triangle CBE$ are similar because of the angle-angle similarity property. Because corresponding sides of similar triangles are proportional, we can solve for $\overline{CE}$ by setting up the proportion $\frac{6}{4} = \frac{x}{14}$. After cross-multiplication we get $4x = 84 \Rightarrow x = 21$.

If you picked **F,** you may have set up the proportion as $\frac{6}{14} = \frac{x}{4}$. If you picked **G,** you may have set up your proportion as $\frac{4}{6} = \frac{x}{14}$. If you picked **H,** you may have assumed that because $\overline{BC}$ was 10 more than $\overline{AB}$, that $\overline{CE}$ would be 10 more than $\overline{AD}$. If you picked **K,** you may have added the given values together without setting up a proportion.

Question 181. The correct answer is C. The minus sign can be rewritten as adding the binomial with a coefficient of -1, thus $7x - (x - 3)$ becomes $7x + (-1)(x - 3)$. Then we must distribute the -1 and combine the like terms: $7x + (-1)(x) + (-1)(-3) = 6 \Rightarrow 7x - x + 3 = 6 \Rightarrow 6x + 3 = 6$. Solving for x we get $6x = 3 \Rightarrow x = \frac{1}{2}$. If you picked **A,** you may have applied the -1 to the $7x$ term instead of the binomial, resulting in $-7x + x - 3 = 6$.

If you picked **B,** you may have subtracted $7x$ from both sides and combined the unlike terms to get $6 - 7x = -1$. Then by not distributing the negative to the binomial the result was $-x - 3 = -1$. If you picked **D,** you may have distributed the -1 to only the x and not to the -3. If you picked **E,** you may have gotten to $6x = 3$ but divided 6 by 3.

Question 182. The correct answer is G. The area of a triangle is $A = \frac{1}{2}b \cdot h$. The area and base of $\overline{XZ}$ are given values, resulting in $\frac{1}{2}8 \cdot h = 32$. Solving for the altitude, or height, we get $4h = 32 \Rightarrow h = 8$.

If you picked **F** or **H,** you may have assumed the height was part of a 6–8–10 right triangle. If you picked **J,** you may have set up the area of the triangle as $b \cdot h$. If you picked **K,** you may have multiplied the area by $\frac{1}{2}$ rather than the $b \cdot h$.

Question 183. The correct answer is D. To evaluate the function for $f(-10)$ plug in -10 into each x variable in the $f(x)$ function: $f(-10) = 2(-10)^2 - 5(-10) + 7 = 2(100) + 50 + 7 = 200 + 57 = 257$.

If you picked **A,** you may have incorrectly calculated $(-10)^2$ as -100 and dropped the negative for the middle term resulting in $-200 - 50 + 7$. If you picked **B,** you may have incorrectly calculated $(-10)^2$ as -100 resulting in $-200 + 50 + 7$. If you picked **C,** you may have dropped the negative for the middle term resulting in $200 - 50 + 7$. If you picked **E**, you may have squared the entire first term: $(2x)^2 = 400$.

Question 184. The correct answer is **J**. The first 200 bars sold would earn $200 \cdot (\$0.40) = \$80$. The next 300 bars sold would earn $300 \cdot (\$0.50) = \$150$. The number of remaining bars sold is unknown and could be represented as $x \cdot (\$0.60)$. Since the goal of the squad was $350.00, the equation can be expressed as $\$80 + \$150 + \$0.60x = \$350.00$, which simplifies to $\$0.60x = 120 \Rightarrow x = 200$. The question asked for the total number of bars sold which would be $200 + 300 + 200 = 700$.

If you answered **F**, you may have assumed the squad received the full price of $1.00 per bar. If you picked **G**, you may have assumed all bars would receive $0.60 per bar and approximated $\$0.60x = \$350.00$. If you answered **H**, you may have applied the $0.50 amount received to the 200 bars and the 300 bars resulting in $\$0.50(500) + \$0.60x = 350.00$, which would give you $x = 166\frac{2}{3}$. When added to the initial 500 bars sold the total would approximately equal 667 bars. If you answered **K**, you may have assumed that all bars would receive $0.40 per bar and solved for $\$0.40x = \$350.00$.

Question 185. The correct answer is **E**. The phrase "at least" represents all possible values greater than or equal to the given value. Thus, the percent of students that are at least 16 would be students 16 and older. Adding the given percentages results in $26\% + 31\% + 9\% = 66\%$.

If you picked **A**, you added the percentages under 16. If you picked **B**, you added percentages over the age of 16. If you picked **C**, you assumed exactly half the students were at least 16. If you picked **D**, you added the percent of students that are "at most" 16, which would be 16 and under.

Question 186. The correct answer is **H**. This can be solved by converting words into math and interpreting "of" as multiply, "is" as equals, and "what" as a variable. This question can be expressed as $x \cdot \frac{2}{3} = \frac{1}{3}$ so that $x = \frac{1}{3} \cdot \frac{3}{2} \Rightarrow x = .5$ which is 50%.

If you picked **F**, you may have multiplied $\frac{1}{3} \cdot \frac{2}{3}$. If you picked **G**, you may have subtracted $\frac{2}{3} - \frac{1}{3}$. If you picked **J**, you may have calculated $\frac{2}{3}$ as a percent. If you picked **K**, you may have incorrectly simplified by calculating $\frac{2}{3} \div \frac{1}{3}$.

Question 187. The correct answer is **B**. To find the sale price of the coat, we need to calculate the original price minus the discount. Since the discount is $\frac{3}{4}$ off, we can find the discounted amount with $\$84 \cdot \frac{3}{4} = \$63.00$. Then by taking the original price minus the discount, we get $\$84.00 - \$63.00 = \$21.00$.

We can also solve this problem by considering how much of the original price we are paying. Since it is $\frac{3}{4}$ off, that means we would pay $\frac{1}{4}$ of the regular price. Multiplying $\frac{1}{4}$ times the original price results in the sale price: $84.00 \cdot \frac{1}{4} = \$21.00$.

If you picked **A**, you may have converted $\frac{3}{4}$ to be 75% but converted that into dollars and subtracted: $84 - 75 = 9$. If you picked **C**, you may have used $\frac{1}{2}$ instead of $\frac{3}{4}$. If you picked **D**, you may have found the amount taken off the original price, but not the sale price itself. If you picked **E**, you may have interpreted $\frac{3}{4}$ to mean $.75¢$ and calculated $84 - .75 = 83.25$.

Question 188. The correct answer is K. With the given ratios, the shapes would be a 2×2 square and a 1×3 rectangle:

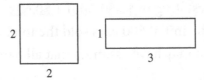

The area of a square is s^2, which results in an area of $2^2 = 4$. The area of the rectangle is $b \cdot h$, which results in an area of $1 \cdot 3 = 3$. Thus, the ratio of the square A to the area of rectangle B is 4:3.

If you picked **F**, you may have used the ratio of the widths. If you picked **G**, you may have given the square A side lengths with a ratio of 2:3 and rectangle B side lengths with a ratio of 2:1. This would give A an area of 6 and B an area of 2; thus, the areas would have a ratio of 3:1. If you picked **H**, you may have made rectangle B with sides of 3 and 2 giving it an area of 6, which would result in the ratio of B to A being 6:4 or 3:2. If you picked **J**, you may have made B into a square with a side length of 1 resulting in a ratio of areas of 4:1.

Question 189. The correct answer is A. A direct variation is defined as $y = k \cdot x$ where x and y are variables and k is a constant. An inverse variation is defined as $y = \frac{k}{x}$. Applying these properties, w^2 and x would be in the numerator as they vary directly while z^3 would be in the denominator as it varies inversely. If you picked **B–E**, you may not have understood the direct and inverse variation definitions.

Question 190. The correct answer is H. If the vertex of the isosceles triangle was x and each base angle is twice the vertex, each base angle can be represented as $2x$. The interior angle measure of a triangle is $180°$; thus, we can set up the equation $x + 2x + 2x = 180°$. Solving for x gives $5x = 180°$, then $x = 36$. Because the question asked for the base angle, which is $2x$, the result is $2 \cdot (36) = 72°$.

If you picked **F**, you may have stopped after solving for x. If you picked **G**, you may have made the figure an isosceles trapezoid and using $2x + 2x + x + x = 360$, solved for x, or you created an equilateral triangle. If you picked **J**, you may have made the figure an isosceles trapezoid and using $2x + 2x + x + x = 360$, solved for $2x$. If you picked **K**, you may have set the interior angles of a triangle to 360° and solved for $2x$.

Question 191. **The correct answer is E.** The given profit equation of $P = n^2 - 300n - 100{,}000$ is a quadratic in the form of $y = ax^2 + bx + c$. Not losing money can be understood as making 0 in profit or $P = 0$; thus, zero profit would occur at $y = 0$, or the x-intercepts. We can find the x-intercepts using the quadratic equation: $x = \dfrac{-b \pm \sqrt{b^2 - 4ac}}{2a} = \dfrac{300 \pm \sqrt{(-300)^2 - 4(1)(-100{,}000)}}{2(1)}$. The equation resolves into $\dfrac{300 \pm \sqrt{90{,}000 + 400{,}000}}{2}$, then $\dfrac{300 \pm \sqrt{490{,}000}}{2}$, then $\dfrac{300 \pm 700}{2}$. This results in two solutions, $\dfrac{300 - 700}{2}$ and $\dfrac{300 + 700}{2}$, which are -200 and 500. Since we can't sell negative items, the point of zero profit would be 500 items sold.

Another way to solve the equation would be to factor. The two factors of $-100{,}000$ whose sum adds to -300 are 200 and -500; thus, the factors of the quadratic are $(x + 200)(x - 500)$. The solutions to those factors, when setting each factor equal to 0, would result in $x = -200$ and $x = 500$. Since we can't sell negative items, the point of zero profit would be 500 items sold.

If you picked **A**, you may have found the x-coordinate of the vertex using $\dfrac{-b}{2a}$. If you picked **B**, you may have found the factor of $(x + 200)$ and interpreted that to mean an x-intercept of 200. If you picked **C**, you may have plugged in values and omitted the last term in the given equation: $(300)^2 - 300(300) = 0$. If you picked **D**, you may have divided $\dfrac{-100{,}00}{-300} = 333\frac{1}{3}$ and chosen the closest answer.

Question 192. **The correct answer is F.** Breaking even, or zero profit, is when *revenue − cost* = 0. This "break even" equation can be rewritten as *revenue = cost*. When two linear equations are set equal, the solution represents where the equations intersect.

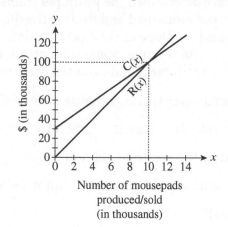

Number of mousepads
produced/sold
(in thousands)

Thus, the intersection is at 10,000 mousepads sold.

If you picked **G,** you may have selected the first number of mousepads on the x-axis scale when the company makes a profit. If you picked **H,** you may have chosen the x-value associated with the highest value on the function $C(x)$. If you picked **J,** you may have averaged the cost and revenue lines at zero mousepads sold. If you picked **K,** you may have assumed the breaking even was paying back the fixed cost of \$30,000.

Question 193. The correct answer is D. The production cost per mousepad is a rate, which can be understood as the slope of a linear equation. Since this rate is being added to a fixed cost, it would look like a linear equation $y = mx + b$ where m is the production cost per mousepad and b is the fixed cost. The value of b, or the fixed cost, can be found by setting the value of x mousepads equal to 0 on the $C(x)$ function. This results in a b value of \$30,000.

If you picked **A,** you may have found the fixed cost, or b value, on the $R(x)$ function. If you picked **B,** you may have found 1,000 to be the unit value of the x-axis and assumed the x-units to be the fixed cost. If you picked **C,** you may have determined the value of each tick mark on the y-axis but overlooked that you needed to multiply by 3 since there are 3 tick marks. If you picked **E,** you may have found the value on the y-axis of the break-even point.

Question 194. The correct answer is H. Using the $R(x)$ function, the price per mousepad can be found using any positive coordinates. Using the x value of 2,000 mousepads sold and a y value of \$20,000 and knowing that "per" means to divide, the price per mousepad would be $\frac{\$}{mousepad} \Rightarrow \frac{\$20,000}{2,000\ mouse\ pad}$, then simplify down to $\frac{\$10}{1\ mousepad}$.

Another way to solve this problem is knowing that the price is the y-axis and mousepads sold is the x-axis. Therefore, the $\frac{\$}{mousepad}$ is also the slope of the function. The slope equation $\frac{y_2 - y_1}{x_2 - x_1}$ can be applied using the origin and coordinate (2,000, 20,000) to get $\frac{20,000 - 0}{2,000 - 0} = 10$.

If you picked **F,** you may have determined the profit per mousepad by calculating the price per mousepad and the cost per mousepad and finding the difference: \$10 − \$7 = \$3. If you picked **G,** you may have found the slope of the $C(x)$ function. If you picked **J,** you may have used the x-value at the maximum revenue. Some students may have chosen **K** because they did not know how to set up the problem and assumed there was not enough information.

Question 195. The correct answer is E. A complete factorization would be finding the greatest common factor among all terms. The greatest common factor from the given expression is $2x$. To factor, each term is divided by the greatest common factor: $\frac{2x}{2x} + \frac{2xy}{2x} + \frac{6x^2y}{2x}$. That expression is simplified and then multiplied by the greatest common factor to get the complete factorization: $2x(1 + y + 3xy)$.

If you picked **A,** you may have made $\frac{2x}{2x} = 0$ rather than 1 when you simplified. If you picked **B,** you did not perform a complete factorization, as the terms in $2x + 2xy$ have a common factor. If you picked **C,** you may have subtracted the coefficients of 6 and 2 rather than dividing. If you picked **D,** you may have simplified the expression and stopped before multiplying by the greatest common factor.

Question 196. The correct answer is G. To find the equation of a line given two points, we first need to find the slope using the equation $\frac{y_2 - y_1}{x_2 - x_1}$. After plugging in the coordinates, the value becomes $\frac{-13 - 3}{-3 - 1}$, then $\frac{-16}{-4}$, and finally 4. Though this is enough to find the answer, we can also use the point-slope equation of $(y - y_1) = m(x - x_1)$ and substitute the slope and one coordinate point to get $(y - 3) = 4(x - 1)$, which becomes $y - 3 = 4x - 4$, then $-3 = 4x - y - 4$, then $1 = 4x - y$ which can be reordered as $4x - y = 1$. If you picked **F,** you may have tested coordinate values in the equation but only substituted the values of $(1, 3)$ for x and y. If you picked **H,** you may have found the slope using the sum of the y values over the sum of the x values rather than the difference. If you picked **J** or **K,** you may have tested coordinate values in the equation but only substituted the values of $(-3, -13)$ for x and y.

Question 197. The correct answer is B. Sketching a picture can be helpful.

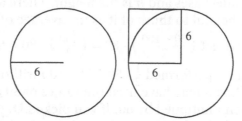

Since the area of the circle is 36π and the area of a circle is $A = \pi r^2$, the radius can be found using $36\pi = \pi r^2$, then $36 = r^2$, and finally $r = 6$. Constructing a square with side lengths that are also 6 will result in a $P = 4s \Rightarrow P = 4(6) \Rightarrow P = 24$.

If you picked **A,** you may have used the circumference formula $36\pi = 2\pi r$ rather than the area formula to find the radius and stopped after finding the radius value. If you picked **C,** you may have found the area of the square rather than the perimeter. If you picked **D,** you may have used the circumference formula $36\pi = 2\pi r$, thus $r = 18$, and then found the perimeter using $4 \cdot 18 = 72$. If you picked **E,** you may have used the circumference formula rather than the area formula to find the radius $36\pi = 2\pi r$ and found the area of the square: $18^2 = 324$.

Question 198. The correct answer is G. A way to solve for x is to use the elimination method. To perform the elimination method, we need to multiply the second equation by -1 so the $6y$ terms cancel:

$$3x + 6y = 52 \Rightarrow \qquad 3x + 6y = 52 \Rightarrow \qquad 3x + 6y = 52$$
$$x + 6y = 24 \qquad (-1)(x + 6y) = 24 \qquad \underline{-x - 6y = -24}$$
$$2x = 28 \Rightarrow \quad x = 14$$

Alternatively, the question can be solved using substitution. First, we would need to solve for one of the variables.

$$x + 6y = 24 \Rightarrow 6y = -x + 24 \Rightarrow y = -\frac{1}{6}x + 4$$

When the y is substituted into the other equation, we would get:

$$3x + 6\left(-\frac{1}{6}x + 4\right) = 52 \Rightarrow 3x - x + 24 = 52 \Rightarrow 2x + 24 = 52 \Rightarrow 2x = 28 \Rightarrow x = 14$$

If you picked **F,** you may have only subtracted the $6y$ when applying the elimination method resulting in $4x = 76 \Rightarrow x = 19$. If you picked **H,** you may have added $3x$ and x and used the second constant, creating $3x + x = 24$. If you picked **J,** you may have used the coefficient of y. If you picked **K,** you may have mistaken the $6y$ in both equations as the slope and assumed that the linear equations were parallel with different y-intercepts, thus no solution.

Question 199. The correct answer is C. The area of trapezoid $BGFC$ is given by $\left(\frac{b_1 + b_2}{2}\right) \cdot h$, where b_1 and b_2 are the parallel bases and h is the height. There are different ways to write this equation, but it can be helpful to think of it as the average of the bases times the height.

When substituting values, we get $\left(\frac{60 + 100}{2}\right) \cdot 80 = \left(\frac{160}{2}\right) \cdot 80 = 80 \cdot 80 = 6{,}400$.

If you picked **A,** you may have performed $\frac{1}{2} \cdot 80 \cdot 60 + 100$ without the parentheses around 60 and 100. If you picked **B,** you may have used the values of 80 and 100 as the bases and found their average and then multiplied by 60. If you picked **D,** you may have used the values of 60 and 80 as the bases and found their average and then multiplied by 100. If you picked **E,** you may have used the sum of the bases times the height.

Question 200. The correct answer is J. To find BC, first, we need to divide $BGFC$ into a rectangle and a triangle. Because $BGFC$ is a right trapezoid the perpendicular, $\overline{GF}$ can translate to the left, connect to B, and form a right triangle. The base of this new triangle would be CF minus BG: $100 - 60 = 40$ and the height is just the length of GF, which is 80. Using the height of 80 and a base of 40, $\overline{BC}$ can be found using the Pythagorean Theorem: $40^2 + 80^2 = c^2$. Solving for c would result in $1600 + 6400 = c^2 \Rightarrow 8000 = c^2 \Rightarrow \sqrt{8000} = c$

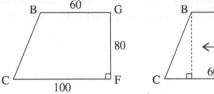
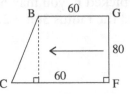
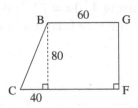

If you picked **F**, you may have averaged *BG* and *GF*. If you picked **G,** you may have performed $60^2 + 80^2 = c^2$. If you picked **H,** you may have performed $60 \cdot 80 = c^2$. If you picked **K,** you may have performed $80^2 + 100^2 = c^2$.

Question 201. The correct answer is A. Sketching the circle in *CFED* can be helpful. To keep all points of the circle inside the trapezoid, the circle will be limited by the shortest side length, which for *CFED* is the height of 80. The bottom and top points of the circle would be limited by and lie on $\overline{DE}$ and $\overline{CF}$. The distance between the bottom and top points of a circles is the diameter, thus the height of *CFED* is the diameter of the circle. Since the radius is $\frac{1}{2}$ of the diameter and the diameter of the circle is 80, the radius is 40.

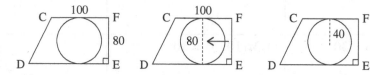

If you picked **B,** you may have assumed that the limit of the circle was the horizontal length of *CF* and divided 100 by 2 to find that radius. If you picked **C,** you may have placed the circle in *BGFC* and used *BG* as the limiting length and thus the diameter without dividing by 2 to find the radius. If you picked **D,** you may have correctly calculated the length of *DE* to be 140 and divided that by 2 to find the radius. If you picked **E,** you may have found the diameter of the circle and stopped short of the answer.

Question 202. The correct answer is J. All the given trigonometric functions use the 15° angle formed by the escape ramp and the ground. Using trigonometric properties of a right triangle and the given angle of 15°, the escape ramp's length is the hypotenuse. The distance vertically from the ground to the emergency exit is the opposite leg. The distance horizontally from the 15° angle to the point where the escape ramp and the ground meet is the adjacent leg. Because the given length is the hypotenuse and the unknown length is the opposite leg, the needed trig function is $\sin x$. The trig ratio for sine is $\sin x = \frac{opposite}{hypotenuse}$. Substituting the given values result in $\sin 15° = \frac{x}{35} \Rightarrow 0.259 = \frac{x}{35} \Rightarrow 35 \cdot 0.259 = x$, therefore $x = 9.065 \approx 9.1$.

If you picked **F,** you may have used the result of $x = \frac{\cos 15°}{35}$. If you picked **G,** you may have used the result of $x = \frac{\sin 15°}{35}$. If you picked **H,** you may have used the result of $x = \frac{\tan 15°}{35}$. If you picked **K,** you may have substituted the decimal approximation for $\tan 15°$ to get $0.268 = \frac{x}{35}$.

Question 203. The correct answer is B. It may be helpful to draw the diagram and test each value of *n* to see if each point is colored.

Another way to solve this problem is to understand the Least Common Multiple (LCM) of 10 and the answer choice values of *n*. If the LCM of two terms equals the product of the two terms, then each dot would be marked before returning to the starting point. If, however, the LCM of the two terms is less than the product of the terms, then the pattern will return to the starting point without hitting each dot.

	Product	LCM	Diagram
A:	$10 \cdot 2 = 20$	$LCM(10, 2) = 10$	
B:	$\mathbf{10 \cdot 3 = 30}$	$\mathbf{LCM(10, 3) = 30}$	
C:	$10 \cdot 4 = 40$	$LCM(10, 4) = 20$	
D:	$10 \cdot 5 = 50$	$LCM(10, 5) = 10$	
C:	$10 \cdot 6 = 60$	$LCM(10, 6) = 30$	

Question 204. The correct answer is H. When a positive real number greater than 1 is raised to an increasing power, the function value increases. For example, if a equals 4 and t is tested at values of 2 and 3, the results would be $4^2 = 16$ and $4^3 = 64$, demonstrating that as t increases, y increases real values of a greater than 1. However, if a is a fraction between 0 and 1 and is raised to increasing powers of t, y will decrease. For example, if a is $\frac{1}{4}$ and t is tested at a value of 2 and 3, the results would be $\frac{1^2}{4^2} = \frac{1}{16}$ and $\frac{1^3}{4^3} = \frac{1}{64}$. Therefore, if $0 < a < 1$, as t increases, a^t decreases. Because C is a positive constant, then the function $y = Ca^t$ will decrease as t increases.

If you picked **F, G,** or **K,** the inequality would include all real values of a greater than 1, and when testing $t = 2$ and $t = 3$, y increases. If you picked **J,** you may not have tested a value between 1 and 2, such as $\frac{3}{2}$, because when testing this value with $t = 2$ and $t = 3$, y increases.

Question 205. The correct answer is D. To find the distance between two points (x_1, y_1) and (x_2, y_2), we can use the distance formula, $d = \sqrt{(x_2 - x_1)^2 + (y_2 - y_1)^2}$. It follows that the distance between $P(-2, -1)$ and $Q(1, 3)$ would be $\sqrt{(1 - (-2))^2 + (3 - (-1))^2} = \sqrt{(3)^2 + (4)^2}$ $= \sqrt{9 + 16} = \sqrt{25} = 5$ coordinate units.

If you picked **A,** you may have added all of the values in the formula: $\sqrt{(3 + (-1))^2 + (1 + (-2))^2}$ $= \sqrt{(2)^2 + (-1)^2} = \sqrt{4 + 1} = \sqrt{5}$. If you picked **B,** you may have forgotten to square the differences: $\sqrt{(1 - (-2)) + (3 - (-1))} = \sqrt{3 + 4} = \sqrt{7}$. If you picked **C,** you may have switched the plus and minus signs in the formula and not used the square root: $(3 + (-1)) - (1 + (-2))$ $= 2 - (-1) = 3$. If you picked **E,** you may have just found the difference between the x and y coordinates and added those values without taking the square root: $(1 - (-2)) + (3 - (-1)) =$ $(1 + 2) + (3 + 1) = 3 + 4 = 7$

Question 206. The correct answer is F. For t seconds Sula was jogging at a rate of 2 meters per second and Jean was jogging at a rate of 2.4 meter per second. Distance can be calculated by multiplying the rate times the time: $D = R \cdot T$. Therefore, after t seconds Sula has jogged a distance of $2 \cdot t$ and Jean has jogged a distance of $2.4 \cdot t$. Because Sula jogs 10 meters ahead, she had a starting distance of $+10$. Thus, Sula's distance would be $2t + 10$. The point at which Jean catches up to Sula is the point of intersection of the two distances, which is when the two equations are equal: $2t + 10 = 2.4t$.

If you picked **G,** you may have subtracted the 10 to take away Sula's head start. If you picked **H,** you may have added 10 to the wrong side of the equation, and then attempted to divide that side by Jean's rate. If you picked **J,** you may have attempted to find the amount of time it took Sula to run the 10 meters ahead. If you picked **K,** you may have assumed that Sula stood still while Jean caught up to the 10-meter head start.

Question 207. The correct answer is D. To solve for a system of inequalities, first isolate the x in each inequality. The first equation is already isolated: $x \le 6$. The second inequality would become $4 + 2x \ge 0 \Rightarrow 2x \ge -4 \Rightarrow x \ge -\frac{4}{2} \Rightarrow x \ge -2$. The solution of inequalities represents the overlap, thus $-2 \le x \le 6$. Another way to combine the inequalities is to express them as overlapping number lines.

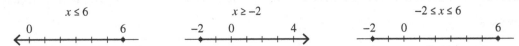

If you picked **A,** you may have solved for the second inequality and stopped short of the answer. If you picked **B,** you may have flipped the direction of the inequality when isolating the x in the second inequality and thought that the solution for $x \le -2$ and $x \le 6$ would be $x \le 6$. If you picked **C,** you may have multiplied by 2 rather than dividing by 2 when isolating x in the second inequality. If you picked **E,** you may have dropped your negative sign when solving the second inequality.

Question 208. The correct answer is K. To find how many of the 120 seniors were NOT enrolled in sociology or drawing, we must first know how many were in each subject only and how many were in both. Because the 55 students in sociology include those that are in both sociology and drawing, we must subtract the 20 seniors enrolled in both classes to determine how many were in sociology only: $55 - 20 = 35$ in sociology only. The same process would be used to determine the number in drawing only: $40 - 20 = 20$ in drawing only. Adding the seniors in drawing only, the seniors in sociology only, and the overlap of seniors in both, the total is $35 + 20 + 20 = 75$ seniors.

These values can also be understood by constructing a Venn Diagram.

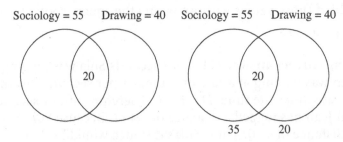

The total number of seniors at Brookfield High School is 120, so the number of seniors NOT in either sociology or drawing would be $120 - 75 = 45$.

If you picked **F,** you may have added the given number of students in sociology, drawing, and both and subtracted those values from 120. If you picked **G,** you may have found the difference between 55 and 40. If you picked **H,** you may have found the number of students in drawing class only and stopped short of the answer. If you picked **J,** you may have found the number of students in sociology class only and stopped short of the answer.

Question 209. The correct answer is C. A perpendicular slope is defined as the negative reciprocal of the slope of the intersecting line. Because the given line has a slope of 3, the slope of the perpendicular line would be the negative reciprocal of 3, which is $-\frac{1}{3}$.

If you picked **A,** you only applied the negative and did not take the reciprocal. If you picked **B,** you may have multiplied the given slope and its perpendicular slope. If you picked **D,** you found the reciprocal without applying the negative. If you picked **E,** you may have misread the question and found the parallel slope.

Question 210. The correct answer is J. A formula for finding the midpoint (x_m, y_m) for points with coordinates (x_1, y_1) and (x_2, y_2) can be expressed as $x_m = \frac{x_1 + x_2}{2}$ and $y_m = \frac{y_1 + y_2}{2}$. To solve for a, either equation will resolve it.

Using the x_m: $12 = \frac{(2a + 4a)}{2} \Rightarrow 12 = \frac{6a}{2} \Rightarrow 12 = 3a \Rightarrow a = 4$.

Using the y_m: $3 = \frac{(a + 3) + (a - 5)}{2} \Rightarrow 3 = \frac{2a - 2}{2} \Rightarrow 3 = a - 1 \Rightarrow a = 4$.

If you picked **F,** you may have calculated $a + 3 = 3$. If you picked **G,** you may have incorrectly set up the equation using $4a$ as the midpoint: $4a = \frac{2a + 12}{2}$. If you picked **H,** you may have calculated $4a = 12$. If you picked **K,** you may have calculated $2a = 12$

Question 211. The correct answer is D. A 3-letter ordering without repetition indicates a permutation without repetition. This can be solved using the permutation formula for n objects taken r objects at a time.

$$\frac{n!}{(n - r)!} \Rightarrow \frac{6!}{(6 - 3)!} \Rightarrow \frac{6!}{3!} = (6 \cdot 5 \cdot 4 \cdot 3 \cdot 2 \cdot 10)/(3 \cdot 2 \cdot 1) = 6 \cdot 5 \cdot 4 = 120$$

This can also be solved visually by representing each letter as a space. The first position would have the maximum number of possibilities: 6. Each space would be one less than the previous because there is no repetition. When each space is filled, apply the fundamental counting principle by multiplying the values together:

$$\underline{6} \cdot \underline{5} \cdot \underline{4}$$

If you picked **A,** you may have used the number of positions in the 3-letter word. If you picked **B,** you may have used 3! as the permutation. If you picked **C,** you may have assumed only three letters for each of the three positions with repetition resulting in $3 \cdot 3 \cdot 3 = 27$. If you picked **E,** you may have performed a permutation with replacement which resulted in $6 \cdot 6 \cdot 6 = 216$.

Question 212. The correct answer is H. Coordinate point H is on the y-axis and would have an x-coordinate of 0. Since coordinate point D is directly above H, moving up along the z-axis, it also has an x-coordinate of 0. Since the figure is a cube, each edge of the cube has a length of 1. As such, $FGHE$ is a square with side of 1. The diagonal $\overline{FH}$ forms $\triangle FEH$ and is a $45°–45°–90°$ right triangle with a side ratio of $x:x:x\sqrt{2}$. Therefore, $\overline{FH}$ is $\sqrt{2}$ and represents the movement along the y-axis, giving coordinate point H a y-coordinate of $\sqrt{2}$. Because D is directly above H, it will also have a y-coordinate of $\sqrt{2}$. Finally, line $\overline{DH}$, which represents a movement along the z-axis, is an edge of the cube and has a given length of 1. Thus, the coordinates of D are $(0, \sqrt{2}, 1)$

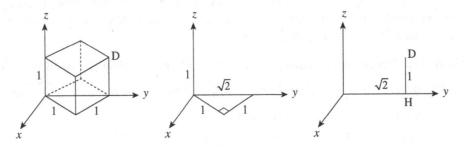

If you picked **F,** you may have assumed the length of $\overline{FH}$ to be 1. If you picked **G,** you may have accidentally solved for the coordinates of H. If you picked **J,** you found the z coordinate by finding the distance from F to D. If you picked **K,** you may have measured edge lengths going from F to E to H to D.

Question 213. The correct answer is B. The logarithmic power rule is $\log_b x^k = k \cdot \log_b x$. The logarithmic product rule is that if the log base values are the same, then $\log_b x + \log_b y = \log_b(x \cdot y)$. Using the power rule, the given expression converts into $\log_3 x^2 + \log_6 y^{\frac{1}{2}} + \log_3 z^{-1} \Rightarrow \log_3 x^2 + \log_6 \sqrt{y} + \log_3 \frac{1}{z}$. Then applying the product rule results in $\log_3\left(x^2 \cdot \frac{1}{z}\right) + \log_6 \sqrt{y} \Rightarrow \log_3\left(\frac{x^2}{z}\right) + \log_6 \sqrt{y}$.

The same result could have been found using the logarithmic quotient rule $\log_b x - \log_b y = \log_b\left(\frac{x}{y}\right)$. This would have resulted in $\log_3 x^2 + \log_6 \sqrt{y} - \log_3 z$ converting directly into $\log_3\left(\frac{x^2}{z}\right) + \log_6 \sqrt{y}$ without needing to give z a negative exponent.

If you picked **A,** you combined terms with different base values. If you picked **C,** you may have incorrectly applied the -1 exponent resulting in $\left(\frac{x^2}{z}\right)^{-1}$ and multiplied y by $\frac{1}{2}$ rather than making $\frac{1}{2}$ an exponent. If you picked **D** or **E,** you incorrectly applied the quotient rule.

Question 214. The correct answer is G. When finding the maximum value of an absolute value, the objective would be to find the greatest magnitude, which is the positive or negative value further away from zero. Due to the given inequality, all values of y must be negative, and all values of x are positive. The given expression can be understood as a negative value minus a positive value. This will result in a negative value. Therefore, the lowest possible value has the greatest magnitude: $|-4 - 2(5)| = |-4 - 10| = |-14| = 14$.

This can also be solved by creating a crosstab of x and y values at the extremes of their inequalities:

	$x = 2$	$x = 5$
$y = -3$	$\|(-3) - 2(2)\| =$ $\|-3 - 4\| = \|-7\| = 7$	$\|(-3) - 2(5)\| =$ $\|-3 - 10\| = \|-13\| = 13$
$y = -4$	$\|(-4) - 2(2)\| =$ $\|-4 - 4\| = \|-8\| = 8$	$\|(-4) - 2(5)\| =$ $\|-4 - 10\| = \|-14\| = 14$

If you picked **H**, **J**, or **K**, you found a value, but not the maximum value.

Question 215. The correct answer is D. Plugging in $n = 5$ into the given equation results in an interior angle measure of $\frac{(n - 2)180°}{n} = \frac{(5 - 2)180°}{5} = \frac{3 \cdot 180°}{5} = \frac{540°}{5} = 108°$. The sum of the designated angle and the interior angle would be $360°$. Therefore, $x + 108° = 360° \Rightarrow x = 252°$.

If you picked **A**, you may have solved for the interior angle and stopped short of the answer.

If you picked **B**, you may have made a math error and performed $\frac{(5 - 1)180°}{5} = 144°$. If you picked **C**, you may have incorrectly made $n - 2$ into $n - \frac{1}{2}$ which would result in $\frac{(5 - \frac{1}{2})180°}{5} = 162°$. This would mistakenly make the designated angle $360° - 162° = 198°$. If you picked **E**, you may have made a math error and performed $\frac{(5 - 3)180°}{5} = 72°$ and then found the designated angle $360° - 72° = 288°$.

Question 216. The correct answer is F. The general form of a trigonometric function is $a \sin(bx - c) + d$ or $a \cos(bx - c) + d$. In this form, $|a|$ represents the amplitude of the function.

If you picked **G**, you identified the $|a|$ but a tangent function has no amplitude because it doesn't have a minimum or maximum value.

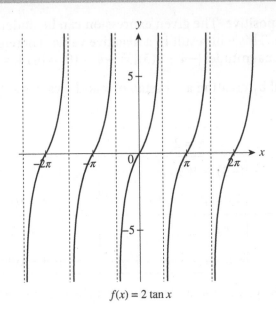

$$f(x) = 2 \tan x$$

If you picked **H**, you may have incorrectly thought that the amplitude of $a\sin(bx - c) + d$ is given by $\frac{1}{|b|}$, or you may have pulled the $\frac{1}{2}$ value from the definition of amplitude and applied it as the b value. If you picked **J**, you may have thought that the amplitude of $a\cos(bx - c) + d$ is given by b. If you picked **K**, you may have pulled the $\frac{1}{2}$ value from the definition of amplitude and applied it as the a value.

Question 217. The correct answer is A. To reevaluate the expression for r in terms of S and t, begin by cancelling the denominator:

$$S = \frac{rt - 3}{r - t} \Rightarrow S \cdot (r - t) = \frac{rt - 3}{r - t} \cdot (r - t) \Rightarrow S \cdot (r - t) = rt - 3$$

Then distribute the S and isolate the r values:

$$S \cdot (r - t) = rt - 3 \Rightarrow Sr - St = rt - 3$$

$$Sr - rt - St = -3 \Rightarrow Sr - rt = St - 3$$

Then factor out the r from the terms and isolate the r by dividing:

$$Sr - rt = St - 3 \Rightarrow r(S - t) = St - 3$$

$$\frac{r(S - t)}{(S - t)} = \frac{St - 3}{(S - t)} \Rightarrow r = \frac{St - 3}{(S - t)}$$

If you picked **B**, you may have replaced t with 1. If you picked **C**, you may have forgotten t on one side of the equation and then switched the numerator and denominator. If you picked **D**, you incorrectly factored the coefficients of r to form $(S + t)$, not $(S - t)$. If you picked **E**, you dropped the St term.

Question 218. The correct answer is G. Given that lines m and l are parallel, we can extend one of the lines to form a complete transversal:

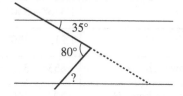

Using the transversal property of alternate interior angles and the property of supplementary angles, we can insert angle values:

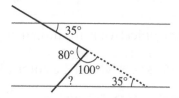

Because the interior angles of a triangle are 180°, the value of x is $180 - 100 - 35 = 45°$.

If you picked **F**, you may have assumed that the unknown angle was congruent with the given 35° angle. If you picked **H**, you may have used a wrong angle for the triangle and performed $180 - 80 - 35 = 65°$. If you picked **J**, you incorrectly used the property of alternate interior angles.

Question 219. The correct answer is E. From the given angle of 20°, the given lengths of 3 and b are the opposite and adjacent legs. This would mean the tangent ratio of $\tan\theta = \dfrac{opposite}{aadjacent}$ is required to solve for b. Using the tangent ratio at the 20° angle, the solution would be $\tan 20° = \dfrac{3}{b} \Rightarrow b = \dfrac{3}{\tan 20°}$. However, this is not an answer choice. The other interior angle of the triangle is $180° - 90° - 20° = 70°$. This changes which sides are the opposite leg and the adjacent leg. Using the 70° angle, side b becomes the opposite leg, and the side length of 3 becomes the adjacent leg. The trig equation now becomes $\tan 70° = \dfrac{b}{3} \Rightarrow 3 \tan 70° = b$.

If you picked **A**, you incorrectly used 3 as the hypotenuse. If you picked **B**, you may have solved for the hypotenuse rather than for b. If you picked **C**, you used the tangent function, but you may have solved the fraction incorrectly or reversed the order by calculating $\dfrac{adjacent}{opposite}$. If you picked **D**, you correctly used the other vertex angle but incorrectly used 3 as the hypotenuse.

Question 220. **The correct answer is K.** Angles that share the same initial side and terminal side are called coterminal angles and can be found by adding or subtracting 360:

	$1{,}573° - 360° = 1{,}213°$
	$1{,}213° - 360° = 853°$
Answer choice J	$853° - 360° = 493°$
Answer choice H	$493° - 360° = 133°$
Answer choice G	$133° - 360° = -227°$
Answer choice F	$-227° - 360° = -587°$

Being an EXCEPT question, the objective is to find an angle measure that cannot be found by adding or subtracting 360° from 1,573°. Since 853° is a coterminal angle and 573° is only 280° from 853°, we know that 573° CANNOT be coterminal to 1573°.

Question 221. **The correct answer is D.** Substituting the given values into the equation $mp - mn$ results in $(4)(9) - (4)(-5)$. Using the proper order of operation resolves to $36 - (-20) \Rightarrow 36 + 20 = 56$

If you picked **A,** you may have dropped a negative and performed $36 - 20 = 16$. If you picked **B,** you may have left off the second m value and dropped a negative, resulting in $(4)(9) - 5 = 31$. If you picked **C,** you may have left off the second m value, resulting in $(4)(9) - (-5) = 41$. If you picked **E,** you may have switched the value of m and p, resulting in $(9 \cdot 4) - (9 \cdot -5)$.

Question 222. **The correct answer is G.** To calculate the gallons of gasoline needed for

Vehicle A, divide the distance of 1,406 miles by the 19 miles per gallon: $\dfrac{1406 \; miles}{19\frac{miles}{gallon}} = 74$ gallons.

The same process can be used for Vehicle B using its 37 miles per gallon: $\dfrac{1406 \; miles}{37\frac{miles}{gallon}} = 38$ gallons.

To determine how many more gallons Vehicle A used, find the difference by subtracting

$74 - 38 = 36$ gallons.

If you picked **F,** you may have averaged the miles per gallon of Vehicle A and B: $\dfrac{37 + 19}{2} = 28$.

If you picked **H,** you may have found the number of gallons Vehicle B uses for the trip and stopped short of the answer. If you picked **J,** you may have found the average, not the difference, of the gallons Vehicle A and Vehicle B would each need. If you picked **K,** you may have found the number of gallons Vehicle A uses for the trip and stopped short of the answer.

Question 223. The correct answer is E. Fractions can be written as a ratio: $\frac{x}{y} = x : y$. A method to solve this problem is to construct a ratio table. From the given information $x : y$ has a ratio of $1 : 9$ and $y : z$ has a ratio of $9 : 8$. The ratio table would be as such:

x	y	z
1	9	
	9	8

Because the y values are the same, the scale factor to multiply and get the second row is 1. Thus, the x value can translate down.

$\times 1$

x	y	z
1	9	
1	9	8

This means the ratio of $z : x$ is $8 : 1$ or written as a fraction $\frac{8}{1} = 8$.

Another way of solving this problem is to find the product that will result in $\frac{z}{x}$. If the terms $\frac{x}{y}$ and $\frac{y}{z}$ are multiplied, the y term cancels, resulting in $\frac{x}{y} \cdot \frac{y}{z} = \frac{x}{z}$. The inverse of this would be $\frac{z}{x}$. Doing this same process with the given equivalent values would result in $\frac{1}{9} \cdot \frac{9}{8} = \frac{1}{8}$ and the inverse would be $\frac{8}{1}$ or 8.

If you picked **A,** you may have multiplied all the values in the given fractions together resulting in $1 \cdot 9 \cdot 9 \cdot 8 = 648$ and placed that in the denominator. If you picked **B,** you may have found the value of $\frac{x}{z}$ and stopped short of the answer. If you picked **C,** you may have multiplied $\frac{1}{9} \cdot \frac{8}{9} = \frac{8}{81}$. If you picked **D,** you may have multiplied $\frac{9}{1} \cdot \frac{9}{8} = \frac{81}{8}$.

Question 224. The correct answer is K. Distributing the 12 in the given equation results in $12x - 84 = -11$. Then isolating x results in $12x = 73 \Rightarrow x = \frac{73}{12}$.

If you picked **F,** you may have subtracted 84 from both sides rather than adding 84 when isolating x. If you picked **G,** you may have forgotten to distribute the 12 to both values of the binomial, resulting in $12x - 7 = -11$. Then you may have subtracted 7 instead of adding 7 when isolating the x: $12x = -18 \Rightarrow x = -\frac{3}{2}$. If you picked **H,** you may have divided both sides by 12 to isolate $(x - 7)$ and stopped short of the answer: $\frac{12(x - 7)}{12} = -\frac{11}{12}$. If you picked **J,** you may have forgotten to distribute the 12 to both values of the binomial, resulting in $12x - 7 = -11 \Rightarrow 12x = -4 \Rightarrow x = -\frac{1}{3}$.

Question 225. The correct answer is B. Given that the triangle is a right triangle, the Pythagorean Theorem of $a^2 + b^2 = c^2$ can be used to determine the hypotenuse. Substituting the value of the given legs results in $18^2 + 24^2 = c^2 \Rightarrow 324 + 576 = c^2 \Rightarrow 900 = c^2 \Rightarrow c = 30$.

If you picked **A,** you may have averaged the lengths of the two legs: $\frac{18 + 24}{2} = 21$. If you picked **C,** you may have added the two legs. If you picked **D,** you may have made 24 the hypotenuse of the right triangle and solved $18^2 + b^2 = 24^2 \Rightarrow 324 + b^2 = 576 \Rightarrow b^2 = 252 \Rightarrow b = \sqrt{252}$. If you picked **E,** you may have made the product of the legs equal to the hypotenuse squared, resulting in $18 \cdot 24 = c^2 \Rightarrow 432 = c^2 \Rightarrow c = \sqrt{432}$.

Question 226. The correct answer is K. The fundamental counting principle allows for the calculation of the total number of outcomes by multiplying together the number of options for each term. Given that, the total number of combinations for a lunch is $4 \cdot 2 \cdot 2 \cdot 2 = 32$.

This can be demonstrated by diagramming each combination of sandwich, soup, salad, and drink.

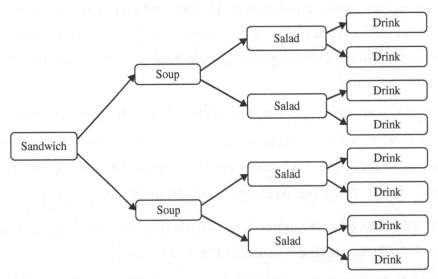

Because the single sandwich option diagrammed above can result in 8 different combinations of soup, salad, and drink, having 4 different sandwich options would result in $4 \cdot 8 = 32$.

If you picked **F,** you may have found the greatest common multiple of the terms. If you picked **G,** you may have just added 1 sandwich + 1 soup + 1 salad + 1 drink or assumed that the number of options was dependent on the largest value. If you picked **H,** you may have added instead of multiplying the values together. If you picked **J,** you may have made a math error and made all the options 2, resulting in $2 \cdot 2 \cdot 2 \cdot 2 = 16$.

Question 227. The correct answer is D. This can be solved by converting words into math and interpreting "of" as multiply, "is" as equals, and "what" as a variable. The question can now be expressed as $x = \frac{1}{9} \cdot 0.63 \cdot \$6,000 \Rightarrow x = 420$.

If you picked **A,** you may have set up the equation as $\frac{1}{9}x = 0.63 \cdot \$6,000$, which results in multlplying both sides by 9. If you picked **B,** you may have used 6.3 instead of 0.63 for 63% or you may have added a zero when figuring $6,000. If you picked **C,** you may have set up the equation as $\frac{1}{9}x = 63\% \cdot \$6,000$ and either used 0.063 for 63% or dropped a zero in $6,000. If you picked **E,** you may have used 0.063 for 63% or dropped a zero in $6,000.

Question 228. The correct answer is K. It was given that "no more than" 250 products can be produced. This would translate to "less than or equal to" 250 or ≤ 250. The sum of DVD players, d, and VCRs, v, must be "no more than" 250 product and would, therefore, be $d + v \le 250$.

If you picked **F,** you set the sum of DVD players and VCRs to be less than or equal to the maximum number of DVD players. If you picked **H,** you set the sum of DVD players and VCRs to be less than or equal to the maximum number of VCRs. If you picked **G** or **J,** you set the value to be greater than the maximum of either the DVD players or the VCRs alone, but it does not account for the limit of 250 products per week. A ≥ would indicate no upward bound of the inequality.

Question 229. The correct answer is A. One way to solve this is to determine $\angle ABC$. Because $\angle ACB = 65°$, $\angle BAC = 90°$, and the sum of interior angles of a triangle equal 180°, $\angle ABC$ can be calculated as $180° - 90° - 65° = 25°$. Because $\angle ADC$ is 50° and forms $\triangle BAD$ with $\angle ABC$ and $\angle BAD$, the unknown angle measure of $\angle BAD$ can be expressed as $\angle BAD + \angle ABC + \angle ADC = 180° \Rightarrow \angle BAD + 25° + 50° = 180° \Rightarrow x = 105°$.

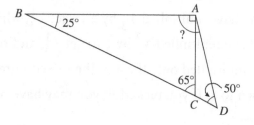

Another way to solve it would be to find $\angle ACD$. Because $\angle ACD$ is supplementary to $\angle ACB$ which is 65°, $\angle ACD$ must be 115°. Because $\angle CAD$, $\angle ACD$, and $\angle ADC$ form a triangle, $\angle CAD$ can be expressed as $\angle CAD + \angle ACD + \angle ADC = 180° \Rightarrow \angle CAD + 115° + 50° = 180°$

⇒ ∠CAD = 15°. Then ∠CAD can be added to the given the 90° of ∠BAC to create ∠BAD, resulting in 90 + 15 = 105°.

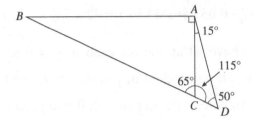

If you picked **B**, you may have assumed that △ABD is similar to △CAD and that ∠ACD ≅ ∠BAD. If you picked **C**, you may have used the 180° of the interior angles of △ABD and only subtracted ∠ADC to isolate ∠BAD. If you picked **D**, you may have added the given angle of ∠ADC and the right angle ∠BAC. If you picked **E**, you may have added the given angle of ∠ACB and the right angle ∠BAC.

Question 230. The correct answer is G. Solving would require binomial multiplication using the FOIL method. The expression $(2x + 3)(x - 7)$ can be FOILed into $(2x)(x) + (2x)(-7) + (3)(x) + (3)(-7) \Rightarrow 2x^2 - 14x + 3x - 21 \Rightarrow 2x^2 - 11x - 21$.

If you picked **F**, you may have multiplied the first and last terms of each binomial. If you picked **H**, you may have reversed the signs of $14x$ and $3x$ to get $11x$ instead of $-11x$. If you picked **J**, you may have dropped the negative with $14x$ which resulted in $14x + 3x = 17x$. If you picked **K**, you may have FOILed $(2x + 3)(x + 7)$.

Question 231. The correct answer is D. The baker has $4\frac{2}{3}$, or $\frac{14}{3}$, cups of sugar and each cake requires $\frac{1}{2}$ cup of sugar. The total amount of sugar can be divided by the amount of sugar per cake to determine how many cakes can be produced. Dividing by a fraction can be simplified by multiplying by the reciprocal. This results in $\frac{14}{3} \div \frac{1}{2} \Rightarrow \frac{14}{3} \cdot \frac{2}{1} = \frac{28}{3} = 9\frac{1}{3}$. Since the question only asked for whole cakes, the $9\frac{1}{3}$ is rounded down to 9 cakes.

If you picked **A**, you may have multiplied $4\frac{2}{3}$ by $\frac{1}{2}$ to get $2\frac{1}{3}$, which would round down to 2. If you picked **B**, you may have multiplied $4\frac{2}{3}$ by $\frac{1}{2}$ to get $2\frac{1}{3}$, and rounded up to 3. If you picked **C**, you may have multiplied only the 4 in the mixed number $4\frac{2}{3}$ times 2 to get $8\frac{2}{3}$ which would round down to 8. If you picked **E**, you may have rounded $9\frac{1}{3}$ up to 10 by counting the $\frac{1}{3}$ as a full cake.

Question 232. The correct answer is J. An $f(-5)$ indicates to substitute -5 for each x value of the function $f(x)$. Doing this substitution would result in $6(-5)^2 + 4(-5) - 11$. Solving this expression results in $6(25) - 20 - 11 = 150 - 20 - 11 = 119$.

If you picked **F,** you may have calculated $(-5)^2 = -25$, which would result in $6(-25) - 20 - 11$ $= -181$. If you picked **G,** you may have reversed your signs. If you picked **H,** you may have forgotten to square the x in $6x^2$, dropped the negative in the $f(-5)$, and added the 11. If you picked **K,** you may have dropped a negative when calculating the $4x$ term, resulting in $4x = 20$.

Question 233. The correct answer is A. The expression can be factored by finding the Greatest Common Factor between the terms. Because $-x^3$ and $-x$ have a leading coefficient of -1 and have an x^1 as the highest common degree of x, when factoring these out the result is $-x(x + 1)$.

If you picked **B,** you may have incorrectly factored the $-x$. When factoring $-x$ from $-x$ the result is 1 instead of -1. If you picked **C,** you may have incorrectly factored $-x$. When factoring $-x$ from $-x^2$ the result is x instead of $-x$. If you picked **D,** you may have factored out the coefficient of -1 from the expression, resulting in the correct $(x + 1)$, but dropped the negative in the greatest common factor. If you picked **E,** you may have incorrectly factored x from the expression. If x is factored from $-x^2$, the result is $-x$ not x.

Question 234. The correct answer is H. A method to solve this problem is to construct a ratio table. From the given information sophomores, juniors, and seniors are in ratio $2:3:4:$ and juniors have 15 members on the council. This would result in the following.

Sophomore	Junior	Senior
2	3	4
	15	

The juniors cross over both rows, so this can be used to find the scale factor, which is the value that when multiplied by the first row, results in the value found in the second row: $3 \cdot x$ $= 15 \Rightarrow x = 5$.

$\times 5$

Sophomore	Junior	Senior
2	3	4
	15	

This means that each value in the ratio can be multiplied by 5.

$\times 5$

Sophomore	Junior	Senior
2	3	4
10	15	20

Therefore, the sum of all the classes would be $10 + 15 + 20 = 45$.

Another way to solve this is to know that a ratio is found by reducing all values by an unknown greatest common factor. If this common factor is represented by x, the sum of each class would be $2x + 3x + 4x$. Juniors are represented by $3x$ and have a given value of 15. The value of x can be found with $3x = 15 \Rightarrow x = 5$. Substituting this value of x into the sum results in $2(5) + 3(5) + 4(5) = 10 + 15 + 20 = 45$.

If you picked **F,** you may have taken the 15 juniors and added the ratio of the other classes, resulting in $15 + 2 + 4 = 21$. If you picked **G,** you may have taken the 15 juniors and added the ratio of all the classes, resulting in $15 + 2 + 3 + 4 = 24$. If you picked **K,** you may have multiplied each value in the ratio by 15 as if it were the common factor, resulting in $2(15) + 3(15) + 4(15) = 135$.

Question 235. The correct answer is B. In an arithmetic sequence, the common difference, d, can be found by finding the difference between any consecutive terms: $a_n - a_{n-1}$ where a_n represents any value within the series and a_{n-1} represents the previous term to a_n. Using the given second and third terms, the common difference is $-34 - (-14) = -20$. The formula for the nth term in an arithmetic sequence is $a_n = a_1 + (n - 1)d$ where a_n is the nth term, a_1 is the first term in the sequence, and n if the number of terms. Because the third term is known, we can solve the equation for a_3 and isolate the a_1, which would result in $a_3 = a_1 + (3 - 1)d$. Then we can substitute the known value of a_3 and the common difference, resulting in $-34 = a_1 + (3 - 1)(-20)$, which becomes $-34 = a_1 + (2)(-20) \Rightarrow -34 = a_1 - 40 \Rightarrow a_1 = 6$.

Another way to solve this question is to create a template and represent each term of the sequence:

$$\_\_\_\_, -14, -34$$

When moving to the next sequential term, a common difference is added. When going backwards to the previous term in the sequence the common difference is subtracted. To go from the second term to the third term is to add -20. Therefore, to go from the second term to the first term would require subtracting -20. Thus, $-14 - (-20) = 6$.

If you picked **A,** you may have worked backward from the second term and calculated the reciprocal of the second term. If you picked **C,** you may have worked backward from the second term using the opposite. If you picked **D,** you may have found the distance between the two given values but stopped short of the answer. If you picked **E,** you may have found the common difference but stopped short of the answer.

Question 236. The correct answer is K. Solving this problem requires translating the words into a mathematical expression. The word "deduct" means to subtract from another value. Because $D was deducted from the annual salary of $S, Tom's take-home pay can be expressed as $S − $D. By translating "represents" to mean equals, "what" to indicate a variable, and "of" to mean multiply, the question can be expressed mathematically as $S − $D = $x \cdot$ $S, which is then solved for x to become $\frac{S - D}{S}$.

If you picked **F,** you may have calculated his deduction as a percent of his salary: $D = $x \cdot$ $S. If you picked **G,** you may have set $S as the take-home pay and divided that by the deductions rather than subtracting. If you picked **H** or **J**, you may have subtracted the annual salary from the deductions.

Question 237. **The correct answer is B.** The distance is the product of rate and time: $D = R \cdot T$. Rearranged to solve for time results in $T = \frac{D}{R}$. The distance between Mara and the starting gun is given as 200 feet and the speed (rate) of sound is given as 1,120 feet per second. Substituting these values results in $T = \frac{200}{1,120} \approx 0.1786$ which would round to 0.2.

If you picked **A**, you may have rounded down to 0.1. If you picked **C**, you may have miscalculated 200 as 2,000, resulting in $\frac{1,120}{2,000} \approx 0.6$. If you picked **D**, you may have subtracted the two distances $1,120 - 200 = 920$ and read it as 0.920, which would round to 0.9. If you picked **E**, you may have added the two distances $200 + 1,120 = 1,320$ and read it as 1.320 which would round to 1.3.

Question 238. **The correct answer is G.** The given equation is in the standard form of a linear equation $Ax + By = C$. A way to solve this is to convert the equation into the slope-intercept form $y = mx + b$, where m is the slope and b is the is the y-intercept. This would mean isolating y in the given equation: $6y - 18x = 6 \Rightarrow 6y = 18x + 6 \Rightarrow y = 3x + 1$. Thus, slope is 3.

If you picked **F**, you may have converted to slope-intercept form but used the b value as the slope instead of the m. If you picked **H**, you may have isolated y to $6y = 18x + 6$ but stopped before dividing out the coefficient of y and then used the b value as the slope. If you picked **J**, you may have isolated y to $6y = 18x + 6$ but stopped before dividing out the coefficient of y. If you picked **K**, you may have used the coefficient of x in the standard form as the slope.

Question 239. **The correct answer is D.** This question is setting up a system of linear equations. If x represents the number of adults and y represents the number of children, the amount spent on adults would be $\$6.95x$ and the amount spent on children would be $\$3.95y$. The sum of those two quantities would be the given total of \$46.60. Given that the 8 people going to the restaurant is the sum of adults and children, this would create the system of equations:

$$6.95x + 3.95y = \$46.60$$

$$x + y = 8$$

A way to solve this is to use the elimination method. To perform the elimination method, we need to multiply the second equation by -3.95 so the y terms cancel which isolates the number of adults, x, in the group:

$$
\begin{aligned}
6.95x + 3.95y = 46.60 \quad &\Rightarrow \quad 6.95x + 3.95y = 46.60 \\
(-3.95)(\quad x + \quad y = 8) \quad &\quad\quad\quad +\; \underline{-3.95x - 3.95y = -31.60} \\
&\quad\quad\quad\quad\quad 3x \quad\quad = 15 \Rightarrow x = 5
\end{aligned}
$$

Because x represents the number of adults, the answer is 5.

Alternatively, the question can be resolved using substitution. First, we isolate a variable in one equation and substitute the solution for that variable in the other equation. We would want to solve for y so x can be solved in the next step.

$$x + y = 8 \Rightarrow y = -x + 8$$

When the expression for y is substituted into the other equation you would get:

$$6.95x + 3.95(-x + 8) = 46.60 \Rightarrow 6.95x - 3.95x + 31.60 = 46.60 \Rightarrow 3x + 31.60 = 46.60 \Rightarrow 3x = 15 \Rightarrow x = 5$$

If you picked **B,** you may have solved for the number of children at the dinner. If you picked **C,** you may have assumed an equal number of adults and children attended the dinner. If you picked **E,** you may have divided the total by the adult price: $46.60 \div 6.95 \approx 6.70$, which would fully cover 6 adults.

Question 240. The correct answer is K. Solving this problem requires translating the words into coordinates and expressing it as a graph.

	Words expressed as a linear equation	Graph of the expression
F:	Starting the walk at home would be 0 hours elapsed and a d distance of 0 miles from home. This results in coordinates (0, 0). After 2 hours and ending 12 miles away would be coordinates (2, 12).	
G:	Starting the walk at home would be 0 hours elapsed and a d distance of 0 miles from home. This results in coordinates (0, 0). After 2 hours and ending 6 miles away would be coordinates (2, 6).	

MATHEMATICS • EXPLANATORY ANSWERS

H:	Starting the walk would be 0 time elapsed and a d distance of 12 miles from home. This results in coordinates (0, 12). After 2 hours and ending at home, which is a distance of 0 miles, would be coordinates (2, 0).	*(graph: line from (0, 12) to (2, 0); d in Miles vs t in Hours)*
J:	Starting the walk would be 0 time elapsed and a d distance of 12 miles from home. This results in coordinates (0, 12). After 2 hours and ending 6 miles from home would be coordinates (2, 6).	*(graph: line from (0, 12) to (2, 6); d in Miles vs t in Hours)*
K:	**Starting the walk would be 0 time elapsed and a d distance of 6 miles from home. This results in coordinates (0, 6).** **After 2 hours and ending 12 miles from home would be coordinates (2, 12).**	*(graph: line from (0, 6) to (2, 12); d in Miles vs t in Hours)*

Question 241. **The correct answer is E.** Because the $\cos Z = \frac{4}{7}$ and the cosine ratio of $\cos\theta = \frac{adjacent}{hypotenuse}$, side $\overline{YZ} = 4$ and side $\overline{XZ} = 7$.

Using the Pythagorean Theorem of $a^2 + b^2 = c^2$, side $\overline{XY}$ is $4^2 + b^2 = 7^2 \Rightarrow 16 + b^2 = 49 \Rightarrow b^2 = 33 \Rightarrow b = \sqrt{33}$. Thus, the length of $\overline{XY} = \sqrt{33}$.

The cos$X$ has an adjacent side of $\overline{XY}$ and the same hypotenuse of $\overline{XZ}$.

Thus the cos $X = \frac{\sqrt{33}}{7}$.

If you picked **A,** you may have assumed that switching corners the reciprocal of the fraction. If you picked **B** or **D,** you may have found the adjacent side by making a mistake in solving the Pythagorean Theorem, resulting in $\sqrt{4^2 + 7^2}$ which would make the adjacent side $\sqrt{65}$. If you picked **C,** you found the adjacent side of $\sqrt{33}$ but used 4 as the hypotenuse instead of 7.

Question 242. The correct answer is F. A power to a power can be solved by multiplying the exponents. Thus $(y^{-5})^3 = y^{-5 \cdot 3} = y^{-15}$. The negative exponent means to take the reciprocal raised to the positive power. Therefore, $y^{-15} = \frac{1}{y^{15}}$.

If you picked **G,** you may have added the exponents to get y^{-2} and then resolved the negative exponent. If you picked **H,** you may have dropped the negative and added the exponents instead of multiplying them. If you picked **J,** you may have dropped the negative when multiplying the exponents. If you picked **K,** you may have dropped the negative and calculated $y^{5^3} = y^{125}$.

Question 243. The correct answer is C. Given two similar triangles, the ratio of two corresponding sides is the same as the ratio of the perimeters. Since the given ratio of corresponding sides is $3 : 5$, the ratio of the perimeter will also be $3 : 5$. The smaller triangle has a perimeter of $5 + 7 + 9 = 21$.

This could be solved by creating a proportion with the ratio of sides equal to the ratio of the perimeters: $\frac{3}{5} = \frac{21}{x}$. Solving for x: $3x = (5)(21) \Rightarrow 3x = 105 \Rightarrow x = 35$.

If you picked **A,** you may have multiplied the perimeter of 21 by the ratio as a fraction, resulting in $21 \cdot \frac{3}{5} = 12\frac{3}{5}$. If you picked **B,** you may have found the perimeter of the smaller triangle and stopped short of the answer. If you picked **D,** you may have multiplied each of the smaller triangle's lengths by 3 and added the products, resulting in $15 + 21 + 27 = 63$. This would be a ratio of $1 : 3$. If you picked **E,** you may have multiplied each of the smaller triangle's lengths by 5 and added the products, resulting in $25 + 35 + 45 = 105$. This would be a ratio of $1:5$.

Question 244. The correct answer is F. The formula for slope is $\frac{y_2 - y_1}{x_2 - x_1}$. Substituting the given coordinates for points R and S results in $\frac{5-4}{-4-6} = \frac{1}{-10} = -\frac{1}{10}$.

If you picked **G**, you may have dropped the negative. If you picked **H**, you may have found the difference between the values of x and y of each coordinate, resulting in $\frac{x_1 - y_1}{x_2 - y_2} = \frac{6-4}{-4-5} = -\frac{2}{9}$. If you picked **J**, you may have found the sum of the x and y values instead of the difference and reversed the fraction, resulting in $\frac{x_2 + x_1}{y_2 + y_1} = \frac{-4+6}{5+4} = \frac{2}{9}$. If you picked **K**, you may have found the sum of the x and y values instead of the difference, resulting in $\frac{y_2 + y_1}{x_2 + x_1} = \frac{5+4}{-4+6} = \frac{9}{2}$.

Question 245. The correct answer is C. The area of a triangle is $\frac{1}{2}(b \cdot h)$. The base of $\triangle DEC$ is $\overline{DC}$ and has a given length of 8. Draw a perpendicular from point E intersecting the base at a new point, F. Because $ABCD$ is a rectangle, $BC = EF$, which means the height of $\triangle DEC$ is also 4.

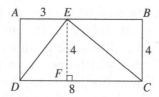

Therefore, the area of $\triangle DEC$ is $\frac{1}{2}(8 \cdot 4) = 16$

If you picked **A**, you may have calculated the area of $\triangle EBC$. If you picked **B**, you may have used the value of AE as the height and DC as the base and calculated $\frac{1}{2}(3 \cdot 8)$. If you picked **D**, you may have calculated $DE = 5$ and used that length as the height of the triangle: $\frac{1}{2}(8 \cdot 5) = 20$. If you picked **E**, you may have dropped the fraction in the area formula, and thus calculated the area of the rectangle $ABCD$.

Question 246. The correct answer is H. The garden is a 10-foot-by-15-foot rectangle. This would give the garden a perimeter of $10 + 15 + 10 + 15 = 50$. The 3-foot-wide opening would mean taking the perimeter minus 3: $50 - 3 = 47$.

If you picked **F**, you may have added the given lengths of 10 and 15 instead of adding the full perimeter and then subtracted 3 for the opening. If you picked **G**, you may have added the given lengths of the rectangle $10 + 15 = 25$ rather than the full perimeter. If you picked **J**, you may have found the perimeter of the garden without subtracting the 3-foot-wide opening. If you picked **K,** you may have found the area of the garden.

Question 247. The correct answer is E. The area of a rectangle is $b \cdot h$. Because the garden is a 10-foot-by-15-foot rectangle, the area would be $10 \cdot 15 = 150$.

If you picked **A,** you may have found the perimeter of the garden instead of the area. If you picked **B,** you may have calculated the rectangular section within the 1-foot border of flowers by subtracting 1 from all four sides of the rectangle, resulting in $8 \cdot 13 = 104$. If you picked **C,** you may have subtracted 1 foot from the two given sides to account for the 1-foot border of flowers and then found the area: $(10 - 1)(15 - 1) = 9 \cdot 14 = 126$. If you picked **D,** you may have calculated the area of the garden and subtracted 1 foot from each side to account for the 1 foot flower border, resulting in $150 - 4 = 146$.

Question 248. The correct answer is F. The garden is a 10-foot-by-15-foot rectangle. Along the inside perimeter of this rectangle is a 1-foot-wide border of flowers, which would effectively make the garden space an 8-foot-by-13-foot rectangle as 1 foot would be subtracted from all four sides. Because the rows of vegetables are 11 feet long, the vegetables will be parallel with the 13-foot side. Each 11-foot row must fit within the 8 feet, or 96 inches, of garden not covered by the flower border. To allow for the 10-inch distance from the flower border the first row would be planted at the 10-inch mark. To allow for the 10-inch distance between the rows, the second row would be planted at the 20-inch mark. This would continue up to the eighth row being planted at 80 inches. The ninth row would need to be planted at 90 inches. However, because the total width of the garden is 96 inches, this ninth row would be only 6 inches from the flower border, which does not allow for the required 10-inch distance between the vegetables and the flower border. Thus, the ninth row cannot be planted, leaving Fran with 8 rows and with 16 inches between the eighth row and the flower border.

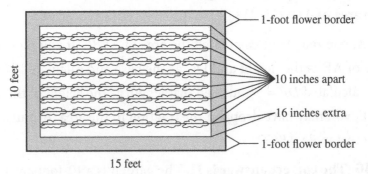

If you picked **G,** you may have calculated that 9 rows can fit 10 inches apart within the 96-inch width but forgot that the last row would be only 6 inches from the flower border. If you picked **H,** you may have started the first row at the perimeter of the flower border and added 9 rows up to 96 inches (for 10 total rows) without accounting for the 10-inch distance between the vegetables and the flower border. If you picked **J,** you may have calculated using the 10-foot, or 120-inch, width of the garden, not accounting for the 1-foot flower border.

Then 11 rows could be planted 10 inches from the perimeter and each row. If you picked **K**, you may have divided the 120-inch width by the 10-inch spacing.

Question 249. The correct answer is A. Once an absolute value expression is isolated, the quantity inside must create two equations: the positive and negative of the other side of the equation. Thus, $|x + 9| = 19$ would be solved by either of the two equations of $x + 9 = 19$ or $x + 9 = -19$.

$$x + 9 = 19 \Rightarrow x = 10$$

$$x + 9 = -19 \Rightarrow x = -28$$

If you picked **B**, you may have subtracted 9 from inside the absolute value expression, resulting in $|x + 9| = 19 \Rightarrow |x| = 10$, which would result in $x = \{-10, 10\}$. If you picked **C**, you may have reversed your positive and negative terms. If you picked **D**, you may have solved the absolute value by setting $x - 9 = 0$ and $x + 9 = 0$. If you picked **E**, you may have dropped a negative or taken the absolute value of the solutions.

Question 250. The correct answer is G. A formula for finding the midpoint (x_m, y_m) for points with coordinates (x_1, y_1) and (x_2, y_2) can be expressed as $x_m = \frac{x_1 + x_2}{2}$ and $y_m = \frac{y_1 + y_2}{2}$. The midpoint M is given as $(9, -8)$ and one endpoint W is given as $(3, 1)$. Substituting those values into the formula solves for the other end point.

$$\text{For } x: \quad 9 = \frac{3 + x}{2} \Rightarrow 18 = 3 + x \Rightarrow x = 15$$
$$\text{For } y: \quad -8 = \frac{1 + y}{2} \Rightarrow -16 = 1 + y \Rightarrow y = -17.$$

Thus, the other endpoint of $\overline{TW}$ is $(15, -17)$.

If you picked **F**, you may have added the y values to find the other end point. If you picked **H**, you may have found the midpoint between M and W. If you picked **J**, you may have found the distance between the x-coordinates and y-coordinates by finding the difference of the x values and y values, resulting in $[(9 - 3), (-8 - 1)] \Rightarrow (6, -9)$.

Question 251. The correct answer is C. The circumference of a circle is $C = 2\pi r$ where r is the radius. The given circumference is 96π, resulting in $96\pi = 2\pi r$. Solving for the radius, r, results in $48\pi = \pi r \Rightarrow r = 48$.

If you picked **A**, you may have used the area formula of πr^2 and solved for r. If you picked **B**, you may have mixed the circumference formulas of $2\pi r$ and πd where d is diameter and formed $2\pi d = 96\pi$. If you picked **D**, you may have solved for the circle's diameter. If you picked **E**, you may have made an algebraic error when isolating the r value and multiplied by 2 instead of dividing.

Question 252. The correct answer is G. When a diagonal connects corners of a rectangle, two right triangles are formed with the length and width becoming the legs of the triangle. The dimensions of the given rectangle are 14 inches wide and 48 inches long; thus, the legs of the right triangle would be 14 and 48. The diagonal of the rectangle is also the hypotenuse and, as such, can be calculated using the Pythagorean theorem: $a^2 + b^2 = c^2$. Substituting the leg values results in $14^2 + 48^2 = c^2 \Rightarrow 196 + 2304 = c^2 \Rightarrow 2500 = c^2 \Rightarrow c = \sqrt{2500} \Rightarrow c = 50$.

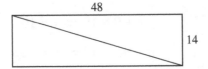

Another method to solve this is to know Pythagorean triplets and their multiples. Because the given tabletop is a rectangle, the diagonal will create a right triangle with legs of 14 and 48. These are the first two legs of a 7-24-25 Pythagorean right triangle times 2. Therefore, the hypotenuse would be $25 \cdot 2 = 50$.

If you picked **F,** you may have found the difference in the leg lengths $48 - 14 = 34$. If you picked **H,** you may have added 48 to half of 14. If you picked **J,** you may have added the two leg lengths together: $48 + 14 = 62$. If you picked **K,** you may have found the difference in the leg lengths $48 - 14 = 34$ and then multiplied by 2.

Question 253. The correct answer is C. A method of solving this question is to follow the translation of the vertices. By finding the difference between the x and y coordinates using $(x' - x)$ and $(y' - y)$, the horizontal and vertical translation of each points can be determined. Substituting A' and A results in $(4 - (-4)) = 8$ and $(-12 - (-2)) = -10$. This means A to A' translates horizontally $+8$ coordinate units and vertically -10 coordinate units. These coordinate translations can be added to the x and y values of any original vertex to find the translated coordinate. Thus, B' is the coordinates of B plus these x and y translations: $(x'-(-4)) = 8 \Rightarrow x' = 4$ and $(y' - 3) = -10 \Rightarrow y' = -7$. Thus $B' = (4, -7)$.

Another method of solving this question involves drawing a graph of the given coordinates.

From the drawing, the rectangle $A'B'C'D'$ is missing its upper left vertex. Using $ABCD$ as a reference, point B is directly vertical to point A and directly horizontal to C. This relationship is true for B'. Being directly vertical from A' would give B' the same x-coordinate of 4 and being directly horizontal from C' would give B' the same y-coordinate of -7. Thus, $B' = (4, -7)$.

If you picked **A,** you may have incorrectly counted or calculated the difference, one unit off in both the x and y-coordinates.

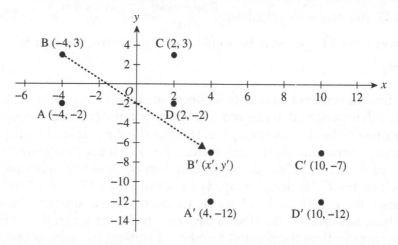

If you picked **B**, you may have reflected B over the y-axis. If you picked **D**, you may have calculated the y translation using the x and y-coordinates from A' resulting in $-12 - (4) = -16$ which results in a y-coordinate of B' of $-16 + 3 = -13$. If you picked **E**, you may have found the translation values but mixed up the x and y values, resulting in a translation of 10 horizontally and -8 vertically which would be $(-4 + 10, 3 - 8) = (6, -5)$.

Question 254. The correct answer is H. The given solutions provided for the quadratic can be expressed as two equations $x = -2$ and $x = 4$. These solutions can then be expressed as factors of the quadratic by setting them equal to 0: $x + 2 = 0$ and $x - 4 = 0$. These factors can be multiplied using the FOIL method of binomial multiplication: $(x + 2)(x - 4) \Rightarrow x^2 - 4x + 2x - 8 \Rightarrow x^2 - 2x - 8$. The n in the given quadratic is the coefficient of x; thus, $n = -2$. Another solution would involve substituting either $x = -2$ or $x = 4$ into the equation: $(4)^2 + n$ $(4) - 8 \Rightarrow 4 - 2n - 8 = 0 \Rightarrow 2n = -4 \Rightarrow n = -2$ or $x^2 \Rightarrow (4)^2 + n(4) - 8 \Rightarrow 16 + 4n - 8 = 0 \Rightarrow$ $4n = -8 \Rightarrow n = -2$

If you picked **F**, you may have multiplied the coefficients of $-4x$ and $2x$ instead of adding the like terms to get $-8x$. If you picked **G**, you may have made the factors $(x - 2)(x - 4)$ and FOILed without comparing back to the given equation to get $x^2 - 6x + 8$, which would have an n of -6. If you picked **J**, you may have made the factors $(x - 2)(x + 4)$ and FOILed to get $x^2 + 2x - 8$, which would have an n value of 2. If you picked **K**, you may have made the factors $(x + 2)(x + 4)$ and FOILed without comparing back to the given equation to get $x^2 + 6x + 8$, which would have an n of 6.

Question 255. The correct answer is C. Percent decrease can be calculated as $\dfrac{final - initial}{initial}$ 100%. The initial, or starting, value is the closing value on August 24, which is 8,600. The final value is the closing value on September 30, which is 7,630. Substituting these values into the equation results in $\dfrac{7,630 - 8,600}{8,600} \cdot 100\%$. This simplifies to $-\dfrac{970}{8,600} \cdot 100\%$ which is approximately $-0.11279 \cdot 100\% \approx -11.3\%$. This is an 11.3% decrease.

If you picked **D**, you may have calculated $\frac{final - intial}{final} = \frac{7{,}630 - 8{,}600}{7{,}630} \approx -12.7\%$, which is a 12.7% decrease. If you picked **E**, you may have subtracted the correct answer from 100% : 100% − 11.3% = 88.7%

Question 256. **The correct answer is K.** Because each answer choice is true, each answer choice must be demonstrated to not prove the significant decline. If a counterexample *could* be true, regardless if the counterexample is true for the data table, then the statement by itself is not sufficient to prove the significant decline. For **F**, having the greatest change as a decline on 8/30 of −510 does not explain the significant loss because multiple smaller advances could offset the decline. For **G**, the least change is an advance of +25 on 9/17 and 9/24 but this does not explain the significant loss because the sum of these smaller advances and other larger magnitude advances could offset a decline. For **H**, the greatest number of consecutive declines being greater than the greatest number of consecutive advances does not explain the significant decline because the magnitude of the values is not accounted for. It is possible to have more and higher magnitude advances but not be consecutive. For **J**, the first change being a decline does not explain the significant decline because subsequent changes could be advances of a greater magnitude. For **K**, the average of the declines times the number of declines equals the sum of the declines: $Average = \frac{sum}{number\ of\ numbers} \Rightarrow average \cdot number\ of$ $numbers = sum$. Likewise, the average of the advances times the number of advances equals the sum of the advances. It was also given that there were 4 more declines than advances. If the magnitude of the average decline was much greater than the average advance and the declines occurred 4 more times than the advances, then the net change would be a decline.

Thus, **K** is the best explanation.

Question 257. **The correct answer is C.** An average is defined as $Average = \frac{sum\ of\ numbers}{number\ of\ numbers}$. Substituting the values for the given 5 days results in $\frac{7{,}945 + 8{,}020 + 8{,}090 + 7{,}870 + 7{,}895}{5} = \frac{39{,}820}{5}$ = 7,964.

If you picked **A**, you may have selected the closing value at the end of the 5-day period. If you picked **B**, you may have selected the closing value at the end of the 5-day period and added the change of −25. If you picked **D**, you may have selected the first day's closing value and added the change from the last day. If you picked **E**, you may have selected the maximum closing value for the 5-day period.

Question 258. **The correct answer is G.** The height of the building would form the leg opposite the given angle of 37°. The given distance of 75 is adjacent to the 37° angle. Using SOHCAHTOA, we can identify that the correct trigonometric ratio is tangent because $\tan \theta$

$= \frac{opposite}{adjacent}$. Substituting the given values results in $\tan 37° = \frac{x}{75}$ and converting using the given trig approximations results in $0.754 = \frac{x}{75}$. When solved, $x = 56.55 \approx 57$.

If you picked **F**, you may have used the $\sin 37°$ approximation instead of the tangent approximation. If you picked **H**, you may have used the $\cos 37°$ approximation instead of the tangent approximation. If you picked **J**, you may have used cosine to find the hypotenuse instead of the height of the building, resulting in $\cos 37° = \frac{75}{x} \Rightarrow x = \frac{75}{\cos 37°} \approx 94$. If you picked **K**, you may have used sine to find the hypotenuse instead of the height of the building, resulting in $\sin 37° = \frac{75}{x} \Rightarrow x = \frac{75}{\sin 37°} \approx 125$.

Question 259. **The correct answer is C.** The area of a trapezoid is $\left(\frac{b_1 + b_2}{2}\right) \cdot h$ where b_1 and b_2 are the length of the parallel bases and h is the height. $\overline{AD}$ and $\overline{BC}$ join with $\overline{DC}$ at a right angle and form the parallel bases, which makes $\overline{DC} = 5$ the height. The given perimeter of the trapezoid can be expressed as $\overline{AD} + \overline{AB} + \overline{BC} + \overline{DC}$. Substituting given values results in $\overline{AD} + 8 + \overline{BC} + 5 = 39 \Rightarrow \overline{AD} + \overline{BC} = 26$. Since $\overline{AD}$ and $\overline{BC}$ are the parallel bases, $\overline{AD} + \overline{BC} = b_1 + b_2$. Therefore, the values can be substituted into the equation $\left(\frac{\overline{AD} + \overline{BC}}{2}\right) \cdot 5 = \left(\frac{26}{2}\right) \cdot 5 = 65$.

If you picked **A**, you may have used the given lengths of $\overline{AB} = 8$ and $\overline{DC} = 5$ as the b_1 and b_2 values, resulting in $\left(\frac{5+8}{2}\right) \cdot 5 = 32\frac{1}{2}$. If you picked **B**, you may have used the given lengths of $\overline{AB} = 8$ and $\overline{DC} = 5$ as the b_1 and b_2 values and then used 8 as the height, resulting in $\left(\frac{5+8}{2}\right) \cdot 8 = 52$. If you picked **D**, you may have calculated $\overline{AD} + \overline{BC} = 26$ but multiplied by the height of 5 without dividing by 2. If you picked **E**, you may have calculated $\overline{AD} + \overline{BC} = 26$ but multiplied by 2 instead of dividing by 2, resulting in $2(\overline{AD} + \overline{BC}) \cdot 5$.

Question 260. **The correct answer is F.** A way to solve this problem is to translate the words into a mathematical expression where "is" means equals, "how many" means the variable x, and "times" means multiply. The result would be $9.3 \cdot \times 10^7 = x \cdot 2.4 \cdot \times 10^5$. When solved for x the result is $x = \frac{9.3 \times 10^7}{2.4 \times 10^5}$. To simply the scientific expression, divide the coefficients and, because of the division, subtract the powers of ten to get $\frac{9.3}{2.4} \times 10^{(7-5)} = 3.875 \times 10^2 \approx 4 \times 10^2$.

If you picked **G**, to simplify the exponents, you may have subtracted to get $7 - 5 = 2$, but you may have also subtracted $9.3 - 2.4$ instead of dividing. If you picked **H**, you may have added the exponents instead of subtracting them when simplifying. If you picked **J**, you may have added the values $9.3 + 2.4 = 11.7$ and added the exponents to get 11.7×10^{12}, which expressed in scientific notation would be approximately 1×10^{13}. If you picked **K**, you may have multiplied the values $9.3 \cdot 2.4 = 22.32$ and added the exponents to get 11.7×10^{12}, which expressed in scientific notation would be approximately 2×10^{13}.

Question 261. **The correct answer is B.** A method for solving the question is to solve the expression with each operation and find which produces the largest result.

		$35 \underline{\hspace{1cm}} \left(-\frac{1}{56}\right)$
A.	Averaged with	$\dfrac{35 + \left(-\frac{1}{56}\right)}{2} \approx 17.5$
B.	**Minus**	$35 - \left(-\frac{1}{56}\right) = 35 + \frac{1}{56} \approx 35.02$
C.	Plus	$35 + \left(-\frac{1}{56}\right) = 35 - \frac{1}{56} \approx 34.98$
D.	Divided by	$35 \div \left(-\frac{1}{56}\right) = 35 \cdot -56 = -1960$
E.	Multiplied by	$35 \cdot \left(-\frac{1}{56}\right) = -\frac{35}{56} = -0.625$

Question 262. **The correct answer is J.** The standard equation of a circle is $(x - h)^2 + (y - k)^2 = r^2$ where (h, k) is the center point and r is the radius. Substituting the given center point and radius into the equation results in $(x - (7))^2 + (y - (-6))^2 = (10)^2$, which simplifies to $(x - 7)^2 + (y + 6)^2 = 100$.

If you picked **F**, you may have assumed that the positive 7 and negative 6 of the center point translated into $(x + 7)^2$ and $(y - 6)^2$ and mistakenly used the difference of the squared binomials instead of the sum or you may have reversed the positive and negative signs in the equation. If you picked **G**, you may have assumed that the positive 7 and negative 6 of the center point translated into $(x + 7)^2$ and $(y - 6)^2$ and mistakenly used the difference of the squared binomials instead of the sum or you may have reversed the positive and negative signs in the equation. Then you forgot to square the radius. If you picked **H**, you may have assumed that the positive 7 and negative 6 of the center point translated into $(x + 7)^2$ and $(y - 6)^2$ and forgot to square the radius. If you picked **K**, you may have forgotten to square the radius.

Question 263. **The correct answer is A.** Drawing $\triangle XYZ$ with $\overline{XY} \cong \overline{XZ}$ and $\angle Y = 22°$ results in

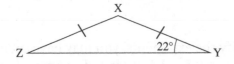

Because $\overline{XY} \cong \overline{XZ}$ the ΔXYZ is isosceles, making $\angle Z = 22°$. The sum of the interior angles of a triangle equal 180°; therefore, $\angle X + \angle Y + \angle Z = 180°$, which after substituting values becomes $\angle X + 22° + 22° = 180°$. Thus, $\angle X = 136°$.

If you picked **B**, you may have made the vertex of the isosceles triangle 22°, resulting in the sum of the base angles to be 158° and each of those angles would be 79°. If you picked **C**, you may have found the 136° solution but mistakenly divided by 2 again thinking that 136° was the sum of the two base angles. If you picked **D**, you may have added the two 22° base angles. If you picked **E**, you may have drawn the figure incorrectly and made $\angle X$ the base angle congruent to $\angle Y$.

Question 264. **The correct answer is G.** The formula for the area of a square is s^2. One face of a cube forms a square with an area of 144; therefore, $s^2 = 144 \Rightarrow s = 12$. The formula for the volume of a cube is s^3. Substituting the side length of 12 results in $12^3 = 1728$.

If you picked **F**, you may have attempted to find the side length by using the perimeter formula instead of the area: $4s = 144 \Rightarrow s = 36$. If you picked **H**, you may have taken the area of the 1 square face of the cube and squared it, resulting in $144^2 = 20{,}736$. If you picked **J**, you may have attempted to find the side length by using the perimeter formula instead of the area and then cubed that value to find the volume: $4s = 144 \Rightarrow s = 36 \Rightarrow s^3 = 46{,}656$.
If you picked **K**, you may have found the side of the cube by dividing the area by 2 instead of finding the square root. This would result in a side length of 72. Then you may have cubed this value to find the volume: $72^3 = 373{,}248$.

Question 265. **The correct answer is C.** The six numbers $\{1, 2, 3, 4, 6, 12\}$ are all factors of 12. There are 12 values in the given set. Therefore, the probability of randomly selecting a factor of 12 would be $\frac{6}{12}$ or $\frac{1}{2}$.

If you picked **A**, you may have forgotten that 1 and 12 are factors of 12. If you picked **B**, you may have forgotten either 1 or 12 as being a factor of 12. If you picked **D**, you may not have recognized the ellipsis in the number set represents the missing values and then determined the probability of selecting one of the 5 values in the given set $\{1, 2, 3, 4, 12\}$ out of the 6 possible factors. If you picked **E**, you may not have recognized the ellipsis in the number set represents the missing values and determined the probability of any of those 5 values being a factor of 12 is $\frac{5}{5}$ because each value $\{1, 2, 3, 4, 12\}$ is a factor of 12.

Question 266. **The correct answer is H.** The I for interest earned, P for the initial money invested, and t for time is all given within the question. However, time is stated to be in years and the given amount of time is in months. Since there are 12 months in a year, the 9 months of the investment can be represented as the fraction $\frac{9}{12}$ years which reduces to $\frac{3}{4}$. Substituting the values into the given equation results in $75 = (1{,}000)(r)\left(\frac{3}{4}\right) \Rightarrow \frac{75}{1{,}000} = r\left(\frac{3}{4}\right) \Rightarrow \left(\frac{4}{3}\right)\left(\frac{75}{1000}\right) = r \Rightarrow r = \frac{1}{10} = 10\%$.

If you picked **F**, you may have omitted January when calculating the number of months accumulating interest because it was invested in that month, resulting in 8 months of interest which would make $t = \frac{2}{3}$ and rounded the 11.25% up to 12%. If you picked **G**, you may have omitted January when calculating the number of months accumulating interest because it was invested in that month, resulting in 8 months of interest which would make $t = \frac{2}{3}$. If you picked **J**, you may have divided $\frac{75}{1000} = 0.075 \approx 8\%$ and stopped short of the answer. If you picked **K**, you may have divided $\frac{75}{1000} = 0.075$, rounded down to 7%, and stopped short of the answer.

Question 267. The correct answer is E. A method for solving the composite $f(f(3))$ would be to find the value of $f(3)$ and substitute that solution into the function again. The given function $f(x) = 2x^2 + x$ when solved for $f(3)$ would result in $f(3) = 2(3)^2 + 3 \Rightarrow 2(9) + 3 = 21$. This means $f(f(3)) = f(21)$. Finally, $f(21) = 2(21)^2 + 21 \Rightarrow 2(441) + 21 = 903$.

Another method is to write out the function inside the other function and then plug in the 3. To do this, take $f(x) = 2x^2 + x$ and substitute this function for every x variable in the $f(x)$ function: $f(f(x)) = 2(2x^2 + x)^2 + (2x^2 + x)$. Then the 3 can be substituted for each variable x and the function can be simplified: $f(f(3)) = 2(2(3)^2 + (3))^2 + (2(3)^2 + (3)) \Rightarrow 2(2(9) + 3)^2 + (2(9) + 3) \Rightarrow 2(21)^2 + (21) \Rightarrow 2(441) + 21 = 903$.

If you picked **A**, you may have calculated $2(2x)^2 + x$. If you picked **B**, you may have calculated $2(x^2)^2 + 2 \cdot x$. If you picked **C**, you may have taken $2x^2 + x$ and made it $4x + x = 5x$, which would make $f(3) = 5(3) = 15$. Therefore, $f(f(3)) = 2(15)^2 + (15)$. If you picked **D**, you may have substituted incorrectly and calculated $2(2x^2 + x)^2 + 3 = 885$.

Question 268. The correct answer is F. To determine possible integer values of x and y from the given equation, find the prime factors of 54. This results in $2 \cdot 3 \cdot 3 \cdot 3 = 54$. Because y is squared, the prime factors represented by y^2 must contain 2 identical primes. Since 3 is the only prime factor with a duplicate, 3 must be one of the answers. Also, because y is squared, y can be a negative value because the product of two negatives will be positive. Thus, -3 and 3 must be the values of y.

If you picked **G** or **H**, you may have thought that y^2 could be 1 because $54 \cdot (1)^2 = 54$; however, x must be less than 10. If you picked **J**, you may have found that y can be 3 but stopped short of recognizing that $(-3)^2 = 3^2$. If you picked **K**, you may have solved for x instead of y.

Question 269. The correct answer is D. Since the angle measures of the quadrilateral have no restrictions, they are not required to be 90°, and so the figure may not be a square or rectangle. A quadrilateral with four equal sides is a rhombus, which is also an equilateral parallelogram. Therefore, parallelogram and rhombus are the only shapes that *must* be described.

If you picked **A**, **B**, **C**, or **E**, you may not have recognized that the angle requirements for squares and rectangles are not stated in the given quadrilateral description.

Question 270. The correct answer is J. The formula for slope is $\frac{y_2 - y_1}{x_2 - x_1}$. Substituting the given coordinate points results in $\frac{1-3}{0-(-2)} = \frac{-2}{2} = -1$. To form a slope-intercept equation from two points, insert one of the points into the point-slope form $(y - y_1) = m(x - x_1)$ which would result in $(y - 3) = -1(x - (-2))$. This would simplify to $y - 3 = -x - 2 \Rightarrow y = -x + 1$.

Alternatively, once you calculate the slope of -1, the slope-intercept equation of $y = mx + b$ becomes $y = (-1)x + b \Rightarrow y = -x + b$. If you recognize that one of the given points, $(0,1)$, is the y-intercept, $(0, b)$, then $b = 1$. So $y = -x + 1$.

If you picked **F**, you may have added instead of subtracted in the slope equation and dropped a negative, resulting in $\frac{3+1}{0+2} = \frac{4}{2} = 2$. If you picked **G** or **H**, you may have reversed corresponding x and y coordinate values, resulting in $\frac{3-1}{0-(-2)} = \frac{2}{2} = 1$. If you picked **K**, you may have added instead of subtracted in the slope equation, resulting in $\frac{3+1}{0+(-2)} = \frac{4}{-2} = -2$.

Question 271. The correct answer is E. If the median of the first list is expressed as M, this median of the second list would be $\frac{M}{10}$ and the median of the third list would be $\frac{M}{10} - 2$. Because the given median of the third list is defined as x; therefore, $\frac{M}{10} - 2 = x$. To find the median of the original list, solve for M: $\frac{M}{10} - 2 = x \Rightarrow \frac{M}{10} = x + 2 \Rightarrow M = 10(x + 2)$.

If you picked **A**, you may have the first list's median to the third list's median, mischaracterizing x. If you picked **B**, you may have figured the modification of the first list's median to the second list's median, mischaracterizing x. If you picked **C**, you may have taken the given median of the third list and figured the median of the second list. If you picked **D**, you may have simplified $\frac{M}{10} = x + 2$ incorrectly.

Question 272. The correct answer is F. The graph of $(x + 4)(x - 3)$ is a parabola. The x-intercepts are the solutions of $(x + 4)(x - 3) = 0$. So, the x-intercepts are -4 and 3. The solution to the inequality $(x + 4)(x - 3) < 0$ will be the x-values for which the function is negative ($y < 0$ on the graph). Knowing if the parabola has a positive maximum value and opens downward to the x-intercepts or has a negative minimum value and opens upward to the x-intercepts would determine what interval values of x would have a solution $y < 0$. A way to find this is to test $x = 0$ and see if the solution is positive or negative: $(0 + 4)(0 - 3) = -12$. Thus, the interval between the x-intercepts of $-4 < x < 3$ will result in $y < 0$.

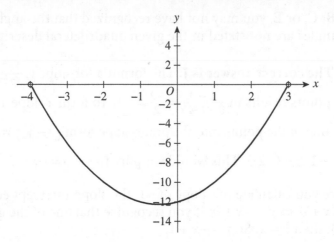

The correct answer choice must have a negative value for all x values in the interval. If the extremes of the interval, $x = -4$ and $x = 3$, are negative for an answer choice, then all function values in the interval $-4 < x < 3$ must also be negative.

	x	$x = -4$	$x = 3$	All $x < 0$?
F.	$x - 5$	$-4 - 5 = -9$	$3 - 5 = -2$	**yes**
G.	$x - 2$	$-4 - 2 = -6$	$3 - 2 = 1$	no
H.	$x + 5$	$-4 + 5 = 1$	$3 + 5 = 8$	no
J.	$2x$	$2(-4) = -8$	$2(3) = 6$	no
K.	$x^2 - 1$	$(-4)^2 - 1 = 15$	$(3)^2 - 1 = 8$	no

The only expression that is negative at both solutions for x and, therefore, negative at all interval values $-4 < x < 3$ would be answer choice **F**.

Question 273. The correct answer is D. Once an absolute value expression is isolated, the quantity inside must create two inequalities: an unchanged solution and the negative of the solution with a reversed inequality sign. Thus, $|x + y| > 1$ would be separated into the two inequalities of $x + y > 1$ and $x + y < -1$. Converting both inequalities to slope-intercept form results in:

$$x + y > 1 \Rightarrow y > -x + 1$$

and

$$x + y < -1 \Rightarrow y < -x - 1$$

The inequality $y > -x + 1$ indicates it has a y-intercept of 1 and a slope of -1. All (x, y) coordinates above that line satisfy the inequality.

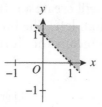

$$x + y < -1 \Rightarrow y < -x - 1$$

The inequality $y < -x - 1$ indicates it has a y-intercept of -1 and a slope of -1. All (x, y) coordinates below that line satisfy the inequality.

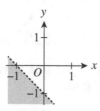

When combining the two inequalities, the result is

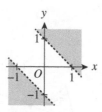

If you picked **A**, you may have reversed the inequalities or interpreted them backwards. If you picked **B**, you may have only solved for $x + y > 1$ and not the negative solution. If you picked **C**, you may have solved for $x + y < -1$ and not the positive solution. If you picked **E**, you may have reversed the inequalities or interpreted them backwards.

Question 274. The correct answer is F. The given expression has $\sin x$ and $\cos x$. Using the trigonometric identity in the note, the only way to simplify to $\sin x \cos x$ is to have $\sin(x + x) = \sin x \cos x + \cos x \sin x$. Because of the commutative property of multiplication, this can be expressed as $\sin x \cos x + \sin x \cos x$, which can simplify to $2 \sin x \cos x$. To make this equal to the given expression, both sides would need to be multiplied by two to result in $2 \sin(x + x) = 2 \cdot (2 \sin x \cos x) \Rightarrow 2 \sin 2x = 4 \sin x \cos x$

If you picked **G** or **K**, you may have used the cosine identity instead of the given sine identity. If you picked **J**, you may have multiplied the correct answer by the coefficient of 4. If you picked **H**, you may have thought that 4 becomes the coefficient of x in the sine function.

Question 275. The correct answer is C. The bottom right corner forms a right triangle with given angles of 90° and 40°. Because the sum of interior angles of a triangle is 180°, the missing angle measure is 50°. This will create a reflected angle of 50° and provide a second angle for the triangle in on the bottom left. The bottom left triangle has a known angle of 50° and a given angle of 75°, which means the third angle is 55° and will create a reflected angle of 55°.

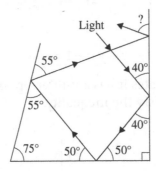

Because angles along one side of a straight line always add to 180°, the angle between each pair of reflected angles can be calculated.

180° − 40° − 40° = 100°

180° − 50° − 50° = 80°

180° − 55° − 55° = 70°

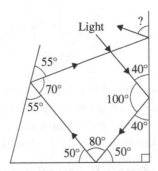

The path of light forms a quadrilateral, and all quadrilaterals have an interior angle measure of 360°. Three of the four corners have been calculated; thus, the fourth corner is 360° − 100° − 80° − 70° = 110°. The supplement to this angle is 70°, which provides the second angle measure for the triangle in the upper right.

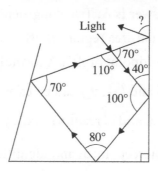

The upper right triangle has a known angle of 70° and a given angle of 40°; thus, the third angle must be 70°. The unknown angle measure indicated is a reflected angle to this 70° angle and, therefore, the indicated angle is also 70°.

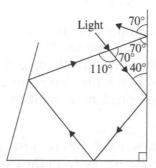

If you picked **A**, **B**, **D**, or **E**, you may have solved for an angle measure along the path of the light and stopped short of the correct answer.

Question 276. The correct answer is K. Once an absolute value expression is isolated, the quantity inside must create two inequalities: an unchanged solution and the negative of the solution with a reversed inequality sign. Thus, $|x - c| \geq 2$ would be separated into the two inequalities of $x - c \geq 2$ OR $x - c \leq -2$. Solving both inequalities for x results in:

$$x - c \geq 2 \Rightarrow x \geq c + 2$$

$c + 2$

$$x - c \leq -2 \Rightarrow x \leq c - 2$$

$c - 2$

If you picked **F**, you may have found the solutions where the absolute value expression equals 2 but stopped short of including the values greater than 2. If you picked **G**, you may have reversed the inequality sign and solved for $|x - c| \leq 2$. If you picked **H** or **J**, you may have divided the absolute value into two equations but only graphed one for the solutions.

Question 277. The correct answer is A. Two congruent regions would have equal areas. Any line cutting a square into two equal area regions must pass through the center of the square. The center can be calculated as the midpoint of $\overline{AC}$. A formula for finding the midpoint (x_m, y_m) for points with coordinates (x_1, y_1) and (x_2, y_2) can be expressed as $(x_m, y_m) = \left(\frac{x_1 + x_2}{2}, \frac{y_1 + y_2}{2}\right)$. Substituting the coordinates of A and C results in $(x_m, y_m) = \left(\frac{0+6}{2}, \frac{1+7}{2}\right) = \left(\frac{6}{2}, \frac{8}{2}\right) = (3, 4)$.

The line $y = ax + 2$ is in slope-intercept form and identifies a y-intercept of 2 and an unknown slope a. The line dividing the square $ABCD$ into two equal area regions along the line $y = ax + 2$ must contain the y-intercept $(0, 2)$ and the center point $(3, 4)$. The slope of the line containing these points would be $a = \frac{y_2 - y_1}{x_2 - x_1} = \frac{4 - 2}{3 - 0} = \frac{2}{3}$.

If you picked **C**, you created a diagonal from the y-intercept $(0, 2)$ to point C, which would not form two equal area regions. If you picked **D**, you may have calculated the slope of the line from the origin to point C inadvertently flipping the fraction, which would not form two equal area regions. If you picked **E**, you may have found the slope of $\overline{AC}$, which does divide the square into two equal area regions but does not have the correct y-intercept of the given line $y = ax + 2$.

Question 278. The correct answer is F. By converting a logarithm into an equivalent exponential form, $\log_b N = a$ can be expressed in the exponential form $b^a = N$. This would convert $\log_3 2 = p$ into $3^p = 2$. Similarly, $\log_3 5 = q$ would convert into $3^q = 5$. The product of these two solutions would be $2 \cdot 5 = 10$. Substituting the solution for the equivalent exponential form would result in $3^p \cdot 3^q = 10$. Because of the product rule for powers, the two bases combine, and the exponents are added, resulting in $3^{p+q} = 10$.

If you picked **G**, you may have performed the product rule and added both values instead of adding just the exponents. If you picked **H**, you may have multiplied the bases when combining the exponents. If you picked **J**, you may have thought $\log_3$ could be canceled out of $(\log_3 2) \cdot (\log_3 5)$ like a common factor, resulting in $pq = 2 \cdot 5 = 10$. If you picked **K**, you may have used the logarithm product rule of $\log_a x + \log_a y = \log_a xy$. This would result in $\log_3 10$ instead of just 10.

Question 279. The correct answer is D. The standard form of a trigonometric cosine function is $a \cos(bx - c) + d$ where a, b, c, and d transforms $\cos x$. Only the a and d values impact the range of the trig function. The range of $\cos x$ has a midline (axis of symmetry) of the x-axis with a maximum value of $+1$ and a minimum value of -1. The amplitude equals $|a|$ and is the vertical distance from the midline to the maximum and from the midline to the minimum. Because the a value in the given equation is 3, the amplitude is $|3| = 3$. So, the maximum becomes $+3$ and the minimum -3.

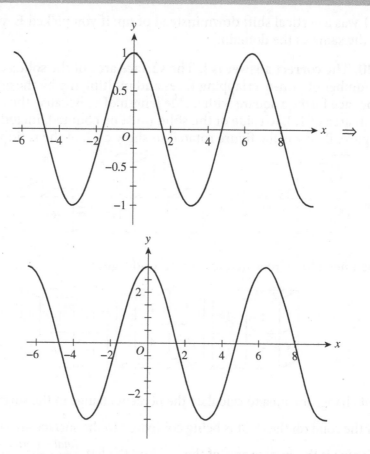

The *d* value performs a vertical shift of the midline. Because *d* in the given equation is 1, the midline shifts up 1 unit, making the minimum value −2 and the maximum value 4.

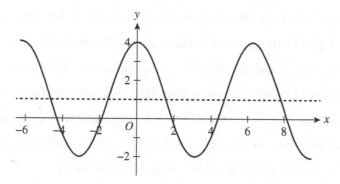

Thus, the range of the given equation is −2 ≤ *y* ≤ 4.

If you picked **A**, you may have calculated the range with an amplitude of 3 but forgot to adjust for the vertical shift. If you picked **B**, you may have used the *a* and *c* values from the equation to compute the minimum and maximum values. If you picked **C**, you may have thought that a value of $d = 1$ was a vertical shift down instead of up. If you picked **E**, you may have thought the range was the same as the domain.

Question 280. The correct answer is J. The surface area of the solids can be calculated by counting the number of non-overlapping faces and multiplying by the area of a single cube face. Each cube face forms a square with a side length of 1. Because the area of a square is s^2, each face has an area of 1. Each side of the solid must be counted, including sides not shown in the given figure. Below is the figure rotated to show each of the solid's faces.

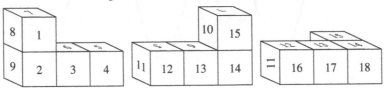

This would then need to be repeated for the second figure:

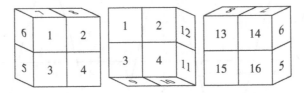

Use the percent change formula to calculate the percent change in the surface area. Because the surface area of the solid on the right is being compared to the surface area of the solid on the left, the initial value is the surface area of the solid on the left. $\frac{final - initial}{initial} \cdot 100\% \Rightarrow \frac{right - left}{left} \cdot 100\% \Rightarrow \frac{16 - 18}{18} \cdot 100\% \Rightarrow -\frac{2}{18} \cdot 100\% = -11.\overline{1}\% \approx -11\%$. This is approximately 11% less. If you picked **F**, you may have counted overlapping faces of the cubes as part of the surface area, which would give both figures a surface area of 24; thus, 0% change. If you picked **G**, you may have calculated the difference in total surface area $18 - 16 = 2$ instead of the percent decrease. If you picked **H**, you may have forgotten to count the faces currently shown on the ground, calculating: $\frac{15 - 14}{14} \cdot 100\% = -6.\overline{6}\%$, and incorrectly rounded to 6%. If you picked **K**, you may have set the figure on the right as the initial value in the percent change calculation: $\frac{18 - 16}{16} \cdot 100\% = 12.5\% \approx 13\%$, which is 13% more.

Question 281. The correct answer is D. To solve the expression, we substitute x and y for the given values: $(x - 2y)(x + 2y) \Rightarrow \left(4 - 2\left(\frac{1}{2}\right)\right)\left(4 + 2\left(\frac{1}{2}\right)\right)$, then we solve $(4 - 1)(4 + 1) \Rightarrow (3)(5) = 15$.

If you picked **A**, you may have incorrectly FOILed the expression into $x^2 - 4xy$ before substituting the values. If you picked **B**, you may have changed the addition into subtraction, resulting in $(x - 2y)(x - 2y)$, which would result in $(4 - 1)(4 - 1) = (3)(3) = 9$. If you picked **C**, you may have incorrectly FOILed the expression into $x^2 - 4y$ before substituting the values. If you picked **E**, you may have changed the subtraction into addition, resulting in $(4 + 1)(4 + 1) = 25$.

Question 282. The correct answer is J. Percent is calculated as the amount earned divided by the total amount and multiplied by 100: $Percent = \frac{earned}{total} \cdot 100$. Substituting the given values results in $80 = \frac{x}{40} \cdot 100$. Then we solve: $\frac{80}{100} = \frac{x}{40} \Rightarrow 0.8 = \frac{x}{40} \Rightarrow 0.8 \cdot 40 = x \Rightarrow x = 32$.

If you picked **F**, you may have misread the question as Tyrone wanting better than 80% rather than 80% or better and found how many can be missed instead of how many must be answered correctly. If you picked **G**, you may have determined how many Tyrone can miss to earn an 80% rather than how many must be answered correctly. If you picked **H**, you may have observed that 40 was half of 80 and assumed the correct answer must be half of 40. If you picked **K**, you may have misread the question as Tyrone wanting better than 80% rather than 80% or better.

Question 283. The correct answer is D. To find the equivalent expression, we can perform binomial multiplication using the FOIL method. The expression $(2x - 3)(3x - 4)$ can be expanded into $(2x)(3x) + (2x)(-4) + (-3)(3x) + (-3)(-4) = 6x^2 - 8x - 9x + 12 = 6x^2 - 17x + 12$.

If you picked **A**, you may have added all the coefficients $6 + (-8) + (-9) + 12 = 1$ as a coefficient of x^2. If you picked **B**, you may have performed the FOIL method but added the First Outer Inner and Last terms rather than multiplying. If you picked **C**, you may have added the coefficients of the first values and omitted the product of the outer and inner terms. If you picked **E**, you may have multiplied $(2x)(3x) + (-3)(-4)$ and omitted the products of the outer and inner terms.

Question 284. The correct answer is J. Adding the probability of an event occurring and the probability of an event not occurring must equal 100% or 1. This can be expressed as $P(A) + P(not\ A) = 1$. Therefore, the probability of an event NOT occurring can be expressed as $P(not\ A) = 1 - P(A)$. Substituting the given probability of an event occurring results in $1 - \frac{2}{9}$, which means the probability of the event NOT happening is $\frac{7}{9}$.

If you picked **H**, you restated the probability of an event occurring. If you picked **K**, you may have thought that the product of an event occurring and an event not occurring must equal 100% or 1, resulting in $\frac{2}{9} \cdot \frac{9}{2} = 1$. However, the probability cannot be greater than 100% or 1.

Question 285. The correct answer is B. The given ratio of servings to liters of sauce is 150 to 4.5. This allows us to create a proportion to determine the liters needed for 80 servings: $\frac{150 \ servings}{4.5 \ liters}$ $= \frac{80 \ servings}{x \ liters}$. We can then cross-multiply and solve $x \cdot 150 = 4.5 \cdot 80 \Rightarrow 150x = 360 \Rightarrow x = 2.4$

If you picked **A**, you may have calculated the difference between how many liters were served for 150 servings compared to 80 servings by subtracting $4.5 - 2.4 = 2.1$. If you picked **D**, you may have created a ratio with 80 servings and 4.5 liters and calculated $\frac{80}{4.5} = \frac{150}{x}$, resulting in $80x = 675$, thus $x \approx 8.4$. If you picked **E**, you may have found the difference of the servings $150 - 80$ and divided that result by the 4.5 liters.

Question 286. The correct answer is F. It should be understood that when a candle burns, the height of the candle is decreasing over time. Therefore, the length of the candle l would be the given total length of 36 inches minus the amount burned. The amount burned is the given rate of 0.48 inches per hour times the amount of time, t, in which it is burning. When expressed as a linear equation $y = mx + b$, this decrease by 0.48 inches per hour can be interpreted as a negative slope and result in the equation $l = 36 - 0.48t$.

If you picked **G**, you mistook the burning rate to be an increasing slope. If you picked **H**, you may have used the amount burned and omitted the initial height of the candle. If you picked **J**, you subtracted the burning rate from the initial height to get $36 - 0.48 = 35.52$ and used that value as the slope. If you picked **K**, you calculated the amount of time it will take for the candle to burn out by calculating $\frac{36}{0.48} = 75$ and used that value as the slope.

Question 287. The correct answer is C. Given that $AB = BC$, the $\triangle ABC$ is an isosceles triangle and by definition $\angle BAC$ and $\angle BCA$ are congruent. If we represent those congruent angles with the variable x and use the knowledge that the sum of interior angles of a triangle equals $180°$, we can create the equation $70 + x + x = 180$, then solve $70 + 2x = 180 \Rightarrow 2x = 110 \Rightarrow x = 55$.

If you picked **A**, you may have mistakenly made $\angle BAC + \angle BCA = 70$, and since they are congruent angles you calculated $2x = 70 \Rightarrow x = 35$. If you picked **D**, you may have assumed that $\angle ABC$ and $\angle BAC$ were the congruent angles of the isosceles triangle. If you picked **E**, you may have solved for $2x$ and stopped short of the solution.

Question 288. The correct answer is H. To determine the number of bags needed, we first need to know the total area of the rectangular regions using the area formula $A = B \cdot H$:

$2 \cdot 8 = 16 \ sq. ft.$

$1 \cdot 4 = 4 \ sq. ft.$

$2 \cdot 20 = 40 \ sq. ft.$

$1 \cdot 5 = 5 \ sq. ft.$

The sum of the rectangular regions would be $16 + 4 + 40 + 5 = 65 \ sq.ft.$ To determine how many bags are needed, divide the total square feet by the square feet per bag: $\dfrac{65 \ sq.ft.}{\frac{10 \ sq.ft.}{bag}} = 6.5$ bags.

To fill the entire area, 7 bags would be needed. If you picked **F**, you may have omitted the 2 by 8 rectangular region when adding up all the areas. If you picked **G**, you may have mistakenly rounded 6.5 down to 6 which does not account for the extra bag needed for the square footage over 60. If you picked **J**, you may have calculated the sum of the perimeters of each of rectangular region to be 86 feet, and divided that by 10 bags to get 8.6, which would round to 9.

Question 289. **The correct answer is D.** The domain of ordered pairs is defined as the set of all x-coordinates from each ordered pair. This can be seen in the given sample. Therefore, the domain of $[(0,2), (2,2), (3,-2)]$ would contain the x-coordinates of each ordered pair: $[0,2,3]$.

If you picked **A**, you may have found the common y-coordinate. If you picked **B**, you may have found the range, or y-coordinates, of the ordered pairs. If you picked **C**, you may have found all the unique, non-repeating values from the x and y coordinates. If you picked **E**, you may have found all unique values within the x and y coordinates.

Question 290. **The correct answer is F.** Breaking the given statement into p and q statements, we get:

$p = $ the lights are on

$q = $ the store is open

Since the converse is given as "If q, then p," then the converse to the statement must be "If the store is open, then the lights are on."

If you picked **G**, you created the inverse. If you picked **H**, you created the contrapositive. If you picked **J** or **K**, you did not form an If-Then statement.

Question 291. **The correct answer is A.** When a point is reflected across an axis of reflection, it is the same distance away from the axis but in the opposite direction. The given axis of reflection is the y-axis. Point (a, b) is a distance a away from the y-axis. Therefore, the reflected point travels the same a distance but in a negative direction, thus $(-a, b)$.

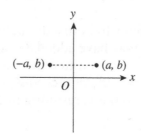

If you picked **B**, you may have reflected over the x-axis. If you picked **C**, you may have reflected over the line $y = x$. If you picked **D**, you calculated a 90° counterclockwise rotation instead of a reflection. If you picked **E**, you calculated a 90° clockwise rotation instead of a reflection.

Question 292. **The correct answer is K.** To solve we will create the equation $(4x^2 + x - 5) + (ax^2 + bx + c) = x^2 + 5x + 1$ where a, b, and c represent the coefficients of the like terms. Solving for the variables results in:

$$ax^2 + bx + c = \begin{array}{r} x^2 + 5x + 1 \\ -(4x^2 + x - 5) \end{array} \Rightarrow \begin{array}{r} x^2 + 5x + 1 \\ -4x^2 - x + 5 \\ \hline -3x^2 + 4x + 6 \end{array}$$

If you picked **F** or **G**, you added the two given expressions rather than thinking of $x^2 + 5x + 1$ as the resulting sum. If you picked **H** or **J**, you may have made a math error when subtracting each term in the expression.

Question 293. **The correct answer is B.** Grocery Garden charges $\frac{\$1.99}{5 \, pound \, bag}$ while Food Fair charges $\frac{\$2.19}{5 \, pound \, bag}$. By dividing the cost by 5, the result is the cost per pound. Therefore, Grocery Garden charges $0.398 per pound and Food Fair charges $0.438 per pound. To find out how much cheaper Grocery Garden is per pound, we find the difference: $0.438 - $0.398 = $0.04.

If you picked **A**, you may have added the pound of potatoes together to get 10, then when you subtracted $2.19 - $1.99, you divided by 10 to get $0.02. If you picked **C**, you may have calculated the difference in the price of a 5-pound bag rather than the difference per pound. If you picked **D**, you may have multiplied the costs by 5 and found their difference: $(5)(2.19) - (5)(1.99) = 10.95 - 9.95 = 1.00$. If you picked **E**, you may have added the pound of potatoes together to get 10, then when you subtracted $2.19 - $1.99, you multiplied by 10 to get $2.00.

Question 294. **The correct answer is F.** Solving requires distribution $12x = -8(10 - x) \Rightarrow 12x = -80 + 8x$, then isolate the variable $12x - 8x = -80 \Rightarrow 4x = -80$, then solve $x = -\frac{80}{4} \Rightarrow x = -20$.

If you picked **G**, you may have added x to both sides before distributing the -8 resulting in $13x = -80$. If you picked **H**, you may have added $8x$ rather than subtracting resulting in $20x = -80$. If you picked **J**, you may have omitted the parentheses and set up the equation as $12x = -8 + 10 - x$, resulting in $13x = 2$. If you picked **K**, you may have distributed the $+8$ to the 10 and distributed the negative to the x, resulting in $12x = 80 + x \Rightarrow 11x = 80$.

Question 295. **The correct answer is B.** The original cost of the small refrigerator plus a 15% profit equals $414. If the original cost is x, the profit would be 15% times the original price or $0.15x$. By substituting these values, the equation is $x + 0.15x = \$414$. This then resolves to $1.15x = \$414 \Rightarrow x = \frac{\$414}{1.15} = \$360$.

If you picked **A,** you may have found the original cost of $360 but solved for the profit the store made: $0.15(360) = 54$. If you picked **C,** you may have mistakenly made the 15% profit into a $15.00 profit and subtracted it from $414. If you picked **D,** you may have mistakenly made the 15% profit into a $15.00 profit and added it to $414. If you picked **E,** you may have estimated a final cost with a 15% profit and an original price of $414.

Question 296. **The correct answer is J.** The area of the shaded region can be calculated using the entire area minus the region NOT shaded. The area of a square is s^2, so the area of $ABCD$ is 10^2 or 100 square centimeters. With the side length of the square given as 10 centimeters and point E given as a midpoint of $\overline{AB}$, the length of $\overline{AE}$ is 5 centimeters. The area of a triangle is $\frac{1}{2}b \cdot h$, so the area of $\triangle ADE$ is $\frac{1}{2}(5)(10) = 25$. Therefore, the area of the shaded region is $100 - 25 = 75$.

Another method of solving this problem is to identify that the shaded region forms a trapezoid. With the side length of the square given as 10 centimeters and point E given as a midpoint of $\overline{AB}$, the length of $\overline{EB}$ is 5 centimeters. The area of a trapezoid is $\left(\frac{b_1 + b_2}{2}\right) \cdot h$ where b_1 and b_2 are the length of the parallel bases and h is the height. This results in a shaded region equaling $\left(\frac{5 + 10}{2}\right) \cdot 10 = \frac{15}{2} \cdot 10 = 75$.

If you picked **F,** you may have found the area of the unshaded region. If you picked **G,** you may have thought that the area of the shaded region was $\frac{1}{2}$ of the area of the square. If you picked **H,** you may have attempted to find the area of the trapezoid by multiplying the base by the slant height $\overline{DE}$, which results in $10 \cdot 5\sqrt{5} = 50\sqrt{5}$. If you picked **K,** you may have calculated the area of the square and stopped short of the solution.

Question 297. **The correct answer is D.** A way to solve for x is to use the elimination method. To perform the elimination method, we need to multiply the second equation by -1 so the x terms cancel:

$$
\begin{array}{llll}
x + 2y = 12 & \Rightarrow & x + 2y = 12 & \Rightarrow \\
x - y = 3 & (-1(x - y = 3)) &
\end{array}
\quad +
\begin{array}{l}
x + 2y = 12 \\
\underline{-x + y = -3} \\
3y = 9 \Rightarrow y = 3
\end{array}
$$

Then substituting the y value into one of the equations to solve for x results in $x + 2(3) = 12$ $\Rightarrow x + 6 = 12 \Rightarrow x = 6$

Alternatively, the question can be resolved using substitution. First, we would need to solve for one of the variables.

$$x + 2y = 12 \Rightarrow 2y = -x + 12 \Rightarrow y = -\frac{1}{2}x + 6$$

When the y is substituted into the other equation you would get:

$$x - \left(-\frac{1}{2}x + 6\right) = 3 \Rightarrow x + \frac{1}{2}x - 6 = 3 \Rightarrow \frac{3}{2}x - 6 = 3 \Rightarrow \frac{3}{2}x = 9 \Rightarrow x = 6$$

Then substituting the x value into one of the equations to solve for y results in $(6) + 2y = 12$ $\Rightarrow 2y = 6 \Rightarrow y = 3$.

If you picked **A,** you may have solved using the equation $x + y = 3$. If you picked **B,** you may have used elimination method and subtracted the x and y terms but added the constants, resulting in $3y = 15 \Rightarrow y = 5$. Then when substituting the y value into the first equation you may have gotten $x + 2(5) = 12 \Rightarrow x = 2$. If you picked **C,** you may have substituted the x and y values into the equation $x + 2y = 12$ and found that $(3, 4.5)$ works as a solution set but didn't substitute into $x - y = 3$. If you picked **E,** you may have incorrectly distributed the negative when substituting, resulting in $x - \left(-\frac{1}{2}x + 6\right) = 3 \Rightarrow x - \frac{1}{2}x - 6 = 3 \Rightarrow \frac{1}{2}x = 9 \Rightarrow x = 18$. Then when substituting into the second equation you may have gotten $18 - y = 3$ to get $y = 15$.

Question 298. The correct answer is H. A composite function is a function written inside another function. Because the given expression has the $g(x)$ function inside the $f(x)$ function, it could be expressed as $f(g(x)) = f(x^2) = 2(x^2)$. Using the function $g(3)$, would result in $f(g(3)) = f(3\,2) = 2(3\,2) = 2 \cdot 9 = 18$.

If you picked **F,** you may have calculated $f(3) = 2(3) = 6$. If you picked **G,** you may have calculated $f(3)$ and substituted that solution into the $f(x)$ function, essentially performing $f(f(x))$, resulting in $2(2(3)) = 2(6) = 12$. If you picked **J,** you may have calculated $g(f(3))$ by reversing which function was inserted into the other, resulting in $(2(3))^2 = 6^2 = 36$. If you picked **K,** you may have multiplied the $f(x)$ and $g(x)$ functions to get $2x \cdot x^2 = 2x^3$ and then substituted 3 for x to get $2(3^3) = 2 \cdot 27 = 54$.

Question 299. The correct answer is E. The fundamental counting principle allows for the calculation of the total number of outcomes by multiplying together the number of options for each term. Given that, the total number of combinations for an appetizer, main course, and dessert would be $5 \cdot 4 \cdot 5 = 100$.

You can visualize this problem by writing it out. A single dinner option can branch into 5 appetizer options. From each appetizer, 4 different main course options would follow. From each main course, 5 different desserts would follow. Depicted below are 20 different paths from 1 of the appetizers. Given that each of the 5 appetizers would have the same 20 paths, it would result in $20 \cdot 5 = 100$.

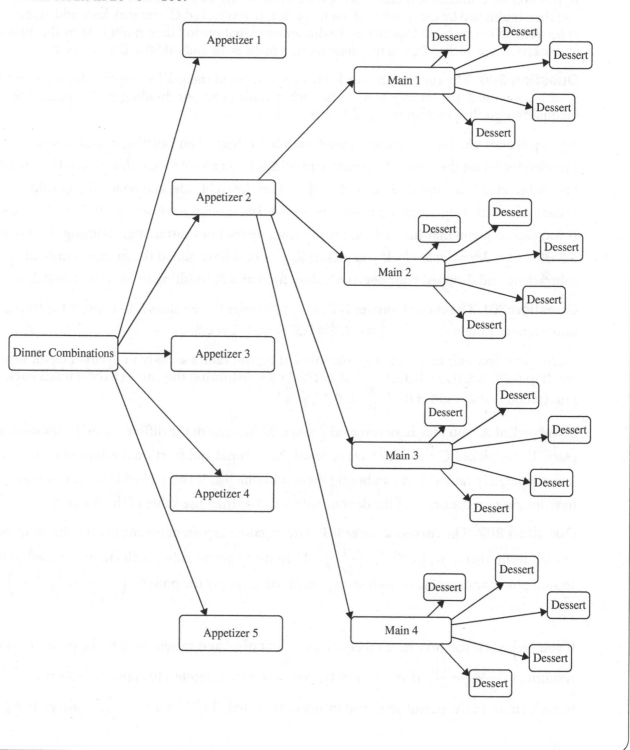

If you picked **A,** you added all the dinner options together rather than multiplying. If you picked **B,** you may have added the number of appetizers and desserts as the dinner combinations and then multiplied by the number of main courses. If you picked **C,** you may have added the appetizer and main course together as the dinner combination and then multiplied by the number of desserts. If you picked **D,** you may have made a math error and calculated $5 \cdot 4 \cdot 4 = 80$.

Question 300. The correct answer is H. The equivalent inequality is solved for m. $-5 + m \leq -4 + 2m \Rightarrow m \leq 1 + 2m \Rightarrow -m \leq 1$. Then when multiplying or dividing by a negative the inequality sign flips direction: $-m \leq 1 \Rightarrow m \geq -1$.

If you picked **F,** you may have subtracted 4 from both sides when isolating m and mistakenly canceled the -4 on the right side, resulting in $-5 \leq -4 + m \Rightarrow -9 \leq m$. If you picked **G,** you may have subtracted 4 on both sides, canceling the -4 on the right side, and added the m values instead of subtracting, resulting in $-5 + m \leq -4 + 2m \Rightarrow -5 \leq -4 + 3m \Rightarrow -9 \leq 3m \Rightarrow m \geq -3$. If you picked **J,** you may have added the m values instead of subtracting, resulting in $-1 + m \leq 2m \Rightarrow -1 \leq 3m \Rightarrow m \geq -\frac{1}{3}$. If you picked **K,** you may have added the m values instead of subtracting and dropped your negative values for 4 and 5, resulting in $3m \geq 9 \Rightarrow m \geq 3$.

Question 301. The correct answer is B. A way to order these values is to convert the fractions into decimal values: $\frac{1}{3} = 0.\overline{33}$, $\frac{2}{5} = 0.4$, $\frac{3}{8} = 0.375$, and $\frac{3}{10} = 0.3$.

Placing the decimals in increasing order, including the values already in decimal form, would result in $0.28, 0.3, 0.\overline{33}, 0.37, 0.375, 0.4$. Then by substituting the converted decimals back into fractions the result is $0.28, \frac{3}{10}, \frac{1}{3}, 0.37, \frac{3}{8}, \frac{2}{5}$.

If you picked **A,** you may have reversed $\frac{3}{8}$ and 0.37 because of the difference in the thousandths place. If you picked **C,** you may have ordered the decimal and fractional values in increasing order separately rather than combining them into one list. If you picked **D** or **E,** you may have focused on the order of the denominators rather than the value of the fraction.

Question 302. The correct answer is F. The negative exponent means to take the reciprocal of each term; therefore, $(3x^3)^{-2} = \left(\frac{1}{3x^3}\right)^2$. Then using power rules, each factor is raised to the second power and any factor with an exponent will multiply the powers: $\left(\frac{1}{3x^3}\right)^2 = \left(\frac{1^2}{3^2 x^{(3 \cdot 2)}}\right) = \frac{1}{9x^6}$.

If you picked **G,** you may have taken the exponent of x^3 and raised the 3 to the power of two, resulting in $\frac{1^2}{3^2 x^{(3^2)}} = \frac{1}{9x^9}$. If you picked **H,** you may have forgotten to apply the -2 exponent to each factor in the parentheses and instead calculated $3(x^3)^{-2} = 3x^{-6} = \frac{3}{x^6}$. If you picked **J,** you may have interpreted the -2 exponent as a multiplier, resulting in $-2(3x^3) = -6x^3$. If you picked **K,** you may have missed the negative in the exponent and just calculated $(3x^3)^2$.

Question 303. The correct answer is C. According to the vertical angle theorem, two angles opposite each other formed by intersecting lines will be congruent. Using this property $\angle 1 \cong \angle 2$ and $\angle 4 \cong \angle 5$.

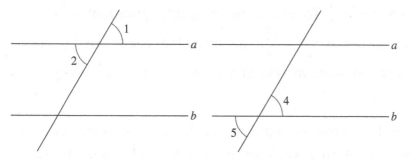

Because of the alternate interior angle property, $\angle 2 \cong \angle 4$.

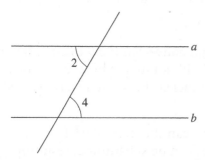

This then means that $\angle 1 \cong \angle 2 \cong \angle 4 \cong \angle 5$. Since $\angle 3$ is connected to a separate transversal than the other angles, it is NOT necessarily congruent.

If you picked **A,** you may have forgotten the property of corresponding angles making $\angle 1 \cong 4$.

If you picked **B,** you may have forgotten the property of alternate exterior angles making $\angle 1 \cong \angle 5$.

If you picked **D,** you may have forgotten the property of alternate interior angles making $\angle 2 \cong \angle 4$.

If you picked **E,** you may have forgotten the property of vertical angles making $\angle 4 \cong \angle 5$.

Question 304. The correct answer is G. To solve for $\log_{10} A$, take the initial equation and log both sides to get $\log_{10} A = \log_{10} 10^{B+C}$. The logarithmic power rule is that $\log_b x^k = k \cdot \log_b x$; therefore, $\log_{10} 10^{B+C} = (B+C) \cdot \log_{10} 10$. The logarithm of any value with a base of the same value will equal 1: $\log_x x = 1$. Therefore, $\log_{10} 10 = 1$. This results in $\log_{10} A = (B+C) \cdot 1$ or simply $\log_{10} A = (B+C)$.

If you picked **F**, you may have forgotten to include C is part of the exponent of 10. If you picked **H**, you may have attempted to convert from logarithmic form to exponential form which should have been $\log_b N = a \Rightarrow b^a = N$. If you picked **J**, you may have incorrectly used the logarithm product rule which is defined as $\log_b x + \log_b y = \log_b (x \cdot y)$. If you picked **K**, you chose the solution for A rather than $\log_{10} A$.

Question 305. The correct answer is B. The quadratic can be solved by isolating the x variable $4x^2 - 9 = 0 \Rightarrow 4x^2 = 9 \Rightarrow x^2 = \frac{9}{4}$. To remove the exponent, square root both sides $\sqrt{x^2} = \sqrt{\frac{9}{4}}$ which can be rewritten as $\sqrt{x^2} = \frac{\sqrt{9}}{\sqrt{4}}$. The square root of a squared variable will result in both a positive and negative solution, resulting in $x = \pm\frac{\sqrt{9}}{\sqrt{4}} \Rightarrow x = \pm\frac{3}{2}$, which can be rewritten as $\left\{-\frac{3}{2}, \frac{3}{2}\right\}$.

Another possible method would be to recognize that the quadratic is the Difference of Squares and can easily factor: $4x^2 - 9 = 0 \Rightarrow (2x - 3)(2x + 3) = 0$. This becomes the two solutions $2x - 3 = 0$ and $2x + 3 = 0$. When solving each equation for x the result is $2x = 3 \Rightarrow x = \frac{3}{2}$ and $2x = -3 \Rightarrow x = -\frac{3}{2}$.

If you picked **A**, you may have made a transposition error and converted the 9 to an 8. If you picked **C**, you may have simplified $\sqrt{4x^2} = \sqrt{9}$ to $2x = 3$ and did not divide by 2. If you picked **D**, you may have focused only on the square root of 4. If you picked **E**, you may have solved for x^2 and stopped short of the answer.

Question 306. The correct answer is G. Using the Pythagorean theorem of $a^2 + b^2 = c^2$ where a and b are the legs of a right triangle, the given values can be substituted, resulting in $1^2 + 2^2 = c^2$. This solves down to $1 + 4 = c^2 \Rightarrow 5 = c^2 \Rightarrow c = \sqrt{5}$.

If you picked **F**, you may have misidentified the given triangle as a 30-60-90 right triangle having the side length in a ratio of $x : x\sqrt{3} : 2x$. However, the $x\sqrt{3}$ represents the longest leg while the hypotenuse is $2x$. Another mistake may have been to use the incorrect formula $a + b = c^2$ instead of the Pythagorean Theorem. If you picked **H**, you may have assumed the hypotenuse had the same length as the longest leg. If you picked **J**, you may have used the formula of $a + b = c$ instead of the correct form of the Pythagorean theorem. If you picked **K**, you may have solved $a^2 + b^2$ and stopped short of the answer.

Question 307. The correct answer is B. The Lehman Heating rate was $22 per hour plus the $30 initial cost for the service call. This linear rate can be expressed as $22x + 30$ where x is the unknown number of hours. The A-1 Heating company was $20 per hour plus the $35 initial cost for the service call. This linear rate can be expressed as $20x + 35$. For the estimates to be the same, the equations can be set equal and solved for x: $22x + 30 = 20x + 35 \Rightarrow 2x + 30 = 35 \Rightarrow 2x = 5 \Rightarrow x = \frac{5}{2} = 2\frac{1}{2}$.

If you picked **A**, you may have identified the difference in their hourly rate: $22 − $20. If you picked **C**, you may have added hourly rate to the initial cost of each heating company and found the difference, resulting in $(35 + 20) − (30 + 22) = 55 − 52 = 3$ or you may have rounded the answer of 2.5 to 3.

Question 308. **The correct answer is H.** The formula for slope is $\frac{y_2 - y_1}{x_2 - x_1}$. Substituting the given coordinate points results in $\frac{3-5}{7-(-3)} = \frac{3-5}{7+3} = -\frac{2}{10} = -\frac{1}{5}$

If you picked **F**, you may have reversed the formula and performed $\frac{7+3}{3-5} = -5$. If you picked **G**, you may have reversed the formula and dropped the negative in the -3: $\frac{7-3}{3-5} = -2$. If you picked **J**, you may have dropped the negative in the -3 and incorrectly ordered the coordinates to $\frac{y_1 - y_2}{x_2 - x_1}$ resulting in $\frac{5-3}{7-3} = \frac{2}{4} = \frac{1}{2}$. If you picked **K**, you may have performed $\frac{7-3}{5-3} = \frac{4}{2} = 2$.

Question 309. **The correct answer is C.** A geometric sequence is created by multiplying the previous term by a common ratio. If the common ratio is defined as x, the second term of the given sequence would be $4 \cdot x$. The third term would take the previous value and multiply it by the common ratio: $(4x) \cdot x$, which is $4x^2$, and the fourth term would be the previous term times the common ratio again: $(4x^2) \cdot x$, which is $4x^3$. The fourth term is given, so the equation would be $4x^3 = 256$. This equation resolves to $x^3 = 64 \Rightarrow \sqrt[3]{x^3} = \sqrt[3]{64} \Rightarrow x = 4$. This common ratio can be applied to determine the second term in the sequence: $4 \cdot x = 4 \cdot (4) = 16$.

If you picked **A**, you may have set up the equation for the fourth term of the sequence as $4 \cdot x \cdot x = 256$ and solved for the common ratio. If you picked **B**, you may have set up the equation for the fourth term of the sequence as $4 \cdot x \cdot x = 256$, which results in a common ratio of 8 and then added that value to the first term as if it were an arithmetic sequence. If you picked **D**, you may have set up the equation for the fourth term of the sequence as $4 \cdot x \cdot x = 256$ and found the second term in that incorrect sequence to be $4 \cdot (8) = 32$. If you picked **E**, you may have found the factor that multiplies times 4 to result in 256.

Question 310. **The correct answer is H.** By doubling the given triangle's lengths, the new lengths are 12 and 5.

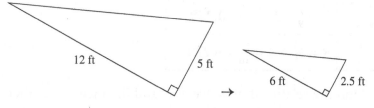

The hypotenuse could be known by memorizing the special right triangles, which, in this instance, is a $5 - 12 - 13$ Pythagorean triplet. Thus, the hypotenuse is 13.

You could also solve this using the Pythagorean Theorem of $a^2 + b^2 = c^2$ and substitute the doubled values to get $5^2 + 12^2 = c^2$ and solve $25 + 144 = c^2 \Rightarrow 169 = c^2 \Rightarrow c = 13$.

If you picked **F**, you may have doubled the shorter side and stopped before resolving for the length of the hypotenuse. If you picked **G**, you may have doubled the longer leg and stopped before resolving for the length of the hypotenuse If you picked **J**, you may have multiplied the given lengths. If you picked **K**, you may have added the doubled lengths to get the length of the hypotenuse.

Question 311. The correct answer is D. A method to isolate the x term is to use reverse order of operations. We would begin by subtracting a from both sides of the equation:

$$\begin{array}{rl} 3x + a &= 9 \\ -a & \quad -a \end{array} \Rightarrow 3x = 9 - a$$

Then we would divide both sides by the coefficient of x, resulting in $\frac{3x}{3} = \frac{9-a}{3} \Rightarrow x = \frac{9-a}{3}$

If you picked **B**, you may have multiplied a to the right side instead of subtracting, resulting in $3x = 9a \Rightarrow x = 3a$. If you picked **C**, you may have divided the 9 by the denominator rather than dividing each term of the binomial which results in $\frac{9}{3} - a$ instead of the correct form of $\frac{9}{3} - \frac{a}{3}$. If you picked **E**, you may have added a to both sides instead of subtracting.

Question 312. The correct answer is J. Distance can be calculated using $D = R \cdot T$ where D is distance, R is the rate, and T is time. When solved for rate (or speed), the equation becomes $R = D \div T$. Since the time is given as 3 minutes, each given distance provided in the answer choices can be plugged into the equation to determine the fastest speed by solving for R.

	$R = D \div T$
F: $\frac{3}{5}$	$R = \frac{3}{5} \div 3 = \frac{1}{5} = 0.2$
G: $\frac{3}{8}$	$R = \frac{3}{8} \div 3 = \frac{1}{8} = 0.125$
H: $\frac{5}{8}$	$R = \frac{5}{8} \div 3 = \frac{5}{24} \approx 0.208$
J: $\frac{7}{9}$	$R = \frac{7}{9} \div 3 = \frac{7}{27} \approx \mathbf{0.259}$
K: $\frac{11}{16}$	$R = \frac{11}{16} \div 3 = \frac{11}{48} \approx 0.229$

Another way to solve is to understand the relationship between D and R. Since $R = \frac{D}{3}$, then R is directly proportional to D. So the largest D results in the largest R.

Question 313. The correct answer is C. To find the equation of a line given two points, we first need to find the slope. To find the slope of the given points requires the equation $\frac{y_2 - y_1}{x_2 - x_1}$, which after plugging in the coordinate values becomes $\frac{3-0}{4-0}$ or $\frac{3}{4}$. We then use the point slope equation of $(y - y_1) = m(x - x_1)$ and substitute the slope and one coordinate point to get $(y - 0) = \frac{3}{4}(x - 0)$, which becomes $y = \frac{3}{4}x$, then converts into the standard form by subtracting y to get $\frac{3}{4}x - y = 0$. To eliminate the fraction, multiply both sides by 4 to get $4\left(\frac{3}{4}x - y\right) = 0 \cdot 4$ and distribute to resolve: $3x - 4y = 0$.

If you picked **A, B,** or **E** you may have substituted the coordinate (4,3) into the equation and stopped without testing (0,0). If you picked **D,** you may have dropped the negative when converting from $y = \frac{3}{4}x$ to standard form.

Question 314. The correct answer is H. This is best solved by illustrating what the question is stating.

If points P, Q, R, and S lie on a line in that order, then

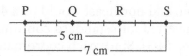

Since R is the midpoint between $\overline{QS}$, then $\overline{QR} \cong \overline{RS}$. The segment $\overline{PR}$ is given as 5 cm long and $\overline{PS}$ is given as 7 cm.

Thus, $PS - PR = RS$ or $7 - 5 = 2$ cm. Because $\overline{QR} \cong \overline{RS}$, the length of $\overline{QR}$ is also 2 cm. Therefore, $QS = 2 + 2 = 4$ cm.

If you picked **F,** you may have solved for the length of $\overline{RS}$ or $\overline{QR}$ and stopped short of the answer. If you picked **G,** you may have solved for the length of $\overline{PQ}$. If you picked **J,** you may have thought $\overline{QS}$ was the same length as $\overline{PR}$ due to a perceived symmetry. If you picked **K,** you may have averaged the given lengths.

Question 315. The correct answer is E. The expression equivalent to the given expression would be its factored form. The greatest common factor of the three terms is 3, which would result in $3(x^4 + 2x^2 - 15)$. This then factors like a quadratic into $(x^2 + 5)(x^2 - 3)$. Then by combining this factored form with the greatest common factor, the result is $3(x^2 + 5)(x^2 - 3)$.

If you picked **A,** you may have dropped the greatest common factor of 3 from the expression. If you picked **B,** you may have reversed the signs within each factor. If you picked **C,** you may have forgotten to factor the 3 from the other two terms. If you picked **D,** you may have reversed your signs when factoring.

Question 316. The correct answer is G. The given scale for the drawing is $1\ cm = 4\ miles$. The given distance between the two schools is $2\frac{1}{2}\ cm$ apart. One way to solve this is to multiply your scale conversion by $2\frac{1}{2}$ to get $2\frac{1}{2}(1\ cm) = 2\frac{1}{2}(4\ miles)$, which equals $2\frac{1}{2}\ cm = 10\ miles$. You could also solve this problem by setting up a proportion:

$$\frac{1\ cm}{4\ miles} = \frac{2\frac{1}{2}\ cm}{x\ miles} \Rightarrow x = 10$$

If you picked **F,** you may have calculated that for each cm, you add 4 miles. Then you used full cm increments and calculated $4 + 4 + 4 = 12$ and forgot to subtract $(4 \cdot \frac{1}{2})$ from the solution to bring it back down to $2\frac{1}{2}$ cm. If you picked **H,** you may have multiplied the 4 miles times the integer value in the distance, resulting in $4 \cdot 2 = 8$ miles. However, when you calculated the $\frac{1}{2}$ cm, you did $2 \cdot \frac{1}{2}$ instead of $4 \cdot \frac{1}{2}$, thus resulting in $8 + 1 = 9$ miles. If you picked **J,** you may have only multiplied 4 times 2 instead of $2\frac{1}{2}$. If you picked **K,** you may have found the difference between the school's distance and the 1 cm distance of the scale graph to get $2\frac{1}{2} - 1 = 1\frac{1}{2}$. Then you multiplied this solution by 4 miles, resulting in $1\frac{1}{2} \cdot 4 = 6$ miles.

Question 317. The correct answer is D. Going "due" northeast of a coordinate point means to go straight in that direction, and northeast would be a 45° direction or a slope of 1. Each landmark location can be converted into standard coordinate points to use the distance formula such as D-3 becoming (4,3). Since each coordinate distance is in centimeters, each will need to be converted into miles using the given scale of $1\ cm = 4\ miles$.

	Coordinate Conversion	Distance Formula	Scale Conversion
A:	E-8 = (5, 8)	$\sqrt{(5-4)^2 + (8-3)^2} \approx 5.1$	$5.1 \cdot 4 = 20.4\ miles$
B:	F-6 = (6, 6)	$\sqrt{(6-4)^2 + (6-3)^2} \approx 3.6$	$3.6 \cdot 4 = 14.4\ miles$
C:	G-6 = (7, 6)	$\sqrt{(7-4)^2 + (6-3)^2} \approx 4.2$	$4.2 \cdot 4 = 16.8\ miles$
D:	**H-7 = (8, 7)**	$\sqrt{(8-4)^2 + (7-3)^2} \approx 5.7$	$5.7 \cdot 4 = \textbf{22.8}\ \textbf{\textit{miles}}$
E:	4 = (9, 4)	$\sqrt{(9-4)^2 + (4-3)^2} \approx 5.1$	$5.1 \cdot 4 = 20.4\ miles$

Answer choices **A, B,** and **E** could have been eliminated for not being due northeast, or 45°, from D-3. Regardless, coordinate point H-7 is closest to the 24 miles distance from D-3 at approximately 22.8 miles.

Question 318. **The correct answer is F.** To convert the given scale of 1 *cm* = 4 *miles* to $\frac{1}{2}$ miles, each side of the equation could be divided by 8, resulting in $\frac{1}{8}$ *cm* = $\frac{1}{2}$ *miles*. This length in centimeters corresponds to a single side of the square park. The area of a square is s^2; therefore, the square area would be $\left(\frac{1}{8}\,cm\right)^2 = \frac{1}{64}\,cm^2$.

If you picked **G,** you may have performed an incorrect scale conversion which resulted in the square's side length to be $\frac{1}{4}$ cm, thus an area of $\frac{1}{16}$ cm. If you picked **H,** you may have found the side length and stopped short of the answer. If you picked **J,** you may have added the length and width in miles. If you picked **K,** you may have found the perimeter in miles.

Question 319. **The correct answer is E.** By definition, any parallelogram will have its diagonals bisect each other. A parallelogram, rectangle, rhombus, and square are all types of parallelograms; thus, their diagonal bisect. Because a trapezoid is not a parallelogram, its diagonals do not bisect.

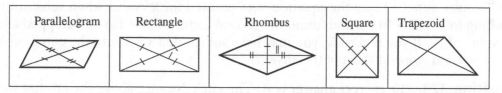

Question 320. **The correct answer is J.** The two medications will be taken at the same time when the elapsed time is a common multiple of the intervals. The time intervals are 6 hours and 4 hours, so the least common multiple between the intervals is 12 hours. Therefore, the next time Mary will take the medications at the same time will be 12 hours after 7:00 A.M.

If you picked **F,** you may have used the greater interval, ignoring that they need to be taken simultaneously. If you picked **H,** you may have added the interval values together. If you picked **K,** you may have multiplied the two times the intervals rather than determining the least common multiple to find the next time she takes both medicines.

Question 321. **The correct answer is B.** The total games won must include the games won at home and the games won away from home. To calculate which team won the most games away from home, the games won at home must be subtracted from the total number of wins.

	Total Wins	Home Wins	Wins Away
A:	92	49	92 − 49 = 43
B:	**88**	**43**	**88 − 43 = 45**
C:	85	47	85 − 47 = 38
D:	74	35	74 − 35 = 39
E:	53	27	53 − 27 = 26

If you picked **A,** you may have selected the team with the highest number of wins or the highest number of wins at home.

Question 322. **The correct answer is F.** Since 1, or $x = 1$, is a given solution of the quadratic, $(x - 1)$ must be a factor. In the standard form of a quadratic $ax^2 + bx + c$, the c value is determined in the FOIL method by multiplying the last term in each factor. Since -1 is the last term in the first factor and the product will be 10, the last term of the other factor must be -10. Thus, the two factors are $(x - 1)(x - 10)$. Using the FOIL method, this would become $x^2 - x - 10x + 10$, which combines to $x^2 - 11x + 10$. Therefore, the value of h must be -11.

Another method for solving this question is to substitute the solution of $x = 1$ into the given equation: $x^2 + hx + 10 = 0 \Rightarrow (1)^2 + h(1) + 10 = 0 \Rightarrow 1 + h + 10 = 0 \Rightarrow h + 11 = 0 \Rightarrow h = -11$.

If you picked **G,** you may have omitted the x^2 value when substituting $x = 1$, resulting in $(1)h + 10 = 0$. If you picked **H,** you may have set up $x = 1$ to be the factor $(x + 1) = 0$ and stopped short of the solution. If you picked **J,** you may have set up $x = 1$ to be the factor $(x + 1)$, substituted -1 into the equation, and omitted the x^2 value when substituting, resulting in $(-1)h + 10 = 0$ and found the second factor of $(x + 10)$ and stopped after finding the value of 10. If you picked **K,** you may have substituted $x = 1$ into the equation to get $h + 11 = 0$ and stopped short of the answer.

Question 323. **The correct answer is A.** The kite's distance above the ground would be the vertical leg of the triangle.

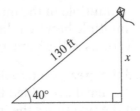

The hypotenuse is the given length of 130 ft because it is opposite the right angle and the unknown side is opposite the given angle. Then using the mnemonic SOHCAHTOA, we can apply the sine ratio because the lengths are opposite and hypotenuse: $\sin 40° = \frac{x}{130}$. When solved for x, the result is $130 \cdot \sin 40°$. Then, substituting the given approximation for $\sin 40°$ results in $130 \cdot 0.643 = 83.59$. The closest approximation for 83.59 is 80.

If you picked **B,** you may have used the given approximation for $\cos 40°$. If you picked **C,** you may have used the given approximation for $\tan 40°$. If you picked **D,** you may have used the given approximation for $\cos 40°$ and solved for x incorrectly, resulting in $\frac{130}{0.766} \approx 170$. If you picked **E,** you may have solved for x incorrectly, resulting in $\frac{130}{0.643}$ which is approximately 200.

Question 324. The correct answer is F. Because the 5 smaller circles have centers lying on the diameter of the larger circle, the diameters of the 5 smaller circles together will form the diameter of the larger circle.

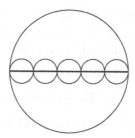

The smaller circles each have a given area of 4π. The area of a circle is defined as $A = \pi r^2$, so $\pi r^2 = 4\pi \Rightarrow r^2 = 4 \Rightarrow r = 2$. Diameter is $2r$, so the diameter of each smaller circle is 4. Because there are 5 circles, the larger circle would have a diameter of $5 \cdot 4 = 20$, which means a radius of 10. Using the area formula again, the larger circle is $A = \pi r^2 = \pi(10)^2 = 100\pi$.

If you picked **G**, when calculating your values, you may have mistaken the radius $r = 10$ of the larger circle as the diameter of the smaller circle. This would give the larger circle a diameter of 50. Then you mistakenly used the circumference formula using that diameter to calculate $C = \pi d = \pi(50)$. If you picked **H**, you may have used the diameter of 20 and applied that to the circumference formula of $C = 2\pi r$ to get $2\pi(20) = 40\pi$. If you picked **K**, you may have found the correct radius but then used the circumference formula to get $2\pi(10) = 20\pi$.

Question 325. The correct answer is A. Rewrite the given expression into a product of separate radical terms: $\sqrt[3]{27} \cdot \sqrt[3]{r^6}$. The number 27 can be expressed as 3^3, so that radical can be written as $\sqrt[3]{3^3}$, which simplifies to 3. The $\sqrt[3]{r^6}$ can be expressed in fractional powers as $r^{\frac{6}{3}}$, which would reduce to r^2. Thus, the equivalent expression would be $3r^2$.

If you picked **B**, you may have incorrectly simplified $\sqrt[3]{r^6}$ ro r^3. If you picked **C**, you may have divided the 27 by 3 instead of determining the cube root of 27. If you picked **D**, you may have divided the 27 by 3 instead of determining the cube root of 27 and incorrectly simplified $\sqrt[3]{r^6}$ to r^3. If you picked **E**, you may have applied the sixth power to 27 and then performed a cube root, resulting in $\sqrt[3]{27^6 r^6} = 27^2 r^2 = 729\,r^2$.

Question 326. The correct answer is K. The given pattern, omitting the sum, is:

$$1^3 + 2^3 = (1 + 2)^2$$

$$1^3 + 2^3 + 3^3 = (1 + 2 + 3)^2$$

Therefore, if 4^3 was added to the sum of cubes, the quantity of the consecutive numbers squared would increase by 4, resulting in $1^3 + 2^3 + 3^3 + 4^3 = (1 + 2 + 3 + 4)^2$. Thus, if the sum continued for the first c consecutive cubes the pattern would be $1^3 + 2^3 + \ldots + c^3 = (1 + 2 + \ldots + c)^2$.

If you picked **F** or **G**, you may have neglected to include the sum of all the integers preceding c. If you picked **H**, you may have assumed that the exponent of the sum of consecutive numbers increased with each term added. If you picked **J**, you may have continued the third power from the left side of the expression.

Question 327. The correct answer is B. If the radius of Earth was defined as x, the radius of Uranus is $4x$. Plugging in each radius value into the given equation for the volume of a sphere results in Earth having a volume of $\frac{4}{3}\pi x^3$ and Uranus having a volume of $\frac{4}{3}\pi(4x)^3$. Simplifying the volume of Uranus results in $\frac{4}{3}\pi 64x^3$, which by the commutative property can be expressed as $64 \cdot \left(\frac{4}{3}\pi x^3\right)$. Because the volume of the Earth is $\left(\frac{4}{3}\pi x^3\right)$, Uranus is 64 times Earth's volume.

If you picked **A**, you may have entered in values incorrectly into your calculator, resulting in $(3x)^4$ instead of $(4x)^3$. If you picked **C**, you may have squared the radius instead of cubing it. If you picked **D**, you may have multiplied the radius of $4x$ by 3 instead of cubing. If you picked **E**, you may have assumed that 4 times the radius would equate to four times the volume.

Question 328. The correct answer is H. The average is defined as $\frac{\text{sum of numbers}}{\text{number of numbers}}$. Using the given information would result in $\frac{a+a+a+b+c}{5} = a$. Isolating for $b + c$ results in $3a + b + c = 5a \Rightarrow b + c = 2a$. Because the question is asking for the value of $\frac{b+c}{2}$, both side of the equation can be divided by 2 to get the answer: $\frac{b+c}{2} = \frac{2a}{2}$. Thus, $\frac{b+c}{2} = a$.

If you picked **G**, you may have mistaken $b + c$ to be equal to a, thus $\frac{b+c}{2}$ would equal $\frac{a}{2}$. If you picked **J**, you may have gotten to $b + c = 2a$ and stopped short of the answer. If you picked **K**, you may have found the sum of the a's.

Question 329. The correct answer is E. The angle of depression is the angle between the horizontal line at the top of the lighthouse and the line of sight from the lighthouse down to the boat. This horizontal line of sight is parallel to the horizontal line from the base of the lighthouse to the boat. This allows the line of sight to act as a transversal across those two parallel lines. Therefore, the angle of depression from the lighthouse equals the angle of elevation from the boat up to the top of the lighthouse.

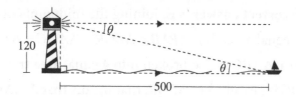

The height of the light tower is opposite the angle of elevation from the boat and the distance between the boat and the light tower is adjacent to that angle. Then using the mnemonic SOHCAHTOA, we can apply the tangent ratio because the lengths are opposite and adjacent, resulting in a tangent ratio: $\tan\theta = \frac{120}{500}$.

If you picked **A,** you may have used the angle complementary to the angle of depression and used 500 as the hypotenuse instead of the horizontal distance. If you picked **B,** you may have used the lengths for the tangent ratio but used the sine function. If you picked **C,** you may have used 500 as the hypotenuse instead of the horizontal distance. If you picked **D,** you may have inverted the opposite and adjacent values.

Question 330. The correct answer is H. This question can be answered by drawing out the figure, drawing the squares, and counting the segments.

Another way of calculating the sides of the 24 squares is to count the number of vertical and horizontal lines that are needed to create the figure.

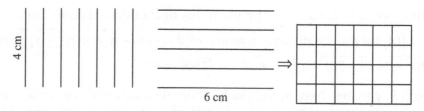

Since the squares are 1 cm on each side, the length of each line corresponds to the number of squares along that length. The length of the vertical lines and the length of the horizontal lines can then be multiplied by the number of lines. The sum of these values would be the total number of 1 cm sides: $(4 \cdot 7) + (6 \cdot 5) = 58$.

If you picked **F,** you may have calculated the area of the rectangle. If you picked **G,** you may have counted the number of horizontal and vertical lines but forgotten the last line of each. $(4 \cdot 6) + (6 \cdot 4) = 48$. If you picked **J,** you may have added the horizontal and vertical lengths and then multiplied that solution by the number of 4 cm lines needed to form the 24 boxes: $(4 + 6) \cdot 7 = 70$. If you picked **K,** you may have calculated that the rectangle can hold 24 squares and each square has four sides without subtracting the duplication of overlapping sides.

Question 331. The correct answer is E. Joining the midpoints of all three sides of a triangle creates 4 triangles of equal area, thus $\triangle PAB = \triangle BCR = \triangle AQC = \triangle ABC$ and each accounts for $\frac{1}{4}$ the triangle's area. $\triangle ABC$ is also broken into 4 equal area triangles; thus, $\triangle MNO$ is $\frac{1}{4}$ of $\triangle ABC$. Since $\triangle ABC$ is already $\frac{1}{4}$ of $\triangle PQR$, that means that $\triangle MNO$ is $\frac{1}{4} \cdot \frac{1}{4} = \frac{1}{16}$ the area of $\triangle PQR$. Adding together the shaded regions of $\triangle PAB + \triangle BCR + \triangle AQC + \triangle MNO = \frac{1}{4} + \frac{1}{4} + \frac{1}{4} + \frac{1}{16} = \frac{13}{16}$.

If you picked **B**, you may have merely counted the number of triangles that are shaded out of the total number of drawn triangles rather than finding the ratio of their areas. If you picked **C**, you may have made a math error when creating a common denominator to add up the fractions and mistakenly converted $\frac{1}{4}$ into $\frac{3}{16}$ instead of $\frac{4}{16}$, thus calculating $\frac{3}{16} + \frac{3}{16} + \frac{3}{16} + \frac{1}{16} = \frac{10}{16} = \frac{5}{8}$. If you picked **D**, you may have determined the shaded areas of $\triangle PAB + \triangle BCR + \triangle AQC$ without $\triangle MNO$.

Question 332. The correct answer is K. A formula for finding the midpoint (x_m, y_m) for points with coordinates (x_1, y_1) and (x_2, y_2) can be expressed as $(x_m, y_m) = \left(\frac{x_1 + x_2}{2}, \frac{y_1 + y_2}{2}\right)$. For coordinate $X(20,100)$ and $Z(120,40)$ the $(x_m, y_m) = \left(\frac{20 + 120}{2}, \frac{100 + 40}{2}\right) = (70, 70)$. To determine the distance between this new midpoint coordinate of $(70, 70)$ and $Y(100,110)$, we use the distance formula of $d = \sqrt{(x_2 - x_1)^2 + (y_2 - y_1)^2}$, resulting in $\sqrt{(100 - 70)^2 + (110 - 70)^2} = \sqrt{30^2 + 40^2} = \sqrt{2500} = 50$.

If you picked **F**, you may have found the horizontal distance between the midpoint and point Y using the x-coordinates: $100 - 70$. If you picked **G**, you may have averaged the horizontal distance of 30 and vertical distances of 40 between the midpoint and point Y. If you picked **H**, you may have found the vertical distance using the y-coordinates: $110 - 70$. If you picked **J**, you may have incorrectly entered the coordinates for point Y as $(100,100)$ when figuring the distance formula.

Question 333. The correct answer is A. The expression $(3t - t^2)$ is a quadratic function. When rearranged into the standard format of $ax^2 + bx + c$, the quadratic would be $-t^2 + 3t$, making the $a = -1$, $b = 3$, and $c = 0$. Because the a value is -1 the parabola created by the quadratic opens downward, giving it a distinct maximum at its vertex. The equation for the x-coordinate of the vertex is $\frac{-b}{2a}$, which results in $\frac{-3}{2(-1)} = \frac{3}{2}$.

If you picked **C**, you may have found the maximum height of the equation by solving for the x-coordinate of the vertex of $\frac{3}{2}$ and substituted that value into the equation to solve for the value of h: $3\left(\frac{3}{2}\right) - \left(\frac{3}{2}\right)^2 = \frac{9}{4}$. If you picked **D**, you may have factored the quadratic into $t(3 - t)$ and set it equal to zero to find the roots of the quadratic. If you picked **E**, you may have set the equation equal to zero: $t^2 - 3t + h = 0$. Then you used the incorrect vertex formula of $\frac{b^2}{2a}$, resulting in $\frac{(-3)^2}{2(1)} = \frac{9}{2}$.

Question 334. **The correct answer is K.** Fractions of unlike denominators must be converted to a common denominator. The common denominator would be $x(x + 1)$. Converting the given expression would require multiplying the numerator and denominator of each term by the missing factor of the common denominator: $\left(\frac{x}{x}\right)\left(\frac{1}{x+1}\right) + \left(\frac{x+1}{x+1}\right)\left(\frac{1}{x}\right)$. After multiplying the terms become $\frac{x}{x(x+1)} + \frac{x+1}{x(x+1)}$. With a common denominator, the numerators can be added $\frac{x + (x+1)}{x(x+1)} \Rightarrow \frac{2x+1}{x(x+1)}$.

If you picked **F**, you may have multiplied the fractions together instead of adding them. If you picked **G**, you may have added the denominators to create the common denominator and multiplied the numerators. If you picked **H**, you may have multiplied the denominators to create the common denominator but merely added the given numerators without converting. If you picked **J**, you may have gotten the $\frac{2x+1}{x(x+1)}$ solution but incorrectly cancelled values, resulting in $\frac{2x+1}{x(x+1)} = \frac{2}{x} + \frac{x+1}{x+1} = \frac{2}{x} + 1$.

Question 335. **The correct answer is D.** The sum of the interior angles of any quadrilateral is $360°$. Because a ratio is reduced by an unknown greatest common factor, each angle's ratio can be multiplied by x, which represents this common factor. Thus, $1x + 2x + 3x + 4x = 360$ $\Rightarrow 10x = 360 \Rightarrow x = 36$. Since the largest angle would be $4x$, the angle measure would be $4(36) = 144°$.

If you picked **B**, you may have found the angle measure for $3x$ instead of the largest angle measure: $3(36) = 108°$. If you picked **C**, you may have calculated the least common multiple of the ratio values and set that equal to the sum of interior angles of a quadrilateral, resulting in $12x = 360 \Rightarrow x = 30$. Thus, $30 \cdot 4 = 120°$. If you picked **E**, you may have combined the ratios to $9x = 360$, resulting in $x = 40$ and thus $40 \cdot 4 = 160°$.

Question 336. **The correct answer is K.** The hypotenuse of a triangle can be expressed as the Pythagorean Theorem solved for c, which would be $c = \sqrt{a^2 + b^2}$. A right triangle with legs of 37 and 45 inches would have a hypotenuse of $\sqrt{37^2 + 45^2}$. Because the smallest angle

MATHEMATICS • EXPLANATORY ANSWERS

of a triangle is opposite the shortest side, the smallest interior angle must be opposite the side length of 37.

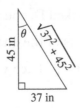

Using the cosine ratio of $\cos\theta = \dfrac{adjacent}{hypotenuse}$ results in $\cos\theta = \dfrac{45}{\sqrt{37^2 + 45^2}}$.

If you picked **F**, you may have used the tangent ratio of $\dfrac{opposite}{adjacent}$. If you picked **G**, you may have calculated the $\dfrac{adjacent}{opposite}$. If you picked **H** or **J**, you may have used the sine ratio of $\dfrac{opposite}{hypotenuse}$.

Question 337. **The correct answer is E.** Solving this problem required translating the words into an inequality and expressing it as a graph.

	Words expressed as an inequality	Graph of the inequalities expressed
A:	Tricycles exceed 30 $\Rightarrow$ $x > 30$ Bicycles exceed 30 $\Rightarrow$ $y > 30$	
B:	Tricycles exceed 30 $\Rightarrow$ $x > 30$ Bicycles less than tricycles $\Rightarrow$ $y < x$	

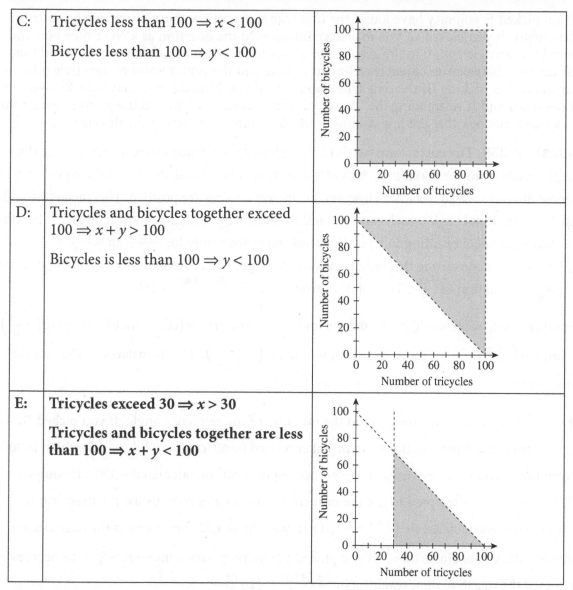

C:	Tricycles less than 100 ⇒ $x < 100$ Bicycles less than 100 ⇒ $y < 100$	
D:	Tricycles and bicycles together exceed 100 ⇒ $x + y > 100$ Bicycles is less than 100 ⇒ $y < 100$	
E:	**Tricycles exceed 30 ⇒ $x > 30$** **Tricycles and bicycles together are less than 100 ⇒ $x + y < 100$**	

Question 338. The correct answer is K. By definition, a circle contains all points in a plane a given distance away from a center point. Therefore, as time elapses while an object travels along a circle's circumference, the distance between the object and the center point does not change—thus, Statement I is correct. Statement III is correct because a fixed point and an object will also not change distance if both remain in a fixed position over time. However, if an object is traveling away from a fixed point over time, the distance between them would increase, resulting in a positive slope. Thus, the only statements that could correspond to the given graph are Statements I and III.

If you picked **F,** you may have found the first true statement without observing other true statements. If you picked **G,** you may have interpreted the question as a NOT question and found the only exception to the graph. If you picked **H,** you may not have understood that the distance between an object traveling in a circle and the center point of the circle remains constant, thus making III the only true statement. If you picked **J,** you may have focused on Statement I and II referencing the "fixed point" and connected that to the point given on the y-axis and mistook that the line coming from that point to represent the distance traveled.

Question 339. The correct answer is D. The given radian value is negative, meaning the angle rotates from the x-axis in a clockwise direction. This would also mean the equivalent degree measure is also negative. However, all answer choices are positive. This means we will use the coterminal angle which can be found in radians by adding or subtracting 2π. Therefore, a coterminal angle resulting in a positive angle measure would be $-\frac{7\pi}{6} + 2\pi = -\frac{7\pi}{6} + \frac{12\pi}{6} = \frac{5\pi}{6}$. Then converting this radian measure to degree measure requires multiplying by the conversion fraction of $\frac{180°}{\pi}$. The solution would then be $\frac{5\pi}{6} \cdot \frac{180°}{\pi} = 150°$.

Another way to solve would be the use the unit circle coordinates $(\cos\theta, \sin\theta)$. Since $\sin\left(-\frac{7\pi}{6}\right) = \frac{1}{2}$ and $\cos\left(-\frac{7\pi}{6}\right) = -\frac{\sqrt{3}}{2}$, the coordinates would be $\left(-\frac{\sqrt{3}}{2}, \frac{1}{2}\right)$. This translates to $150°$ on the unit circle.

If you picked **A,** you may have found the measure of the reference angle. If you picked **B,** you may have reversed the functions and mistakenly used $(\sin\theta, \cos\theta) \Rightarrow \left(\frac{1}{2}, -\frac{\sqrt{3}}{2}\right)$, which is $300°$. From there, you may have used the reference angle of $60°$ or calculated $-300°$. If you picked **C,** you may have attempted to use the unit circle coordinates but mistakenly used $(\sin\theta, \cos\theta)$ and miscalculated $\sin\left(\frac{7\pi}{6}\right) = -\frac{1}{2}$. Then you chose $120°$ because it is the only answer choice with x-coordinate of $-\frac{1}{2}$. If you picked **E,** you may have converted $-\frac{7\pi}{6}$ into degrees but dropped the negative sign, resulting in $\frac{7\pi}{6} \cdot \frac{180°}{\pi} = 210°$.

Question 340. The correct answer is G. The standard equation of a circle is $(x - h)^2 + (y - k)^2 = r^2$ where (x, y) is any point on the circle, (h, k) is the center point, and r is the radius. Substituting the given center point and radius values results in $(x + 2)^2 + (y - 3)^2 = 25$. Then by using the FOIL method to expand this equation results in $(x^2 + 4x + 4) + (y^2 - 6y + 9) = 25$, then combining like terms and reordering results in $x^2 + y^2 + 4x - 6y + 13 = 25 \Rightarrow x^2 + y^2 + 4x - 6y = 12$.

If you picked **F,** you may have dropped the constant values when using FOIL and forgot to square the radius. If you picked **H,** you may have dropped the constant values when using

FOIL. If you picked **J**, you may have reversed the signs in the equation of a circle, resulting in $(x - 2)^2 + (y + 3)^2 = 25$. If you picked **K**, you may have reversed the signs in the equation of the circle and dropped a value when simplifying.

Question 341. **The correct answer is D.** If 6 people pay $10.00 each to pay for a boat rental, the total cost would then be $6 \cdot 10 = \$60.00$. If 1 person didn't attend, the 5 people that did attend would evenly pay the $60.00 rental fee, and each person would pay $\frac{\$60.00}{5} = \$12.00$.

If you picked **A**, you may have correctly found that each would be affected by $2 but subtracted it from the original amount. If you picked **B**, you may have calculated the cost as $50.00, 5 people at $10.00 each, and divided that by the 6 original people planning on attending. If you picked **C**, you may have mistakenly thought that the 1 person not attending means the original number of people was 7 and calculated the cost as $\$10.00 \cdot 7 = \$70.00$. Then the 1 person not attended reduced the number to 6 people, resulting in $\frac{\$70.00}{6} \approx \$11.67$. If you picked **E**, you may have recognized the need to pay $10.00 to cover the missing person but added that to the initial cost of $10.00 per person rather than distributing that cost evenly.

Question 342. **The correct answer is G.** To determine the price reduction, the original price can be multiplied by the percent discount and then subtracted from the original price. This would result in $\$58.95 - (\$58.95 \cdot 0.20) \Rightarrow \$58.95 - 11.79 = \$47.16$.

If you picked **F**, you may have mistakenly calculated 20% as $\frac{100}{20}$ and subtracted that value from the original cost: $\$58.95 - \frac{100}{20} = 53.95$. If you picked **H**, you may have subtracted 20 from the original price instead of calculating a 20% discount. If you picked **J**, you may have calculated half of the original price of $58.95. If you picked **K**, you may have calculated the amount discounted and stopped short of the answer.

Question 343. **The correct answer is C.** The conversion of miles per hour to feet per second can be expressed using the given numbers as a ratio $\frac{30 \text{ } mph}{44 \text{ } fps}$. This ratio can be used in a proportion to determine the feet per second when Melissa drives 70 miles per hour. This would result in $\frac{30 \text{ } mph}{44 \text{ } fps} = \frac{70 \text{ } mph}{x \text{ } fps}$. After cross-multiplication, this would solve to $30x = 44 \cdot 70 \Rightarrow 30x = 3080 \Rightarrow x \approx 103$.

If you picked **B**, you may have incorrectly set up the proportion as $\frac{30 \text{ } mph}{44 \text{ } fps} = \frac{x \text{ } fps}{70 \text{ } mph}$.

Question 344. **The correct answer is F.** Substituting the given values into the equation $(r + b - g)(b + g)$ would result in $(5 + 2 - (-3))(2 + (-3)) \Rightarrow (5 + 2 + 3)(2 - 3) \Rightarrow (10)(-1) = -10$.

If you picked **G**, you may have dropped a negative for the first value of g, resulting in $(5 + 2 - 3)(2 - 3) = -4$. If you picked **H**, you may have dropped a negative for the first value of g and dropped a negative when solving $(2 - 3)$, resulting in $(5 + 2 - 3)(2 - 3) = 4 \cdot 1 = 4$. If you picked **J**, you may have added the quantities instead of multiplying, resulting in $(5 + 2 - (-3)) + (2 + (-3)) = 9$. If you picked **K**, you may have dropped the negative in the solution or maybe solved for $(r + b - g)$ without solving for $(b + g)$.

Question 345. The correct answer is A. To make x the largest value, y must be the smallest value. The values of x and y are squared and will result in a non-negative value. The smallest non-negative number is 0. If $y = 0$, then the equation would be $x^2 + 0^2 = 256 \Rightarrow x^2 = 256 \Rightarrow x = 16$

If you picked **B**, you may have divided 256 by 2 instead of performing a square root. If you picked **C**, you may have found the answer of 16 and subtracted that from 256. If you picked **D**, you may have solved for the largest value of x^2 instead of x. If you picked **E**, you may have mistakenly multiplied 256 by 2 instead of performing a square root.

Question 346. The correct answer is J. The idea of NOT being more than 4 feet tall resulting in NOT riding the roller coaster is a statement with a double negative. This means it can be expressed as the positive statement "a person that IS more than 4 feet tall CAN ride the roller coaster." Because Antoine rode the roller coaster, then Antoine must be more than (greater than) 4 feet tall.

If you picked **F**, you may have evaluated the phrase "not more than 4 feet tall" to mean less than 4 feet tall and then went to the next integer value below 4 feet. If you picked **G**, you may have evaluated the phrase "not more than 4 feet tall" to mean less than 4 feet tall and stopped short of the answer. If you picked **H**, you may have interpreted Antoine riding the roller coaster to mean that Antoine was 4 feet tall and missed the phrase "more than 4 feet." If you picked **K**, you may have assumed that "greater than 4 feet tall" would start at 5 feet; however, 4 feet 1 inch would be greater than 4 feet and, thus, could ride the roller coaster.

Question 347. The correct answer is C. The variable t is defined as the week. Because the question asked for Week 4, the function can be expressed as $N(4) = \dfrac{1{,}200\,(4)^2 + 10}{(4)^2 + 1}$, which simplifies to $\dfrac{1{,}200(16) + 10}{16 + 1} \Rightarrow \dfrac{19{,}200 + 10}{17} \Rightarrow \dfrac{19{,}210}{17} = 1{,}130$

If you picked **B**, you may have mistaken t^2 to be $t \cdot 2$.

Question 348. The correct answer is J. When multiplying terms, begin with multiplying the coefficients: $3 \cdot 7 = 21$. Because the variables have the same base, the exponents are added: $x^5 \cdot x^9 = x^{5+9} = x^{14}$. This results in $21\,x^{14}$.

If you picked **F, G,** or **H**, you may have added the coefficients instead of multiplying. If you picked **K**, you may have multiplied the exponents instead of adding.

Question 349. The correct answer is B. The probability of a certain event occurring is $\frac{\text{occurrence of desired event}}{\text{all possible events}}$. The desired event is selecting one of the 3 green jellybeans, and there are 12 total jellybeans. Thus, the probability can be expressed as $\frac{3}{12} \Rightarrow \frac{1}{4}$.

If you picked **A,** you may have calculated the probability of selecting 1 jellybean out of the 12 total jellybeans. If you picked **C,** you may have calculated the probability of selecting a red jellybean. If you picked **D,** you may have calculated the probability of selecting a yellow jellybean. If you picked **E,** you may have thought the probably of a selecting a green jellybean is the same as not selecting a red jellybean, forgetting to remove the yellow jellybeans and resulting in $\frac{12-4}{12}$.

Question 350. The correct answer is G. To find the least common denominator for the fractions, each denominator must be broken into their prime factors (with exponents). Each unique prime number is isolated, and the highest exponent is chosen. The product of these listed values is the least common denominator of the fraction.

$$
\begin{aligned}
35 &= \underline{} \times 5^1 \times 7^1 \\
56 &= 2^3 \times \underline{} \times 7^1 \\
16 &= 2^4 \times \underline{} \times \underline{} \\
\\
\text{LCD} &= 2^4 \times 5^1 \times 7^1 = 560
\end{aligned}
$$

If you picked **F,** you may have found the prime factors of 2 and 5 (missing 7) and used their highest exponents to get $2^4 \cdot 5^1 = 80$. If you picked **H,** you may have found the common denominator by multiplying $35 \cdot 56 = 1{,}960$. If you picked **J,** you may have added the powers of 2 (making $2^{3+4} = 2^7$) rather than choosing the highest power, resulting in $2^7 \cdot 5^1 \cdot 7^1 = 4480$. If you picked **K,** you may have found the common denominator by multiplying all of the denominators $35 \cdot 56 \cdot 16 = 31{,}360$.

Question 351. The correct answer is B. The sum of the interior angles of a triangle is $180°$. Therefore, $\angle CBA + 70° + 45° = 180°$ and solves to $\angle CBA = 180° - 70° - 45° = 65°$. Because it is given that $\triangle ABC \cong \triangle DEC$, their corresponding angles must also be congruent. This means that $\angle CBA \cong \angle CED$. Because $\angle CBA \cong \angle CED$, the measure of $\angle CED = 65°$.

If you picked **A,** you may have mistaken $\angle CED$ to be congruent to $\angle ECD$. If you picked **C,** you may have thought that $\angle CED$ is congruent to $\angle CDE$. If you picked **D,** you may have calculated $\angle ABC = 70° + 45°$ and used that value for $\angle ABC \cong \angle CED$. If you picked **E,** you may have calculated $\angle CED = 180° - 45° = 135°$.

Question 352. The correct answer is F. The terms in the numerator can be simplified by finding the common denominator: $8 + \frac{1}{7} = \frac{56}{7} + \frac{1}{7} = \frac{57}{7}$. Likewise, the terms in the denominator can be simplified by finding the common denominator: $1 + \frac{1}{14} = \frac{14}{14} + \frac{1}{14} = \frac{15}{14}$. Dividing by a

fraction can be simplified by multiplying by the reciprocal, which would result in $\frac{\frac{57}{7}}{\frac{15}{14}} = \frac{57}{7} \cdot \frac{14}{15}$.

This then simplifies to $\frac{57}{1} \cdot \frac{2}{15} = \frac{19}{1} \cdot \frac{2}{5} = \frac{38}{5}$.

If you picked **G,** you may have meant to multiply by the reciprocal of $\left(1 + \frac{1}{14}\right)$ but, instead,

converted it into $\frac{1}{1} + \frac{14}{1}$, which simplifies to 15 and results in $\frac{57}{7} \cdot 15 = \frac{855}{7}$. If you picked **H,**

you may have misread the plus sign for a division sign and calculated $\dfrac{8 \div \frac{1}{7}}{1 \div \frac{1}{14}} = \frac{56}{14} = 4$.

If you picked **K,** you may have divided terms individually and added the results:

$\frac{8}{1} + \dfrac{\frac{1}{7}}{\frac{1}{14}} = 8 + 2 = 10$.

Question 353. The correct answer is D. Solving this problem requires translating the words into a mathematical expression where "sum" means addition, "is" means equals, and "difference" means subtraction. The first equation can be expressed as $x + y = 15$ and the second equation can be expressed as $x - y = 9$. The values of x and y can be found by setting up a system of linear equations. To perform the elimination method, we do not need to multiply either equation by a value because the y values will already cancel:

$$
\begin{aligned}
x + y &= 15 \\
+ \quad x - y &= 9 \\
\hline
2x \phantom{{}+ y} &= 24 \Rightarrow \quad x = 12
\end{aligned}
$$

Alternatively, the question can be solved using substitution. First, we would need to solve for one of the variables.

$x + y = 15 \Rightarrow y = -x + 15$

When the y is substituted into the other equation you would get:

$x - (-x + 15) = 9 \Rightarrow x + x - 15 = 9 \Rightarrow 2x - 15 = 9 \Rightarrow 2x = 24 \Rightarrow x = 12$

Since $x = 12$ using either method, this value can be substituted into one of the equations to find the y value: $12 + y = 15 \Rightarrow y = 3$. Therefore, the value of $xy = 12 \cdot 3 = 36$.

If you picked **A,** you may have found the value of x and stopped short of the answer. If you picked **B,** you may have confused the word "sum" to mean multiply and stopped with the given "sum" is 15. If you picked **C,** you may have added $15 + 9 = 24$. If you picked **E,** you may have multiplied: $15 \cdot 9 = 135$.

Question 354. The correct answer is J. If point A is placed at the top of the circle, a clockwise rotation would be traveling along the 17-unit circumference to the right and a counterclockwise rotation would be to the left. Because C is a clockwise rotation of 2 from A and point D is a clockwise rotation of 9 away from A, point D must be after point C. Point B is a left (counterclockwise) rotation of 6 from and D is a left rotation of 8 from A. This means that point B is closer to A and would, therefore, be the last point if ordering points clockwise. Thus, the clockwise order would be A, C, D, B.

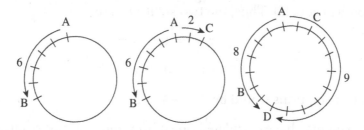

If you picked **F,** you may have assumed that the naming of the points given in the question was already sequenced in a clockwise format. If you picked **G,** you may have found the counterclockwise ordering of points. If you picked **H,** you may have rotated point B clockwise instead of counterclockwise, which would result in B being between C and D. If you picked **K,** you may have added the given clockwise and counterclockwise rotations of D to get $9 - 8 = 1$, which would result in a clockwise rotation of 1, resulting in D being between A and C.

Question 355. The correct answer is D. An average is defined as $Average = \dfrac{sum\ of\ numbers}{number\ of\ numbers}$. Because Ms. Rainwater is deleting the lowest score, the test score of 81 is removed from the total and the number of tests is decreased by 1. The result is $\dfrac{83 + 88 + 92 + 99}{4} = 90.5$.

If you picked **A,** you may have found the median of the 5 given tests instead of calculating the average. If you picked **B,** you may have calculated the average of the current 5 test scores without deleting the lowest test score. If you picked **C,** you may have removed the test score of 83 instead of 81 or you may have gotten the correct answer of 90.5 and rounded down to the nearest whole number. If you picked **E,** you may have found the correct answer of 90.5 but rounded to the nearest whole number.

Question 356. The correct answer is K. Slope-intercept form is $y = mx + b$ and requires isolating the y value. In the given equation $6x - y - 2 = 0$ the value of y can be added on both sides to get $6x - 2 = y$. This can be rewritten as $y = 6x - 2$.

If you picked **F,** you may have correctly subtracted the $6x$ and added 2 on both sides to isolate the y but dropped the -1 coefficient of y. If you picked **G,** you may have inserted a negative when adding 2 to both sides and dropped the -1 coefficient of y. If you picked **H,** the 2 and the 6 switched positions. The 2 became the coefficient and 6 became the constant. If you picked **J,** when isolating y and multiplying both sides by -1 to eliminate the -1 coefficient,

MATHEMATICS • EXPLANATORY ANSWERS

you may have only multiplied the -1 times $6x$ instead of the entire binomial, resulting in $-y = -6x + 2 \Rightarrow y = (-1)(-6x) + 2 \Rightarrow y = 6x + 2$.

Question 357. The correct answer is B. A way to find the solutions of a quadratic in the form of $ax^2 + bx + c$ with an a value of 1 is to determine what two values have a product of c and a sum of b. The product of $-7 \cdot 4$ is -28 and the sum of $-7 + 4$ is -3. Thus, the factors of the given quadratic are $(x - 7)(x + 4) = 0$. The solutions of a quadratic are any value of x that will result in the quadratic function being equal to 0. If either factor is set equal to 0, then the entire expression will equal 0. Thus, the two solutions are:

$$x - 7 = 0 \Rightarrow x = 7$$

$$x + 4 = 0 \Rightarrow x = -4$$

The sum of the two solutions would be $7 + (-4) = 3$.

If you picked **A**, you may have calculated one of the solutions but stopped short of the answer. If you picked **C**, you may have seen that $x^2 - 3x - 28$ is set equal to 0 and assumed it was the sum of the solutions. If you picked **D**, you may have calculated one of the solutions but stopped short of the answer. If you picked **E**, you may have calculated the product of the solutions instead of the sum.

Question 358. The correct answer is G. Using the proper order of operations, the values inside the absolute value must be multiplied: $|5(-4) + 3(6)| = |-20 + 18|$. Then the values are added, and the absolute value makes the sum a non-negative number: $|-20 + 18| = |-2| = 2$.

If you picked **F**, you may have solved inside the absolute value but forgot to apply the absolute value. If you picked **H**, you may have added all the values inside the absolute value, resulting in $|5 + (-4) + 3 + (6)| = 10$. If you picked **J**, you may have interpreted $5(-4)$ as $5 - 4$, resulting in $|5 - 4 + 3(6)| = |1 + 18| = 19$. If you picked **K**, you may have either dropped the negative or applied the absolute value to each term prior to the multiplication and addition steps, resulting in $20 + 18 = 38$.

Question 359. The correct answer is C. If the $\frac{3}{8}$-inch wrench is too large and the $\frac{5}{16}$-inch wrench is too small, this can be expressed as an inequality $\frac{5}{16} < x < \frac{3}{8}$. To identify a fractional value in the middle, each fraction can be expressed with a common denominator: $\frac{5}{16} < x < \frac{6}{16}$. Because the numerators are consecutive, the only value of x with a denominator of 16 would need to be a decimal. So, the denominators can be increased to the next common multiple: $\frac{10}{32} < x < \frac{12}{32}$.

This would mean the value in the middle would be $\frac{11}{32}$.

For **A**, the $\frac{1}{4}$-inch wrench would convert to $\frac{4}{16}$-inch and, therefore, would be smaller than the already too small $\frac{5}{16}$-inch wrench. For **B,** the too small $\frac{5}{16}$-inch wrench can be expressed as $\frac{10}{32}$, so a smaller $\frac{9}{32}$-inch wrench would also be too small. For **D,** the too large $\frac{3}{8}$-inch wrench can be expressed as $\frac{24}{64}$, so the larger $\frac{25}{64}$-inch wrench would also be too large. If you picked **E,** the too large $\frac{3}{8}$-inch wrench can be expressed as $\frac{12}{32}$, so the larger $\frac{13}{32}$-inch wrench would also be too large.

Question 360. The correct answer is K. The formula for slope is $\frac{y_2 - y_1}{x_2 - x_1}$. Substituting the given coordinate points results in $\frac{10 - 8}{-2 - 3} = \frac{2}{-5} = -\frac{2}{5}$.

If you picked **F,** you may have calculated the sum of the x coordinates over the sum of the y coordinates: $\frac{x_2 + x_1}{y_2 + y_1}$. If you picked **G,** you may have calculated $\frac{y_2 - x_2}{y_1 - x_1}$. If you picked **H,** you may have calculated the sum of the y-coordinates over the sum of the x-coordinates instead of the difference: $\frac{y_2 + y_1}{x_2 + x_1}$.

If you picked **J,** you may have reversed the x and y values in the formula and calculated the change in x over the change of y : $\frac{x_2 - x_1}{y_2 - y_1}$.

Question 361. The correct answer is E. By the commutative and associative property of addition, the given expression can be expressed as $(a + a) + (b + b) + (c + c)$. This can be simplified to $2a + 2b + 2c$.

If you picked **A,** you may have mistakenly added each of the coefficients of $2a + 2b + 2c$ to get 6 and combined the variables with multiplication. If you picked **B,** you may have mistaken the given equation to be the product of each term. If you picked **C,** you may have counted 6 terms and multiplied all the variables. If you picked **D,** you may have mistaken that the sum of like terms to be squared.

Question 362. The correct answer is H. Percent can be calculated with $\frac{part}{whole} \cdot 100\%$ where the number of houses sold in the 5-year period is the whole and the number of houses sold in 1993 is part of that total. Using the given bar graph, 250 houses were sold in 1993. It is also given that a total of 875 houses were sold in the 5-year period. Thus, the percent is $\frac{250}{875} \cdot 100\% = 0.285 \cdot 100\% = 28.5\%$. Among the answer choices, the closest percent is 30%.

If you picked **F,** you may have calculated the percent for 1994. If you picked **G,** you may have rounded 28.5% down to 25% or you may have calculated the percent for 1992 or you misinterpreted the 250 houses built to correspond to 25%. If you picked **J,** you may have misread the number of houses built in 1993 as 350 instead of 250 and misinterpreted the 350 houses built to correspond to 35%. If you picked **K,** you may have misread the number of housed built in 1993 as 350 instead of 250, resulting in $\frac{350}{875} \cdot 100\% = 40\%$.

Question 363. The correct answer is B. A way to solve this question is to write out the terms in the arithmetic sequence up to 37 and count the number of terms between 13 and 37, exclusive of 13 and 37. In an arithmetic sequence, the common difference can be found by finding the difference between any consecutive terms: $a_n - a_{n-1}$ where a_n represents any value within the series and a_{n-1} represents the previous term to a_n. Using the given first and second terms, the common difference is $7 - 4 = 3$. This allows the other values to be filled in.

Term	1st	2nd	3rd	4th	5th	6th	7th	8th	9th	10th	11th	12th
Value	4	7	10	13	16	19	22	25	28	31	34	37

The terms between 13 and 37, exclusive of 13 and 37, are the 5th through the 11th terms. That amounts to 7 terms.

If you picked **A,** you may have misinterpreted the ellipsis as having no values between 13 and 37 instead of interpreting the ellipsis as a shorthand representation of the omitted values. If you picked **C,** you may have found that 13 is the 4th term and 37 is the 12th term and then found the different between those two terms: $12 - 4 = 8$. If you picked **D,** you may have mistakenly found the number of terms between 13 and 27 but inclusive of 13 and 27, resulting in 9. Then you found the 9th term of the sequence, which is 28. If you picked **E,** you may have calculated the number of positive integers below 37.

Question 364. The correct answer is F. Every difference of squares can be expressed as $a^2 - b^2 = (a + b)(a - b)$. The denominator of the given expression is the difference of squares and can be expressed as $(x + 7)(x - 7)$. The given expression can be expressed as $\frac{(x-7)(x-7)}{(x+7)(x-7)}$. Because it was given that $x^2 \neq 49$, resulting in a defined solution, common factors can be cancelled: $\frac{(x-7)\cancel{(x-7)}}{(x+7)\cancel{(x-7)}} = \frac{(x-7)}{(x+7)}$.

If you picked **G,** you may have incorrectly factored $x^2 - 49$ into $(x - 7)(x - 7)$ and omitted that the numerator was a squared binomial. This would result in $\frac{(x-7)}{(x-7)(x-7)}$. If you picked **H,** you may have omitted that numerator was a squared binomial, and when you cancelled common factors, it simplified the numerator to 1: $\frac{(x-7)}{(x-7)(x+7)}$. If you picked **J** or **K,** you may have cancelled the x and the exponent of two.

Question 365. The correct answer is C. For two similar triangles, corresponding sides will be proportional. Using the shortest side of the first and second triangle creates a ratio of $\frac{12}{8}$.

The longest side of the first triangle is 15. This would create the proportion equation $\frac{12}{8} = \frac{15}{x}$. Cross-multiplying and solving for x results in $12x = 120 \Rightarrow x = 10$.

If you picked **A**, you may have set up a proportion with non-corresponding sides: $\frac{15}{8} = \frac{12}{x}$. If you picked **B**, you may have used 14 inches as the longest side of the first triangle: $\frac{12}{8} = \frac{14}{x}$. If you picked **D**, you may have assumed that because the second triangle's shortest leg was 4 less than the first triangle that the longest side must also be 4 less: $15 - 4 = 11$. If you picked **E**, you may have mistakenly used 18 instead of 8 as the length of the second triangle's side, and mistakenly set up $\frac{15}{12} = \frac{18}{x}$.

Question 366. The correct answer is H. According to the zero power rule, any real number other than zero raised to the zero power equals 1. Therefore, $(x + 2)^0 = 1$.

If you picked **F**, you may have applied the power of 1 instead of the power of zero. If you picked **G**, you may have interpreted the expression as multiplying by zero, which would result in 0. If you picked **J**, you may have applied the exponent only to the x and mistakenly made $x^0 = 0$ If you picked **K**, you may have applied the exponent only to the x, resulting in $x^0 + 2 = 1 + 2 = 3$.

Question 367. The correct answer is B. The perimeter of a polygon is the sum of all side lengths. For the given pentagon, this would result in $z + 2(z + 2) + 5 + 3z$. Distributing the 2 and combining like terms results in $z + 2z + 4 + 5 + 3z \Rightarrow z + 2z + 3z + 9 \Rightarrow 6z + 9$.

If you picked **A**, you may have reversed your values of 6 and 9. If you picked **C**, you may have omitted the side length of 5. If you picked **D**, you may have incorrectly calculated the two sides of $x + 2$ to be $x + 4$ instead of $2x + 4$. If you picked **E**, you may have omitted the second $x + 2$ side length.

Question 368. The correct answer is G. To find the location of the water fountain located halfway between points B and D, it would be best to give coordinates to the points relative to point A (see the following diagram). The first coordinate is the number of blocks east, and the second coordinate is the number of blocks north.

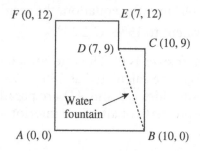

The water fountain is at the midpoint of $\overline{BD}$, and so the midpoint formula applies. For points with coordinates (x_1, y_1) and (x_2, y_2), the midpoint has coordinates $\left(\frac{x_1 + x_2}{2}, \frac{y_1 + y_2}{2} \right)$.

For B (10, 0) and D (7, 9), the midpoint is $\left(\frac{10+7}{2}, \frac{0+9}{2}\right) \Rightarrow \left(\frac{17}{2}, \frac{9}{2}\right) \Rightarrow \left(8\frac{1}{2}, 4\frac{1}{2}\right)$. The y-coordinate of $4\frac{1}{2}$ translates to $4\frac{1}{2}$ blocks north and the x-coordinate of $8\frac{1}{2}$ translates to $8\frac{1}{2}$ blocks east.

If you picked **F**, you may have found the midpoint between A and C. If you picked **H**, you may have found the midpoint between A and E. If you picked **J**, you may have found the midpoint between B and F. If you picked **K**, you may have found the wrong coordinates for C, D, or E.

Question 369. The correct answer is E. When $a = 2c$ is solved for c the result is $c = \frac{a}{2}$. This value of c can be substituted into the second equation, resulting in $b = 6\left(\frac{a}{2}\right)$, which simplifies to $b = 3a$. When solved for a the equation becomes $a = \frac{1}{3}b$.

If you picked **A**, you may have reversed the variables and mistaken $b = 3a$ for $a = 3b$. If you picked **B**, you may have used the given equation of $a = 2c$ and substituted c for b without using the equation $b = 6c$. If you picked **C**, you may have misread nonzero as zero and set $c = 0$. This would make $a = 0$ and $b = 0$, thus $a = b$. If you picked **D**, you may have substituted a for c instead of $\frac{a}{2}$ resulting in $b = 6(a) \Rightarrow a = \frac{1}{6}b$.

Question 370. The correct answer is J. If the given formula for Celsius conversion was solved for F then that solution could be substituted into the given inequality $59° \le F \le 68°$. Solved for F, the equation becomes $C = \frac{5}{9}(F - 32) \Rightarrow \frac{9}{5}C = F - 32 \Rightarrow F = \frac{9}{5}C + 32$. When the solution for F is substituted into the inequality the result is $59° \le \frac{9}{5}C + 32 \le 68°$. This then simplifies to $27° \le \frac{9}{5}C \le 36° \Rightarrow \frac{5}{9}(27°) \le C \le \frac{5}{9}(36°) \Rightarrow 15° \le C \le 20°$.

Another way to solve this question would be to plug in the extremes of the inequality into the given equation. If we plug in $F = 59°$ into the equation, the result is $C = \frac{5}{9}((59) - 32) \Rightarrow \frac{5}{9}$ $(27) = 15°$. If we plug in $F = 68°$ into the equation, the result is $C = \frac{5}{9}((68) - 32) \Rightarrow \frac{5}{9}(36) = 20°$. So $59° \le F \le 68°$ is equivalent to $15° \le C \le 20°$.

Question 371. The correct answer is C. The interior angles of a triangle equal $180°$. For $\triangle BCD$, the angle $\angle CBD$ can be calculated as $180° - 98° - 38° = 44°$. Because $ABCD$ is a parallelogram, the opposite sides $\overline{CB}$ and $\overline{AD}$ are parallel and the diagonal $\overline{BD}$ acts as a transversal. Because of the property of alternate interior angles, $\angle CBD \cong \angle BDA$, which means that $\angle BDA$ is also $44°$.

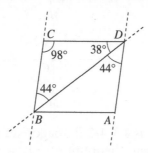

If you picked **A,** you may have assumed that $\overline{BD}$ bisects $\angle CDA$. If you picked **B,** you may have correctly determined that $\angle DCB + \angle CBA = 180$, and since $\angle DCB = 98°$, $\angle CBA$ would be 82°. Then you incorrectly assumed that BD bisected $\angle CBA$, making $\angle CBD = 41°$. Since $\angle CBD \cong \angle BDA$ by alternate interior angle, you chose 41°. If you picked **D,** you may have assumed that $\angle DBA = 41°$ by assuming that BD bisected $\angle CBA$. Then, while trying to calculate $\angle CBD$, you assumed $\angle CBA = 90°$; therefore, $\angle CBD = 49°$. Since $\angle CBD \cong \angle BDA$ by alternate interior angle, you chose 49°. If you picked **E,** you may have assumed that $\angle CDA = 90°$, so $\angle BDA = 90° - 38° = 52°$.

Question 372. The correct answer is J. Because each line segment intersects at a right angle, segment lengths can be translated to cut the figure into standard shapes.

This would create 5 squares with a side length of 6. Since the area of a square is s^2 and there are 5 squares, the solution could be expressed as $5(s^2) = 5(6^2) = 5(36) = 180$.

If you picked **F,** you may have found the perimeter of the figure instead of the area. If you picked **G,** you may have determined the perimeter of 1 square to be $4 \cdot 6 = 24$ and counted 5 squares within the figure to get $5 \cdot 24 = 120$. If you picked **H,** you may have calculated the area of one square to be 36 but omitted the square in the center. If you picked **K,** you may have extended the figure to be 3 squares by 3 squares and calculated the area with 9 squares instead of the given 5.

Question 373. The correct answer is E. A rhombus is a parallelogram with all equal side lengths. Since $\overline{HR} = 5$, then $\overline{HO}$, $\overline{OM}$, and $\overline{MR}$ must also equal 5. Because RHOM is a rhombus, the diagonals of $\overline{HM}$ and $\overline{OR}$ intersect at the center, which will be labeled C. By definition, these diagonals will form right angles and bisect each other, and because $\overline{HM} = 6$ and is bisected by $\overline{RO}$, $\overline{HC} = 3$.

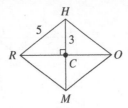

ΔRCH forms a right triangle and is a 3-4-5 Pythagorean triplet, making $\overline{RC} = 4$. This could also be calculated with the Pythagorean theorem: $a^2 + b^2 = c^2 \Rightarrow 3^2 + b^2 = 5^2 \Rightarrow 9 + b^2 = 25 \Rightarrow b^2 = 16 \Rightarrow b = 4$. Since $\overline{RO}$ is bisected by $\overline{HM}$, $\overline{RC} \cong \overline{CO}$. Thus, $\overline{RO}$ is 2 times $\overline{RC}$: $2 \cdot 4 = 8$.

If you picked **A**, you may have found the bisected length of $\overline{HM}$ and stopped short of the answer. If you picked **B**, you may have found $\overline{RC}$ and stopped short of the solution. If you picked **C**, you may have solved for a side length. If you picked **D**, you may have assumed that, like a square, the diagonals of a rhombus are congruent in length.

Question 374. The correct answer is H. Having the shaded regions symmetrical about the *y*-axis means that all shaded squares on the right of the axis must have a shaded reflection left of the axis. If not, they must be added. Similarly, shaded squares left of the axis must have a shaded reflection right of the axis. If not, they too will be added to create symmetry.

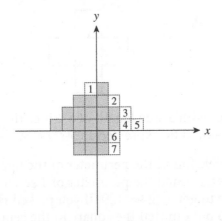

If you picked **F**, you may have found that the outer perimeter of the shaded region off the *y*-axis to the left is 13 and to the right is 10. This would mean three additional edges would be needed to have an equal number of edges on both sides. If you picked **G**, you may have calculated that the shaded area on the left was 13 and the shaded area on the right was 8. This would only require 5 addition squares to make the areas even, but it would not be symmetrical. If you picked **J**, you may have found the average of the areas of 13 and 8. If you picked **K**, you may have found the average of the areas on the left and right of the *y*-axis $\frac{8 + 13}{2} = 11$ and then doubled that value to create symmetry on both sides of the axis.

Question 375. The correct answer is C. A ratio is reduced by an unknown greatest common factor. This common factor can be represented by the variable x. Since the ratio of side lengths is $4 : 1$, the area of the rectangle can be expressed with the greatest common factor as $4x \cdot 1x = 80$. This would result in $4x^2 = 80 \Rightarrow x^2 = 20 \Rightarrow x = \sqrt{20}$. Because the question asked about the approximate length of the longest side of the rectangle, $4x$, the longest side would be $4(\sqrt{20}) = 17.8885 \approx 18$.

If you picked **A,** you may have set the sum of the two longer sides equal to 80 and solved for x. If you picked **B,** you may have added the ratio values instead of multiplying, resulting in $4x + 1x = 80$, and then solved for x. If you picked **D,** you may have solved for the common factor by using 80 as the perimeter, which results in $10x = 80 \rightarrow x = 8$. This would then make the longest side $4x = 4(8) = 32$. If you picked **E,** you may have set the sum of the two longer sides equal to 80 and solved for x, and then calculated the longer sides using the ratio of $4x$.

Question 376. The correct answer is K. The formula for the volume of a rectangular prism is $V = l \cdot w \cdot h$. Substituting the given binomials for the length, width and height results in $(x + 2)(x - 2)(x + 1)$. Using the FOIL method to multiply the first binomials results in $(x + 2)(x - 2) \Rightarrow x^2 - 2x + 2x - 4 \Rightarrow x^2 - 4$. This product can then be multiplied by the last binomial, also using the FOIL method because both terms are binomials: $(x^2 - 4)(x + 1) \Rightarrow x^3 + x^2 - 4x - 4$.

If you picked **F,** you may have added the x values in each binomial and multiplied the numeric values: $2 \cdot (-2) \cdot (1) = -4$. If you picked **G,** you may have added the length values. If you picked **H,** you may have multiplied the x values and multiplied the numeric values: $(x \cdot x \cdot x) + 2 \cdot (-2) \cdot (1) = x^3 - 4$. If you picked **J,** you may have multiplied $(x - 2)(x + 1)$ and mistakenly got $(x^2 - 2)$ and then properly FOILed $(x^2 - 2)(x + 2)$.

Question 377. The correct answer is B. If the median of the first list is expressed as M, the median of the second list would be $10(M)$ and the median of the third list would be $10(M) - 20$. The given median of the third list is defined as 50; therefore, $10(M) - 20 = 50$. To find the median of the original list, isolate M: $10(M) - 20 = 50 \Rightarrow 10(M) = 70 \Rightarrow M = 7$.

If you picked **A,** you may have identified the decrease of each element by 20 and stopped short of the answer. If you picked **C,** you may have added the number of elements in the first and second sets to the amount of change to the third set: $15 + 15 + 20 = 50$. If you picked **D,** you may have solved for the median of the second set. If you picked **E,** you may have multiplied the median of 50 times the 15 elements of the set: $50 \cdot 15 = 750$.

Question 378. The correct answer is G. If Jamal was directly across from the tree and turned 90° to walk 100 meters, Jamal must have initially been at the right angle of the given triangle. This also means that Jamal's initial distance to the tree is the side opposite the given 25°.

MATHEMATICS • EXPLANATORY ANSWERS

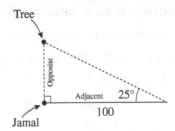

The distance from Jamal's initial location to the tree can be found by using the tangent ratio: $\tan\theta = \dfrac{opposite}{adjacent}$. Substituting given values results in $\tan 25° = \dfrac{x}{100} \Rightarrow 100\tan 25° = x$. Then using the given $\tan 25°$ approximation results in $100(0.47) = 47$.

If you picked **F**, you may have set up the tangent ratio but substituted the approximation for $\sin 25°$ in the last step. If you picked **H**, you may have set up the tangent ratio but substituted the approximation for $\cos 25°$ in the last step. If you picked **J**, you may have incorrectly set up the tangent ratio as $\dfrac{adjacent}{opposite}$. If you picked **K**, you may have incorrectly set up the tangent ratio as $\dfrac{adjacent}{opposite}$ and substituted the approximation for $\sin 25°$.

Question 379. The correct answer is E. Coordinate point (3, 4) is horizontal from (−3, 4) because it shares a y-coordinate and is vertical from (3, −4) because it shares an x-coordinate. The intersection of a vertical and horizontal line will form a right angle, making (3, 4) the right angle vertex of the triangle.

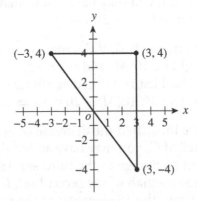

Because a hypotenuse is defined as being opposite the right angle, the line connecting (−3, 4) and (3, −4) must form the hypotenuse. Using the distance formula $d = \sqrt{(x_2 - x_1)^2 + (y_2 - y_1)^2}$ and substituting the coordinate points results in $\sqrt{(3 - (-3))^2 + (-4 - 4)^2}$. This simplifies to $\sqrt{6^2 + (-8)^2} = \sqrt{36 + 64} = \sqrt{100} = 10$.

If you picked **A**, you may have used the x-coordinate from the given points, which is the horizontal distance from the point to the y-axis. If you picked **B**, you may have used the y-coordinate from the given points, which is the vertical distance from the point to the x-axis. If you picked **C**, you may have found the distance between (3, 4) and (−3, 4), which is the shorter leg of the right triangle. If you picked **D**, you may have found the distance between (3, 4) and (3, −4), which is the longer leg of the right triangle.

Question 380. The correct answer is **J**. The formula for the volume of a cube is s^3. The first cube has a side length of 4 inches; thus, it has a volume of $4^3 = 64$. The second cube has each side length triple the first cube's side length: $3 \cdot 4 = 12$. This would mean the second cube has a volume of $12^3 = 1{,}728$. To determine how much bigger the second cube is compared to the first, we find the difference: $1{,}728 − 64 = 1{,}664$.

If you picked **F**, you may have tripled only one of the three dimensions of the larger cube's sides, resulting in $12 \cdot 4 \cdot 4 = 192$, and then subtracted the smaller cube's volume: $192 − 64 = 128$. If you picked **G**, you may have tripled only two of the three dimensions of the larger cube's sides, resulting in $12 \cdot 12 \cdot 4 = 576$, and then subtracted the smaller cube's volume: $576 − 64 = 512$. If you picked **H**, you may have tripled only two of the three dimensions of the larger cube's sides, resulting in $12 \cdot 12 \cdot 4 = 576$. If you picked **K**, you may have found the volume of the larger cube and stopped short of the answer.

Question 381. The correct answer is **E**. The standard equation of a circle is $(x − h)^2 + (y − k)^2 = r^2$ where (h, k) is the center point and r is the radius. The given equation $(x − 8)^2 + y^2 = 15$ has an (h, k) of (8, 0). Since the formula is set equal to r^2 and the given equation is equal to 15, the radius would be $r^2 = 15 \Rightarrow r = \sqrt{15}$.

If you picked **A**, you may have assumed that the term $(x − 8)^2$ resulted in an h value of −8 instead of positive 8 and that the radius is $\frac{1}{2}$ of 15 instead of the square root of 15. If you picked **B**, you may have assumed that the radius is $\frac{1}{2}$ of 15 instead of the square root of 15. If you picked **C**, you may have assumed that the equation is set equal to the radius rather than set equal to r^2. If you picked **D**, you may have assumed that the term $(x − 8)^2$ resulted in an h value of −8 instead of positive 8.

Question 382. The correct answer is **J**. The perimeter of a rectangle is $2A + 2B$. The given dimensions of the park is 60 feet by 150 feet. Substituting these values into the perimeter equation results in $2(60) + 2(150) = 120 + 300 = 420$.

If you picked **F**, you may have found the longest side of the rectangle, but not the perimeter. If you picked **G**, you may have added the two given lengths and performed $A + B$, which is a semi-perimeter. If you picked **H**, you may have added the given lengths of the rectangle, $A + B$, and added the given lengths of the square picnic shelter, resulting in $60 + 150 + 30 + 30 = 270$. If you picked **K**, you may have added the perimeter of the park and the perimeter of the square picnic shelter, resulting in $2(60) + 2(150) + 4(30) = 540$.

Question 383. The correct answer is A. Given that there are 6 squares stacked vertically and this distance is given as being 60, one square must equal 10. It is also given that the picnic shelter is 30 feet by 30 feet. Using the given graph, the picnic shelter must be a 3 by 3 square. The picnic shelter cannot be placed on any of the shaded squares. The edge of the shelter can be built along the edge of the 10-foot shaded border, and because there are 4 vertical blocks, there are two possible orientations of the shelter: aligning the top edge with the border or aligning the bottom edge with the border.

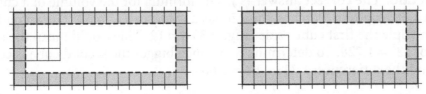

These two orientations can then shift over one block, 10 feet, and create two more orientations.

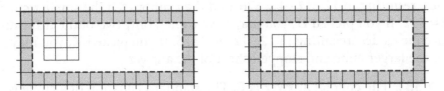

This shifting over one square, 10 feet, can be repeated until the right most edge of the picnic shelter aligns with the edge of the border. This results in the picnic shelter having 22 possible locations within the unshaded grid.

If you picked **B,** you may have made the picnic shelter a 2 by 2 square instead of a 3 by 3 and counted the total number of orientations. If you picked **C,** you may have included in the calculation the number of 10-foot by 10-foot squares within the 10-foot border. If you picked **D,** you may have calculated the number of 10-foot by 10-foot squares in the diagram, including the right and bottom sides of the border where the shelter cannot be built. If you picked **E,** you may have calculated the number of 10-foot by 10-foot squares in the diagram, including the border where the shelter cannot be built.

Question 384. The correct answer is F. This can be solved by converting words into math and interpreting "doubling" to mean multiply by 2 and "extend" to mean add. The dimensions of the park are given as 60 feet and 150 feet; thus, the area would be $60 \cdot 150 = 9{,}000$. "Doubling the area" results in $2(9{,}000)$. To double this area, the length and width are "extended by d feet," which would result in $60 \cdot 150$ becoming $(d + 60)(d + 150)$. Since it is given that $x = d$, the new area can be expressed as $(x + 60)(x + 150) = 2(9{,}000)$.

If you picked **G** or **H,** you may have doubled the given length and width instead of, or in addition to, doubling the area. If you picked **J,** you may have multiplied the extension of the length and width by 2. If you picked **K,** you may have attempted to double the new area and set it equal to the original area.

Question 385. **The correct answer is E.** The standard form of a trigonometric cosine function is $a\cos(bx - c) + d$ where a, b, c, and d transforms $\cos x$. When $b = 1$, the value of c is the phase shift and moves the function left or right, where a positive c value moves the functions to the right and a negative c value moves it to the left. The given transformation function is $g(x) = \cos\left(x - \frac{\pi}{4}\right) + 1$. The transformation by c can be isolated $(x - c) \Rightarrow \left(x - \left(\frac{\pi}{4}\right)\right)$, so $c = \frac{\pi}{4}$, indicating a shift to the right of $\frac{\pi}{4}$. The d value in the equation represents the vertical shift and moves the function up or down. A positive d value moves the function up, and a negative d value moves it down. Because the given transformed function has a d value of $+1$, the function transforms up 1 unit.

If you picked **A, B,** or **C,** you may have reversed the phase (horizontal) shift and the vertical shift in the equation. If you picked **D,** you may have assumed that $\left(x - \frac{\pi}{4}\right)$ was a phase shift of $-\frac{\pi}{4}$.

Question 386. **The correct answer is K.** It is given that $0 < p < q$, which means that p and q are both positive values and that q is larger than p. If the inequality of $0 < p < q$ is multiplied by -1, the inequality symbol changes directions, resulting in $0 > -1(p) > -1(q) \Rightarrow -p > -q$.

Another way to find this solution is to select values of p and q that satisfy the given inequality $0 < p < q$ to see if each answer choices would be true:

If $p = 3$ and $q = 5$ then:

F.	$p + 1 > q + 1$	$3 + 1 > 5 + 1 \Rightarrow 4 > 6$	FALSE
G.	$\frac{p}{q} > 1$	$\frac{3}{5} > 1 \Rightarrow 0.6 > 1$	FALSE
H.	$\frac{1}{q} > \frac{1}{p}$	$\frac{1}{5} > \frac{1}{3} \Rightarrow 0.2 > 0.\overline{33}$	FALSE
J.	$p^2 > q^2$	$3^2 > 5^2 \Rightarrow 9 > 25$	FALSE
K.	$-p > -q$	$-3 > -5$	TRUE

Question 387. **The correct answer is D.** This can be solved by converting words into math and interpreting "is" as equals, "of" as multiply, and "what" as a variable. The question can now be expressed as "if $a = 0.25 \cdot b$ then $1.35 \cdot b = x \cdot a$". Substituting the solution for a into the second equation results in $1.35b = x(0.25b)$. Solving for x results in $x = \frac{1.35b}{0.25b} = 5.40 = 540\%$.

If you picked **A,** you may have added the percentages together: $25\% + 135\% = 160\%$. If you picked **C,** you may have incorrectly converted 135% and 25% into decimal form and multiplied the values together instead of dividing. If you picked **E,** you may have mistakenly calculated 135% as 35% and multiplied $25 \cdot 35 = 875$.

Question 388. The correct answer is H. In trigonometry, one of the Pythagorean identities is defined as $\sin^2 \theta + \cos^2 \theta = 1$. From the commutative property of addition, the given expression can be expressed as $\sin^2 \theta + \cos^2 \theta - 4$, which by substituting the Pythagorean identity results in $1 - 4 = -3$.

If you picked **F,** you may have mistakenly replaced $\sin^2 \theta + \cos^2 \theta$ with -1. If you picked **G,** you may have assumed that the trig identity cancelled out or that $\sin^2 \theta + \cos^2 \theta = 0$. If you picked **J,** you may have dropped the negative in the result. If you picked **K,** you may have dropped a negative when rearranging the expression, resulting in $\sin^2 \theta + \cos^2 \theta + 4$.

Question 389. The correct answer is E. For any point reflected across the line $x = y$, the coordinates (x, y) would transform to (y, x). If point F is estimated to have coordinates $(-4, 3)$, the coordinates of F' when reflected over $x = y$ would be $(3, -4)$. This accurately demonstrates the transformation seen in the given figure.

For each line of reflection found in the answer choices, the correct resulting graph is given below:

	Line of Reflection	Resulting Graph
A.	$y = 0$	
B.	$y = \frac{1}{2}$	

	Line of Reflection	Resulting Graph
C.	$y = -x$	*not all points are represented
D.	$x = 0$	
E.	$x = y$	

You may have picked **C** because the figures $ABCDEF$ and $A'B'C'D'E'F'$ appear to be symmetrical about the line $y = -x$.

Question 390. The correct answer is H. An arc is a portion, or percentage, of a circle's circumference. The given arc is 144° and a circle has a total of 360°; thus, the arc as a percent of the circle can be expressed as $\frac{144}{360} = \frac{2}{5}$. The circle's given circumference is 60. The arc is $\frac{2}{5}$ of the circle's circumference and can be expressed as $\frac{2}{5} \cdot 60$, which equals 24.

Another way to solve this problem is to use the formula for arc length: $s = r \cdot \theta$ where s is the arc length, r is the radius, and θ is the central angle in radians. If the central angle is the total angle measure of a circle in radians of 2π, the resulting arc length would be the circumference of the circle. Using the arc length formula with the given circumference would yield the circle's radius: 60 inches $= r \cdot 2\pi$ radians $\Rightarrow r = \frac{60}{2\pi} = \frac{30 \text{ inches}}{\pi \text{ radians}}$. Then converting $144°$ to radians results in $144° \cdot \frac{\pi \text{ radians}}{180°} = \frac{4}{5}\pi$ radians. So, $s = r \cdot \theta \Rightarrow s = \frac{30 \text{ inches}}{\pi \text{ radians}} \cdot \frac{4}{5}\pi$ radians $\Rightarrow s = 24$ inches.

If you picked **G**, you may have mistaken 60 for the diameter, which would make $r = 30$. Then you multiplied that by the ratio of the central angle to the total number of degrees in a circle to get $30 \cdot \frac{144°}{360°} = 12$. If you picked **J**, you may have calculated the correct arc length of 24 inches but subtracted it from the circumference: $60 - 24 = 36$. If you picked **K**, you may have mistakenly found the radius to be $r = 30\pi$ then multiplied that by the ratio of the central angle to the total number of degrees in a circle to get $30\pi \cdot \frac{144°}{360°} = 12\pi$.

Question 391. **The correct answer is B.** A right circular cone will have a flat base perpendicular to the height. A perpendicular plane passing through the center point will have created a shape with a flat base that will also be the diameter of the cone. Also, a perpendicular plane passing through the vertex and the center of its base will cut the cone along the slant height (of the cone. Thus, the 2-dimensional shape formed from a perpendicular plane through the vertex of a cone would have three straight edges, which forms a triangle.

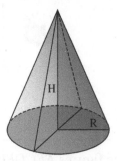

If you picked **A** or **E**, you may have assumed from the given image that the base of the cone was curved. If you picked **D**, you may have used your knowledge that a vertical plane through a cone would form a hyperbola with curved edges, but a vertical plane passing through the vertex does not form a hyperbola.

Question 392. **The correct answer is F.** By converting logarithms into exponential form, $log_b N = a$ can be expressed as the exponent $b^a = N$. This would convert $log_b\left(\frac{1}{81}\right) = -4$ into $b^{-4} = \left(\frac{1}{81}\right)$. The negative exponent means to raise the reciprocal to the positive power. Therefore, $b^{-4} = \frac{1}{b^4}$. Since $\frac{1}{b^4} = \frac{1}{81}$, we can take the reciprocal of both sides: $b^4 = 81$. This solves to $\sqrt[4]{b^4} = \sqrt[4]{81} \Rightarrow b = 3$.

Another way to solve would be to get to $b^{-4} = \left(\frac{1}{81}\right)$ and then raise both sides to the -1 power. This would result in $(b^{-4})^{-1} = \left(\frac{1}{81}\right)^{-1} \Rightarrow b^4 = \frac{1}{81^{-1}} \Rightarrow b^4 = 81$. Which, like the other method, solves to $\sqrt[4]{b^4} = \sqrt[4]{81} \Rightarrow b = 3$.

If you picked **G**, you may have calculated the square root of 81 instead of the fourth root. If you picked **H**, you may have added 4 to 81 instead of taking the fourth root. If you picked **J**, you may have solved to $b^{-4} = \left(\frac{1}{81}\right)$ and calculated the fourth root of both sides but dropped the negative in the exponent. If you picked **K**, you may have solved to $b^{-4} = \left(\frac{1}{81}\right)$ but dropped the negative and calculated the square root of both sides instead of the fourth root.

Question 393. The correct answer is D. A standard function transformation of $y = f(x)$ to $y = f(x + c)$ will shift the graph left c units while $y = f(x - c)$ will shift the graph to the right by c units. Also, a standard transformation of $y = f(x)$ to $y = f(x) + d$ will shift the graph up d units while $y = f(x) - d$ will shift the graph down d units. Since the given function transformation is $y = f(x - 3) + 2$, the graph would transform to the right by 3 units and up 2 units, resulting in choice D.

If you picked **A**, you may have interpreted $f(x - 3)$ as a shift to the left. If you picked **B**, you may have interpreted $f(x - 3)$ as a shift to the left and the $+2$ as a shift down. If you picked **E**, you may have interpreted the $+2$ as a shift down.

Question 394. The correct answer is F. The angle supplementary to the given $70°$ is calculated $180° - 70° = 110°$. Because lines c and d are parallel lines and, therefore, the property of corresponding angles applies, $\angle 1$ is congruent to the supplementary angle to the given $70°$ and is, therefore, also $110°$. Since a and b are also parallel, $\angle 2$ would be congruent to this supplementary angle because they are alternate interior angles. Therefore, $\angle 1 \cong \angle 2$ and the sum of $\angle 1$ and $\angle 2$ is $110° + 110° = 220°$.

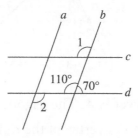

If you picked **G**, you may have made an error in identifying congruent angles made by a transversal across parallel lines and made either $\angle 1$ or $\angle 2$ congruent to the given $70°$ angle. If you picked **H**, you may have made an error in identifying congruent angles made by a transversal across parallel lines and made both $\angle 1$ and $\angle 2$ congruent to the given $70°$ angle. If you picked **J**, you may have found measure of either $\angle 1$ or $\angle 2$ and stopped short of the answer.

Question 395. **The correct answer is D.** $P(x, y) = 4x + 3y$ is an objective function in linear programming. The constrained area of $P(x, y) = 4x + 3y$ is the shaded regions of the given figure. The maximum and minimum values of an objective function will always be at the vertex points and not along the edges or within the shaded region. Therefore, plugging in the coordinates of points A, B, and C into the $P(x, y)$ function will find the maximum value.

A $(-2, 0)$	$4(-2) + 3(0) = -8 + 0 = -8$
B $(0, 4)$	$4(0) + 3(4) = 0 + 12 = 12$
C $(4, 0)$	$4(4) + 3(0) = 16 + 0 = 16$

The largest value when plugging in each vertex point into the $P(x, y)$ function was 16 and is, therefore, the maximum value.

If you picked **A,** you may have assumed that the maximum value to be the largest x or the largest y-coordinate. If you picked **B,** you may have plugged in the coordinates of point A and ignored the negative. If you picked **C,** you may have plugged in the coordinates of point B and stopped short without testing point C. If you picked **E,** you may have added the results of plugging in point B and C to get $12 + 16 = 28$.

Question 396. **The correct answer is F.** The domain of an objective function with 2 variables is defined as the area constrained by the inequalities, not just the set of x values. Also, any points on the x or y axes, by definition, are not in any quadrant. Therefore, none of the points along $\overline{AC}$ lie in any quadrant. The shaded constrained area lies in quadrants I and II; therefore, the answer is F.

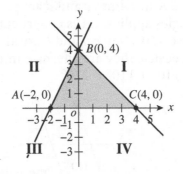

Question 397. **The correct answer is A.** The trigonometric ratios in SOHCAHTOA only apply to a right triangle. If $\angle BCA$ is a vertex of the right triangle, coordinate point B and the origin could create the other vertices. The tangent ratio is $\tan \theta = \dfrac{opposite}{adjacent}$. From $\angle BCA$, the distance from the origin to point C would be the adjacent side and the distance from the origin to point B would be the opposite side. This would result in $\tan \angle BCA = \dfrac{4}{4} = 1$.

If you picked **C** or **D,** you may have used $\overline{AC}$ and $\overline{AB}$ as legs for the tangent function, though $\triangle ABC$ is not a right triangle. If you picked **E,** you may have found $\tan \angle ABC$, though $\triangle ABC$

is not a right triangle, and used the length of $\overline{AC}$ for the opposite leg and the length of $\overline{BC}$ for the adjacent leg.

Question 398. The correct answer is K. The given solutions for the cubic polynomial are 0, 3, and −5. Each solution can be converted into a factor by making them a binomial equal to zero. Therefore, $x = 0$, $x = 3$, and $x = -5$ become the factors x, $(x - 3)$, and $(x + 5)$. The product of these factors is the cubic polynomial: $x(x - 3)(x + 5)$. By testing the $f(1)$ of this cubic, the result is $f(1) = 1 \cdot (1 - 3) \cdot (1 + 5) = 1 \cdot (-2) \cdot (6) = -12$. This does not equal the given value of $f(1) = -24$. Because −24 is twice the calculated result, both sides of the cubic can be multiplied by 2 to get the solution: $2 \cdot x(x - 3)(x + 5) = 2 \cdot -12 \Rightarrow 2x(x - 3)(x + 5) = -24$

If you picked **F**, you may have selected this cubic because it satisfied the $f(1) = -24$; however, none of the given solutions of 0, 3, or −5 result in 0. If you picked **G**, you may have dropped a negative when calculating the $f(1)$, resulting in 12 and needing to multiply both sides by −2 to have a final solution of −24. If you picked **H**, you may have created the correct factors but didn't test the value of $f(1)$. If you picked **J**, you may have made an error when converting the solutions into factors, resulting in the factors having reversed signs.

Question 399. The correct answer is C. Scientific notation is expressed as $m \times 10^n$, where $1 \leq m < 10$ and n is the power of ten that moves the decimal point. A shift of the decimal to the right would result in a negative n and a shift of the decimal to the left would result in a positive n. By translating the word "per" to mean divide, the result is $5 \div 1{,}000{,}000$, which equals 0.000005. To get the m value to be between 1 and 10, the decimal would need to move 6 places to the right, resulting in 5×10^{-6}.

If the terms are expressed in scientific notation before division, you would need to apply exponent rules: $\dfrac{5 \times 10^0}{1 \times 10^6}$. To simply the scientific expression, divide the coefficient and, because of the division, subtract the powers of ten to get $5 \times 10^{0-6}$, which equals 5×10^{-6}.

If you picked **A**, you may have misread or incorrectly calculated the water value as billion instead of million If you picked **B**, you may have counted the number of places incorrectly. If you picked **D** or **E**, you may have thought that a shift to the right resulted in a positive power of 10.

Question 400. The correct answer is F. The binomial $(a^2 - b^2)$ is the difference of perfect squares and can be factored into the two binomial conjugates $(a - b)(a + b)$. Substituting the conjugates into the inequality results in $(a - b) > (a - b)(a + b)$. Both sides can be divided by the common binomial $\dfrac{(a - b)}{(a - b)} > \dfrac{(a - b)(a + b)}{(a - b)} \Rightarrow 1 > (a + b)$. Since $a > b$, the divisor is a positive term; thus, $a + b$ must be less than 1.

If you picked **G**, you may have flipped the inequality when dividing both sides by $(a - b)$. If you picked **H**, you may have assumed that b was a positive value and that adding a positive value to a would make it larger than a by itself. If you picked **J**, you may have assumed that b was a positive value and that adding a positive value to a would make it larger than a. If you picked **K**, you may have only divided the right side, and mistakenly changed the sign to equals.

$$(a - b) = \frac{(a - b)(a + b)}{(a - b)} \Rightarrow (a - b) = (a + b).$$

NOTES

NOTES

NOTES

NOTES

NOTES

NOTES

NOTES

NOTES

NOTES

NOTES